The Hebraic Tongue Restored

[Volume One]

The Hebraic Tongue Restored

And the True Meaning of the Hebrew
Words Re-established and Proved
by their Radical Analysis

[Volume One]

By

Fabre d'Olivet

Done into English by

Nayán Louise Redfield

יתות

"He who can rightly pronounce it, causeth
heaven and earth to tremble, for it is the
NAME
which rusheth through the universe."

Hermetica

San Rafael, Ca

Second, facsimile edition
Hermetica, 2007
First edition, G.P. Putnam's Sons, 1921

For information, address:
Hermetica, P.O. Box 151011
San Rafael, California 94915, USA

Library of Congress Cataloging-in-Publication Data

Fabre d'Olivet, Antoine, 1767–1825.
The Hebraic tongue restored and the true meaning of the
Hebrew words re-established and proved by their radical analysis/
Fabre d'Olivet; translated by Nayán Redfield. — Reprint ed.

v. cm.
Originally published: New York: G.P. Putnam's Sons, 1921.
ISBN 978-1-59731-204-2 (vol 1, pbk.: alk. paper)
ISBN 978-1-59731-205-9 (vol 1, hardback: alk. paper)
ISBN 978-1-59731-206-6 (vol 2, pbk.: alk. paper)
ISBN 978-1-59731-207-3 (vol 2, hardback: alk. paper)
1. Hebrew language—Grammar. I. Redfield, Nayán Louise. II. Title.
PJ4563.F25 2007
492.4'82421—dc22   2007027592

To the Torch-bearers of the Seven-Tongued-Flame
who have ever been the Path-Finders and
Lights on the Way-of-Knowing
and Being, I offer at the
Dawn-of-the-New-Day
this volume

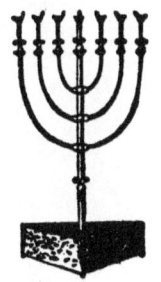

TO THE READER

I would direct attention to the English word-for-word translation given in the Literal Version of the Cosmogony of Moses. This translation is *d'Olivet's,* and in the footnotes which accompany it I have retained his selection of words some of which are now obsolete. In the "Correct Translation" at the close of the volume I have, however, set aside some of the quaint words making choice of more modern ones.

N. L. R.

TRANSLATOR'S FOREWORD.

THE HEBRAIC TONGUE RESTORED is a strong appeal to those who, realizing that the time of philosophy is past and the time of religion at hand, are seeking for those higher truths the spreading knowledge of which has already altered the complexion of the world and signalled the approaching end of materialism.

In this prodigious work of Fabre d'Olivet, which first appeared in 1815, he goes back to the origin of speech and rebuilds upon a basis of truly colossal learning the edifice of primitive and hieroglyphic Hebrew, bringing back the Hebraic tongue to its constitutive principles by deriving it wholly from the *Sign,* which he considers the symbolic and living image of the generative ideas of language. He gives a neoteric translation of the first ten chapters of the SEPHER OF MOSES (*Genesis*) in which he supports each with a scientific, historic and grammatical commentary to bring out the three meanings: literal, figurative and hieroglyphic, corresponding to the natural, psychic and divine worlds. He asserts plainly and fearlessly that the Genesis of Moses was symbolically expressed and ought not to be taken in a purely literal sense. Saint Augustine recognized this, and Origen avers that "if one takes the history of the creation in the literal sense, it is absurd and contradictory."

Fabre d'Olivet claims that the Hebrew contained in Genesis is the *pure idiom of the ancient Egyptians,* and considering that nearly six centuries before Jesus Christ, the Hebrews having become Jews no longer spoke nor understood their original tongue, he denies the value of the Hebrew as it is understood today, and has undertaken to restore this tongue lost for twenty-five centuries. The truth of this opinion does not appear doubtful, since the Hebrews according to *Genesis* itself remained some four hundred years in Egypt. This idiom, therefore, having become separated from a tongue which had attained its highest perfection and was composed entirely of universal, intellectual, abstract expressions, would naturally fall from degeneracy to degeneracy, from restriction to restriction, to its most material elements; all that was spirit would become substance; all that was intellectual would become sentient; all that was universal, particular.

According to the Essenian tradition, every word in this *Sepher of Moses* contains three meanings—the positive or simple, the comparative or figurative, the superlative or hieratic. When one has penetrated to this last meaning, all things are disclosed through a radiant illumination and the soul of that one attains to heights which those bound to the narrow limits of the positive meaning and satisfied with the letter which killeth, never know.

The learned Maimonides says "Employ you reason, and you will be able to discern what is said allegorically, figuratively and hyperbolically, and what is meant literally."

NAYÁN LOUISE REDFIELD

HARTFORD, CONN.,
October, 1918.

NOTE.

It may be noted by the careful student that the Syriac characters in this volume are in some instances not exactly correct. Unfortunately, the impossibility of securing better types necessitated the use of these unsatisfactory forms. For this the author and the publishers ask the indulgence of the reader.

THE HEBRAIC TONGUE RESTORED
AND THE TRUE MEANING OF THE HEBREW
WORDS RE-ESTABLISHED AND PROVED
BY THEIR RADICAL ANALYSIS.

In this work is found:

> 1st.—INTRODUCTORY DISSERTATION upon the Origin of Speech, the study of the tongues which can lead to this origin and the purpose that the Author has in view;

> 2nd.—HEBRAIC GRAMMAR founded upon new principles, and made useful for the study of tongues in general;

> 3rd.—SERIES OF HEBRAIC ROOTS considered under new relations, and destined to facilitate the understanding of language, and that of etymological science;

> 4th.—PRELIMINARY DISCOURSE;

> 5th.—Translation into English of the first ten chapters of the Sepher, containing the COSMOGONY OF MOSES.

This translation, destined to serve as proof of the principles laid down in the Grammar and in the Dictionary, is preceded by a LITERAL VERSION, in French and in English, made upon the Hebrew Text presented in the original with a transcription in modern characters and accompanied by critical and grammatical notes, wherein the interpretation given to each word is proved by its radical analysis and its comparison with the analogous word in Samaritan, Chaldaic, Syriac, Arabic or Greek.

CONTENTS

OF PART FIRST

INTRODUCTORY DISSERTATION.

PAGE

§I.   Upon the Origin of Speech and upon the Study of the Tongues which can lead to it 3

§II. Hebraic Tongue: Authenticity of the Sepher of Moses; Vicissitudes experienced by this book.. 21

§III. Continuation of the Revolutions of the Sepher. Origin of the Principal Versions which have been made 37

HEBRAIC GRAMMAR.

Chapter I. General Principles.

§I.   The Real Purpose of this Grammar............ 55
§II. Etymology and Definition.................... 60
§III. Division of Grammar: Parts of Speech......... 65
§IV. Hebraic Alphabet: Comparative Alphabet 70-71

Chapter II. Signs Considered as Characters.

§I.   Hebraic Alphabet: its vowels: its origin........ 73

		PAGE
§II.	Origin of the Vowel Points...................	77
§III.	Effects of the Vowel Points. Samaritan Text....	84

Chapter III. Characters Considered as Signs.

§I.	Traced Characters, one of the elements of Language: Hieroglyphic Principle of their Primitive Form	89
§II.	Origin of Signs and Their Development: Those of the Hebraic Tongue...................	93
§III.	Use of the Signs: Example drawn from the French	99

Chapter IV. The Sign Producing the Root.

§I.	Digression on the Principle and the Constitutive Elements of the Sign...................	103
§II.	Formation of the Root and of the Relation......	107
§III.	Preposition and Interjection...................	114

Chapter V. The Noun.

§I	The Noun Considered under seven relations: Etymology	119
§II.	Quality	124
§III.	Gender	132
§IV.	Number	135
§V.	Movement	139
§VI.	Construct State	147
§VII.	Signification	150

Chapter VI. Nominal Relations.

§I.	Absolute Pronouns...........................	151
§II.	Affixes	155
§III.	Use of the Affixes...........................	161

Chapter VII. The Verb.

§I.	Absolute Verb and Particular Verbs............	167

CONTENTS

		PAGE
§II.	Three Kinds of Particular Verbs	172
§III.	Analysis of Nominal Verbs: Verbal Inflection	177

Chapter VIII. Modifications of the Verb.

§I.	Form and Movement	183
§II.	Tense	187
§III.	Formation of Verbal Tenses by Means of Pronominal Persons	192

Chapter IX. Conjugations.

§I.	Radical Conjugation	197
	Remarks upon the Radical Conjugation	207
§II.	Derivative Conjugation	212
	Remarks upon the Derivative Conjugation	220
§III.	Compound Radical Conjugation with the Initial Adjunction '	225
	Remarks on the Compound Radical Conjugation. Initial Adjunction '	230
§IV.	Compound Radical Conjugation with the Initial Adjunction נ	233
	Remarks on the Compound Radical Conjugation	238
§V.	Compound Radical Conjugation with the Terminative Adjunction	241
	Remarks on the Compound Radical Conjugation	246
§VI.	Irregular Conjugations	250

Chapter X. Construction of Verbs: Adverbial Relations: Paragogic Characters: Conclusion.

§I.	Union of Verbs with Verbal Affixes	255
§II.	Adverbial Relations	262
§III.	Paragogic Characters	271
§IV.	Conclusion	275

CONTENTS

Radical Vocabulary : Prefatory Note............... 279

HEBRAIC ROOTS.

		PAGE
א	A.	287
ב	B.	300
ג	G.	310
ד	D.	318
ה	H. E.	326
ו	O. OU. W.	334
ז	Z.	339
ח	E. H. CH.	345
ט	T.	356
י	I.	361
כ	CH. KH.	368
ל	L.	377
מ	M.	385
נ	N.	394
ס	S.	405
ע	U. H. WH.	413
פ	PH.	422
צ	TZ.	430
ק	KQ.	438
ר	R.	446
ש	SH.	455
ת	TH.	465

The Hebraic Tongue Restored

PART FIRST

I

INTRODUCTORY DISSERTATION

INTRODUCTORY DISSERTATION.

§ I.

UPON THE ORIGIN OF SPEECH AND UPON THE STUDY OF THE TONGUES WHICH CAN LEAD TO IT.

The origin of speech is generally unknown. It is in vain that savants of the centuries past have endeavoured to go back to the hidden principles of this glorious phenomenon which distinguishes man from all the beings by which he is surrounded, reflects his thought, arms him with the torch of genius and develops his moral faculties; all that they have been able to do, after long labours, has been to establish a series of conjectures more or less ingenious, more or less probable, founded in general, upon the physical nature of man which they judged invariable, and which they took as basis for their experiments. I do not speak here of the scholastic theologians who in order to extricate themselves from perplexity upon this difficult point, taught that man had been created possessor of a tongue wholly formed; nor of Bishop Walton who, having embraced this convenient opinion, gave as proof, the conversation of God Himself with the first man, and the discourses of Eve with the serpent;[1] not reflecting that this so-called serpent which conversed with Eve, and to which God also spoke, might, therefore, have drawn from the same source of speech and participated in the tongue of the Divinity. I refer to those savants who, far from the dust and clamours of the school, sought in good faith the truth that the school no longer possessed. Moreover, the theologians themselves had been abandoned long since by their disciples. Richard Simon, the priest,[2] from

[1] Walton, *Prolegom* I.
[2] Rich. Sim. *Histoire crit.* L. I, ch. 14 et 15.

whom we have an excellent critical history of the Old Testament, did not fear, relying upon the authority of Saint Gregory of Nyssa, to reject theological opinion in this respect, and to adopt that of Diodorus Siculus and even that of Lucretius, who attribute the formation of language to the nature of man and to the instigation of his needs.[3]

It is not because I here oppose the opinion of Diodorus Siculus or Lucretius to that of the theologians, that one should infer that I consider it the best. All the eloquence of J. J. Rousseau could not make me approve of it. It is one extreme striking another extreme, and by this very thing departing from the just mean where truth abides. Rousseau in his nervous, passionate style, pictures the formation of society rather than that of language: he embellishes his fictions with most vivid colours, and he himself, drawn on by his imagination, believes real what is only fantastic.[4] One sees plainly in his writing a possible beginning of civilization but no probable origin of speech. It is to no purpose that he has said that the meridional tongues are the daughters of pleasure and those of the North, of necessity: one still asks, how pleasure or necessity can bring forth simultaneously, words which an entire tribe agrees in understanding and above all agrees in adopting. Is it not he who has said, with cold, severe reason, that language could be instituted only by an agreement and that this agreement could not be conceived without language? This vicious circle in which a modern theosophist confines it, can it be eluded? "Those who devote themselves to the pretension of forming our tongues and all the science of our understanding, by the expedients of natural circumstances alone, and by our human means alone," says this theosophist,[5] "expose

[3] Diod-Sic. L. II. "At varios linguæ sonitus natura subegit
　　　Mittere, et utilitas expressit nomina rerum."
　　　　　　　　　　　　　　　　　—Lucret.

[4] *Essai sur l'origine des Langues.*
[5] St.-Martin *Esprit des choses,* T. II p. 127.

themselves voluntarily to this terrible objection that they themselves have raised; for he who only denies, does not destroy, and he does not refute an argument because he disapproves of it: if the language of man is an agreement, how is this agreement established without language?"

Read carefully both Locke and his most painstaking disciple Condillac;⁶ you will, if you desire, have assisted at the decomposition of an ingenious contrivance; you will have admired, perhaps, the dexterity of the decomposer; but you will remain as ignorant as you were before, both concerning the origin of this contrivance, the aim proposed by its author, its inner nature and the principle which moves its machinations. Whether you reflect according to your own opinion, or whether long study has taught you think according to others, you will soon perceive in the adroit analyst only a ridiculous operator who, flattering himself that he is explaining to you how and why such an actor dances in the theatre, seizes a scalpel and dissects the legs of a cadaver. Your memory recalls Socrates and Plato. You hear them again rebuking harshly the physicists and the metaphysicians of their time;⁷ you compare their irresistible arguments with the vain jactancy of these empirical writers, and you feel clearly that merely taking a watch to pieces does not suffice to give reason for its movement.

But if the opinion of the theologians upon the origin of speech offends reason, if that of the historians and the philosophers cannot hold out against a severe examination, it is therefore not given to man to know it. Man, who according to the meaning of the inscription of the temple of Delphi,* can know nothing only so far as he

---

6 Locke. *Essay concern. Human Understand.* B. III; Condillac *Logique.*

7 Plat. *dial Theaet. Phaedon. Crat.*

* This famous inscription, *Know thyself* was, according to Pliny, a saying of the sage Chilo, a celebrated Greek philosopher who lived about 560 B. C. He was from Lacedæmon and died of joy, it was said, embracing his son, victor in the Olympic games.

knows himself, is therefore condemned to be ignorant of what places him in the highest rank among sentient beings, of what gives him the sceptre of the earth, of what constitutes him veritably man,—namely Speech! no! that cannot be, because Providence is just. Quite a considerable number of the sages among all nations have penetrated this mystery, and if, notwithstanding their efforts, these privileged men have been unable to communicate their learning and make it universal, it is because the means, the disciples or the favourable conditions for this, have failed them.

For the knowledge of speech, that of the elements and the origin of language, are not attainments that can be transmitted readily to others, or that can be taken to pieces after the manner of the geometricians. To whatever extent one may possess them, whatever profound roots they may have thrown into the mind, whatever numerous fruits they may have developed there, only the principle can ever be communicated. Thus, nothing in elementary nature is propagated at the same time: the most vigorous tree, the most perfect animal do not produce simultaneously their likeness. They yield, according to their specie, a germ at first very different from them, which remains barren if nothing from without coöperates for its development.

The archæological sciences, that is to say, all those which go back to the principles of things, are in the same category. Vainly the sages who possess them are exhausted by generous efforts to propagate them. The most fertile germs that they scatter, received by minds uncultivated or badly prepared, undergo the fate of seeds, which falling upon stony ground or among thorns, sterile or choked die there. Our savants have not lacked aid; it is the aptitude for receiving it that has been lacking. The greater part of them who ventured to write upon tongues, did not even know what a tongue was; for it is not enough merely to have compiled grammars, or to have toiled laboriously to find the difference between a supine and a gerund; it is necessary to have explored many idioms, to have compared them assiduously and without prejudices; in order to penetrate, through the points of contact of their particular genius, to the universal genius which presides over their formation, and which tends to make only one sole and same tongue.

Among the ancient idioms of Asia, are *three* that it is absolutely imperative to understand if one would proceed with assurance in the field of etymology and rise by degrees to the source of language. These idioms, that I can justly name tongues, in the restricted meaning which one has given to this word, are Chinese, Sanskrit and Hebrew. Those of my readers who are familiar with the works of the savants of Calcutta and particularly those of Sir William Jones, may perhaps be astonished that I name Hebrew in place of the Arabic from which this estimable writer derives the Hebraic idiom, and which he cites as one of the mother-tongues of Asia. I shall explain my thought in this respect, and at the same time state why I do not name either Persian, or Uigurian Tataric, which one might think I had forgotten.

When Sir William Jones, glancing with observant eye over the vast continent of Asia and over its numerous dependent isles, placed therein the five ruling nations, among which he divided the heritage, he created a geographical tableau of happy conception and great interest that the historian ought not to overlook.[8] But in establishing this division his consideration was rather of the power and extent of the peoples that he named, than of their true claims to anteriority; since he did not hesitate to say that the Persians, whom he ranked among the five ruling nations, draw their origin from the Hindus and Arabs,[9] and that the Chinese are only an Indian colony;[10]

[8] *Asiat. Research.* T. I.
[9] *Ibid.* T. II. p. 51.
[10] *Asiat. Research.* T. II. p. 368, 379.

therefore, recognizing only three primordial sources, viz., that of the Tatars, that of the Hindus and that of the Arabs.

Although I may not agree wholly with him in this conclusion, I infer nevertheless, as I have already said, that this writer, in naming the five principal nations of Asia, considered their power more than their true rights to anteriority. It is evident, to say the least, that if he had not been obliged to yield to the *éclat* with which the Arabic name is surrounded in these modern times, due to the appearance of Mohammed, to the propagation of the cult, and of the Islamic empire, Sir William Jones would not have chosen the Arabic people instead of the Hebrew people, thus making the former one of the primordial sources of Asia.

This writer had made too careful a study of the Asiatic tongues not to have known that the names which we give to the Hebrews and to the Arabs, however much dissimilar they may appear, owing to our manner of writing them, are in substance only the same epithet modified by two different dialects. All the world knows that both these peoples attribute their origin to the patriach Heber:* now, the name of this so-called patriarch, signifies nothing less than that which is placed *behind* or *beyond*, that which is *distant, hidden, deceptive, deprived of light;* that which *passes*, that which *terminates*, that which is *occidental*, etc. The Hebrews, whose dialect is evidently anterior to that of the Arabs, have derived from it *hebri* and the Arabs *harbi*, by a transposition of letters which is a characteristic of their language. But whether it be pronounced *hebri*, or *harbi*, one or the other word expresses always that the people who bear it are found placed either beyond, or at the extremity, at the confines, or at the occidental borders of a country. From

* Following the Hebraic orthography עבר *habar*, following the Arabic عبر *habar*. The Hebraic derivative is עברי *habri*, a Hebrew: the Arabic derivative is عربي *harbi*, an Arab.

the most ancient times, this was the situation of the Hebrews or the Arabs, relative to Asia, whose name in its primitive root signifies the unique continent, the land, in other words, the Land of God.

If, far from all systematic prejudice, one considers attentively the Arabic idiom, he discovers there the certain marks of a dialect which, in surviving all the dialects emanated from the same branch, has become successively enriched from their *débris*, has undergone the vicissitudes of time, and carried afar by a conquering people, has appropriated a great number of words foreign to its primitive roots; a dialect which has been polished and fashioned upon the idioms of the vanquished people, and little by little shown itself very different from what it was in its origin; whereas the Hebraic idiom on the contrary (and I mean by this idiom that of Moses), long since extinct in its own country and lost for the people who spoke it, was concentrated in one unique book, where hardly any of the vicissitudes which had altered the Arabic had been able to assail it; this is what distinguishes it above all and what has made it my choice.

This consideration has not escaped Sir William Jones. He has clearly seen that the Arabic idiom, toward which he felt a strong inclination, had never produced any work worthy of fixing the attention of men prior to the Koran,[11] which is, besides, only a development of the Sepher of Moses; whereas this Sepher, sacred refuge of the Hebrew tongue, seemed to him to contain, independent of a divine inspiration,[12] more true sublimity, exquisite beauties, pure morals, essential history and traits of poetry and eloquence, than all the assembled books written in any tongue and in any age of the world.

However much may be said and however much one may, without doing the least harm to the Sepher, compare and even prefer certain works equally famous among

---

[11] *Asiat. Research.* T. II. p. 13.
[12] *Ibid.* T. II. p, 15.

the nations, I affirm that it contains for those who can read it, things of lofty conception and of deep wisdom; but it is assuredly not in the state in which it is shown to the vulgar readers, that it merits such praise. Sir William Jones undoubtedly understood it in its purity and this is what I like to believe.

Besides, it is always by works of this nature that a tongue acquires its right to veneration. The books of universal principles, called *King*, by the Chinese, those of divine knowledge, called *Veda* or *Beda*, by the Hindus, the Sepher of Moses, these are what make illustrious the Chinese, the Sanskrit and the Hebrew. Although Uigurian Tataric may be one of the primitive tongues of Asia, I have not included it as one that should be studied by the student who desires to go back to the principle of speech; because nothing could be brought back to this principle in an idiom which has not a sacred literature. Now, how could the Tatars have had a sacred or profane literature, they who knew not even the characters of writing? The celebrated Genghis Khan, whose empire embraced an immense extent, did not find, according to the best writers, a single man among his Mongols capable of writing his dispatches.[13] Tamerlane, ruler in his turn of a part of Asia, knew neither how to read nor write. This lack of character and of literature, leaving the Tataric idioms in a continual fluctuation somewhat similar to that which the rude dialects of the savage peoples of America experienced, makes their study useless to etymology and can only throw uncertain and nearly always false lights in the mind.

One must seek the origin of speech only from authentic monuments, whereon speech itself has left its ineffaceable imprint. If time and the scythe of revolutions had respected more the books of Zoroaster, I doubtless might have compared with the Hebrew, the ancient tongue of the Parsees, called *Zend*, in which are written the fragments

[13] *Traduct. franc. des Recher. Asiat.* T. II. P. 49. *Notes.*

which have come down to us; but after a long and impartial examination, I cannot refrain from believing, notwithstanding all the recognition that I feel for the extraordinary labours of Anquetil-Duperron who has procured them for us, that the book called today, the *Zend-Avesta*, by the Parsees, is only a sort of breviary, a compilation of prayers and litanies wherein are mingled here and there certain fragments from the sacred books of Zeradosht, the ancient Zoroaster, translated in the living tongue; for this is precisely what the word *Zend* signifies—living tongue. The primitive Avesta was divided into twenty-one parts, called *Nosk*, and entered into all the details of nature,[14] as do the Vedas and Pouranas of the Hindus, with which it had perhaps more affinity than one imagines. The Boun-Dehesh, which Anquetil-Duperron has translated from the *Pehlevi*, a sort of dialect more modern still than the *Zend*, appears to be only an abridgment of that part of the Avesta which treated particularly of the origin of Beings and the birth of the Universe.

Sir William Jones, who believes as I do that the original books of Zoroaster were lost, thinks that the Zend, in which are written the fragments that we possess, is a dialect of Sanskrit, in which Pehlevi, derived from the Chaldaic and from the Cimmerian Tatars, has mingled many of its expressions.[15] This opinion, quite comformable with that of the learned d'Herbelot who carries the Zend and Pehlevi back to Nabatæan Chaldaic,[16] that is, to the most ancient tongue of Assyria, is therefore most probable since the characters of Pehlevi and Zend are obviously of Chaldaic origin.

I do not doubt that the famous inscriptions which are found in the ruins of ancient Isthakr,[17] named Persepolis by the Greeks, and of which no savant, up to this time,

[14] *Zend-Avesta*, T. I. *part* II. p. 46.
[15] *Asiat. Research*, T. II. p. 52 *et suiv.*
[16] *Bibl. ori.* p. 514.
[17] Millin: *Monumens inédits.*

has been able to decipher the characters, belong to the tongue in which the sacred books of the Parsees were originally written before they had been abridged and translated in Pehlevi and Zend. This tongue, whose very name has disappeared, was perhaps spoken at the court of those monarchs of Iran, whom Mohsenal-Fany mentions in a very curious book entitled *Dabistan*,* and whom he assures had preceded the dynasty of the Pishdadians, which is ordinarily regarded as the earliest.

But without continuing further upon this digression, I believe I have made it sufficiently understood that the study of Zend cannot be of the same interest, nor produce the same results as that of Chinese, Sanskrit or Hebrew, since it is only a dialect of Sanskrit and can only offer sundry fragments of the sacred literature translated from an unknown tongue more ancient than itself. It is enough to make it enter as a sort of supplement in the research of the origin of speech, considering it as a link which binds Sanskrit to Hebrew.

It is the same with the Scandinavian idiom, and the Runic poetry preserved in the Edda.[18] These venerable relics of the sacred literature of the Celts, our ancestors, ought to be regarded as a medium between the tongues of ancient Asia and that of modern Europe. They are not to be disdained as an auxiliary study, the more so since they are all that remains to us really authentic pertaining to the cult of the ancient Druids, and as the other Celtic dialects, such as Basque, Armoric Breton, Welsh Breton or *Cymraeg*, possessing no writings, can merit no sort of confidence in the important subject with which we are engaged.

But let us return to the three tongues whose study I recommend: Chinese, Sanskrit and Hebrew; let us

---

* This work which treats of the manners and customs of Persia, is not known except for a single extract inserted in the *New Asiatic Miscellany*, published by Gladwin, at Calcutta, 1789.

[18] *Edda Islandorum* Haoniæ, 1665, in-4.°

glance at them without concerning ourselves for the present, with their grammatical forms; let us fathom their genius and see in what manner they principally differ.

The Chinese tongue is, of all the living tongues today, the most ancient; the one whose elements are the simplest and the most homogeneous. Born in the midst of certain rude men, separated from other men by the result of a physical catastrophe which had happened to the globe, it was at first confined to the narrowest limits, yielding only scarce and material roots and not rising above the simplest perceptions of the senses. Wholly physical in its origin, it recalled to the memory only physical objects: about two hundred words composed its entire lexicon, and these words reduced again to the most restricted signification were all attached to local and particular ideas. Nature, in thus isolating it from all tongues, defended it for a long time from mixture, and when the men who spoke it, multiplied, spread abroad and commingled with other men, art came to its aid and covered it with an impenetrable defense. By this defense, I mean the symbolic characters whose origin a sacred tradition attributes to Fo-Hi. This holy man, says the tradition, having examined the heavens and the earth, and pondered much upon the nature of intermediate things, traced the eight *Koua*, the various combinations of which sufficed to express all the ideas then developed in the intelligence of the people. By means of this invention, the use of knots in cords, which had been the custom up to that time, ceased.*

Nevertheless, in proportion as the Chinese people extended, in proportion as their intelligence made progress and became enriched with new ideas, their tongue followed these different developments. The number of its words fixed by the symbolic *Koua*, being unable to be augmented, was modified by the accent. From being par-

* This tradition is drawn from the great history *Tsee-tchi-Kien-Kang-Mou*, which the Emperor *Kang-hi* ordered translated into Tataric and embellished with a preface.

ticular they became generic; from the rank of nouns they were raised to that of verbs; the substance was distinguished from the spirit. At that time was felt the necessity for inventing new symbolic characters, which, uniting easily, the one with the other, could follow the flight of thought and lend themselves to all the movements of the imagination.[19] This step taken, nothing further arrested the course of this indigenous idiom, which, without ever varying its elements, without admitting anything foreign in its form, has sufficed during an incalculable succession of ages for the needs of an immense nation; which has given it sacred books that no revolution has been able to destroy, and has been enriched with all the profoundness, brilliancy and purity that moral and metaphysical genius can produce.

Such is this tongue, which, defended by its symbolic forms, inaccessible to all neighbouring idioms, has seen them expiring around it, in the same manner that a vigorous tree sees a host of frail plants, which its shade deprives of the generating heat of day, wither at its feet.

Sanskrit did not have its origin in India. If it is allowable for me to express my thought without promising to prove it, since this would be neither the time nor the place; I believe that a people much older than the Hindus, inhabiting another region of the earth, came in very remote times to be established in *Bharat-Wersh*, to-day Hindustan, and brought there a celebrated idiom called *Bali* or *Pali*, many indications of which are found in *Singhala*, of the island of Ceylon, in the kingdoms of Siam, of Pegu, and in all that part which is called the empire of the Burmans. Everywhere was this tongue considered sacred.[20] Sir William Jones, whose opinion is the same as mine relative to the exotic origin of Sanskrit, without however giving the Pali tongue as its primitive source,

---

[19] *Mém. concer. les Chinois.* T. I. p. 273 *et suiv. Ibid.* T. VIII. p 133 *et suiv. Mém. de l'Acad. des Inscrip.* T. XXXIV. in-4. p. 25.

[20] *Descript. de Siam.* T. I. p. 25. *Asiat. Resear.* T. VI. p. 307.

shows that the pure Hindi, originating in Tatary, rude jargon of the epoch of that colonization, has received from some sort of foreign tongue its grammatical forms, and finding itself in a convenient position to be, as it were, grafted by it, has developed a force of expression, harmonious and copious, of which all the Europeans who have been able to understand it speak with admiration.[21]

In truth, what other tongue ever possessed a sacred literature more widespread? How many years shall yet pass ere Europeans, developed from their false notions, will have exhausted the prolific mine which it offers!

Sanskrit, in the opinion of all the English writers who have studied it, is the most perfect tongue that men have ever spoken.[22] It surpasses Greek and Latin in regularity as in richness, and Persian and Arabic in poetic conceptions. With our European tongues it preserves a striking analogy that holds chiefly to the form of its characters, which being traced from left to right have served, according to Sir William Jones, as type or prototype of all those which have been and which still are in use in Africa and in Europe.

Let us now pass on to the Hebraic tongue. So many abstract fancies have been uttered concerning this tongue, and the systematic or religious prejudice which has guided the pen of its historians, has so obscured its origin, that I scarcely dare to say what it is, so simple is what I have to say. This simplicity will, nevertheless, have its merit; for if I do not exalt it to the point of saying with the rabbis of the synagogue or the doctors of the Church, that it has presided at the birth of the world, that angels and men have learned it from the mouth of God Himself, and that this celestial tongue returning to its source, will become that which will be spoken by the blessed in heaven; neither shall I say with the modern philosophists, that

[21] *Ibid.* T. I. p. 307.
[22] Wilkin's *Notes on the Hitopadesa,* p. 294. Halhed, *dans la préface de la Gramm. du Bengale, et dans le Code des lois des Gentoux.*

it is a wretched jargon of a horde of malicious, opinionated, suspicious, avaricious and turbulent men; I shall say without any partiality, that the Hebrew contained in the Sepher, is the pure idiom of the ancient Egyptians.

This truth will not please those prejudiced *pro* or *con*, I am certain of this; but it is no fault of mine if the truth so rarely flatters their passions.

No, the Hebraic tongue is neither the first nor the last of the tongues; it is not the only one of the mother-tongues, as a modern theosophist, whom I esteem greatly otherwise, has inopportunely believed, because it is not the only one that has sprung from the divine wonders;[23] it is the tongue of a powerful, wise and religious people; of a thoughtful people, profoundly learned in moral sciences and friend of the mysteries; of a people whose wisdom and laws have been justly admired. This tongue separated from its original stem, estranged from its cradle by the effect of a providential emigration, an account of which is needless at the moment, became the particular idiom of the Hebrew people; and like a productive branch, which a skillful agriculturist has transplanted in ground prepared for this purpose, so that it will bear fruit long after the worn out trunk whence it comes has disappeared, so has this idiom preserved and brought down to us the precious storehouse of Egyptian learning.

But this storehouse has not been trusted to the caprice of hazard. Providence, who willed its preservation, has known well how to shelter it from storms. The book which contains it, covered with a triple veil, has crossed the torrent of ages respected by its possessors, braving the attention of the profane, and never being understood except by those who would not divulge its mysteries.

With this statement let us retrace our steps. I have said that the Chinese, isolated from their birth, having departed from the simplest perceptions of the senses, had reached by development the loftiest conceptions of intel-

[23] St-Martin: *Esprit des choses*, T. II. p. 213.

ligence; it was quite the contrary with the Hebrew: this distinct idiom, entirely formed from a most highly perfected tongue, composed wholly of expressions universal, intelligible and abstract, delivered in this state to a sturdy but ignorant people, had, in its hands fallen from degeneracy to degeneracy, and from restriction to restriction, to its most material elements; all that was intelligible had become sentient; all that was universal had become particular.

Sanskrit, holding a sort of mean between the two, since it was the result of a formed tongue, grafted upon an unformed idiom, unfolded itself at first with admirable promptness: but after having, like the Chinese and the Hebrew, given its divine fruits, it has been unable to repress the luxury of its productions: its astonishing flexibility has become the source of an excess which necessarily has brought about its downfall. The Hindu writers, abusing the facility which they had of composing words, have made them of an excessive length, not only of ten, fifteen and twenty syllables, but they have pushed the extravagance to the point of containing in simple inscriptions, terms which extend to one hundred and even one hundred and fifty.[24] Their vagabond imagination has followed the intemperance of their elocution; an impenetrable obscurity has spread itself over their writings; their tongue has disappeared.

But this tongue displays in the *Vedas* an economical richness. It is there that one can examine its native flexibility and compare it with the rigidity of the Hebrew, which beyond the amalgamation of root and sign, does not admit of any composition: or, compare it with the facility with which the Chinese allows its words, all monosyllables, to be joined without ever being confused. The principal beauties of this last idiom consist in its characters, the symbolic combination of which offers a tableau more or less perfect, according to the talent of the writer. It

[24] *Asiat. Research.* T. I. p. 279, 357, 366, etc.

can be said without metaphor, that they paint pictures in their discourse.[25] The written tongue differs essentially from the spoken tongue.[26] The effect of the latter is very mediocre, and as it were, of no importance; whereas, the former, carries the reader along presenting him with a series of sublime pictures. Sanskrit characters say nothing to the imagination, the eye can run through them without giving the least attention; it is to the happy composition of its words, to their harmony, to the choice and to the blending of ideas that this idiom owes its eloquence. The greatest effect of Chinese is for the eyes; that of Sanskrit, for the ears. The Hebrew unites the two advantages but in a less proportion. Sprung from Egypt where both hieroglyphic and literal characters were used at the same time,[27] it offers a symbolic image in each of its words, although its sentence conserves in its *ensemble* all the eloquence of the spoken tongue. This is the double faculty which has procured for it so much eulogy on the part of those who felt it and so much sarcasm on the part of those who have not.

Chinese characters are written from top to bottom, one under the other, ranging the columns from right to left; those of Sanskrit, following the direction of a horizontal line, going from left to right; Hebraic characters, on the contrary, proceed from right to left. It appears that in the arrangement of the symbolic characters, the genius of the Chinese tongue recalls their origin, and makes them still descend from heaven as, it was said, their first inventor had done. Sanskrit and Hebrew, in tracing their lines in an opposite way, also make allusion to the manner in which their literal characters were invented; for, as Leibnitz very well asserted, everything has its sufficient reason; but as this usage pertains especially to the history of peoples, this is not the place to enter in-

---

[25] *Mém. concern. les Chinois.* T. I.
[26] *Ibid.* T. VIII. p. 133 à 185.
[27] Clem. Alex. *Strom.* L. V. Herodot. L. II. 36.

to the discussion that its examination would involve. I shall only observe that the method which the Hebrew follows was that of the ancient Egyptians, as related by Herodotus.[28] The Greeks, who received their letters from the Phœnicians, wrote also for some time from right to left; their origin, wholly different, made them soon modify this course. At first they traced their lines in forms of furrows, going from right to left and returning alternately from left to right;[29] afterward, they fixed upon the sole method that we have to-day, which is that of Sanskrit, with which the European tongues have, as I have already said, much analogy. These three styles of writing merit careful consideration, as much in the three typical tongues as in the derivative tongues which are directly or indirectly attached to them. I conclude here this parallelism: to push it further would be useless, so much the more as, not being able to lay before the reader at once the grammatical forms of Chinese, Sanskrit and Hebrew, I should run the risk of not being understood.

If I had felt sure of having the time and the assistance necessary, I should not have hesitated to take first the Chinese, for basis of my work, waiting until later to pass on from Sanskrit to Hebrew, upholding my method by an original translation of the King, the Veda and the Sepher; but being almost certain of the contrary, I have decided to begin with the Hebrew because it offers an interest more direct, more general, more within the grasp of my readers and promises besides, results of an early usefulness. I trust that if the circumstances do not permit me to realize my idea in regard to Sanskrit and Chin-

[28] Herodot. *Ibid.*
[29] *Mém. de l'Acad. des Inscript.* T. XXXIX. in-12 p. 129. Court-de-Gébelin, *Orig. du Lang.* p. 471.

ese, that there will be found men sufficiently courageous, sufficiently obedient to the impulse which Providence gives toward the perfecting of the sciences and the welfare of humanity, to undertake this laborious work and terminate what I have commenced.

§ II.

HEBRAIC TONGUE: AUTHENTICITY OF THE SEPHER OF MOSES; VICISSITUDES EXPERIENCED BY THIS BOOK.

In choosing the Hebraic tongue, I have not been ignorant of any of the difficulties, nor any of the dangers awaiting me. Some knowledge of speech, and of tongues in general, and the unusual course that I had given to my studies, had convinced me long since that the Hebraic tongue was lost, and that the Bible which we possess was far from being the exact translation of the Sepher of Moses. Having attained this original Sepher by other paths than that of the Greeks and Latins, and carried along from the Orient to the Occident of Asia by an impulse contrary to the one ordinarily followed in the exploration of tongues, I saw plainly that the greater part of the vulgar interpretations were false, and that, in order to restore the tongue of Moses in its primitive grammar, it would be necessary to clash violently with the sc'entific or religious prejudices that custom, pride, interest, the rust of ages and the respect which it attached to ancient errors, concurred in consecrating, strengthening and preserving.

But if one had to listen always to these pusillanimous considerations, what things would ever be perfected? Has man in his adolescence the same needs that he has in his infancy? Does he not change his apparel as well as his nourishment? Are not the lessons of manhood different from those of youth? Do not the savage nations advance toward civilization and those which are civilized toward the acquisition of sciences? Does not one see the cave of the troglodyte make way for the lodge of the hunter, the tent of the herdsman, the hut of the agriculturist, and this cabin transformed successively, thanks to the progressive development of commerce and the arts, into a commodious house, castle, magnificent palace or sumptuous temple? This superb city that we inhabit and this Louvre which spreads before our eyes such rich architecture, do not these all repose upon the same soil where a few miserable hovels of fishermen stood not long ago?

Be not deceived: there are moments indicated by Providence, when the impulse that it gives toward new ideas, undermining precedents useful in their beginning but now superfluous, forces them to yield, even as a skillful architect clears away the rough framework which has supported the arches of his edifice. It would be just as foolish or culpable to attack these precedents or to disturb this framework, when they still support either the social edifice or the particular one, and proceeding, under pretext of their rusticity, their ungracefulness, their necessary obstruction, to overthrow them as out of place; as it would be ridiculous or timid to leave them all there by reason of a foolish or superannuated respect, or a superstitious and condemnatory weakness, since they are of no further use, since they encumber, since they are an obstruction, since they detract from the wisest institutions or the noblest and loftiest structures. Undoubtedly, in the first instance, and following my comparison, either the prince or the architect should stop the audacious ignoramus and prevent him from being buried beneath the inevitable ruins: but in the second instance, they should, on the contrary, welcome the intrepid man who, presenting himself with either torch or lever in hand, offers them, notwithstanding certain perils, a service always difficult.

Had I lived a century or two earlier, even if fortunate circumstances assisted by steadfast labour had placed the same truths within my grasp, I would have kept silent about them, as many savants of all nations have been obliged to do; but the times are changed. I see in looking about me that Providence is opening the portals of a New Day. On all sides, institutions are putting themselves in harmony with the enlightenment of the century. I have not hesitated. Whatever may be the success of my efforts, their aim has been the welfare of humanity and this inner consciousness is sufficient for me.

I am about therefore, to restore the Hebraic tongue in its original principles and show the rectitude and force of these principles, giving by their means a new translation of that part of the Sepher which contains the Cosmogony of Moses. I feel myself bound to fulfill this double task by the very choice that I have made, the motives of which it is useless to explain further. But it is well, perhaps, before entering into the details of the Grammar, and of the numerous notes preceding my translation which prepare and sustain it, that I reveal here the true conditions of things, so as to fortify upright minds against the wrong direction that might be given them, showing the exact point of the question to exploring minds, and make it clearly understood to those whose interests or prejudices, of whatever sort, might lead them astray, that I shall set at naught all criticism which may come from the limits of science, whether supported by delusory opinions or authorities, and that I shall recognize only the worthy champion who shall present himself upon the field of truth, armed with *truth*.

It is well known that the Fathers of the Church have believed, until Saint Jerome, that the Hellenistic version called the *Septuagint*, was a divine work written by prophets rather than by simple translators, often even unaware, from what Saint Augustine says, that another original existed;[30] but it is also known that Saint Jerome, judging this version corrupt in innumerable passages, and by no means exact,[31] substituted a Latin version for it

---

[30] Walton. *Proleg.* IX. Rich. Simon, *Hist. crit.* L. II. ch. 2, August. L. III. c. 25.

[31] Hieron. *in quæst. hebr.* Rich. Simon. *Ibid.* L. II. ch. 3.

that was considered the only authentic one by the Council of Trent, and in defense of which the Inquisition has not feared to kindle the flames of the stake.[32] Thus the Fathers have contradicted beforehand the decision of the Council, and the decision of the Council has, in its turn, condemned the opinion of the Fathers; so that one could not find Luther entirely wrong, when he said that the Hellenistic interpreters had not an exact knowledge of Hebrew, and that their version was as void of meaning as of harmony,[33] since he followed the sentiment of Saint Jerome, sanctioned in some degree by the Council; nor even blame Calvin and the other wise reformers for having doubted the authenticity of the Vulgate, notwithstanding the infallible decision of the Council,[34] since Saint Augustine had indeed condemned this work according to the idea that every Church had formed in his time.

It is therefore, neither the authority of the Fathers, nor that of the Councils that can be used against me; for the one destroying the other, they remain ineffectual. It will be necessary to demonstrate by a complete and perfect knowledge of Hebrew, and not by Greek and Latin citations to which I take exception, but by interpretations founded upon better principles than mine, to prove to me that I have misunderstood this tongue, and that the bases upon which I place my grammatical edifice are false. One clearly realizes, at this time in which we are living, that it is only with such arguments one can expect to convince me.*

[32] Mariana: *pr. Edit. vulg.* c. I.
[33] Luther *sympos. Cap. de Linguis.*
[34] Fuller, *in miscell.* Causabon. *adv. Baron.*

* The Fathers of the Church can unquestionably be quoted like other writers, but it is upon things *de facto*, and in accordance with the rules of criticism. When it is a question of saying that they have believed that the translation of the Septuagint was a work inspired of God, to quote them in such case is unobjectionable; but if one pretends thus to prove it, the quotation is ridiculous. It is necessary, before engaging in a critical discussion, to study the excellent rules

But if honest minds are astonished that after more than twenty centuries, I alone have been able to penetrate the genius of the tongue of Moses, and understand the writings of this extraordinary man, I shall reply frankly that I do not believe that it is so; I think, on the contrary, that many men have, at different times and among different peoples, possessed the understanding of the Sepher in the way that I possess it; but some have prudently concealed this knowledge whose divulgence would have been dangerous at that time, while others have enveloped it with veils so thick as to be attacked with difficulty. But if this explanation will not be accepted, I would invoke the testimony of a wise and painstaking man, who, being called upon to reply to a similar objection explained thus his thought: "It is very possible that a man, secluded in the confines of the Occident and living in the nineteenth century after Christ, understands better the books of Moses, those of Orpheus, and the fragments which remain to us of the Etruscans, than did the Egyptian, Greek and Roman interpreters of the age of Pericles and Augustus. The degree of intelligence required to understand the ancient tongues is independent of the mechanism and the material of those tongues. It is not only a question of grasping the meaning of the words, it is also necessary to enter into the spirit of the ideas. Often words offer in their vulgar relation a meaning wholly opposed to the spirit that has presided at their *rapprochement*...." [35]

I have said that I consider the Hebraic idiom contained in the Sepher, as a transplanted branch of the Egyptian tongue. This is an assertion the historic proof of which I cannot give at this moment, because it would draw me into details too foreign to my subject; but it seems to me that plain, common sense should be enough

laid down by Fréret the most judicious critic that France has possessed. Voyez *Acad. de Belles-Let.* T. VI. *Mémoir.* p. 146. T. IV. p. 411. T. XVIII. p. 49. T. XXI. *Hist.* p. 7.

[35] Court-de Gébelin: *Mond. primit.* T. I, p. 88.

here: for, in whatever manner the Hebrews may have escaped, one cannot deny that they made a long sojourn in Egypt. Even though this sojourn were of only four or five centuries duration as everyone is led to believe;* I ask in all good faith, whether a rude tribe deprived of all literature, without civil or religious institutions that might hold it together, could not assume the tongue of the country in which it lived; a tribe which, transported to Babylon for only seventy years, and while it formed a corps of the nation, ruled by its particular law, submissive to an exclusive cult, was unable to preserve its maternal tongue and bartered it for the Syriac-Aramæan, a sort of Chaldaic dialect;[36] for it is well known that Hebrew, lost from this epoch, ceased to be the vulgar tongue of the Jews.

Therefore, I believe that one cannot, without voluntarily ignoring the evidence, reject so natural an assertion and refuse to admit that the Hebrews coming out from Egypt after a sojourn of more than four hundred years, brought the tongue with them. I do not mean by this to destroy what Bochart, Grotius, Huet, Leclerc,[37] and other erudite moderns have advanced concerning the radical identity which they have rightly admitted between Hebrew and Phœnician; for I know that this last dialect brought into Egypt by the Shepherd kings became identified with the ancient Egyptian long before the arrival of the Hebrews at the banks of the Nile.

Thus the Hebraic idiom ought therefore to have very close relations with the Phœnician, Chaldaic, Arabic and all those sprung from the same source; but for a long time cultivated in Egypt, it had acquired intellectual developments which, prior to the degeneracy of which I have spoken, made it a moral tongue wholly different

* In the Second Book of the Sepher, entitled ואלה שמות *W'âleh-Shemoth* ch. 12 v. 40, one reads that this sojourn was 430 years.

[36] Walton *Proleg.* III. Rich. Simon: *Hist. crit. L.* II. ch. 17.

[37] Bochart, *Chanaan* L. II. ch. I. Grotius: *Comm. in Genes.* c. II. Huet: *Démonst. Evan. prop.* IV. c. 3. Leclerc: *Diss. de Ling. hebr.*

from the vulgar Canaanitish tongue. Is it needful to say to what degree of perfection Egypt had attained? Who of my readers does not know the stately eulogies given it by Bossuet, when, laying aside for a moment his theological partiality, he said, that the noblest works and the most beautiful art of this country consisted in moulding men;[38] that Greece was so convinced of this that her greatest men, Homer, Pythagoras, Plato, even Lycurgus and Solon, those two great legislators, and others whom it is unnecessary to name, went there to acquire wisdom.

Now, had not Moses been instructed in all the sciences of the Egyptians? Had he not, as the historian of the Acts of the Apostles insinuated,[39] begun there to be "mighty in words and deeds?" Think you that the difference would be very great, if the sacred books of the Egyptians, having survived the *débris* of their empire, allowed you to make comparison with those of Moses? Simplicius who, up to a certain point had been able to make this comparison, found so much that was conformable,[40] that he concluded that the prophet of the Hebrews had walked in the footsteps of the ancient *Thoth*.

Certain modern savants after having examined the Sepher in incorrect translations, or in a text which they were incapable of understanding, struck with certain repetitions, and believing they detected in the numbers taken literally, palpable anachronisms, have imagined, now, that Moses had never existed, and then, that he had worked upon scattered memoirs, whose fragments he himself or his secretaries had clumsily patched together.[41] It has also been said that Homer was an imaginary being; as if the existence of the Iliad and the Odyssey, these master-pieces of poetry, did not attest the existence of

[38] Bossuet: *Hist. Univers.* III. part. § 3.
[39] Act. VII. v. 22.
[40] Simplic. *Comm. phys. arist.* L. VIII p. 268.
[41] Spinosa: *tract. theol.* c. 9. Hobbes: *Leviath. Part.* III, c. 33. Isaac de la Peyrère: *Syst. theol. Part.* I. L. IV. c. I. Leclerc, Bolinbroke, Voltaire, Boulanger, Fréret, etc.

their author! He must have little poetic instinct and poor understanding of the arrangement and plan of an epic work, who could conceive such a false idea of man and his conceptions, and be persuaded that a book like the Sepher, the King or the Veda could be put forward as genuine, be raised by fraud to the rank of divine Writings, and be compiled with the same heedlessness that certain authors display in their crude libels.

Undoubtedly certain notes, certain commentaries, certain reflections written at first marginally, have slipped into the text of the Sepher; Esdras has restored badly some of the mutilated passages; but the statue of the Pythian Apollo on account of a few slight breaks, remains none the less standing as the master-piece of an unrivalled sculptor whose unknown name is a matter of less consequence. Not recognizing in the Sepher the stamp of a grand man shows lack of knowledge; not wishing that this grand man be called Moses shows lack of criticism.

It is certain that Moses made use of more ancient books and perhaps of sacerdotal memoirs, as has been suspected by Leclerc, Richard Simon and the author of Conjectures upon Genesis.[42] But Moses does not hide it; he cites in two or three passages of the Sepher the title of the works which are before his eyes: the book of the *Generations of Adam;*[43] the book of the *Wars of the Lord;*[44] the book of the *Sayings of the Seers.*[45] The book of *Jasher* is mentioned in Joshua.[46] The compiling of old memoirs the causing of them to be compiled by scribes as these writers have advanced, or indeed the abridging them as Origen supposed, is very far from that.[47] Moses created in copying: this is what a real genius does. Can one im-

---

[42] Leclerc, *in Diss.* III. *de script. Pentateuch.* Richard Simon: *Hist. crit.* L. I. c. 7.
[43] *Gen.* c. 5. v. 1.
[44] *Num.* c. 21. v. 14.
[45] *Chron.* II. c. 33, v. 19.
[46] *Jos.* c. 10. v. 13.
[47] *Epist. ad Affric.*

AUTHENTICITY OF THE SEPHER

agine that the sculptor of the Pythian Apollo had no models? Can one imagine, by chance, that Homer imitated nothing? The opening lines of the Iliad were copied from the *Demetréide* of Orpheus. The history of Helen and the war of Troy were preserved in the sacerdotal archives of Tyre whence this poet took it. It is asserted that he changed it to such an extent, that, of the simulacrum of the Moon he made a woman, and of the Eons, or celestial Spirits who contended for its possession, the men whom he called Greeks and Trojans.[48]

Moses had delved deeply into the sanctuaries of Egypt, and he had been initiated into the mysteries; it is easily discovered in examining the form of his Cosmogony. He undoubtedly possessed a great number of hieroglyphics which he explained in his writings, as asserted by Philo;[49] his genius and particular inspiration produced the rest. He made use of the Egyptian tongue in all its purity.* This tongue had at this time attained its highest degree of perfection. It was not long becoming deteriorated in the hands of a rude tribe left to their own fate in the deserts of Idumea. It was a giant that found itself suddenly among a troop of pygmies. The extraordinary movement which this tongue had stamped upon its nation could not last, but in order that the plans of Providence should be fulfilled it was sufficient that the sacred storehouse in the Sepher should be guarded carefully.

It appears, in the opinion of the most famous rabbis,[50] that Moses himself, foreseeing the fate to which his

[48] Beausobre, *Hist. du Manich.* T. II. p. 328.
[49] *De vitâ Mos.*

* I shall not stop to contend with the opinion of those who seem to believe that the Coptic differs not in the least from the ancient Egyptian; for can one imagine such an opinion as serious? One might as well say that the tongue of Boccaccio and Dante is the same as that of Cicero and Vergil. One can display his wit in upholding such a paradox; but he could prove it neither by criticism nor even by common sense.

[50] Moyse de Cotsi: *Pref. au grand Livre des Command. de la Loi.* Aben-Esra, *Jesud Mora*, etc.

book must be submitted and the false interpretations that must be given it in the course of time, had recourse to an oral law which he gave by word of mouth to reliable men whose fidelity he had tested, and whom he charged to transmit it in the secret of the sanctuary to other men who, transmitting it in their turn from age to age might insure its thus reaching the remotest posterity.[51] This oral law that the modern Jews are confident they still possess, is named Kabbala,* from a Hebrew word which signifies, that which *is received,* that which *comes from elsewhere,* that which *is passed from hand to hand,* etc. The most famous books that they possess, such as those of the *Zohar,* the *Bahir,* the *Medrashim,* the two *Gemaras,* which compose the *Talmud,* are almost entirely kabbalistic.

It would be very difficult to say today whether Moses has really left this oral law, or whether, having left it, it has not become altered, as the learned Maimonides seems to insinuate when he writes that his nation has lost the knowledge of innumerable things, without which it is almost impossible to understand the Law.[52] Be that as it may, it is quite possible that a like institution might have been in the mind of the Egyptians whose inclination for the mysteries is quite well known.

Besides, chronology, cultivated but little before the conquest of Chosroes, that famous Persian monarch whom we call Cyrus, hardly permits fixing the epoch of the appearance of Moses. It is only by approximation that one can place, about fifteen centuries before the Christian era, the issue of the Sepher. After the death of this theocratic lawgiver, the people to whom he had confided this sacred storehouse, remained still in the desert for some time and were established only after many struggles. Their wandering life influenced their lang-

[51] Boulanger: *Antiq. dev.* L. I. c. 22.

* קבל

[52] Rambam. *More. Nebuch.* Part. I. c. 21.

uage which degenerated rapidly. Their character became harsh; their spirit was roused. They turned hands against each other. One of the twelve tribes, that of Benjamin, was almost wholly destroyed. Nevertheless, the mission that this people had to fulfill and which had necessitated their exclusive laws, alarmed the neighbouring peoples; their customs, their extraordinary institutions, their pride irritated them; they became the object of their attacks. In less than four centuries they were subjected six times to slavery, and six times they were delivered by the hand of Providence who willed their preservation. In the midst of these terrible catastrophes, the Sepher was respected: covered with a providential obscurity it followed the vanquished, escaped the victors, and for a long time remained unknown to its possessors themselves. Too much publicity would have brought about its loss. Whether it is true that Moses had left oral instructions for evading the corruption of the text, it is not to be doubted that he did not take all possible precaution to guard its preservation. It can therefore be regarded as a very probable thing that those who handed down in silence and in the most inviolable secrecy, the thoughts of the prophet, confided his book to each other in the same manner, and in the midst of troubles preserved it from destruction.

But at last after four centuries of disasters, a more peaceful day seemed to shine upon Israel. The theocratic sceptre was divided; the Hebrews gave themselves a king, and their empire although restricted by neighbouring powers did not remain without some glory. Here a new danger appeared. Prosperity came to do what the most frightful reverses had been unable to achieve. Indolence seated upon the throne crept into the lowest ranks of the people. Certain indifferent chronicles, certain misunderstood allegories, chants of vengeance and of pride, songs of voluptuousness, bearing the names of Joshua, Ruth, Samuel, David and Solomon, usurped the place of the

Sepher. Moses was neglected; his laws were unheeded. The guardians of his secrets, invested with luxury, a prey to all the temptations of avarice gradually forgot their oaths. The arm of Providence raised against this intractable people, struck them at the moment least suspected. They were stirred by intestine struggles, they turned against each other. Ten tribes separated themselves and kept the name of Israel. The other two tribes took the name of Judah. An irreconcilable hatred spread between these two rival peoples; they erected altar against altar, throne against throne; Samaria and Jerusalem had each its sanctuary. The safety of the Sepher was the outcome of this division.

Amid the controversies born of this schism each people recalled its origin, invoked its unheeded laws, cited the forgotten Sepher. Everything proves that neither one nor the other possessed this book any longer and that it was only by favour of heaven that it was found long afterward,[53] at the bottom of an old coffer covered with dust, but happily preserved beneath a heap of pieces of money, which avarice had in all probability accumulated secretly and hidden from all eyes. This event decided the fate of Jerusalem. Samaria deprived of her palladium, having been struck a century before by the power of the Assyrians, had fallen, and her ten tribes, captive, dispersed among the nations of Asia, having no religious bond, or to speak more clearly, entering no more in the conservative plans of Providence, were dissolved there; whereas Jerusalem, having recovered her sacred code in the moment of her greatest peril, attached herself to it with a strength that nothing could break. In vain were the peoples of Judah led away into bondage; in vain was their royal city destroyed as Samaria had been, the Sepher which followed them to Babylon was their safe-guard. They could indeed lose, during the seventy years of their captivity, even their mother tongue, but they could not

---

[53] Voyez *Chroniq.* II. c. 34. v. 14. *et suiv.;* et conférez *Rois* II. ch. 12.

AUTHENTICITY OF THE SEPHER

be detached from the love of their laws. It was only needful that a man of genius should deliver these laws to them. This man was found; for genius never fails to come forth when summoned by Providence.

Esdras was the name of this man. His soul was strong and his constancy unflinching. He saw that the time was favourable, that the downfall of the Assyrian empire, overthrown by the hands of Cyrus, gave him the means for reëstablishing the Kingdom of Judah. He skillfully profited by this. From the Persian monarch he obtained the liberty of the Jews and led them to the ruins of Jerusalem. But previous even to their captivity, the politics of the Assyrian kings had reanimated the Samaritan schism. Certain tribes, Cuthæans or Scythians, brought into Samaria, had intermarried with certain surviving members of Israel and even with certain remnants of the Jews who had taken refuge there. At Babylon the plan had been conceived of opposing them to the Jews, whose religious obstinacy was disturbing.[54] A copy of the Hebraic Sepher had been sent to them with a priest devoted to the interests of the court. Accordingly when Esdras appeared, these new Samaritans opposed its establishment with all their strength.[55] They accused him before the great king, of fortifying a city and of making a citadel rather than a temple. It was even said that not content with calumniating him they advanced to fight.

But Esdras was hard to intimidate. Not only did he repulse these adversaries and thwart their intrigues, but anathematizing them, raised up between them and the Jews an insurmountable barrier. He did more: being unable to take away from them the Hebraic Sepher, a copy of which they had received from Babylon, he conceived the idea of giving another form to his and resolved upon the change of its characters.

This was comparatively easy, since the Jews, having

[54] *Kings* II ch. 17. v. 27.
[55] Joseph: *Hist. Jud.* L. XI. c. 4.

at that time not only become denaturalized, but having lost completely the idiom of their forefathers, read the ancient characters with difficulty, accustomed as they were to the Assyrian dialect and to the modern characters of which the Chaldeans had been the inventors. This innovation that politics alone seemed to order, and which without doubt was done from the loftiest motives, had most fortunate results for the preservation of the text of Moses, as I shall relate in my Grammar. It called forth between the two peoples an emulation which has contributed not inconsiderably to bring down to us a book to which the highest interests must ever be attached.

Furthermore, Esdas did not act alone in this matter. The anathema which he had hurled against the Samaritans having been approved by the doctors of Babylon, he convoked them and held with them that great synagogue, so famous in the books of the rabbis. [56] It was there that the changing of the characters was arrested; that the vowel points were admitted in the writing for the use of the vulgar, and the ancient Masorah began, which one should guard against confusing with the modern Masorah, a work of the rabbis of Tiberias, the origin of which does not go back beyond the fifth century of the Christian era.*

[56] R. Eleasar.

* The first *Mashorah*, whose name indicates Assyrian origin as I shall show in my Grammar, regulates the manner in which one should write the Sepher, as much for usage in the temple as for its particular use; the characters that should be employed, the different divisions in books, chapters and verses that should be admitted in the works of Moses; the second *Masorah*, that I write with a different orthography in order to distinguish it from the first, aside from the characters, vowel points, books, chapters and verses with which it is likewise occupied, enters into the most minute details pertaining to the number of words and letters which compose each of these divisions in particular, and of the work in general; it notes those of the verses where some letter is lacking, is superfluous, or else has been changed for another; it designates by the word *Kere* and *Ketib*, the diverse renditions that should be substituted in the reading of each; it marks the

Esdras did still more. As much to estrange the Samaritans as to humour the Jews, whom long custom and their sojourn at Babylon had attached to certain writings more modern than those of Moses and much less authentic, he made a choice from them, retouched those which appeared to him defective or altered, and made up a collection which he joined to the Sepher. The assembly over which he presided approved of this labour that the Samaritans deemed impious; for it is well to know that the Samaritans received absolutely only the Sepher of Moses,[57] and rejected all the other writings as apocryphal. The Jews themselves have not today the same veneration for all the books which constitute what we call the Bible. They preserved the writings of Moses with a much more scrupulous attention, learned them by heart and recited them much oftener than the others. The savants, who have been in a position to examine their various manuscripts, state that the part consecrated to the books of the Law is always much more exact and better treated than the rest.[58]

number of times that the same word is found at the beginning, the middle or the end of a verse; it indicates what letters should be pronounced, understood, inverted, suspended, etc., etc. It is because they have not studied to distinguish these two institutions from each other, that the savants of the past centuries have laid themselves open to such lively discussions: some, like Buxtorf who saw only the first *Mashorah* of Esdras, would not grant that it had anything of the modern, which was ridiculous when one considers the minutiæ of which I have just spoken: others, like Cappell, Morin, Walton and even Richard Simon who saw only the *Masorah* of the rabbis of Tiberias, denied that it had anything of the ancient, which was still more ridiculous, when one considers the choice of characters, vowel points, and the primitive divisions of the Sepher. Among the rabbis, all those who have any name, have upheld the antiquity of the *Mashorah;* there has been only Elijah Levita who has attributed it to more modern times. But perhaps he heard only the *Masorah* of Tiberias mentioned. Rarely do the rabbis say all that they think.

[57] Walton. *Proleg.* XI. Richard Simon. *Hist. crit.* L. I. ch. 10.

[58] Rich. Simon: *Hist. Crit.* L. I. ch. 8.

This revision and these additions have given occasion in later times for thinking that Esdras had been the author of all the writings of the Bible. Not only have the modern philosophists embraced this opinion,[59] which favoured their skepticism, but many Fathers of the Church, and many thinkers have ardently sustained it, believing it more consistent with their hatred of the Jews:[60] they rely chiefly upon a passage attributed to Esdras himself.[61] I think I have sufficiently proved by reasoning, that the Sepher of Moses could be neither a supposition nor a compilation of detached fragments: for one never takes for granted nor compiles works of this nature, and as to its integrity in the time of Esdras, there exists a proof *de facto* that cannot be challenged: this is the Samaritan text. It is well known, however little one may reflect, that considering the condition of things, the Samaritans, mortal enemies of the Jews, anathematized by Esdras, would never have received a book of which Esdras had been the author. They were careful enough not to receive the other writings, and it is also this which can make their authenticity doubted.[62] But it is not my plan here to enter into a discussion in regard to this. It is only with the writings of Moses that I am occupied; I have designated them expressly by the name Sepher, in order to distinguish them from the Bible in general, the Greek name of which, recalls the translation of the Septuagint and comprises all the additions of Esdras and even some more modern ones.

[59] Bolingbroke, Voltaire, Fréret, Boulanger, etc.

[60] St. Basil. *Epist. ad Chil.* St. Clém. Alex. *Strom.* I. Tertull. *de habit. mulier.* c. 35. St. Iren. L. XXXIII. c. 25. Isidor. *Etymol.* L. VI c. 1. Leclerc. *Sentim. de quelq. théolog.* etc.

[61] Esdras ch. IV. v. 14. This book is regarded as **apocryphal**.

[62] Rich. Simon. *Hist. crit.* L. I. ch. 10.

§ III.

CONTINUATION OF THE REVOLUTIONS OF THE SEPHER. ORIGIN OF THE PRINCIPAL VERSIONS WHICH HAVE BEEN MADE.

Let us rely firmly upon this important truth: the Hebraic tongue already corrupted by a gross people, and intellectual as it was in its origin, brought down to its most material elements, was entirely lost after the captivity of Babylon. This is an historic fact impossible to be doubted, whatever skepticism we may profess. The Bible shows it;[63] the Talmud affirms it;[64] it is the sentiment of the most famous rabbis;[65] Walton cannot deny it;[66] the best critic who has written upon this matter, Richard Simon, never wearies of repeating it.[67] Thus therefore, nearly six centuries before Jesus Christ, the Hebrews, having become Jews, no longer either spoke or understood their original tongue. They used a Syriac dialect called Aramaic, formed of the union of several idioms of Assyria and Phœnicia, and quite different from the Nabathæan which according to d'Herbelot was pure Chaldaic.[68]

On and after this epoch, the Sepher of Moses was always paraphrased in the synagogues. It is known that after the reading of each verse, an interpreter was charged with explaining it to the people, in the vulgar tongue. From this came the name of *Targum*.* It is somewhat

---

[63] *Nehem.* ch. 8.
[64] Thalm. *devot.* ch. 4.
[65] Elias, Kimchi, Ephode, etc.
[66] *Proleg.* III et XII.
[67] *Hist. crit.* L. I. ch. 8, 16, 17, etc.
[68] *Biblioth. ori.* p. 514.

* From the Chaldaic word, תַּרְגּוּם, *version, translation*: R. Jacob: *in compend. thalm.*

difficult to say today, whether these versions were at first written by the doctors or entrusted to the sagacity of the interpreters. However that may be, it appears certain that the meaning of the Hebraic words, becoming more and more uncertain, violent discussions arose concerning the diverse interpretations which were given to the Sepher. Some, claiming to possess the oral law secretly given by Moses, wished to introduce it for everyone in these explanations; others, denied the existence of this law, rejected all kinds of traditions and required that they hold to the most literal and the most material explanations. Two rival sects were born of these disputes. The first, that of the Pharisees was the most numerous and the most esteemed: it admitted the spiritual meaning of the Sepher, treated as allegories what appeared to be obscure, believed in divine Providence and in the immortality of the soul.[69] The second, that of the Sadducees, treated as fables all the traditions of the Pharisees, scorned their allegories, and as it found nothing in the material meaning of the Sepher which might prove or even express the immortality of the soul, denied it; seeing nothing in what their antagonists called soul, only a consequence of the organization of the body, a transient faculty which must become extinguished with it.[70] In the midst of these two contending sects, a third was formed, less numerous than the other two, but infinitely more learned: it was that of the Essenes. These held a median position between the Pharisees, who made every thing give way to the allegorical, and the Sadducees who, by the dryness of their interpretations perverted the dogmas of Moses. They preserved the letter and the material meaning outwardly, but guarded the tradition and the oral law for the secret of the sanctuary. The Essenes, living far from cities, formed particular societies, and in no wise

---

[69] Joseph. *Antiq.* L. XII. 22. XVII. 3.

[70] Joseph. *Ibid.* L. XIII. 9. Budd. *Introd. ad phil. hebr.* Basnage: *Hist. des Juifs.* T. I.

jealous of the sacerdotal charges filled by the Pharisees, or of the civil honours intrigued for by the Sadducees, they applied themselves much to ethics and the study of nature. All that has been written upon the mode of life and intelligence of this sect has redounded greatly to its credit. [71] Wherever there were Jews, there were Essenes; but it was in Egypt that they were mostly found. Their principal retreat was in the environs of Alexandria, toward the lake, and Mount Moriah.

I beg the reader seriously interested in ancient secrets to give attention to this name;* for if it is true, as everyone attests, that Moses has left an oral law, it is among the Essenes that it has been preserved. The Pharisees who boasted so haughtily that they possessed it, had only its semblances, for which Jesus constantly reproaches them. It is from these Pharisees that the modern Jews descend, with the exception of certain true savants through whom the secret tradition goes back to that of the Essenes. The Sadducees have brought forth the present Karaites, otherwise called *Scripturalists.*

But even before the Jews possessed their Chaldaic targums, the Samaritans had a version of the Sepher made in the vulgar tongue; for they were even less able than the Jews to understand the original text. This version which we possess entire, being the first of all those which had been made, merits consequently more confidence than the targums, which succeeding and destroying one another do not appear of great antiquity: besides, the dialect in which the Samaritan version is written has more affinity with the Hebrew than with the Aramaic or the Chaldaic of the targums. To a rabbi, named Onkelos, has ordinarily been attributed the targum of the Sepher,

---

[71] Joseph: *de bello Jud.* L. II. c. 12. Phil. *de vitâ contempl.* Budd: *Introd. ad phil. hebr.* etc.

* It is unnecessary, I think, for me to say that Mount Moriah has become one of the symbols of Adonhiramite masonry. This word signifies *the reflected light, the splendour.*

properly so-called, and to another rabbi named Jonathan, that of the other books of the Bible; but the epoch of their composition has not been fixed. It can only be inferred that they are more ancient than the Talmud, because the dialect is more correct and less disfigured. The Talmud of Jerusalem particularly, is in a barbarous style, mixed with a quantity of words borrowed from neighbouring tongues and chiefly from Greek, Latin and Persian.[72] This was the vulgar idiom of the Jews in the time of Jesus Christ.

Nevertheless, the Jews, protected by the Persian monarchs, had enjoyed some moments of tranquillity; they had rebuilt their temples; they had raised again the walls of their city. Suddenly the face of things was changed: the empire of Cyrus crumbled; Babylon fell into the power of the Greeks; all bent beneath the laws of Alexander. But this torrent which burst forth in a moment, both upon Africa and upon Asia, soon divided its waves and turned them in different channels. Alexander died and his captains parcelled out his heritage. The Jews fell into the power of the Seleucidæ. The Greek tongue carried everywhere by the conquerors, modified the new idiom of Jerusalem and drew it further away from the Hebrew. The Sepher of Moses already disfigured by the Chaldaic paraphrases disappeared gradually in the Greek version.

Thanks to the discussions raised by the savants of the last centuries upon the famous version of the Hellenist Jews, vulgarly called the Septuagint version, nothing had become more obscure than its origin.[73] They questioned among themselves, at what epoch, and how, and why it had been done;[74] whether it was the first of all, and whether there did not exist an earlier version in Greek,

[72] *Hist. crit.* L. II. ch. 18.

[73] *Hist. crit.* L. II. c. 2.

[74] Despierres: *Auctor, script. tract.* II. Walton. *Proleg.* IX.

from which Pythagoras, Plato and Aristotle had drawn their knowledge;[75] who the seventy interpreters were and whether they were or were not, in separate cells while labouring at this work;[76] whether these interpreters were, in short, prophets rather than simple translators.[77]

After having examined quite at length the divergent opinions which have been put forth on this subject, these are what I have judged the most probable. Anyone can, if he is so inclined, do this difficult labour over again, which after all will produce only the same results, if he is careful to exercise the same impartiality that I have shown.

It cannot be doubted that Ptolemy, son of Lagus, notwithstanding some acts of violence which marked the beginning of his reign and into which he was forced by the conspiracy of his brothers, was a very great prince. Egypt has not had a more brilliant epoch. There, flourished at the same time, peace, commerce, the arts, and the cultivation of the sciences, without which there is no true grandeur in an empire. It was through the efforts of Ptolemy that the splendid library in Alexandria was established, which Demetrius of Phalereus, to whom he had confided its keeping, enriched with all the most precious literature of that time. The Jews had long since been settled in Egypt.[78] I cannot conceive by what spirit of contradiction the modern thinkers insist that, in the course of circumstances such as I have just presented, Ptolemy did not have the thought that has been attributed to him of making a translation of the Sepher in order to place it in his library.[79] Nothing seems to me so simple. The

---

[75] Cyril. Alex. L. I. Euseb. *præp. evan.* c. 3. Ambros. *Epist.* 6. Joseph *Contr. Api.* L. I. Bellarmin. *de verbo Dei.* L. II. c. 5.

[76] St. Justin, *orat. par. ad gent.* Epiph. *Lib. de mens. et ponder.* Clem. Alex. *Strom.* L. I. Hieron. *Præf. in Pentat.* J. Morin. *Exercit.* IV.

[77] St. Thomas: *quæst.* II. art. 3. St. August. *de Civit. dei.* L. XVIII. c. 43. Iren. *adv. hæres.* c. 25, etc.

[78] Joseph. *Antiq.* L. XII. c. 3.

[79] *Horæ Biblicæ*: § 2.

historian Josephus is assuredly believable on this point as well as the author of the letter of Aristeas, [80] notwithstanding certain embellishments with which he loads this historic fact.

But the execution of this plan might offer difficulties; for it is known that the Jews communicated with reticence their books, and that they guarded their mysteries with an inviolable secrecy. [81] It was even a customary opinion among them, that God would punish severely those who dared to make translations in the vulgar tongue. The Talmud relates that Jonathan, after the appearance of his Chaldaic paraphrase, was sharply reprimanded by a voice from heaven for having dared to reveal to men the secrets of God. Ptolemy, therefore, was obliged to have recourse to the intercession of the sovereign pontiff Eleazar, showing his piety by freeing certain Jewish slaves. This sovereign pontiff whether touched by the bounty of the king, or whether not daring to resist his will, sent him an exemplar of the Sepher of Moses, permitting him to make a translation of it in the Greek tongue. It was only a question of choosing the translators. As the Essenes of Mount Moriah enjoyed a merited reputation for learning and sanctity, everything leads me to believe that Demetrius of Phalereus turned his attention upon them and transmitted to them the orders of the king. These sectarians lived as anchorites, secluded in separate cells, being occupied, as I have already said, with the study of nature. The Sepher was, according to them, composed of spirit and substance: by the substance they understood the material meaning of the Hebraic tongue; by the spirit, the spiritual meaning lost to the vulgar.[82] Pressed between the religious law which forbade the communication of the divine mysteries and the authority of the prince who ordered them to translate

[80] Joseph. *Ibid. præf.* et L. XII. c. 2.
[81] *Hist. crit.* L. II. ch. 2.
[82] Joseph. *de Bello Jud.* L. II. ch. 12. Phil. *de vitâ contempl.* Budd. *introd. ad phil. hebr.*

ORIGIN OF PRINCIPAL VERSIONS

the Sepher, they were astute enough to extricate themselves from such a hazardous step: for, in giving the substance of the book, they obeyed the civil authority, and in retaining the spirit, obeyed their conscience. They made a verbal version as exact as they could in the restricted and material expression, and in order to protect themselves still further from the reproaches of profanation, they made use of the text of the Samaritan version whenever the Hebraic text did not offer sufficient obscurity.

It is very doubtful whether there were seventy in number who performed this task. The name of the *Septuagint Version* comes from another circumstance that I am about to relate.

The Talmud states that at first there were only five interpreters, which is quite probable; for it is known that Ptolemy caused only the five books of Moses to be translated, those contained in the Sepher, without being concerned with the additions of Esdras.[83] Bossuet agrees with this in saying that the rest of the books were, in the course of time, put into Greek for the use of the Jews who were spread throughout Egypt and Greece, where they had not only forgotten their ancient tongue, the Hebrew, but even the Chaldaic which they had learned during captivity.[84] This writer adds, and I beg the reader to note this, that these Jews made a Greek mixture of Hebraisms which is called the Hellenistic tongue, and that the *Septuagint* and all the New Testament are written in this language.

It is certain that the Jews, dispersed throughout Egypt and Greece, having entirely forgotten the Aramaic dialect in which their Targums were written, and finding themselves in need of a paraphrase in the vulgar tongue, would naturally take the version of the Sepher which already existed in the royal library at Alexandria: this is

---

[83] Joseph. *Antiq.* L. XII. ch. 2.
[84] *Disc. sur l'Hist. univ.* I. part. 8.

what they did. They joined to it a translation of the additions of Esdras and sent the whole to Jerusalem to be approved as a paraphrase. The sanhedrin granted their demand, and as this tribunal happened to be of seventy judges in conformity with the law, [85] this version received the name of *Septuagint version,* that is to say, approved by the seventy. [86]

Such is the origin of the Bible. It is a copy in the Greek tongue of the Hebraic writings wherein the material forms of the Sepher of Moses are well enough preserved, so that those who see nothing beyond the material forms may not suspect the spiritual. In the state of ignorance in which the Jews were at that time, this book thus disguised suited them. It suited them to such an extent, that in many of the Greek synagogues, it was read not only as paraphrase, but in place of and in preference to the original text. [87] Of what use was the reading of the Hebrew text? The Jewish people had long since ceased to understand it even in its most restricted acceptance,* and among the rabbis, if one excepts certain

[85] Sepher. L. IV. c. 11. Elias Levita: *in Thisbi.*
[86] *Hist. crit.* L. II. c. 2.
[87] Walton: *Proleg.* IX. *Horœ biblicœ.* §. 2. *Hist. Crit.* L. I. c. 17.

* Philo, the most learned of the Jews of his time, did not know a word of Hebrew although he wrote a history of Moses. He praises much the Greek version of the Hellenists, which he was incapable of comparing with the original. Josephus himself, who has written a history of his nation and who should have made a special study of the Sepher, proves at every step that he did not understand the Hebrew text and that he often made use of the Greek. He laboured hard in the beginning of his work to understand why Moses, wishing to express the first day of creation, used the word *one* and not the word *first,* without making the very simple reflection that the word אחד in Hebrew, signifies both. It is obvious that he pays less attention to the manner in which the proper names were written, than to that in which they were pronounced in his time, and that he read them not by the Hebraic letter, but by the Greek letter. This historian who promises to translate and to render the meaning of Moses, without adding or diminishing anything, is however far from accomplishing this purpose. In the very first chapter of his book, he says that God

ORIGIN OF PRINCIPAL VERSIONS 45

Essenes initiated in the secrets of the oral law, the most learned scarcely pretended to go back of the Greek, the Latin, or the barbarous jargon of Jerusalem, to the Chaldaic Targums which had become for them almost as difficult as the text.*

It was during this state of ignorance and when the Greek Bible usurped everywhere the place of the Hebraic Sepher, that Providence wishing to change the face of the world and operating one of those necessary movements whose profound reason I believe it useless to reveal, raised up Jesus. A new cult was born. Christianity, at first obscure, considered as a Jewish sect, increased, was spread abroad and covered Asia, Africa and Europe. The Roman empire was enveloped by it. Jesus and his disciples had always quoted the Greek Bible, the Fathers of the Church attaching themselves to this book with a religious respect, believing it inspired, written by the prophets, scorned the Hebraic text, and as Saint Augustine clearly says,[88] were even ignorant of its existence. Nevertheless the Jews, alarmed at this movement which was beyond their comprehension, cursed the book which caused it. The rabbis, either by politics or because the oral law became known, openly scoffed it as an illusory version, decried it as a false work, and caused it to be considered by the Jews as more calamitous for Israel than the golden calf. They publicly stated that the earth had been enveloped in darkness during three days on account of this profanation of the holy Book, and as one

took away speech from the serpent, that he made its tongue venomous, that he condemned it henceforth to have feet no more; that he commanded Adam to tread upon the head of this serpent, etc. Now, if Philo and Josephus showed themselves so ignorant in the understanding of the sacred text, what must have been the other Jews? I make exception always of the Essenes.

* It is related in St. Luke that Jesus Christ read to the people a passage from Isaiah paraphrased in Chaldaic and that he explained it (ch. 4. v. 17). It is Walton who has made this observation in his Prolegomena. *Dissert.* XII.

[88] "Ut an alia esset ignorarent." August. L. III. c. 25.

can see in the Talmud, ordained an annual fast of three days in memory of this event.

These precautions came too late; the storehouse badly guarded had changed hands. Israel, resembling a crude coffer closed with a triple lock but worn out by time, afforded no longer a sufficiently sure shelter. A terrible revolution drew nigh: Jerusalm fell, and the Roman empire, a political moribund body, was destined to the vultures of the North. Already the clouds of ignorance were darkening the horizon; already the cries of the barbarians were heard in the distance. It was necessary to oppose these formidable enemies with an insurmountable obstacle. That obstacle was this same Book which was to subdue them and which they were not to understand.

Neither the Jews nor the Christians were able to enter into the profoundness of these plans. They accused each other of ignorance and of bad faith. The Jews, possessors of an original text which they could no longer comprehend, anathematized a version which rendered only the gross and exterior forms. The Christians, content with these forms which at least they grasped, went no further and treated with contempt all the rest. It is true that from time to time there appeared among them men who, profiting by a last gleam of light in those dark days, dared to fix the basis of their belief, and judging the version in its spirit to be identical with its forms, detached themselves abruptly and disdainfully from it. Such were Valentine, Basil, Marcion, Apelles, Bardesane, and Manes, the most terrible of the adversaries that the Bible has encountered. All treated as impious the author of a book wherein the Being, preëminently good, is represented as the author of evil; wherein this Being creates without plan, prefers arbitrarily, repents, is angered, punishes an innocent posterity with the crime of one whose downfall he has prepared.[89] Manes, judging Moses by the book that the Christians declared to be from him,

---

[89] Beausobre: *Hist. du Manich.* Passim. Epiphan, *hœres*, passim.

regarded this prophet as having been inspired by the Genius of evil. [90] Marcion, somewhat less severe saw in him only the instrument of the Creator of the elementary world, very different from the Supreme Being.[91] All of them caused storms, more or less violent; according to the force of their genius. They did not succeed, because their attack was imprudent, unseasonable, and because without knowing it they brought their light to bear inopportunely upon a rough structure prepared for sustaining a most true and imposing edifice.

Those Fathers of the Church whose eyes were not wholly bli ded, sought for expedients to evade the greatest difficulties. Some accused the Jews of having foisted upon the books of Moses things false and injurious to the Divinity;[92] others had recourse to allegories.[93] Saint Augustine acknowledged that there was no way of conserving the literal meaning of the first three chapters of Genesis, without attributing to God things unworthy of him. [94] Origen declared that if the history of the creation was taken in the literal sense it was absurd and contradictory.[95] He complained of the ignorant ones who, led astray by the letter of the Bible, attributed to God sentiments and actions that one would not wish to attribute to the most unjust, the most barbarous of men.[96] The wise Beausobre in his *Histoire du Manichéisme*, and Pétau in his *Dogmes théologiques*, cite numerous similar examples.

The last of the Fathers who saw the terrible mistake of the version of the Hellenists and who wished to remedy it, was Saint Jerome. I give full justice to his inten-

[90] *Act. disput. Archel.* § 7.
[91] Tertull. *Contr. Marci.*
[92] *Recognit.* L. II. p. 52. *Clément. Homel.* III. p. 642-645.
[93] Pétau: *Dogm. théol. de opif.* L. II. 7.
[94] August. *Contr. Faust.* L. XXXII. 10. *De Genes. Contr. Manich.* L. II. 2.
[95] Origen. *philocal.* p. 12.
[96] Origen. *Ibid.* p. 6 et 7.

tions. This Father, of an ardent character and searching mind, might have remedied the evil, if the evil had been of a nature to yield to his efforts. Too prudent to cause a scandal like that of Marcion or of Manes; too judicious to restrict himself to vain subtleties as did Origen or Saint Augustine, he felt deeply that the only way of arriving at the truth was to resort to the original text. This text was entirely unknown. The Greek was everything. It was from the Greek, strange and extraordinary fact, that had been made, according as was needed, not only the Latin version, but the Coptic, Ethiopic, Arabic, and even the Syriac, Persian and others.

But in order to resort to the original text it would be necessary to understand the Hebrew. And how was it possible to understand a tongue lost for more than a thousand years? The Jews, with the exception of a very small number of sages from whom the most horrible torments were unable to drag it, understood it hardly better than Saint Jerome. Nevertheless, the only way that remained for this Father was to turn to the Jews. He took a teacher from among the rabbis of the school of Tiberias. At this news, all the Christain church cried out in indignation. Saint Augustine boldly censured Saint Jerome. Rufinus attacked him unsparingly. Saint Jerome, exposed to this storm, repented having said that the version of the Septuagint was wrong; he used subterfuges; sometimes, to flatter the vulgar, he said that the Hebraic text was corrupt; sometimes, he extolled this text concerning which, he declared that the Jews had not been able to corrupt a single line. When reproached with these contradictions, he replied that they were ignorant of the laws of dialectics, that they did not understand that in disputes one spoke sometimes in one manner and sometimes in another, and that one did the opposite of what one said.[97] He relied upon the example of Saint Paul; he quoted Origen. Rufinus charged him with

[97] P. Morin. *Exercit. Bibl.* Rich. Simon. *Hist. crit.*

ORIGIN OF PRINCIPAL VERSIONS 49

impiety, and replied to him that Origen had never forgotten himself to the point of translating the Hebrew, and that only Jews or apostates could undertake it.[98] Saint Augustine, somewhat more moderate, did not accuse the Jews of having corrupted the sacred text; he did not treat Saint Jerome as impious and as apostate; he even agreed that the version of the Septuagint is often incomprehensible; but he had recourse to the providence of God,[99] which had permitted that these interpreters should translate the Scripture in the way that was judged to be the most fitting for the nations who would embrace the Christian religion.

In the midst of these numberless contradictions, Saint Jerome had the courage to pursue his plan; but other contradictions and other obstacles more alarming awaited him. He saw that the Hebrew which he was so desirous of grasping escaped from him at each step; that the Jews whom he consulted wavered in the greatest uncertainty; that they did not agree upon the meaning of the words, that they had no fixed principle, no grammar; that, in fact, the only lexicon of which he was able to make use was that very Hellenistic version which he aspired to correct.[100] What was the result of his labour? A new translation of the Greek Bible in Latin, a little less barbarous than the preceding translations and compared with the Hebraic text as to the literal forms. Saint Jerome could do nothing further. Had he penetrated the inner principles of the Hebrew; had the genius of that tongue been unveiled to his eyes, he would have been constrained by the force of things, either to keep silence or to restrict it within the version of the Hellenists. This version, judged the fruit of a divine inspiration, dominated the minds in such a manner, that one was obliged to lose one's way like Marcion, or follow it into its necessary

[98] Ruffin. *Invect.* Liv. II. Richard Simon. *Ibid.* L. II. chap. 2.
[99] August. *de doct. Christ.* Walton: *Proleg.* X.
[100] Rich. Simon. *Ibid.* L. II. ch. 12.

obscurity. This is the Latin translation called ordinarily, the Vulgate.

The Council of Trent has declared this translation authentic, without nevertheless, declaring it infallible; but [101] the Inquisition has sustained it with all the force of its arguments,[102] and the theologians with all the weight of their intolerance and their partiality.*

I shall not enter into the irksome detail of the numberless controversies which the version of the Hellenists and that of Saint Jerome have brought about in the more modern times. I shall pass over in silence the translations which have been made in all the tongues of Europe, whether before or after the Reformation of Luther, because they were all alike, only copies more or less removed from the Greek and Latin.

No matter how much Martin Luther and Augustine Eugubio say about the ignorance of the Hellenists, they still use their lexicon in copying Saint Jerome. Though Santes Pagnin or Arias Montanus endeavour to discredit the Vulgate; though Louis Cappell pass thirty-six years of his life pointing out the errors; though Doctor James or Father Henri de Bukentop, or Luc de Bruges, count minutely the mistakes of their work, brought according to some to two thousand, according to others, four thousand; though Cardinal Cajetan, or Cardinal Bellarmin perceive them or admit them; they do not advance one iota the

[101] *Hist. crit.* L. II. ch. 12.
[102] Palavic. *Hist.* M. VI. ch. 17. Mariana: *pro. Edit. vulg.* c. I.

* Cardinal Ximenes having caused to be printed in 1515, a polyglot composed of Hebrew, Greek and Latin, placed the Vulgate between the Hebraic text and the Septuagint version: comparing this Bible thus ranged in three columns, to Jesus Christ between the two robbers: the Hebrew text according to his sentiment, represented the wicked robber, the Hellenistic version the good robber and the Latin translation Jesus Christ! The editor of the Polyglot of Paris, declares in his preface that the Vulgate should be regarded as the original source wherein all the other versions and the text itself should agree. When one has such ideas, one offers little access for truth.

intelligence of the text. The declamations of Calvin, the labours of Olivetan, of Corneille, Bertram, Ostervald and a host of other thinkers do not produce a better effect. Of what importance the weighty commentaries of Calmet, the diffuse dissertations of Hottinger? What new lights does one see from the works of Bochard, Huet, Leclerc, Lelong and Michaelis? Is the Hebrew any better understood? This tongue, lost for twenty-five centuries, does it yield to the researches of Father Houbigant, or to the indefatigable Kennicott? Of what use is it to either or both, delving in the libraries of Europe, examining, compiling and comparing all the old manuscripts? Not any. Certain letters vary, certain vowel points change, but the same obscurity remains upon the meaning of the Sepher. In whatever tongue one turns it, it is always the same Hellenistic version that one translates, since it is the sole lexicon for all the translators of the Hebrew.

It is impossible ever to leave the vicious circle if one has not acquired a true and perfect knowledge of the Hebraic tongue. But how is one to acquire the knowledge? How? By reëstablishing this lost tongue in its original principles: by throwing off the Hellenistic yoke: by reconstructing its lexicon: by penetrating the sanctuaries of the Essenes: by mistrusting the exterior doctrine of the Jews: by opening at last that holy ark which for more than three thousand years, closed to the profane, has brought down to us, by a decree of Divine Providence, the treasures amassed by the wisdom of the Egyptians.

This is the object of a part of my labours. With the origin of speech as my goal, I have found in my path Chinese, Sanskrit and Hebrew. I have examined their rights. I have revealed them to my readers, and forced to make a choice between these three primordial idioms I have chosen the Hebrew. I have told how, being composed in its origin of intellectual, metaphorical and universal expressions, it had insensibly become wholly gross in its nature because restricted to material, literal and particular expressions. I have shown at what epoch and how it was entirely lost. I have followed the revolutions of the Sepher of Moses, the unique book which contains this tongue. I have developed the occasion and the manner in which the principal versions were made. I have reduced these versions to the number of four; as follows: the Chaldaic paraphrases or targums, the Samaritan version, that of the Hellenists, called the Septuagint version, and finally that of Saint Jerome, or the Vulgate. I have indicated sufficiently the idea that one ought to follow.

It is now for my Grammer to recall the forgotten principles of the Hebraic tongue, to establish them in a solid manner, and to connect them with the necessary results: it is for my translation of the Cosmogony of Moses and the notes which accompany it, to show the force and concordance of these results. I shall now give myself fearlessly to this difficult labour, as certain of its success as of its utility, if my readers vouchsafe to follow me with the attention and the confidence that is required.

Hebraic Grammar

HEBRAIC GRAMMAR

CHAPTER I.

GENERAL PRINCIPLES.

§ I.

THE REAL PURPOSE OF THIS GRAMMAR.

Long ago it was said, that grammar was the art of writing and of speaking a tongue correctly: but long ago it ought also to have been considered that this definition good for living tongues was of no value applied to dead ones.

In fact, what need is there of knowing how to speak and even write (if composing is what is meant by writing) Sanskrit, Zend, Hebrew and other tongues of this nature? Does one not feel that it is not a question of giving to modern thoughts an exterior which has not been made for them; but, on the contrary, of discovering under a worn-out exterior ancient thoughts worthy to be revived under more modern forms? Thoughts are for all time, all places and all men. It is not thus with the tongues which express them. These tongues are appropriate to the customs, laws, understanding and periods of the ages; they become modified in proportion as they advance in the centuries; they follow the course of the civilization of peoples. When one of these has ceased to be spoken it can only be understood through the writings which have survived. To continue to speak or even to write it when its genius is extinguished, is to wish to resuscitate a dead body; to affect the Roman toga, or to appear in the streets of Paris in the robe of an ancient Druid.

I must frankly say, despite certain scholastic precedents being offended by my avowal, that I cannot approve of those sorry compositions, whether in prose or in verse, where modern Europeans rack their brains to clothe the forms long since gone, with English, German or French thoughts. I do not doubt that this tendency everywhere in public instruction is singularly harmful to the advancement of studies, and that the constraint of modern ideas to adapt themselves to ancient forms is an attitude which checks what the ancient ideas might pass on in the modern forms. If Hesiod and Homer are not perfectly understood; if Plato himself offers obscurity, for what reason is this so? For no other reason save that instead of seeking to understand their tongue, one has foolishly attempted to speak or write it.

The grammar of the ancient tongues is not therefore, either the art of speaking or even of writing them, since the sound is extinct and since the signs have lost their relations with the ideas; but the grammar of these tongues is the art of understanding them, of penetrating the genius which has presided at their formation, of going back to their source, and by the aid of the ideas which they have preserved and the knowledge which they have procured, of enriching modern idioms and enlightening their progress.

So then, while proposing to give an Hebraic grammar, my object is assuredly not to teach anyone either to speak or to write this tongue; that preposterous care should be left to the rabbis of the synagogues. These rabbis, after tormenting themselves over the value of the accents and the vowel points, have been able to continue their cantillation of certain barbarous sounds; they have been indeed able to compose some crude books, as heterogeneous in substance as in form, but the fruit of so many pains has been to ignore utterly the signification of the sole Book which remained to them, and to make themselves more and more incapable of defending their lawmaker, one of the noblest men that the earth has produced, from the increased attacks that have never ceased to be directed against him by those who knew him only through the thick clouds with which he had been enveloped by his translators.* For, as I have sufficiently intimated, the Book of Moses has never been accurately translated. The most ancient versions of the Sepher which we possess, such as those of the Samaritans, the Chaldaic Targums, the Greek version of the Septuagint and the Latin Vulgate, render only the grossest and most exterior forms without attaining to the spirit which animates them in the original. I might compare them appropriately with those disguises which were used in the ancient mysteries,[1] or even with those symbolic figures which were used by the initiates; the small figures of satyrs and of Sileni that were brought from Eleusis. There was nothing more absurd and grotesque than their outward appearance, upon opening them, however, by means of a secret spring, there were found all the divinities of Olympus. Plato speaks of this pleasing allegory in his dialogue of the Banquet and applies it to Socrates through the medium of Alcibiades.

It is because they saw only these exterior and material forms of the Sepher, and because they knew not how to make use of the secret which could disclose its spiritual and divine forms, that the Sadducees fell into materialism and denied the immortality of the soul.[2] It is well known how much Moses has been calumniated by modern philosophers upon the same subject.[3] Fréret has not failed to quote all those who, like him, have ranked him among the materialists.

* The most famous heresiarchs, Valentine, Marcion and Manes rejected scornfully the writings of Moses which they believed emanated from an evil principle.

[1] Apul. I. XL.
[2] Joseph. *Antiq.* I. XIII. g.
[3] Fréret: *des Apol. de la Rel. chrét.* ch. II.

When I say that the rabbis of the synagogues have put themselves beyond the state of defending their lawgiver, I wish it to be understood that I speak only of those who, holding to the most meticulous observances of the *Masorah*, have never penetrated the secret of the sanctuary. Doubtless there are many to whom the genius of the Hebraic tongue is not foreign. But a sacred duty imposes upon them an inviolable silence.[4] It is said, that they hold the version of the Hellenists in abomination. They attribute to it all the evils which they have suffered. Alarmed at its use against them by the Christians in the early ages of the Church, their superiors forbade them thereafter to write the Sepher in other characters than the Hebraic, and doomed to execration those among them who should betray the mysteries and teach the Christians the principles of their tongue. One ought therefore to mistrust their exterior doctrine. Those of the rabbis who were initiated kept silence, as Moses, son of Maimon, called Maimonides, expressly said:[5] those who were not, had as little real knowledge of Hebrew, as the least learned of the Christians. They wavered in the same incertitude over the meaning of the words, and this incertitude was such that they were ignorant even of the name of some of the animals of which it was forbidden them, or commanded by the Law, to eat.[6] Richard Simon who has furnished me with this remark, never wearies of repeating how obscure is the Hebraic tongue:[7] he quotes Saint Jerome and Luther, who are agreed in saying, that the words of this tongue are equivocal to such an extent that it is often impossible to determine the meaning.[8] Origen, according to him, was persuaded of this truth; Calvin felt it and Cardinal Cajetan himself, was convinced.[9] It

[4] Richard Simon, *Hist. Crit.* L. I. ch. 17
[5] *Mor. Nebuc.* P. II. ch. 29.
[6] Bochart: *de Sacr. animal.*
[7] *Ibid.* I. III. ch. 2.
[8] Hieron. *Apelog. adv. Ruff.* I. 1. Luther, *Comment. Genes.*
[9] Cajetan, *Comment. in Psalm.*

was Father Morin who took advantage of this obscurity to consider the authors of the Septuagint version as so many prophets;[10] for, he said, God had no other means of fixing the signification of the Hebrew words.

This reason of Father Morin, somewhat far from being decisive, has not hindered the real thinkers, and Richard Simon particularly, from earnestly wishing that the Hebraic tongue lost for so long à time, might finally be reëstablished.[11] He did not conceal the immense difficulties that such an undertaking entailed. He saw clearly that it would be necessary to study this tongue in a manner very different from the one hitherto adopted, and far from making use of the grammars and dictionaries available, he regarded them, on the contrary, as the most dangerous obstacles; for, he says, these grammars and these dictionaries are worth nothing. All those who have had occasion to apply their rules and to make use of their interpretations have felt their insufficiency.[12] Forster who had seen the evil sought in vain the means to remedy it. He lacked the force for that: both time and men, as well as his own prejudices were too much opposed.*

I have said enough in my Dissertation concerning what had been the occasion and the object of my studies. When I conceived the plan with which I am now occupied, I knew neither Richard Simon nor Forster, nor any of the thinkers who, agreeing in regarding the Hebraic tongue as lost, had made endeavours for, or had hoped to succeed in its reëstablishment; but truth is absolute, and it is truth which has engaged me in a difficult undertaking; it is truth which will sustain me in it; I now pursue my course.

[10] *Exercit. Bibl.* L. I. ex. VI. ch. 2.
[11] *Hist. crit.* I. III. ch. 2.
[12] *Hist. Crit.* I. III. ch. 3.

* The rabbis themselves have not been more fortunate, as one can see in the grammar of Abraham de Balmes and in several other works.

§ II.

ETYMOLOGY AND DEFINITION.

The word *grammar* has come down to us from the Greeks, through the Latins; but its origin goes back much further. Its real etymology is found in the root קר, כר, גר (*gre, cre, kre*), which in Hebrew, Arabic or Chaldaic, presents always the idea of engraving, of character or of writing, and which as verb is used to express, according to the circumstances, the action of engraving, of characterizing, of writing, of proclaiming, of reading, of declaiming, etc. The Greek word γραμμάτική signifies properly the science of characters, that is to say, of the characteristic signs by means of which man expresses his thought.

As has been very plainly seen by Court de Gébelin, he who, of all the archæologists has penetrated deepest into the genius of tongues, there exist two kinds of grammars: the one, universal, and the other, particular. The universal grammar reveals the spirit of man in general; the particular grammars develop the individual spirit of a people, indicate the state of its civilization, its knowledge and its prejudices. The first, is founded upon nature, and rests upon the basis of the universality of things; the others, are modified according to opinion, places and times. All the particular grammars have a common basis by which they resemble each other and which constitutes the universal grammar from which they emanate:[13] for, says this laborious writer, "these particular grammars, after having received the life of the universal grammar, react in their turn upon their

---

[13] *Mond. prim. Gramm. univ.* t. I, ch. 13, 14 et 15.

ETYMOLOGY AND DEFINITION

mother, to which they give new force to bring forth stronger and more fruitful off-shoots."

I quote here the opinion of this man whose grammatical knowledge cannot be contested, in order to make it understood, that wishing to initiate my readers into the inner genius of the Hebraic tongue, I must needs give to that tongue its own grammar; that is to say, its idiomatic and primitive grammar, which, holding to the universal grammar by the points most radical and nearest to its basis, will nevertheless, be very different from the particular grammars upon which it has been modelled up to this time.

This grammar will bear no resemblance to that of the Greeks or that of the Latins, because it is neither the idiom of Plato nor that of Titus Livius which I wish to teach, but that of Moses. I am convinced that the principal difficulties in studying Hebrew are due to the adoption of Latin forms, which have caused a simple and easy tongue to become a species of scholastic phantom whose difficulty is proverbial.

For, I must say with sincerity, that Hebrew is not such as it has ordinarily been represented. It is necessary to set aside the ridiculous prejudice that has been formed concerning it and be fully persuaded that the first difficulties of the characters being overcome, all that is necessary is six months closely sustained application.

I have said enough regarding the advantages of this study, so that I need not dwell further on this subject. I shall only repeat, that without the knowledge of this typical tongue, one of the fundamental parts of universal grammar will always be unknown, and it will be impossible to proceed with certainty in the vast and useful field of etymology.

As my intention is therefore to differ considerably from the method of the Hebraists I shall avoid entering into the detail of their works. Besides they are sufficiently well known. I shall limit myself here to indicate summarily, those of the rabbis whose ideas offer some analogy to mine.

The Hebraic tongue having become absolutely lost during the captivity of Babylon, all grammatical system was also lost. From that time nothing is found by which we can infer that the Jews possessed a grammar. At least, it is certain that the crude dialect which was current in Jerusalem at the time of Jesus Christ, and which is found employed in the Talmud of that city, reads more like a barbarous jargon than like an idiom subject to fixed rules. If anything leads me to believe that this degenerated tongue preserved a sort of grammatical system, before the captivity and while Hebrew was still the vulgar tongue, it is the fact that a great difference is found in the style of writing of certain writers. Jeremiah, for example, who was a man of the people, wrote evidently without any understanding of his tongue, not concerning himself either with gender, number or verbal tense; whilst Isaiah, on the contrary, whose instruction had been most complete, observes rigorously these modifications and prides himself on writing with as much elegance as purity.

But at last, as I have just said, all grammatical system was lost with the Hebraic tongue. The most learned Hebraists are agreed in saying, that although, from the times of the earliest Hellenist interpreters, it had been the custom to explain the Hebrew, there had been, however, no grammar reduced to an art.

The Jews, dispersed and persecuted after the ruin of Jerusalem, were buried in ignorance for a long time. The school of Tiberias, where Saint Jerome had gone, possessed no principle of grammar. The Arabs were the first to remedy this defect. Europe was at that time plunged in darkness. Arabia, placed between Asia and Africa, reanimated for a moment their ancient splendour.

The rabbis are all of this sentiment. They assert that those of their nation who began to turn their attention to grammar did so only in imitation of the Arabs. The first books which they wrote on grammar were in Arabic. After Saadia-Gaon, who appears to have laid the foundation, the most ancient is Juda-Hayyuj. The opinion of the latter is remarkable.[14] He is the first to speak, in his work, of the letters which are hidden and those which are added. The greatest secret of the Hebraic tongue consists, according to him, of knowing how to distinguish these sorts of letters, and to mark precisely those which are of the substance of the words, and those which are not. He states that the secret of these letters is known to but few persons, and in this he takes up again the ignorance of the rabbis of his time, who, lacking this understanding were unable to reduce the words to their true roots to discover their meaning.

The opinion of Juda-Hayyuj is confirmed by that of Jonah, one of the best grammarians the Jews have ever had. He declares at the beginning of his book, that the Hebraic tongue has been lost, and that it has been reëstablished as well as possible by means of the neighbouring idioms. He reprimands the rabbis sharply for putting among the number of radicals, many letters which are only accessories. He lays great stress upon the intrinsic value of each character, relates carefully their various peculiarities and shows their different relations with regard to the verb.

The works of Juda-Hayyuj and those of Jonah have never been printed, although they have been translated from the Arabic into rabbinical Hebrew. The learned Pocock who has read the books of Jonah in Arabic, under the name of Ebn-Jannehius, quotes them with praise. Aben Ezra has followed the method indicated by these two ancient grammarians in his two books entitled *Zahot* and *Moznayim*. David Kimchi diviates more. The Christian Hebraists have followed Kimchi more willingly than they have Aben Ezra, as much on account of the clear-

[14] Richard Simon, *Hist. Crit.* L. I. ch. 31.

ness of his style, as of his method which is easier. But in this they have committed a fault which they have aggravated further by adopting, without examining them, nearly all of the opinions of Elijah Levita, ambitious and systematic writer, and regarded as a deserter and apostate by his nation.

I dispense with mentioning other Jewish grammarians.* I have only entered into certain details with regard to Juda-Hayyuj, Jonah and Aben Ezra, because I have strong reasons for thinking, as will be shown in the development of the work, that they have penetrated to a certain point, the secret of the Essenian sanctuary, either by the sole force of their genius or by the effect of some oral communication.

* Although Maimonides is not, properly speaking, a grammarian, his way of looking at things coincides too well with my principles to pass over them entirely in silence. This judicious writer teaches that as the greater part of the words offer, in Hebrew, a generic, universal and almost always uncertain meaning, it is necessary to understand the sphere of activity which they embrace in their diverse acceptations, so as to apply that which agrees best with the matter of which he is treating. After having pointed out, that in this ancient idiom, very few words exist for an endless series of things, he recommends making a long study of it, and having the attention always fixed upon the particular subject to which the word is especially applied. He is indefatigable in recommending, as can be seen in the fifth chapter of his book, long meditation before restricting the meaning of a word, and above all, renunciation of all prejudices if one would avoid falling into error.

§ III.

DIVISION OF GRAMMAR:

PARTS OF SPEECH.

I have announced that I was about to reëstablish the Hebraic tongue in its own grammar. I claim a little attention, since the subject is new, and I am obliged to present certain ideas but little familiar, and also since it is possible that there might not be time for me to develop them to the necessary extent.

The modern grammarians have varied greatly concerning the number of what they call, parts of speech. Now, they understand by parts of speech, the classified materials of speech; for if the idea is one, they say, the expression is divisible, and from this divisibility arises necessarily in the signs, diverse modifications and words of many kinds.

These diverse modifications and these words of many kinds have, as I have said, tried the sagacity of the grammarian. Plato and his disciples only recognized two kinds, the noun and the verb;[15] neglecting in this, the more ancient opinion which, according to the testimony of Dionysius of Halicarnassus and Quintilian, admitted three, the noun, the verb and the conjunction.[16] Aristotle, more to draw away from the doctrine of Plato than to approach that of the ancients, counted four: the noun, the verb, the article and the conjunction.[17] The Stoics acknowledged five, distinguishing the noun as proper and appellative.[18] Soon the Greek grammarians, and after

---

[15] Plat. *in Sophist*. Prisc. L. ĪI. Apollon. *Syn.*
[16] Denys Halyc, *de Struct. orat.* 2. Quint. *Inst.* L. I. ch. 4.
[17] Arist. *Poet.* ch. 20.
[18] Diog. Lært. L. VIII, §. 57.

them the Latins, separated the pronoun from the noun, the adverb from the verb, the preposition from the conjunction and the interjection from the article. Among the moderns, some have wished to distinguish the adjective from the noun; others, to join them; again, some have united the article with the adjective, and others, the pronoun with the noun. Nearly all have brought into their work the spirit of the system or prejudices of their school. Court de Gébelin [19] who should have preferred the simplicity of Plato to the profusion of the Latin grammatists, has had the weakness to follow the latter and even to surpass them, by counting ten parts of speech and giving the participle as one of them.

As for me, without further notice of these vain disputes, I shall recognize in the Hebraic tongue only three parts of speech produced by a fourth which they in their turn produce. These three parts are the Noun, the Verb, and the Relation: שם *shem,* פעל *phahal,* מלה *millah.* The fourth is the Sign, אות *aoth.**

Before examining these three parts of speech, the denomination of which is quite well known, let us see what

[19] *Gramm. univ.* L. II. ch. 2. 3 et 4.

* An English grammarian named Harris, better rhetorician than able dialectician, has perhaps believed himself nearer to Plato and Aristotle, by recognizing at first only two things in nature, the *substance* and the *attribute*, and by dividing the words into *principals* and *accessories.* According to him one should regard as principal words, the *substantive* and the *attributive*, in other words, the noun and the verb; as accessory words, the *definitive* and the *connective*, that is to say, the article and the conjunction. Thus this writer, worthy pupil of Locke, but far from being a disciple of Plato, regards the verb only as an attribute of the noun. "*To think,*" he said, "is an attribute of man; *to be white*, is an attribute of the swan; *to fly*, an attribute of the eagle, etc." (*Hermes,* L. I. ch. 3.) It is difficult by making such grammars, to go far in the understanding of speech. To deny the absolute existence of the verb, or to make it an attribute of the substance, is to be very far from Plato, who comprises in it the very essence of language; but very near to Cabanis who makes the soul a faculty of the body.

is the fourth, which I have just mentioned for the first time.

By *Sign,* I understand all the exterior means of which man makes use to manifest his ideas. The elements of the sign are voice, gesture and traced characters: its materials, sound, movement and light. The universal grammar ought especially to be occupied with, and to understand its elements: it ought, according to Court de Gébelin, to distinguish the sounds of the voice, to regulate the gestures, and preside at the invention of the characters.[20] The more closely a particular grammar is related to the universal grammar, the more it has need to be concerned with the *sign.* This is why we shall give very considerable attention to this in regard to one of its elements,— the traced characters; for, as far as the voice and gesture are concerned, they have disappeared long ago and the traces they have left are too vague to be taken up by the Hebraic grammar, such as I have conceived it to be.

Every sign produced exteriorly is a noun; for otherwise it would be nothing. It is, therefore, the noun which is the basis of language; it is, therefore, the noun which furnishes the substance of the verb, that of the relation, and even that of the sign which has produced it. The noun is everything for exterior man, everything that he can understand by means of his senses. The verb is conceived only by the mind, and the relation is only an abstraction of thought.

There exists only one sole Verb, absolute, independent, creative and inconceivable for man himself whom it penetrates, and by whom it allows itself to be felt: it is the verb *to be-being,* expressed in Hebrew by the intellectual sign ו *o,* placed between a double root of life הוה, *hoeh.*

It is this verb, unique and universal, which, penetrating a mass of innumerable nouns that receive their

---

[20] *Gramm. univ.* L. I, ch. 8. et 9.

existence from the sign, forms particular verbs. It is the universal soul. The particular verbs are only animated nouns.

The relations are abstracted by thought from signs, nouns or verbs, and incline toward the sign as toward their common origin.

We shall examine in particular each of these four parts of speech in the following order: the *Sign*, the *Relation*, the *Noun* and the *Verb*, concerning which I have as yet given only general ideas. In terminating this chapter, the Hebrew alphabet, which it is indispensable to understand before going further, is now added. I have taken pains to accompany it with another comparative alphabet of Samaritan, Syriac, Arabic and Greek characters; so as to facilitate the reading of words in these tongues, which I shall be compelled to cite in somewhat large number, in my radical vocabulary and in my notes upon the Cosmogony of Moses.

It must be observed, as regards the comparative Alphabet, that it follows the order of the Hebraic characters. This order is the same for the Samaritan and Syriac; but as the Arabs and Greeks have greatly inverted this order, I have been obliged to change somewhat the idiomatic arrangement of their characters, to put them in relation to those of the Hebrews. When I have encountered in these last two tongues, characters which have no analogues in the first three, I have decided to place them immediately after those with which they offer the closest relations.

Hebraic Alphabet
and
Comparative Alphabet

Hebraic Alphabet

א	A, a.	{ as mother-vowel, this is *a*: as consonant, it is a very soft aspiration.
ב	B, b, bh.	English *b*.
ג	G, g, gh.	English *g* before a, o, u.
ד	D, d, dh.	English *d*.
ה	H, hè, h.	{ as mother-vowel, this is *è*: as consonant, it is a simple aspiration: *h*.
ווו	{ O, o, W or { U, u, y.	{ as mother-vowel, this is *o, u, ou*: as consonant, it is *v, w* or *f*.
ז	Z, z.	English *z*.
ח	H, hê, h, ch.	{ as mother-vowel, this is *hê*: as consonant, it is a chest aspiration: *h,* or *ch*.
ט	T, t.	English *t*.
י	I, i, J, j.	{ as mother-vowel, this is *i* or *aï*: as consonant, it is a whispering aspiration: *j*.
כך	C, c, ch.	German *ch,* Spanish iota, Greek χ.
ל	L, l.	}
מם	M, m.	} same as English analogues.
נן	N, n.	}
ס	S, s.	}
ע	H, ho, gh, gho	{ as mother-vowel, it is the Arabic ع *ho*: as consonant, it is a guttural aspiration, the nasal *gh,* the Arabic غ.
פ	PH, ph.	Greek φ.
צץ	TZ, tz.	}
ק	K, k, qu.	} Same as English.
ר	R, r.	}
ש	SH, sh.	French *ch* or English *sh*.
ת	TH, th.	English *th* or Greek θ.

COMPARATIVE ALPHABET

Hebrew		Samaritan	Syriac	Arabic	Greek	French
א	aleph.	א	ܐ	ا	A α	A a.
ב	beth.	ב	ܒ	ب	B β ϐ	B b.
ג	ghimel.	ג	ܓ	ج	Γ γ Γ	G g gh.
ד	daleth.	ד	ܕ	د	Δ δ	D d.
				ذ		DZ dz, d *weak*.
				ض ظ		DH dh, d *strong*.
ה	hè.	ה	ܗ	ه	E ε	E, Hè.
ו	wao.	ו	ܘ	و	O o, Ω ω, Υ υ	O o, OU ou, U u.
ז	zaïn.	ז	ܙ	ز	Z ζ	Z z.
ח	heth.	ח	ܚ	ح	H η	Ḣ hè.
				خ	X χ	CH ch.
ט	teth.	ט	ܛ	ت	T τ	T t.
				ط		TH th, t *strong*.
י	ïod.	י	ܝ	ي	I ι	I i.
כ ך	caph.		ܟ	ق ك		KH kh.
ל	lamed.	ל	ܠ	ل	Λ λ	L l.
מ ם	mëm.		ܡ	م	M μ	M m.
נ ן	noun.		ܢ	ن	N ν	N n.
ס	samech.		ܣ	س	Σ ς σ	S s.
				ص		SS ss- s *strong*.
ע	haïn.	ע		ع	O υ	Ḣ ho, wh.
				غ		GH gh.
פ ף	phè.		ܦ	ف	Φ φ	PH ph, F f.
					Π π	P p.
					Ψ ψ	PS ps.
צ ץ	tzad.			ط		TZ tz.
ק	coph.	ק		ض	K κ	C c, K k, Q q.
ר	resch.	ר		ر	P ρ	R r.
ש	shin.			ش		SH sh.
ת	thâo.	ת		ت	Θ θ	TH th.

CHAPTER II.

SIGNS CONSIDERED AS CHARACTERS.

§ I.

HEBRAIC ALPHABET: ITS VOWELS: ITS ORIGIN.

Before examining what the signification of the characters which we have just laid down can be, it is well to see what is their relative value.

The first division which is established here is that which distinguishes them as vowels and as consonants. I would have much to do if I related in detail all that has been said, for and against the existence of the Hebraic vowels. These insipid questions might have been solved long ago, if those who had raised them had taken the trouble to examine seriously the object of their dispute. But that was the thing concerning which they thought the least. Some had only a scholastic erudition which took cognizance of the material of the tongue; others, who had a critical faculty and a philosophic mind were often ignorant even of the form of the Oriental characters.

I ask in all good faith, how the alphabet of the Hebrews could have lacked the proper characters to designate the vowels, since it is known that the Egyptians who were their masters in all the sciences, possessed these characters and made use of them, according to the report of Demetrius of Phalereus, to note their music and to solmizate it; since it is known, by the account of Horus-Apollonius, that there were seven of these characters;[1] since it is known that the Phœnicians, close neighbours of the Hebrews, used these vocal characters to designate the seven planets.[2] Porphyry testifies positively to this in his

[1] *Hyeroglyph.* L. II. 29.
[2] Cedren. p. 169.

Commentary upon the grammarian Dionysius Thrax,[3] which confirms unquestionably, the inscription found at Milet, and concerning which we possess a learned dissertation by Barthelemy.[4] This inscription includes invocations addressed to the seven planetary spirits. Each spirit is designated by a name composed of seven vowels and beginning with the vowel especially consecrated to the planet which it governs.

Let us hesitate no longer to say that the Hebrew alphabet has characters whose primitive purpose was to distinguish the vowels; these characters are seven in number.

א soft vowel, represented by *a*.

ה stronger vowel, represented by *e, h*.

ח very strong pectoral vowel, represented by *e, h, ch*.

ו indistinct, dark vowel, represented by *ou, u, y*.

ו brilliant vowel, represented by *o*.

י hard vowel, represented by *i*.

ע deep and guttural vowel, represented by *ho, who*.

Besides these vocal characters, it is further necessary to know that the Hebrew alphabet admits a vowel which I shall call consonantal or vague, because it is inherent in the consonant, goes with it, is not distinguishable, and attaches to it a sound always implied. This sound is indifferently *a, e, o,* for we ought not to believe that the vocal sound which accompanies the consonants has been as fixed in the ancient tongues of the Orient as it has become in the modern tongues of Europe. The word מלך, which signifies a *king*, is pronounced indifferently *malach, melech, moloch,* and even *milich;* with a faint sound of the voice. This indifference in the vocal sound would not have existed if a written vowel had been inserted between the consonants which compose it; then the sound would have become fixed and striking, but of

[3] *Mém. de Gotting.* T. I. p. 251. *sur l'ouvrage de Démétrius de Phal* Περὶ 'Ερμηνείας.

[4] *Mém. de l'Acad. des Belles-Lettres,* T. XLI. p. 514.

ten the sense would also have been changed. Thus, for example, the word מֶלֶךְ, receiving the mother vowel א, as in מַלְאָךְ, signifies no longer simply *a king,* but a divine, eternal emanation; *an eon, an angel.*

When it was said that the Hebrew words were written without vowels, it was not understood, and Boulanger who has committed this mistake in his encyclopædic article, proves to me by this alone, that he was ignorant of the tongue of which he wrote.

All Hebrew words have vowels expressed or implied, that is to say, mother vowels or consonantal vowels. In the origin of this tongue, or rather in the origin of the Egyptian tongue from which it is derived, the sages who created the alphabet which it has inherited, attached a vocal sound to each consonant, a sound nearly always faint, without aspiration, and passing from the *œ* to the *œ,* or from the *a* to the *e,* without the least difficulty; they reserved the written characters for expressing the sounds more fixed, aspirate or striking. This literal alphabet, whose antiquity is unknown, has no doubt come down to us as far as its material characters are concerned; but as to its spirit, it has come down in sundry imitations that have been transmitted to us by the Samaritans, Chaldeans, Syrians and even the Arabs.

The Hebraic alphabet is that of the Chaldeans. The characters are remarkable for their elegance of form and their clearness. The Samaritan much more diffuse, much less easy to read, is obviously anterior and belongs to a more rude people. The savants who have doubted the anteriority of the Samaritan character had not examined it with sufficient attention. They have feared besides, that if once they granted the priority of the character, they would be forced to grant the priority of the text; but this is a foolish fear. The Samaritan text, although its alphabet may be anterior to the Chaldaic alphabet, is nevertheless only a simple copy of the Sepher of Moses, which the politics of the kings of Assyria caused to pass into Samaria, as I have already said in my Dissertation; if this copy differs it is because the priest who was charged with it, as one reads in the Book of Kings,[5] either conformed to the ideas of the Samaritans with whom he wished to keep up the schism, or he consulted manuscripts by no means accurate. It would be ridiculous to say with Leclerc,[6] that this priest was the author of the entire Sepher; but there is not the least absurdity in thinking that he was the author of the principal different readings which are encountered there; for the interest of the court of Assyria which sent him was, that he should estrange as much as possible the Samaritans and the Jews, and that he should stir up their mutual animosity by all manner of means.

It is therefore absolutely impossible to deny the Chaldean origin of the characters of which the Hebraic alphabet is composed today. The very name of this alphabet demonstrates it sufficiently. This name written thus כתיבה אשׁורית (*chathibah ashourith*) signifies, Assyrian writing: an epithet known to all the rabbis, and to which following the genius of the Hebraic tongue, nothing prevents adding the formative and local sign מ to obtain כתיבה מאשׁורית (*chathibah mashourith*), writing in the Assyrian style. This is the quite simple denomination of this alphabet; a denomination in which, through a very singular abuse of words, this same Elijah Levita, of whom I have had occasion to speak, insisted on seeing the Masorites of Tiberias; thus confusing beyond any criticism, the ancient Mashorah with the modern Masorah, and the origin of the vowel points with rules infinitely newer, that are followed in the synagogues relative to their employment.*

[5] *Kings* L. II. ch. 17. v. 27.

[6] Leclerc: *Sentimens de quelq. theol. de Hollande.* L. VI.

* No one is ignorant of the famous disputes which were raised among the savants of the last centuries concerning the origin of the vowel points. These points had always been considered as contem-

§ II.

ORIGIN OF THE VOWEL POINTS.

Thus therefore, the Hebraic alphabet, whatever might have been the form of its characters at the very remote epoch when Moses wrote his work, had seven written vowels: א, ה, ח, ו, וֹ, י, ע; besides a vague vowel attached to each consonant which I have called on account of this, consonantal vowel. But by a series of events which hold to principles too far from my subject to be explained here, the sound of the written vowels became altered, materialized, hardened as it were, and changed in such a way that the characters which expressed them were con-

poraries of the Hebraic characters and belonging to the same inventors; when suddenly, about the middle of the sixteenth century, Elijah Levita attacked their antiquity and attributed the invention to the rabbis of the school of Tiberias who flourished about the fifth century of our era. The entire synagogue rose in rebellion against him, and regarded him as a blasphemer. His system would have remained buried in obscurity, if Louis Cappell, pastor of the Protestant Church at Saumur, after having passed thirty-six years of his life noting down the different readings of the Hebraic text, disheartened at being unable to understand it, had not changed his idea concerning these same points which had caused him so much trouble and had not taken to heart the opinion of Elijah Levita.

Buxtorf, who had just made a grammar, opposed both Elijah Levita and Cappell, and started a war in which all the Hebrew scholars have taken part during the last two centuries, never asking themselves, in their disputes for or against the points, what was the real point of question. Now, this is the real point. Elijah Levita did not understand Hebrew, or if he did understand it, he was very glad to profit by an equivocal word of that tongue to start the war which drew attention to him.

The word אשורי (*ashouri*), signifies in Hebrew, as in Chaldaic, *Assyrian*, that which belongs to Assyria, its root שר or שור indicates all that which tends to rule, to be lifted up; all that which emanates from an original principle of force, of grandeur and of *éclat*. The

fused with the other consonants. The vowels א ,ה and
ח offered only an aspiration more or less strong, being
deprived of all vocal sound; ו and ו became the consonants *v* and *w*; י was pronounced *ji*, and ע took a
raucous and nasal accent.*

If, as has very well been said by the ancients, the
vowels are the soul and the consonants the body of the
words,[7] the Hebraic writing and all which, generally
alphabet of which Esdras made use in transcribing the Sepher, was
called כתיבה אשורית *Assyrian writing*, or in a figurative sense, sovereign,
primordial, original writing. The addition of the sign מ having reference to the intensive verbal form, only gives more force to the expression. כתיבה מאשורית, signifies therefore, *writing in the manner of
the Assyrian*, or writing emanated from the sovereign radiant principle.
This is the origin of the first *mashorah*, the real mashorah to which
both the Hebraic characters and vowel points which accompany them
must be related.

But the word אסור *assour*, signifies all that which is *bound, obliged*
and *subject to rules*. אסירה *a college, a convention*, a thing which
receives or which gives certain laws in certain circumstances. This
is the origin of the second *Masorah*. This latter does not invent the
vowel points; but it fixes the manner of using them; it treats of everything which pertains to the rules that regulate the orthography as
well as the reading of the Sepher. These *Masorites* enter, as I have
said, into the minutest details of the division of the chapters, and the
number of verses, words and letters which compose them. They know,
for example, that in the first book of the Sepher called *Berœshith*, the
Parshioth, or great sections, are twelve in number; those named *Sedarim* or orders, forty-three in number; that there are in all one thousand
five hundred and thirty-four verses, twenty thousand seven hundred
and thirteen words, seventy-eight thousand, one hundred letters; and
finally, that the middle of this book is at chapter 27, v. 40, at the
centre of these words: וְעַל חַרְבְּךָ תִחְיֶה "And by thy sword (extermination) shalt thou live."

* I render it by *gh* or *wh*.

[7] Priscian L. I.

ORIGIN OF THE VOWEL POINTS 79

speaking, belonged to the same primitive stock, became by this slow revolution a kind of body, if not dead, at least in a state of lethargy wherein remained only a vague, transitory spirit giving forth only uncertain lights. At this time the meaning of the words tended to be materialized like the sound of the vowels and few of the readers were capable of grasping it. New ideas changed the meaning as new habits had changed the form.

Nevertheless, certain sages among the Assyrians, called Chaldeans, a lettered and savant caste which has been inappropriately confused with the corps of the nations;* certain Chaldean sages, I say, having perceived the successive change which had taken place in their tongue, and fearing justly that notwithstanding the oral tradition which they strove to transmit from one to the other, the meaning of the ancient books would become lost entirely, they sought a means to fix the value of the vocal characters, and particularly to give to the implied consonantal vowel, a determined sound which would prevent the word from fluctuating at hazard among several significations.

For it had come to pass that at the same time that the mother vowels, that is to say, those which were designated by the written characters, had become consonantal, the consonants, so to speak, had become vocalized by means of the vague vowel which united them. The

---

* The Chaldeans were not a corps of the nations, as has been ridiculously believed; but a corps of savants in a nation. Their principal academies were at Babylon, Borseppa, Sippara, Orchoe, etc. Chaldea was not, properly speaking, the name of a country, but an epithet given to the country where the Chaldeans flourished. These sages were divided into four classes, under the direction of a supreme chief. They bore, in general, the name of כשראין, *Chashdain* or of כלדאין, *Chaldain*, according to the different dialects. Both of these names signified alike, *the venerables, the eminent ones, those who understand the nature of things.* They are formed of the assimilative article ל, and the words שדי or חלד which have reference to excellence, to eminence, to infinite time and to eternal nature.

many ideas which were successively attached to the same root, had brought about a concourse of vowels that it was no longer possible to blend as formerly with the spoken language, and as the written language afforded no assistance in this regard, the books became from day to day more difficult to understand.

I beg the readers but little familiar with the tongues of the Orient, to permit me to draw an example from the French. Let us suppose that we have in this tongue, a root composed of two consonants *bl*, to which we attach an idea of roundness. If we conceive trifling objects under this form, we say indifferently *bal, bel, bil, bol, bul, boul;* but in proportion as we distinguish the individuals from the species in general, we would know that a *bale* is neither a *bille*, nor a *boule;* we would be careful not to confuse the *bol* of an apothecary, with the *bôl* which is used for liquors, nor the *bill* of the English parliament with a *bulle* of the pope; in short, we make a great difference between this last *bulle* and a *bulle* of soap and a *balle* of merchandize, etc.

Now it is in this manner that the Chaldeans thought to obviate the ever growing confusion which was born of the deviation of the mother vowels and of the fixation of the vague vowels. They invented a certain number of small accents, called today vowel points, by means of which they were able to give to the characters of the alphabet under which they placed them, the sound that these characters had in the spoken language. This invention, quite ingenious, had the double advantage of preserving the writing of the ancient books, without working any change in the arrangement of the literal characters, and of permitting the noting of its pronunciation such as usage had introduced.

Here is the form, value and name of these points, which I have placed under the consonant ב solely for the purpose of serving as example; for these points can be

ORIGIN OF THE VOWEL POINTS

placed under all the literal characters, consonants as well as vowels.

Long Vowels	Short Vowels
בָ bâ—*kametz*	בַ ba—*patah*
בֵ bê—*zere*	בֶ be—*segol*
בִ bî—*hirek*	בֻ bu—*kibbuz*
בֹ bô—*holem*	בָ bo—*kamez-hatef*

The point named *shewa*, represented by two points placed perpendicularly under a character, in this manner בְ, signifies that the character under which it is placed lacks the vowel, if it is a consonant, or remains mute if it is a vowel.

The consonant שׁ always bears a point, either at the right of the writer, שׁ, to express that it has a hissing sound as in *sh*; or at the left שׂ, to signify that it is only aspirate. This difference is of but little importance; but it is essential to remark that this point replaces on the character שׁ, the vowel point called *holem*, that is to say *o*. This vocal sound precedes the consonant שׁ when the anterior consonant lacks a vowel, as in מֹשֶׁה *moshe*, it follows it when this same consonant שׁ is initial, as in שָׁנָה *shone*.

Besides these points, whose purpose was to fix the sound of the vague vowels and to determine the vocal sound which remained inherent, or which was attached to the mother vowels either as they were by nature or as they became consonants, the Chaldeans invented still another kind of interior point, intended to give more force to the consonants or to the mother vowel, in the bosom of which it is inscribed. This point is called *dagesh*, when applied to consonants, and *mappik*, when applied to vowels. The interior point *dagesh,* is inscribed in all of the consonants except ר. It is soft in the following six, ת‎, פ‎, כ‎, ך‎, ג‎, ב when they are initial or preceded by the mute point called *shewa;* it is hard in all the others and even in those alluded to, when they are preceded by any vowel whatever; its effect is to double their value. Certain Hebrew grammarians declare that this point, inscribed in the bosom of the consonant פ, pronounced ordinarily *ph,* gives it the force of the simple *p;* but here their opinion is sharply contested by others who assert that the Hebrews, as well as the Arabs, have never known the articulation of our *p*. But as my object is not to teach the pronunciation of Hebrew, I shall not enter into these disputes.

Indeed it is of no importance whatever in understanding the sole Hebrew book which remains to us, to know what was the articulation attached to such or such character by the orators of Jerusalem; but rather, what was the meaning that Moses, and the ancient writers who have imitated him, gave to these characters.

Let us return to the point *mappik*. This inner point is applied to three vowels ה‎, ו‎, י‎, and gives them a new value. The vowel ה, is distinguished from the word, and takes an emphatic or relative meaning; the vowel ו ceases to be a consonant, and becomes the primitive vowel *ou*, and if the point is transposed above it, וֹ it takes the more audible sound of *o* or *u*. The vowel י, is distinguished from the word, even as the vowel ה, and takes an emphatic sound or becomes audible from the mute that it had been.

The diphthongs, however, are quite rare in Hebrew. Nevertheless, according to the Chaldaic pronunciation, when the pure vowels ו or י, are preceded by any vowel point, or joined together, they form real diphthongs as in the following words: עָשׂוּ *heshaou,* שָׁלוּ *shaleou,* פָּנַי *phanai* גּוֹי *goi,* גָּלוּי *galoui,* etc.

The reading of the Hebraic text which I give further on in the original, and its carefully made comparison with the transcription in modern characters, will instruct those who desire to familiarize themselves with the Hebrew characters, much more than all that I might be able to tell them now, and above all they will acquire these same characters with less *ennui.*

§ III.

EFFECTS OF THE VOWEL POINTS.

SAMARITAN TEXT.

Such was the means invented by the Chaldeans to note the pronunciation of the words without altering their characters. It is impossible, lacking monuments, to fix today even by approximation, the time of this invention; but one can without deviating from the truth, determine when it was adopted by the Hebrews. Everything leads to believe that this people, having had occasion during its long captivity in Babylon to become acquainted with the Assyrian characters and the Chaldaic punctuation, found in its midst men sufficiently enlightened to appreciate the advantage of each, and to sacrifice the pride and national prejudice which might hold them attached to their ancient characters.

To Esdras is due the principal honour; a man of great genius and uncommon constancy. It was he who, shortly after the return of the Jews to Jerusalem, revised the sacred Book of his nation, repaired the disorder brought upon it by the numerous revolutions and great calamities, and transcribed it completely in Assyrian characters. It is needless to repeat here the motives and occasion of the additions which he judged proper to make. I have spoken sufficiently of this in my Introductory Dissertation. If any fault was committed in the course of a work so considerable, the evil which resulted was slight; while the good of which it became the source was immense.

For if we possess the very work of Moses in its integrity, we owe it to the particular care of Esdras and to his bold policy. The Samaritan priests who remained obstinately attached to the ancient character, finally corrupted the original text and this is how it was done.

Since they no longer pronounced the words in the same manner, they believed the changing of the orthography immaterial, and since they were deprived of means for determining the sound of the vague vowels which were fixed, they inserted mother vowels where there were none.* These vowels whose degeneration was rapid, became consonants; these consonants were charged with new vague vowels which changed the meaning of the words, besides taking from them what had been hieroglyphic, and finally the confusion became such that they were forced, in order to understand their Book, to have recourse to a translation in the language of the time. Then all was lost for them; for the translators, whatever scruples they might have brought to bear in their work, could translate only what they understood and as they understood.

What happened, however, to the rabbis of the Jewish synagogue? Thanks to the flexibility of the Chaldaic punctuation, they were able to follow the vicissitudes of

*Only a glance at the Samaritan text is sufficient to see that it abounds in the added mother vowels. Father Morin and Richard Simon have already remarked this: but neither has perceived how this text could in that way lose its authenticity. On the contrary, Morin pretended to draw from this abundance of mother vowels, a proof of the anteriority of the Samaritan text. He was ignorant of the fact that the greater part of the mother vowels which are lacking in the Hebraic words, are lacking designedly and that this want adds often an hieroglyphic meaning to the spoken meaning, according to the Egyptian usage. I know well that, particularly in the verbs, the copyists prior to Esdras, and perhaps Esdras himself, have neglected the mother vowels without other reason than that of following a defective pronunciation, or through indolence; but it was an inevitable misfortune. The Masorites of Tiberias may also have followed bad rules, in fixing definitely the number of these vowels. One ought in this case to supply them in reading, and an intelligent person will do so.

the pronunciation without changing anything in the substance, number or arrangement of the characters. Whereas the greater part yielding to the proneness of their gross ideas, lost as had the Samaritans, the real meaning of the sacred text; this text remained entirely concealed in its characters, the knowledge of which was preserved by an oral tradition. This tradition called Kabbala, was especially the portion of the Essenes who communicated it secretly to the initiates, neglecting the points or suppressing them wholly.

This has been the fate of the Sepher of Moses. This precious Book more and more disfigured from age to age, at first by the degeneration of the tongue, afterward by its total loss, given over to the carelessness of the ministers of the altars, to the ignorance of the people, to the inevitable digressions of the Chaldaic punctuation, was preserved by its characters which like so many of the hieroglyphics have carried the meaning to posterity. All of those whom the synagogue has considered as enlightened men, all of those whom the Christian church itself has regarded as true savants, the sages of all the centuries, have felt this truth.

Therefore, let us leave to the Hebraist grammarians the minute and ridiculous care of learning seriously and at length, the rules, wholly arbitrary, which follow the vowel points in their mutations. Let us receive these points in the Hebraic tongue, as we receive the vowels which enter in the composition of the words of other tongues, without concerning ourselves as to their origin or their position. Let us not seek, as I have already said, to speak Hebrew, but to understand it. Whether such or such word is pronounced in such or such fashion in the synagogue, matters not to us. The essential thing is to know what it signifies. Let us also leave the musical notes which the rabbis call the accents, and without disturbing ourselves as to the tones in which the first chapters of the Sepher were cantillated at Jerusalem, let us consider what profound meaning was attached to it by Moses, and with that object let us seek to penetrate the inner genius of the Egyptian idiom which he has employed under its two relations, literal and hieroglyphic. We shall attain this easily by the exploration of the roots, few in number, which serve as the basis of this idiom and by an understanding of the characters, still fewer in number, which are as their elements.

For, even in the richest tongues, the roots are few in number. The Chinese tongue, one of the most varied in the whole earth, which counts eighty-four thousand characters, has scarcely more than two hundred or two hundred and thirty roots, which produce at the most, twelve or thirteen hundred simple words by variations of the accent.

CHAPTER III.

CHARACTERS CONSIDERED AS SIGNS.

§ I.

TRACED CHARACTERS, ONE OF THE ELEMENTS OF LANGUAGE:

HIEROGLYPHIC PRINCIPLE OF THEIR PRIMITIVE FORM.

We are about to examine the alphabetical form and value of the Hebrew characters; let us fix our attention now upon the meaning which is therein contained. This is a matter somewhat novel and I believe it has not been properly investigated.

According to Court de Gébelin, the origin of speech is divine. God alone can give to man the organs which are necessary for speaking; He alone can inspire in him the desire to profit by his organs; He alone can establish between speech and that multitude of marvelous objects which it must depict, that admirable *rapport* which animates speech, which makes it intelligible to all, which makes it a picture with an energy and truthfulness that cannot be mistaken. This estimable writer says, "How could one fail to recognize here the finger of the All Powerful? how could one imagine that words had no energy by themselves? that they had no value which was not conventional and which might not always be different; that the name of lamb might be that of wolf, and the name of vice that of virtue, etc."[1]

---

[1] *Monde primi. Orig. du lang.* p. 66.

Indeed a person must be the slave of system, and singularly ignorant of the first elements of language to assert with Hobbes and his followers, that there is nothing which may not be arbitrary in the institution of speech;[2] that "we cannot from experience conclude that anything is to be called just or unjust, true or false, or any proposition universal whatsoever, except it be from remembrance of the use of names imposed arbitrarily by men."[3]

Again if Hobbes, or those who have followed him, having delved deeply in the elements of speech, had demonstrated the nothingness or absolute indifference of it by a rational analysis of tongues or even simply by the analysis of the tongue that they spoke; but these men, compilers of certain Latin words, believed themselves so wise that the mere declaration of their paradox was its demonstration. They did not suspect that one could raise his grammatical thoughts above a supine or a gerund.

May I be pardoned for this digression which, distant as it appears from the Hebraic grammar, brings us, however, back to it; for it is in this grammar that we shall find the consoling proof, stated above by Gébelin and the response to the destructive paradoxes of Hobbes and all his acolytes. It is even one of the motives which has caused me to publish this grammar, and which, being connected with that of giving to my translation of the Cosmogony of Moses an incontrovertible basis, engages me in a work to which I had not at first destined myself.

I shall show that the words which compose the tongues in general, and those of the Hebraic tongue in particular, far from being thrown at hazard, and formed by the explosion of an arbitrary caprice, as has been asserted, are, on the contrary, produced by a profound reason. I shall prove that there is not a single one that may not, by means of a well made grammatical analysis,

[2] Hobb. *de la nat. hum.* ch. 4. 10.
[3] *Ibid*: ch. 5. § 10. **Leviath.** ch. 4.

CHARACTERS CONSIDERED AS SIGNS 91

be brought back to the fixed elements of a nature, immutable as to substance, although variable to infinity as to forms.

These elements, such as we are able to examine here, constitute that part of speech to which I have given the name of *sign*. They comprise, as I have said, the voice, the gesture, and the traced characters. It is to the traced characters that we shall apply ourselves; since the voice is extinct, and the gesture disappeared. They alone will furnish us a subject amply vast for reflections.

According to the able writer whom I have already quoted, their form is by no means arbitrary. Court de Gébelin proves by numerous examples that the first inventors of the literal alphabet, unique source of all the literal alphabets in actual use upon the earth, and whose characters were at first only sixteen in number, drew from nature itself the form of these characters, relative to the meaning which they wished to attach to them. Here are his ideas upon this subject, to which I shall bring only some slight changes and certain developments necessitated by the extent of the Hebraic alphabet and the comparison that I am obliged to make of several analogous letters; in order to reduce the number to the sixteen primordial characters, and make them harmonize with their hieroglyphic principle.

א A.—Man himself as collective unity, principle: master and ruler of the earth.

פ ב B. P. PH.—The mouth of man as organ of speech; his interior, his habitation, every central object.

כ ג G. C. CH.—The throat: the hand of man half closed and in action of taking: every canal, every enclosure, every hollow object.

ת ד D. DH. TH.—The breast: every abundant, nutritive object: all division, all reciprocity.

ה H. EH. AH.—The breath: all that which animates: air, life, being.

ו O. U.—The eye: all that which is related to the light, to brilliancy, to limpidness, to water.

עוו OU. W. WH.—The ear: all that which is related to sound, to noise, to wind: void, nothingness.

שסן Z. S. SH.—A staff, an arrow, a bow; the arms, the instruments of man: every object leading to an end.

ח H. HE. CH.—A field, image of natural existence: all that which requires work, labour, effort: all that which excites heat.

ץ ט T. TZ.—A roof: a place of surety, of refuge: a haven, a shelter; a term, an aim: an end.

י I.—The finger of man, his extended hand: all that which indicates the directing power and which serves to manifest it.

ל L.—The arm: everything which is extended, raised, displayed.

מ M.—The companion of man, woman: all that which is fruitful and creative.

נ N.—The production of woman: a child: any fruit whatsoever: every produced being.

ק Q. K.—A positive arm: all that which serves, defends, or makes an effort for man.

ר R.—The head of man: all that which possesses in itself, a proper and determining movement.

Now it must be observed that these characters received these symbolic figures from their first inventors only because they already contained the idea; that in passing to the state of signs, they present only abstractly to the thought the faculties of these same objects: but, as I have stated, they can fulfill the functions of the *signs*, only after having been veritable *nouns:* for every *sign* manifested exteriorly is at first a *noun*.

§ II.

ORIGIN OF SIGNS AND THEIR DEVELOPMENT:

THOSE OF THE HEBRAIC TONGUE.

Let us try to discover how the *sign*, being manifested exteriorly, produced a *noun*, and how the *noun*, characterized by a figured type produced a *sign*. Let us take for example, the sign מ M, which, expressing by means of its primordial elements, the sound and organs of the voice, becomes the syllable aM or Ma, and is applied to those faculties of woman which eminently distinguish her, that is to say, to those of mother. If certain minds attacked by skepticism ask me why I restrict the idea of mother in this syllable aM or Ma, and how I am sure that it is applied effectively there, I shall reply to them that the sole proof that I can give them, in the material sphere which envelops them is, that in all the tongues of the world from that of the Chinese to that of the Caribs, the syllable aM or Ma is attached to the idea of mother, and aB, Ba, or aP, Pa, to that of father. If they doubt my assertion let them prove that it is false; if they do not doubt it, let them tell me how it is that so many diverse peoples, thrown at such distances apart, unknown to each other, are agreed in the signification of this syllable, if this syllable is not the innate expression of the sign of maternity.

This is a grammatical truth that all the sophisms of Hobbes and his disciples knew not how to overthrow.

Let us settle upon this fundamental point and proceed. What are the relative or abstract ideas which are attached to, or which follow from, the primordial idea represented by the syllable aM or Ma? Is it not the idea of fecundity, of multiplicity, of abundance? Is it not the idea of fecundation, of multiplication, of formation? Does not one see from this source, every idea of excited and passive action, of exterior movement, of plastic force, of characteristic place, of home, of means, etc?

It is useless to pursue this examination: the mass of ideas contained in the primordial idea of mother, is either attached to the figured sign, to the typical character which represents it, or is derived from and follows it.

Each *sign* starts from the same principles and acquires the same development. Speech is like a sturdy tree which, shooting up from a single trunk begins with a few branches; but which soon extends itself, spreads, and becomes divided in an infinity of boughs whose interlaced twigs are blended and mingled together.

And do not wonder at this immense number of ideas following from so small a number of *signs*. It is by means of the eight keys called *Koua*, that the Chinese tongue, at first reduced to two hundred and forty primordial characters, is raised to eighty and even eighty-four thousand derivative characters, as I have already said.

Now the newer a tongue is and closer to nature, the more the *sign* preserves its force. This force dies out insensibly, in proportion as the derivative tongues are formed, blended, identified and mutually enriched with a mass of words which, belonging to several tribes at first isolated and afterward united, lose their synonymy and finally are coloured with all the nuances of the imagination, and adapt themselves to every delicacy of sentiment and expression. The force of the *sign* is the grammatical touchstone by means of which one can judge without error the antiquity of any tongue.

In our modern tongues, for example, the *sign*, because of the idiomatic changes brought about by time, is very difficult to recognize; it yields only to a persistent analysis. It is not thus in Hebrew. This tongue, like a vigorous shoot sprung from the dried trunk of the pri-

ORIGIN OF SIGNS OF HEBRAIC TONGUE 95

mitive tongue, has preserved on a small scale all the forms and all the action. The *signs* are nearly all evident, and many even are detached: when this is the case, I shall give them name of *relations* for I understand by *sign* only the constitutive character of a root, or the character which placed at the beginning or at the end of a word, modifies its expression without conserving any in itself.

I now pass, after these explanations, to what the Hebraic *signs* indicate, that is to say, to a new development of the literal characters of the Hebraic tongue considered under the relation of the primitive ideas which they express, and by which they are constituted representative *signs* of these same ideas.

א   A.—This first character of the alphabet, in nearly all known idioms, is the sign of power and of stability. The ideas that it expresses are those of unity and of the principle by which it is determined.

ב   B. P.—Virile and paternal sign: image of active and interior action.

ג   G.—This character which offers the image of a canal, is the organic sign; that of the material covering and of all ideas originating from the corporeal organs or from their action.

ד   D.—Sign of nature, divisible and divided: it expresses every idea proceeding from the abundance born of division.

ה   H. He.—Life and every abstract idea of being.

ו   OU. W.—This character offers the image of the most profound, the most inconceivable mystery, the image of the knot which unites, or the point which separates nothingness and being. It is the universal, convertible sign which makes a thing pass from one nature to another; communicating on the one side, with the sign of light and of spiritual sense ו, which is itself more elevated, and connecting on the other side, in its degeneration, with the sign of darkness and of material sense ע which is itself still more abased.

ז   Z. C. S.—Demonstrative sign: abstract image of the link which unites things: symbol of luminous refraction.

ח   H. HE. CH.—This character, intermediary between ה and כ, the former designating life, absolute existence; the latter, relative life, assimilated existence, —is the sign of elementary existence: it offers the image of a sort of equilibrium, and is attached to ideas of effort, of labour, and of normal and of legislative action.

ט   T.—Sign of resistance and of protection. This character serves as link between ד and ת, which are both much more expressive.

י   I.—Image of potential manifestation: of spiritual duration, of eternity of time and of all ideas relating thereunto: remarkable character in its vocal nature, but which loses all of its faculties in passing to the state of consonant, wherein it depicts no more than a material duration, a sort of link as ו, or of movement as ש.

כ   C. CH.—Assimilative sign: it is a reflective and transient life, a sort of mould which receives and makes all forms. It is derived from the character ח which proceeds itself from the sign of absolute life ה. Thus holding, on the one side, to elementary life, it joins to the signification of the character ח, that of the organic sign ג, of which it is, besides, only a kind of reinforcement.

ל   L.—Sign of expansive movement: it is applied to all

ORIGIN OF SIGNS OF HEBRAIC TONGUE 97

ideas of extension, elevation, occupation, possession. As final sign, it is the image of power derived from elevation.

מ M.—Maternal and female sign: local and plastic sign: image of exterior and passive action. This character used at the end of words, becomes the collective sign ם. In this state, it develops the being in indefinite space, or it comprises, in the same respect, all beings of an identical nature.

נ N.—Image of produced or reflected being: sign of individual and of corporeal existence. As final character it is the augmentative sign ן, and gives to the word which receives it all the individual extension of which the expressed thing is susceptible.

ס S. X.—Image of all circumscription: sign of circular movement in that which has connection with its circumferential limit. It is the link ו reinforced and turned back upon itself.

ע H. WH.—Sign of material meaning. It is the sign ו considered in its purely physical relations. When the vocal sound ע, degenerates in its turn into consonant, it becomes the sign of all that which is bent, false, perverse and bad.

פ PH. F.—Sign of speech and of that which is related to it. This character serves as link between the characters ב and ו, B and V, when the latter has passed into state of consonant; it participates in all their significations, adding its own expression which is the emphasis.

צ TZ.—Final and terminative sign being related to all ideas of scission, of term, solution, goal. Placed at the beginning of words, it indicates the movement which carries toward the term of which it is the sign: placed at the end, it marks the same term where it has tended; then it receives this form ץ, It is derived from the character ם and from the character ן, and it marks equally scission for both.

ק Q. K.—Sign eminently compressive, astringent and trenchant; image of the agglomerating or repressive form. It is the character כ wholly materialized and is applied to objects purely physical. For this is the progression of the signs: ה, universal life; ח, elementary existence, the effort of nature; כ, assimilated life holding the natural forms; ק material existence giving the means of forms.

ר R.—Sign of all movement proper, good or bad: original and frequentative sign: image of the renewal of things as to their movement.

ש SH.—Sign of relative duration and of movement therewith connected. This character is derived from the vocal sound ׳, passed into the state of consonant; it joins to its original expression the respective significations of the characters ז and ם.

ת TH.—Sign of reciprocity: image of that which is mutual and reciprocal. Sign of signs. Joining to the abundance of the character ר, to the force of the resistance and protection of the character ט, the idea of perfection of which it is itself the symbol.

Twenty-two signs: such are the simple bases upon which reposes the Hebraic tongue, upon which are raised the primitive or derivative tongues which are attached to the same origin. From the perfect understanding of these bases, depends the understanding of their genius: their possession is a key which unlocks the roots.

§ III.

USE OF THE SIGNS: EXAMPLE DRAWN FROM

THE FRENCH.

I might expatiate at length upon the signification of each of these characters considered as *Signs*, especially if I had added to the general ideas that they express, some of the particular, relative or abstract ideas which are necessarily attached; but I have said enough for the attentive reader and he will find elsewhere in the course of this work quite a considerable number of examples and developments to assure his progress and level all doubts which he might have conceived.

As I have not yet spoken of the *noun*, fundamental part of speech, and as it would be difficult for those of my readers, who have of the Hebraic tongue only the knowledge that I am giving them, to understand me if I proceeded abruptly to the composition or the decomposition of the Hebraic words by means of the sign, I shall put off demonstrating the form and utility of this labour. In order, however, not to leave this chapter imperfect and to satisfy the curiosity as much as possible, without fatiguing too much the attention, I shall illustrate the power of the sign by a French word, taken at hazard, of a common acceptation and of obvious composition.

Let it be the word *emplacement*.* Only a very super-

* At the very moment of writing this, I was at the *Bureau des Opérations militaires du Ministère de la guerre*, where I was then employed. Just as I was seeking for the French word announced in the above paragraph, the chief of the division interrupted me, in order to give me some work to do relative to an *emplacement* of troops. My administrative labour terminated, I again took up my grammatical work, retaining the same word which had engaged my attention.

ficial knowledge of etymology is necessary to see that the simple word here is *place*. Our first task is to connect it with the tongue from which it is directly derived; by this means we shall obtain an etymology of the first degree, which will set to rights the changes which might be effected in the characters of which it is composed. Now, whether we go to the Latin tongue, or whether we go to the Teutonic tongue, we shall find in the one *platea*, and in the other *platz*. We shall stop there without seeking the etymology of the second degree, which would consist in interrogating the primitive Celt, common origin of the Latin and the Teutonic; because the two words that we have obtained suffice to enlighten us.

It is evident that the constitutive root of the French word *place*, is *aT* or *aTz*. Now, the sign in *at*, indicates to us an idea of resistance or of protection, and in *atz* an idea of term, of limit, of end. It is, therefore, a thing resisting and limited, or a thing protective and final. But what is the sign which governs this root and which makes it a noun, by proceeding from right to left following the Oriental manner? It is the sign L, that of all extension, of all possession. *Lat* is therefore, a thing extended as **lat,** or extended and possessed as *latitude*. This is unimpeachable.

Next, what is the second sign which stamps a new meaning on these words? It is the sign P, that of active and central action; inner and determinative character; which, from the word *lat*, an extended thing, makes a thing of a fixed and determined extent, a *plat*, or a *place* by changing the *t* into *c*, as the etymology of the first degree has proved to us the reality of this change.

Now that we understand clearly in the word *em-placement*, the simple word *place* of which it is composed, let us search for the elements of its composition. Let us examine first the termination *ment*, a kind of adverbial relation, which added to a noun, determines, in French, an action implied. The etymology of the first degree gives us *mens,* in Latin, and *mind* in Teutonic. These two words mutually explain each other, therefore it is unnecessary for us to turn to the second degree of etymology. Whether we take *mens* or *mind,* it remains for us to explore the root *eN* or *iN,* after dropping the initial character M, and the final S or D, that we shall take up further on. To the root *en,* expressing something even in the tongue of the Latins, we shall now direct our attention.

Here we see the sign of absolute life E, and that of reflective or produced existence N, joined together to designate every particular being. This is precisely what the Latin root EN, signfies, *lo, behold;* that is to say, *see; examine* this individual existence. It is the exact translation of the Hebrew הן *hen!* If you add to this root the luminous sign as in the Greek αἰών (*æon*), you will have the individual being nearest to the absolute being; if, on the contrary, you take away the sign of life and substitute that of duration as in the Latin *in,* you will have the most restricted, the most centralized, the most interior being.

But let the root EN be terminated by the conscriptive and circumferential sign S, and we shall obtain *ens,* corporeal mind, the intelligence peculiar to man. Then let us make this word rule by the exterior and plastic sign M, and we shall have the word *mens,* intelligence manifesting itself outwardly and producing. This is the origin of the termination sought for: it expresses the exterior form according to which every action is modified.

As to the initial syllable *em,* which is found at the head of the word *em-place-ment,* it represents the root EN, and has received the character M, only because of the consonant P, which never allows N in front of it, and this, as though the being generated could never be presented prior to the generating being. This syllable comes therefore from the same source, and whether it be derived from the corresponding Latin words *en* or *in,* it always characterizes restricted existence in a determined or inner point.

According to these ideas, if I had to explain the French word *em-place-ment*, I would say that it signifies the proper mode according to which a fixed and determined extent, as *place*, is conceived or is presented exteriorly.

Moreover, this use of the sign which I have just illustrated by a word of the French tongue, is much easier and more sure in the Hebrew, which, possessing in itself nearly all the constitutive elements, only obliges the etymologist on very rare occasions to leave his lexicon; whereas, one cannot analyze a French word without going back to Latin or Teutonic, from which it is derived, and without making frequent incursions into Celtic, its primitive source, and into Greek and Phœnician, from which it has received at different times a great number of expressions.

CHAPTER IV.

THE SIGN PRODUCING THE ROOT.

§ I.

DIGRESSION ON THE PRINCIPLE AND THE CONSTITUTIVE ELEMENTS OF THE SIGN.

I have endeavoured to show in the preceding chapter, the origin of the sign and its power: let us again stop a moment upon this important subject, and though I might be accused of lacking method, let us not fear to retrace our steps, the better to assure our progress.

I have designated as elements of speech, the voice, the gesture and the traced characters; as means, the sound, the movement and the light: but these elements and these means would exist in vain, if there were not at the same time a creative power, independent of them, which could take possession of them and put them into action. This power is the Will. I refrain from naming its principle; for besides being difficult to conceive, it would not be the place here to speak of it. But the existence of the will cannot be denied even by the most determined skeptic; since he would be unable to call it in question without willing it and consequently without giving it recognition.

Now the articulate voice and the affirmative or negative gesture are, and can only be, the expression of the will. It is the will which, taking possession of sound and movement, forces them to become its interpreters and to reflect exteriorly its interior affections.

Nevertheless, if the will is absolute, all its affections although diverse, must be identical; that is to say, be respectively the same for all individuals who experience them. Thus, a man willing and affirming his will by gesture or vocal inflection, experiences no other affection than any man who wills and affirms the same thing. The gesture and sound of the voice which accompany the affirmation are not those destined to depict negation, and there is not a single man on earth who can not be made to understand by the gesture or by the inflection of the voice, that he is loved or that he is hated; that he wishes or does not wish the thing presented. There would be nothing of agreement here. It is an identical power which is manifested spontaneously and which radiating from one volitive centre reflects itself upon the other.

I would it were as easy to demonstrate that it is equally without agreement and by the sole force of the will, that the gesture or vocal inflection assigned to affirmation or negation is transformed into different words, and how it happens, for example, that the words לא, *no*, and כה, *yes*, having the same sound and involving the same inflection and the same gesture, have not, however, the same meaning; but if that were so easy, how has the origin of speech remained till now unknown? How is it that so many savants armed with both synthesis and analysis, have not solved a question so important to man? There is nothing conventional in speech, and I hope to prove this to my readers; but I do not promise to prove to them, a truth of this nature in the manner of the geometricians; its possession is of too high an importance to be contained in an algebraic equation.

Let us return. Sound and movement placed at the disposition of the will is modified by it; that is to say, that by certain appropriate organs, sound is articulated and changed into voice; movement is determined and changed into gesture. But voice and gesture have only an instantaneous, fugitive duration. If it is of importance to the will of man, to make the memory of the affections that it manifests exteriorly survive the affections themselves (for this is nearly always of importance to him); then, finding no resource to fix or to depict the sound, it takes possession of movement and with the aid of the hand, its most expressive organ, finds after many efforts, the secret of drawing on the bark of trees or cutting on stone, the gesture upon which it has at first determined. This is the origin of traced characters which, as image of the gesture and symbol of the vocal inflection, become one of the most fruitful elements of language, which extend its empire rapidly and present to man an inexhaustible means of combination. There is nothing conventional in their principle; for *no* is always *no,* and *yes* always *yes:* a man is a man. But as their form depends much upon the designer who first tests the will by depicting his affections, enough of the arbitrary can be insinuated, and it can be varied enough so that there may be need of an agreement to assure their authenticity and authorize their usage. Also, it is always in the midst of a tribe advanced in civilization and subject to the laws of a regular government, that the use of some kind of writing is encountered. One can be sure that wherever traced characters are found, there also are found civilized forms. All men, however savage they may be, speak and impart to each other their ideas; but all do not write, because there is no need of agreement for the establishment of a language, whereas there is always need of one for writing.

Nevertheless, although traced characters infer an agreement, as I have already said, it must not be forgotten that they are the symbol of two things which are not inferred, the vocal inflection and the gesture. These are the result of the spontaneous outburst of the will. The others are the fruit of reflection. In tongues similar to Hebrew, where the vocal inflection and the gesture have long since disappeared, one must devote himself to the characters, as the sole element which remains of the language, and regard them as the complete language itself, not considering the agreement by which they have been established. This is what I have done, in constituting them representative signs of the fundamental ideas of the Hebraic tongue. I shall follow the same method showing successively how this small quantity of signs has sufficed for the formation of the roots of this tongue, and for the composition of all the words which have been derived therefrom. Let us examine first what I mean by a root.

§ II.

FORMATION OF THE ROOT AND OF THE RELATION.

A root is, and can never be anything but, monosyllabic: it results from the union of two signs at the least, and of three at the most. I say two signs at the least, for a single sign cannot constitute a root, because the fundamental idea that it contains, being, as it were, only in germ, awaits the influence of another sign in order to be developed. It is not that the sign before being constituted such, may not have represented a noun, but this noun becomes effaced, as I have said, to constitute the sign. When the sign is presented alone in speech, it becomes, in Hebrew, what I call an article; that is to say, a sort of relation whose expression entirely abstract, determines the diverse relations of nouns and verbs to each other.

The root cannot be composed of more than three signs, without being dissyllabic and consequently without ceasing to be of the number of primitive words. Every word composed of more than one syllable is necessarily a derivative. For, two roots are either united or contracted; or else one or several signs have been joined to the radical root for its modification.

Although the etymological root may be very well employed as noun, verb or relation, all that, however, does not matter, so long as one considers it as root; seeing that it offers in this respect no determined idea of object, action or abstraction. A noun designates openly a particular object of whatever nature it may be, a verb expresses some sort of action, a relation determines a *rapport:* the root presents always a meaning universal as noun, absolute as verb, and indeterminate as relation.

Thus the root אִי, formed of the signs of power and of manifestation, designates, in general, the centre toward which the will tends, the place where it is fixed, its sphere of activity. Employed as noun, it is a desire, a desired object: a place distinct and separate from another place; an isle, a country, a region, a home, a government: as verb, it is the action of desiring a thing eagerly, of tending toward a place, of delighting therein: as relation, it is the abstract connection of the place where one is, of the object to which one tends, of the sphere wherein one acts.

Thus the root אוֹ, which unites to the sign of power, the universal, convertible sign, image of the mysterious knot which brings nothingness to being, offers even a vaguer meaning than the root אִי, of which I have spoken, and of which it seems to be a modification. Nor is it yet a desire, even in general; it is, so to speak, the germ of a desire, a vague appetence, without aim and without object; a desirous uneasiness, an obtuse sense. Employed as noun, it designates the uncertainty of the will; if it is made a verb, it is the indeterminate action of willing; if it is used as relation, it is the abstract expression of the affinity that the uncertainty or indetermination of the will, establishes between one or the other object which attracts it. This root, considered rightly as primitive, produces a great number of derivative roots by becoming amalgamated with other primitive roots, or receiving them by the adjunction of the signs which modify it. One finds, for example, the following, which are worthy of closest attention.

אָב All desire acting inwardly and fructifying. It is, as noun, the matrix of the Universe, the vessel of Isis, the Orphic egg, the World, the Pythonic spirit; etc.

אוֹר Every desire acting outwardly and being propagated. As noun, it is that which binds cause to effect, the causality; any sort of emanation; as verb, it is the action of emanating, of passing from cause to effect; as relation, it is the abstract affinity according to which one

FORMATION OF ROOT AND RELATION 109

conceives that a thing exists, or takes place *because* of another.

אֵל Every expansive desire being projected into space. As noun, it is an interval of time or place; a duration, a distance; as verb, it is the action of being extended, of filling, of invading time or space; that of waiting or lasting; as relation, it is the abstract affinity expressed by *perhaps*.

אֵן Every desire spreading into infinity, losing itself in vacuity, vanishing: as noun, it is everything and nothing according to the manner in which one considers infinity.

אַף Every desire subjugating another and drawing it into its vortex: as noun, it is the sympathetic force, the passion; a final cause: as verb, it is the action of drawing into its will, of enveloping in its vortex: as relation, it is the abstract affinity expressed by *same, likewise*.

אֵץ Every desire leading to a goal. As noun, it is the very limit of desire; the end to which it tends; as verb, it is the action of pushing, of hastening, of pressing toward the desired object: as relation, it is the abstract affinity expressed by *at*.

אוּר Every desire given over to its own impulse. As noun, it is ardour, fire, passion: as verb, it is that which embraces, burns, excites, literally as well as figuratively.

אוֹת All sympathizing desire; being in accord with another. As noun it is a symbol, a character, any object whatever: as verb, it is the action of sympathizing, of being in accord with, of agreeing, of being *en rapport,* in harmony; as relation it is the abstract affinity expressed by *together*.

I shall give no more examples on this subject since my plan is to give, in the course of this Grammar, a series of all the Hebraic roots. It is there that I invite the reader to study their form. I shall be careful to distinguish the primitive roots from the compound, intensive or onomatopoetic roots. Those of the latter kind are quite rare in

Hebrew. One finds them in much greater numbers in Arabic where many local circumstances have called them into existence. This concurrence of imitative sounds, very favourable to poetry and to all the arts of imitation, must have been greatly prejudicial to the development of universal ideas toward which the Egyptians directed their greatest efforts.

It is an unfortunate mistake to imagine that the examination of Hebraic roots is as difficult as it is in the modern idioms. In these idioms, raised, for the most part, upon the *débris* of many united idioms, the roots deeply buried beneath the primitive materials, can deceive the eye of the observer; but it cannot do thus in Hebrew. This tongue, thanks to the form of the Chaldaic characters which have changed scarcely anything but its punctuation, offers still to an observant reader who does not wish to concern himself with the vowel points, the terms used by Moses in their native integrity. If, notwithstanding the precautions of Esdras, there have crept in certain alterations in the mother vowels and even in the consonants, these alterations are slight and do not prevent the root, nearly level with the ground, if I may thus express it, from striking the eye of the etymologist.

Let us examine now what I mean by the relations.

The relations are, as I have said, extracted by thought from the signs, nouns or verbs. They express always a connection of the sign with the noun, of the noun with the noun, or of the noun with the verb. Thence, the simple and natural division which I establish, in three kinds, according to the part of speech with which they preserve the greatest analogy. I call designative relation or *article,* that which marks the connection of the sign with the noun: nominal relation or *pronoun,* that which indicates the connection of the noun with the noun, or of the noun with the verb; and finally adverbial relation or *adverb,* that which characterizes the connection of the verb with the verb, or of the verb with the noun. I use here these denominations known as article, pronoun and adverb to avoid prolixity; but without admitting in Hebrew the distinctions or the definitions that grammarians have admitted in other tongues.

The relations, forming together a kind of grammatical bond which circulates among the principal parts of speech, must be considered separately, kind by kind, and according as they are connected with the sign, noun or verb. I am about to speak of the designative relation or article, since I have already made known the sign: but I shall put off speaking of the nominal relation, because I have already spoken of the noun, and shall deal later with the adverbial relation having already dealt with the verb.

The designative relation or article, is represented under three headings in the Hebraic tongue, namely: under that of the relation properly speaking, or *article,* of the prepositive relation, or *preposition,* and of the interjective relation, or *interjection.* The article differs principally from the sign, by what it preserves of its own peculiar force, and by what it communicates to the noun to which it is joined; a sort of movement which changes nothing of the primitive signification of this noun; nevertheless it is strictly united there and is composed of but one single character.

I enumerate six articles in Hebrew, without including the designative preposition את, of which I shall speak later. They have neither gender nor number. The following are the articles with the kind of movement that they express.

ה DETERMINATIVE ARTICLE.—It determines the noun; that is to say, that it draws the object which it designates from a mass of similiar objects and gives it a local existence. Derived from the sign ה, which contains the idea of universal life, it presents itself under several acceptations as article. By the first, it points out simply the noun that it modifies and is rendered by the corresponding articles *the; this, that, these, those:*

by the second, it expresses a relation of dependence or division, and is translated *of the; of this, of that, of these, of those:* by the third, it adds to the noun before which it is placed, only an emphatic meaning, a sort of exclamatory accent. In this last acceptation, it is placed indifferently at the beginning or at the end of words and is joined with the greater part of the other articles without being harmful to their movement. Therefore I call it *Emphatic article,* and when I translate it, which I rarely do lacking means, I render it by *o! oh! ah!* or simply by the exclamation point (!).

ל DIRECTIVE ARTICLE.—It expresses, with nouns or actions whose movement it modifies, a direct relation of union, of possession, or of coincidence. I translate it by *to, at, for, according to, toward,* etc.

מ EXTRACTIVE OR PARTITIVE ARTICLE.—The movement which this article expresses, with nouns or actions that it modifies, is that by which a noun or an action is taken for the means, for the instrument, by which they are divided in their essence, or drawn from the midst of several other nouns or similar actions. I render it ordinarily by *from, out of, by; with, by means of, among, between,* etc.

ב MEDIATIVE OR INTEGRAL ARTICLE.—This article characterizes with nouns or actions, almost the same movement as the extractive article מ, but with more force, and without any extraction or division of the parts. Its analogues are: *in, by, with, while,* etc.

כ ASSIMILATIVE ARTICLE.—The movement which it expresses, with nouns or actions is that of similitude, of analogy, and of concomitance. I render it by: *as, similar; such as, according to,* etc.

ו CONJUNCTIVE OR CONVERTIBLE ARTICLE.—This article. in uniting nouns, causes the movement of nothingness, of which the character ו becomes the sign, as we have seen: in making actions pass from one time to another.

FORMATION OF ROOT AND RELATION

it exercises upon them the convertible faculty of which this same character is the universal emblem. Its conjunctive movement can be rendered by: *and, also, thus, then, afterward, that,* etc. But its convertible movement is not expressible in our tongue and I do not know of any in which it can be expressed. In order to perceive it one must feel the Hebraic genius.

The chapters wherein I shall treat of the noun and the verb will contain the necessary examples to illustrate the use of these six articles whether relative to the noun or the verb.

§ III.

PREPOSITION AND INTERJECTION.

Articles, which we shall now examine, remain articles, properly speaking, only so far as they are composed of a single literal character and as they are joined intimately to the noun, the verb or the relation which they govern; when they are composed of several characters and when they act apart or are simply united to words by a hyphen, I call them prepositive articles or *prepositions*: they become *interjections* when, in this state of isolation, they offer no longer any relation with the noun or the verb, and express only a movement of the mind too intense to be otherwise characterized.

Prepositions, intended to serve as link between things, and to show their respective function, lose their meaning when once separated from the noun which they modify. Interjections, on the contrary, have only as much force as they have independence. Differing but little in sound, they differ infinitely in the expression, more or less accentuated, that they receive from the sentiment which produces them. They belong, as a learned man has said, "to all time, to all places, to all peoples": they form an universal language.[1]

I am about to give here, the prepositions and interjections which are the most important to understand, so as to fix the ideas of the reader upon the use of these kinds of relations. I am beginning with those prepositions which take the place of the articles already cited.

חַאֽ׃ *determinative prep.* replaces the article הֽ.
אַל, אֵלִי׳ or עַל׃ *directive* " " " " לֽ.
מִן, מָנִי׳ or מָמֶנִי׃ *extractive* " " " " מֽ.

[1] Court de Geb: *Gramm. Univ.* p. 353.

PREPOSITION AND INTERJECTION

בְּ, *mediative* prep. replaces the article בִּי, בְּדִי or בְּמוֹ:
כְּ, *assimilative* " " " " כִּי, כֵּה or כְּמוֹ:

The conjunctive and convertible article וְ is not replaceable.

אֵת, אוֹת: *designative preposition:* **has no corresponding article.**

גַּם, גַם כִּי: same, also, as ⎫
כִּי: that ⎬ *conjunctive prepositions*
עִם, עָמַד: with ⎪
אַף: likewise, even ⎭

אוֹ either, or ⎫
בַּל: neither, nor ⎬ *disjunctive prepositions*
בְּלִי, בִּלְתִּי, מִבְּלִי: without ⎭

אַךְ: but, except ⎫
אוּלָם: nevertheless ⎬ *restrictive prepositions*
רַק: save, at least ⎭

אִם, כִּי אִם: if, but if ⎫ *conditional prepositions*
אוּלַי: perhaps ⎭

יוֹתֵר: besides, moreover ⎫ *additive prepositions*
מְאֹד: very, more ⎭

אֵצֶל: near, with ⎫ *final prepositions*
עַד עֲדֵי: at, as far as ⎭

בַּעַד: for ⎫
כְּפִי, לְפִי: according to ⎪
כִּי: for, because ⎪
חֵלֶף: on account of ⎬ *discursive prepositions*
יַעַן כִּי: since ⎪
לָכֵן: therefore ⎪
עַל־כֵּן: now then, so ⎪
לְמַעַן: as ⎭

etc., etc.,

INTERJECTIONS.

אָח, אוֹי, אוֹיחַ׃	ah! woe! alas!
הָ, הָא׃	oh! heavens!
חֶאָח׃	now then! come **now**!
הָבָה׃	take care! mind!
הוֹי׃	indeed!
לוּ, אַחֲלַי׃	would to God!
	etc., etc.,

I believe it quite useless to prolong this list and to dwell upon the particular signification of each of these relations; however, there is one of which I must speak, because its usage is very frequent in the tongue of Moses, and also because we shall see it soon figuring in the nominal inflection, and joining its movement to that of the articles. This is the designative preposition אֵת, which I have mentioned as having no corresponding article.

The movement which expresses this preposition with the nouns which it modifies, is that by which it puts them *en rapport* as governing or governed, as independent one of the other and participating in the same action. I name it *designative*, on account of the sign of signs, ת, from which it is derived. It characterizes sympathy and reciprocity when it is taken substantively. Joined to a noun by a hyphen אֶת־, it designates the substance proper and individual, the identity, the selfsameness, the seity, the *thou-ness*, if I may be permitted this word; that is to say, that which constitutes *thou*, that which implies something apart from *me*, a thing that is not *me;* in short, the presence of another substance. This important preposition, of which I cannot give the exact meaning, indicates the coincidence, the spontaneity of actions, the liaison, the *ensemble* and the dependence of things.

The designative relation that I am considering in connection with the article, preposition and interjection, will be easily distinguished from the nominal relation concerning which I shall speak later on; because this relation is not intended either to modify nouns or to set forth the confused and indeterminate movements of the mind; but serves as supplement to nouns, becomes their lieutenant, so to speak, and shows their mutual dependence. This same relation will not be, it is true, so easy to distinguish from the adverbial relation, and I admit that often one will meet with some that are, at the same time, prepositions and adverbs. But this very analogy will furnish the proof of what I have advanced, that the relation extracted by thought, from the sign, the noun and the verb, circulates among these three principal parts of speech and is modified to serve them as common bond.

One can observe, for example, that the designative relation tends to become adverbial and that it becomes thus whenever it is used in an absolute manner with the verb, or when the article is joined, making it a sort of adverbial substantive. Therefore one can judge that *upon, in, outside,* are designative relations, or prepositions when one says: *upon that; in the present; outside this point:* but one cannot mistake them for adverbials when one says: *I am above; I am within; I am without.* It is in this state that they are taken to be inflected with the article. *I see the above, the within, the without; I come from above, from within, from without; I go above, within, without;* etc. The Hebraic tongue, which has not these means of construction, makes use of the same words עַל, חוּץ, בֵּית to express equally *upon, above, the upper part; in, the inside; out, beyond, the outside.* It is to these fine points that great attention must be given in translating Moses.

As to the vowel points which accompany the different relations of which I shall speak, they vary in such a way, that it would be vainly wasting precious time to consider them here; so much the more as these variations change nothing as to the meaning, which alone concerns me, and alters only the pronunciation, which does not concern me.

I am always surprised, in reading the majority of the Grammars written upon the Hebraic tongue, to see with what scruples, with what tedious care they treat a miserable *kamez,* or a still more miserable *kamez-hatif;* whereas they hardly deign to dwell upon the meaning of the most important words. Numberless pages are found jumbled with the uncouth names of *zere, segol, patah, holem,* and not one where the sign is mentioned, not one where it is even a question of this basis, at once so simple and so fecund, both of the Hebraic language and of all the languages of the world.

CHAPTER V.

THE NOUN.

THE NOUN CONSIDERED UNDER SEVEN RELATIONS.

§ I.

ETYMOLOGY

The noun, I repeat, is the basis of speech; for, although it may be the product of the sign, the sign without it would have no meaning, and if the sign had no meaning, there would exist neither relations nor verbs.

We shall consider the nouns of the Hebraic tongue, under seven relations, namely: under the first six, of Etymology, Quality, Gender, Number, Movement and Construction, and then, under the seventh relation of Signification, which includes them all.

The Hebraist grammarians, dazzled by the *éclat* of the verb and by the extensive use of the verbal faculties, have despoiled the noun of its etymological rank to give it to the verb, thus deriving from the verb not only the equi-literal substantives, that is to say, compounds of the same number of characters, but even those which offer less: claiming, for example, that גַל *a heap*, is formed from גָלל *he heaps up;* that אָב *father*, is derived from אָבָה *he willed;* that אֵשׁ *the fire*, finds its origin in אָשַׁשׁ *he was strong and robust*, etc.

It is needless for me to say into how many errors they have fallen by this false course, and how far distant they are from the real etymological goal. The lexicons also, of these Hebraists, all constructed after this method, are only crude vocabularies, where the simplest words, thrown more or less far from their root, according as the verb bids it, are presented almost never in their real place, or in the true light which would facilitate their comprehension.

I have spoken sufficiently of the sign and its value, of the root and its formation; I now intend to give certain simple rules to lead to the etymological understanding of the noun.

Often a *noun* properly speaking, is, in the tongue of the Hebrews, only its root used in a more restricted sense: as when uniting the idea of paternity and maternity upon a single subject, one pronounces אב, *father,* or אם *mother.* It is then a movement of the thought upon itself, which makes of a thing that it had conceived in general, a determined thing, by which it qualifies a particular subject. This movement is very common in the idiom of Moses, and it merits so much the more attention, because, not having observed it, the greater part of the translators have been mistaken in the meaning of the words and have ridiculously particularized what was universal. As when, for example, in עץ, a vegetable substance, a vegetation in general, they have seen *a wood,* or *a tree:* or in גן , an enclosure, a circumscription, a sphere, only a *garden*: or even in דם, the universal idea of an assimilation of homogeneous parts, they have seen only *blood;* etc.

When a noun is composed of three or more consonants, and when it is of more than one syllable, it is obviously a derivative. It is in the examination of its root that the art of the etymologist shines. He must master both the value of each sign and the position that it takes, whether at the beginning or the end of words, and the different modifications which it brings about; for, to understand the root clearly, it is necessary to know how to distinguish it from the sign, or from the article by which it is modified. If the etymologist would acquire a science which opens the door to the loftiest conceptions, he must be provided with the faculties and the necessary means. If long study of tongues in general, and the Hebraic tongue in particular, can lend a little confidence in my abilities, I beg the reader, interested in an art too little cultivated, to study carefully, both the series of Hebraic roots which I give him at the close of this Grammar and the numerous notes which accompany my translation of the Cosmogony of Moses.

The work of Court de Gébelin is a vast storehouse of words, which one ought to possess without being a slave to it. This painstaking man had intellect rather than etymological genius; he searched well; he classed well his materials; but he constructed badly. His merit, is having introduced the Primitive tongue; his fault, is having introduced it to his reader in a thousand scattered fragments. The genius will consist in reassembling these fragments to form a whole. I offer in this Grammar an instrument to attain this end. It is THE HEBRAIC TONGUE DERIVED WHOLLY FROM THE SIGN.

Here are the general principles which can be drawn from the work of Gébelin relative to etymological science. I add some developments that experience has suggested to me.

Particular tongues are only the dialects of an universal tongue founded upon nature, and of which a spark of the Divine word animates the elements. This tongue, that no people has ever possessed in its entirety, can be called *the Primitive tongue.* This tongue, from which all others spring as from an unique trunk, is composed only of monosyllabic roots, all adhering to a small number of signs. In proportion as the particular tongues become mingled with one another and separated from their primitive stock, the words become more and more altered: therefore it is essential to compare many languages in order to obtain the understanding of a single one.

It is necessary to know that all vowels tend to become consonants, and all consonants to become vowels;

to consider this movement; to follow it in its modifications; to distinguish carefully the mother vowel from the vague vowel and when one is assured that the vocal sound which enters into the composition of a word, descends from a vague vowel, give it no further attention. One will attain to this final understanding, by the study of the Hebraic tongue, where the difference which exists between these two sorts of vowels is decisive.

It is necessary to consider besides, that, in the generation of tongues, the consonants are substituted for one another, particularly those of the same organic sound. Therefore it is well to classify them by the sound and to know them under this new relation.

Labial sound: ב, פ, ו: B, P, PH, F, V. This sound, being the easiest, is the first of which children make use; it is generally that of gentleness and mildness considered as onomatopoetic.

Dental sound: ד, ט : D, T. It expresses, on the contrary, all that which touches, thunders, resounds, resists, protects.

Lingual sound: ל, ר : L, LL, LH, R, RH. It expresses a rapid movement, either rectilinear or circular, in whatever sense one imagines it, always considered as onomatopoetic.

Nasal sound: מ, נ : M, N, GN. It expresses all that which passes from without within, or which emerges from within without.

Guttural sound: ג, כ, ע, ק: GH, CH, WH, K, Q. It expresses deep, hollow objects, contained one within the other, or modelled by assimilation.

Hissing sound: ז, ס, צ : Z, S, X, TZ, DZ, PS. It is applied to all hissing objects, to all those which have relation with the air, or which cleave it in their course.

Sibilant sound: י, ש, ת: J, G, CH, SH, TH. It expresses light movements, **soft and durable** sounds; all pleasing objects.

The consonants thus distinguished by sound, become the general signs from which the onomatopoetic roots of which I have spoken, are formed, and are very easily put one in the place of the other. In the derivative tongues they even lend mutual aid in passing from one sound to another, and it is then that they render the etymology of the words more and more uncertain. The etymologist can only surmount the numerous obstacles in the modern idioms, by having stored in his mind a number of tongues whose radical words can assist him readily in going back to the idiomatic or primitive root of the word which he analyzes. Never can one hope by the aid of a single tongue, to form good etymology.

As to the mother vowels, א, ה, ח, ו, י, ׳, ע; A, E, Ê, OU, O, I, HO; they are substituted successively one for the other, from א to ע; they all incline to become consonants and to become extinct in the deep and guttural sound כ, which can be represented by the Greek χ or the German *c̀h*. I always mark this *c̀h* with an *accent grave* in order to distinguish it from the French *ch*, which is a hissing sound like the ש of the Hebrews, or the *sh* of the English.

After having set forth these etymological principles, I pass on to the next rules, relative to their employment; very nearly such as Court de Gébelin gives them.

One should not take for granted any alteration in a word that one may not be able to prove by usage or by analogy; nor confuse the radical characters of a word with the accessory characters, which are only added signs or articles. The words should be classified by families and none admitted unless it has been grammatically analyzed: primitives, should be distinguished from compounds and all forced etymology carefully avoided: and finally, an historical or moral proof should corroborate the etymology; for the sciences proceed with certain step only as they throw light upon each other.

§ II.

QUALITY

I call Quality, in the Hebraic nouns, the distinction which I establish among them and by means of which I divide them into four classes, namely: substantives, qualificatives, modificatives, and facultatives.

Substantives are applied to all that has physical or moral substance, the existence of which the thought of man admits either by evidence of the senses, or by that of the intellectual faculties. Substantives are proper or common: *proper* when they are applied to a single being, or to a single thing in particular, as מֹשֶׁה *Mosheh* (Moses), נֹחַ *Noah*, מִצְרַיִם *Mitzraim* (Egypt) etc.; *common*, when they are applied to all beings, or to all things of the same kind, as אִישׁ *man* (intelligent being); רֹאשׁ *head* (that which rules or enjoys by its own movement); מֶלֶךְ *king* (a temporal and local deputy); etc.

Qualificatives express the qualities of the substantives and offer them to the imagination under the form which characterizes them. The grammarians in naming them *adjectives,* have given them a denomination too vague to be preserved in a grammar of the nature of this one. This class of nouns expresses more than a simple adjunction; it expresses the very quality or the form of the substance, as in טוֹב *good,* גָּדוֹל *great,* צַדִּיק *just,* עִבְרִי *Hebrew;* etc.

The tongue of Moses is not rich in qualificatives, but it obviates this lack by the energy of its articles, by that of its verbal facultatives and by the various extensions which it gives to its substantives by joining them to certain initial or terminative characters. It has, for example, in the emphatic article ה, a means of intensity of which it

QUALITY 125

makes great use, either in placing it at the beginning or the end of words. Thus, of נָחַל *a torrent*, it makes נָחֲלָה *a very rapid torrent;* of קָפַד *disappearance, absence,* it makes קְפָדָה *an eternal absence, a total disappearance:* מוֹת *death*, it makes הַמּוֹתָה *a violent, cruel, sudden death,* etc. Sometimes it adds to this article, the sign of reciprocity ת, to augment its force. Then one finds for עֵזֶר *a support, an aid,* עֶזְרָתָה *a firm support, an accomplished aid;* for אֵימָה *terror,* אֵימָתָה *extreme terror, frightful terror;* for יְשׁוּעָה *safety, refuge,* יְשׁוּעָתָה *an assured safety, an inaccessible refuge;* etc.

The assimilative article כְ, forms a kind of qualificative of the noun which it governs. It is thus that one should understand כֵּאלֹהִים *like unto the Gods,* or *divine;* כַּכֹּהֵן *like unto the priest,* or *sacerdotal;* כְּעָם *like unto the people,* or *vulgar;* כְּהַיּוֹם *like to-day,* or *modern;* etc.

On the other hand, the sign ת placed at the beginning of a word expresses reciprocity. אֲנִיָּה *signifies pain,* תַּאֲנִיָּה *mutual pain.*

The sign מ, when it is initial, is related to exterior action; when final, on the contrary, it becomes expansive and collective. אוּל signifies *any force whatever,* מָאוּל *a circumscribed and local force;* אוּלָם *an exterior, invading force.*

The sign נ, is that of passive action when it is at the head of words; but at the end, it constitutes an augmentative syllable which extends its signification. אֲפֻדָּה signifies *a veil,* אֹפֶן *an immense veil, the enclosure of a tent;* גֵּוָא characterizes *an extension,* and גַּוָּאן *an unlimited extension, inordinate;* הֵם expresses *a noise,* and הָמוֹן *a frightful noise, a terrible tumult, a revolt;* etc.

I pass over these details of which my footnotes on

the Cosmogony of Moses will afford sufficient examples. It will be enough for me here to indicate the grammatical forms.

The rabbis, in writing modern Hebrew, form the qualificatives by the addition of the character י to the masculine, and the syllable ית, to the feminine. They say, for example, אלהי *divine* (mas.) and אלהית *divine* (fem.). נפשי *spiritual* (mas.) and נפשית *spiritual* (fem.). Then they draw from these qualificatives a mass of substantive nouns, such as אלהות *the divinity;* אולות *fortitude;* נפשות *spirituality;* ידירות *tenderness;* etc. These forms do not belong to primitive Hebrew.

The comparative among qualificatives is not strictly characterized in the Hebraic tongue. When it is established, which is somewhat rare, it is by means of the extractive article מ, or by the preposition מן which corresponds.

The superlative is expressed in many ways. Sometimes one finds either the substantive or the qualificative doubled, in order to give the idea that one has of their force or their extent; sometimes they are followed by an absolute relative to designate that nothing is comparable to them. At other times the adverbial relation מְאֹד *very, very much, as much as possible,* indicates that one conceives them as having attained their measure in good or in evil, according to their nature. Finally one meets different periphrases and different formulas of which I herewith offer several examples.

QUALITY 127

נֹחַ אִישׁ צַדִּיק תָּמִים.....	Noah, intelligent being (man), just with integrity (as just as upright).
טוֹב שֵׁם מִשֶּׁמֶן טוֹב:	a good name, of good essence (a name of high repute is the best essence).
טוֹבִים הַשְּׁנַיִם מִן־הָאֶחָד.	good the two of a single one (two are better than one).
רַע רָע : מַטָּה מָטָּה:	bad, evil (wicked); down, down (beneath).
מִן־הָאָדוֹם הָאָדוֹם:	among the red, red (much redder).
קָטֹן בַּגּוֹיִם:	small among people (very small).
הָהָר הַטּוֹב הַזֶּה:	a mountain, the good, that one (the best of all).
טוֹב מְאֹד:	good exceedingly (as much as possible).
הַשָּׁמַיִם וּשְׁמֵי הַשָּׁמָיִם:	the heavens and the heaven of heavens.
אֱלֹהֵי אֱלֹהִים וַאֲדֹנֵי הָאֲדֹנִים:	God of Gods and Lord of Lords.
עֶבֶד עֲבָדִים:	servant of the servants.
חֹשֶׁךְ־אֲפֵלָה:	the obscurity of darkness.
שַׁלְהֶבֶתְיָה : מַאְפֵּלְיָה:	the flame of Jah! the darkness of Jah! (extremes).
אַרְזֵי־אֵל :	the cedars of God! (admirable, very beautiful).
עִיר גְּדוֹלָה לֵאלֹהִים:	a great city! according to Him-the-Gods!
אַמִּץ לַאדֹנָי:	strong according to the Lord! (very strong).
בְּעֵרָה : בִּמְאֹד מְאֹד :	a burning; with might of might.

Modificatives are the substantives or the qualificatives modified either by a simple abstraction of thought, or by the addition of an adverbial relation, so as to become the expression of an action understood. It is not unusual to find in Hebrew, nouns which can be taken, at the same time, as substantives, qualificatives or modificatives; all by a movement of abstraction, and this is easy when the idiom is not far removed from its source. Thus, for example טוֹב *good*, signifies equally *the good*, and the *good* manner in which a thing is done: רָע *evil*, signifies equally that which is *evil*, and the *evil* manner in which a thing is done. One perceives that the words *good* and *evil*, have exactly the same signification as the Hebraic words טוֹב and רָע, as substantives, and that they contain the same qualificative and modificative faculties. I have chosen them expressly so as to show how this abstraction of thought of which I have spoken, is accomplished.

Modificative nouns which are formed by the addition of a designative or adverbial relation as in French, *à-la-mode* (in the fashion), *à-outrance* (to the utmost), *fortement* (strongly), *douce-ment* (gently), are very rare in Hebrew. One finds, however, certain ones such as בְּ־רֵאשִׁ־ית, *in the beginning, in-principle;* יְהוּד־ית, *in Jewish;* מֵ־אַשּׁוּר־ית *from the Assyrian;* etc. The nouns of number belong at the same time to substantives, qualificatives and modificatives. אחד, *one*, can signify alike, *unity, unique* and *uniquely*.

Facultative nouns are the substantives, *verbalized*, as it were, and in which the absolute verb הוה, *to be-being*, begins to make its influence felt. The grammarians have called them up to this time *participles*, but I treat this weak denomination, as I have treated the one which they have given to qualificatives. I replace it by another which I believe more just.

Facultatives merit particular attention in all tongues, but especially in that of Moses, where they present more openly than in any other, the link which unites the substantive to the verb, and which, by an inexplicable power, makes of a substance inert and without action, an animated substance being carried suddenly toward a determined end. It is by means of the sign of light and of intellectual sense, ו, that this metamorphosis is accomplished. This is remarkable. If I take, for example, the substantive רֶגֶן, which expresses all physical movement all moral affection; if I introduce between the first and second character which compose it, the verbal sign ו, I obtain immediately the *continued* facultative, רוֹגֵן, *to be-moving, affecting, agitating*. If I modify this sign, that is to say, if I give it its convertible nature ו, and if I place it between the second and third character of the substantive in question, I obtain then the *finished* facultative רָגוֹן, *to be-moved, affected, agitated*. It is the same with מֶלֶךְ *a king*, whose continued and finished facultatives are מוֹלֵךְ *to be-ruling, governing;* מָלוּךְ *to be-ruled, governed*, and many others.

It can be observed that I name *continued facultative*, what the grammarians call *present participle*, and *finished* that which they call *past;* because in effect, the action expressed by these facultatives is not, properly speaking, present or past, but continued or finished in any time whatever. One says clearly *it was burning, it is burning, it will be burning; it was burned, it is burned, it will be burned*. Now who cannot see that the facultatives *burning* and *burned*, are by turns, both past, present and future? They both participate in these three tenses with the difference, that the first is always continued and the other always finished.

But let us return. It is from the finished facultative that the verb comes, as I shall demonstrate later on. This facultative, by means of which speech receives verbal life, is formed from the primitive root by the introduction of the sign וֹ, between the two characters of which it is composed. Thus, for example:

The root שׁם contains every idea of elevation, erection, or monument, raised as indication of a place or thing:

thence: שָׁם or שׁוֹם to be erecting, stating, decreeing, designating:

שׁוּם to be erected, stated, etc., whence the verb שׁוּם *to erect*.

The root כל contains every idea of consummation, of totalization, of agglomeration, of absorption:

thence: כָּל or כּוּל to be consummating, totalizing, agglomerating:

כּוּל to be consummated, agglomerated: whence the verb כּוּל, *to consummate*.

The root גל expresses every idea of heaping up, lifting up, of movement which carries upward from below:

thence: גָּל or גּוֹל to be heaping up, lifting up, pushing, leaping:

גּוּל to be heaped up, lifted up; whence the verb גּוּל, *to heap up*.

As I shall be obliged to return to this formation of the facultatives, in the chapter in which I shall treat of the verb, it is needless for me to dwell further upon it now. I cannot, however, refrain from making the observation that since the institution of the Chaldaic punctuation, the points *kamez, holem*, and even *zere*, have often **replaced the verbal sign** וֹ in the continued facultative,

QUALITY

whether of compound or radical origin, and that one finds quite commonly רָגז *to be moving;* מֶלֶךְ *to be ruling;* קָם *to be establishing;* מֵת *to be dying;* etc. But two things prove that this is an abuse of punctuation. The first is, that when the continued facultative presents itself in an absolute manner, and when nothing can determine the meaning, then the sign reappears irresistibly; as in the following examples, קוֹם *the action of establishing,* or *to be establishing:* מוֹת *the action of dying,* or *to be dying.* The second thing which proves the abuse of which I am speaking, is that the rabbis who preserve to a certain point the oral tradition, never fail to make the mother vowel וֹ, appear in these same facultatives unless they deem it more suitable to substitute its analogues ' or אִ, writing קוֹם, קִים or קאִים, *to be establishing, to establish, the action of establishing.*

I shall terminate this paragraph by saying that facultatives both continued and finished, are subject to the same inflections as the substantive and qualificative nouns, that is, of gender, number, movement and construction. The modificative noun does not have the inflections of the others because it contains an implied action, and since it has, as I shall demonstrate, the part of itself which emanates from the verb *to be,* wholly immutable and consequently inflexible.

§ III.

GENDER

Gender is distinguished at first by the sex, male or female, or by a sort of analogy, of similitude, which appears to exist among things, and the sex which is assigned to them by speech. The Hebraic tongue has two genders only, the masculine and the feminine; notwithstanding the efforts that the grammarians have made to discover in it a third and even a fourth which they have called common or epicene. These so-called genders are only the liberty allowed the speaker of giving to such or such substantive the masculine or feminine gender, indifferently, and according to the circumstance: if these genders merit any attention, it is when passing into the derivative tongues, and in taking a particular form there, that they have constituted the neuter gender which one encounters in many of them.

The feminine gender is derived from the masculine, and is formed by adding to the substantive, qualificative or facultative noun, the sign ה which is that of life. The modificative nouns have no gender, because they modify actions and not things, as do the other kinds of words.

I beg the reader who follows me with any degree of interest, to observe the force and constancy with which is demonstrated everywhere, the power that I have attributed to the *sign*, a power upon which I base the whole genius of the tongue of Moses.

I have said that the feminine gender is formed from the masculine by the addition of the sign of life ה: was it possible to imagine a sign of happier expression, to indicate the sex by which all beings appear to owe life, this blessing of the Divinity?

GENDER

Thus מֶלֶךְ *a king,* produces מַלְכָּה *a queen;* חָכָם *a wise man,* חֲכָמָה *a wise woman;* דָּג *a male fish,* דָּגָה *a female fish.*

Thus טוֹב *good* (mas.), becomes טוֹבָה *good* (fem.); גָּדוֹל *great* (mas.), גְּדוֹלָה *great* (fem.).

Thus מוֹלֵךְ *to be ruling* (mas.), becomes מוֹלְכָה *to be ruling* (fem.): שׂוֹם or שָׂם *to be raising* (mas.), שׂוֹמָה *to be raising* (fem.).

It must be observed, in respect to this formation, that when the qualificative masculine is terminated with the character ה, which is then only the emphatic sign, or by the character י, sign of manifestation, these two characters remain wholly simple, or are modified by the sign of reciprocity ת, in the following manner: יָפֶה *beautiful* (mas.), יָפָה or יָפָת (fem.); שֵׁנִי *second* (mas.), שְׁנִיָה or שֵׁנִית (fem.).

Besides, this sign ת, image of all that is mutual, replaces in almost every case the character ה, when it is a question of the feminine termination of qualificative or facultative nouns; it seems even, that the genius of the Hebraic tongue is particularly partial to it in the latter. One finds נוֹפֶלֶת, rather than נוֹפְלָה, *to be falling;* בּוֹרַחַת, rather than בּוֹרְחָה *to be fleeing;* etc.

It is useless, in a Grammar which treats principally of the genius of a tongue, to expatiate much upon the application of the genders; that is a matter which concerns the dictionary. Let it suffice to know, that, in general, the proper names of men, of occupations, of titles, peoples, rivers, mountains and months, are masculine; whereas the names of women, of countries, of cities, the members of the body, and all substantives terminating with the sign ה, are feminine.

As to the common gender, that is to say, that of the substantive nouns which take the masculine and feminine alike, it is impossible to apply any rule even approximately; it is by use alone that it can be shown. These are the substantives of the common gender which come to my mind at the moment: גַן *enclosure, organic sphere;* שֶׁמֶשׁ *sun;* אֶרֶץ *earth;* אוֹת *sign;* עֵת *time;* רוּחַ *spirit, expansive breath;* נֶפֶשׁ *soul;* אָרוֹן *chain of mountains;* חֲזִיר *pig;* אֲרִי *lion;* etc.

§ IV.

NUMBER

There exist only two characteristic numbers in Hebrew; these are *the singular* and *the plural;* the third number, called *dual,* is but a simple restriction of thought, a modification of the plural which tradition alone has been able to preserve by aid of the Chaldaic punctuation. This restricted number, passing into certain derivative tongues, has constituted in them a characteristic number, by means of the forms which it has assumed; but it is obvious that the Hebraic tongue, had it at first either alone, or else distinguished it from the plural only by a simple inflection of the voice, too little evident to be expressed by the sign; for it should be carefully observed that it is never the sign which expresses it, but the punctuation, at least in masculine nouns: as to feminine nouns, which, in the *dual* number, assume the same characters which indicate the masculine plural, one might, strictly speaking, consider them as belonging to common gender.

Masculine nouns, whether substantive, qualificative or facultative, form their plural by the addition of the syllable ם׳, which, uniting the signs of manifestation and of exterior generation. expresses infinite succession, the immensity of things.

Feminine nouns of the same classes form their plural by the addition of the syllable ni, which, uniting the signs of light and of reciprocity, expresses all that is mutual and similar, and develops the idea of the identity of things.

The two genders of the dual number are formed by the addition of the same syllable ם׳, designating the masculine plural, to which one adds, according to the Chaldaic punctuation, the vague vowel named *kamez* or *patah,* in this manner: יָם, or יִם. One should realize now that this number is not really characteristic, as I have stated, since, if we remove the Chaldaic punctuation, and if we read the tongue of Moses without points, which should always be done in order to go back to its hieroglyphic source, this number disappears entirely; the dual masculine being absorbed in the plural of the same gender, and the feminine being only an extension of the common number. The modern rabbis who have clearly seen this difficulty (considering the disadvantage of the Chaldaic punctuation, and furthermore, not wishing to loose this third number which presented certain beauties, and had been orally transmitted to them), have adopted the plan of expressing the inflection of the voice which constituted it in its origin, by doubling the sign of manifestation י, in this manner: רַגְלַיִם *the two feet* יָדַיִם *the two hands.* This number, furthermore, is usually applied to the things which nature has made double, or which the mind conceives as double, as the following examples will demonstrate.

Examples of the masculine plural.

מֶלֶךְ *king,* מְלָכִים *kings;* סֵפֶר *book,* סְפָרִים *books;* צַדִיק *just one,* צַדִיקִים *just ones;* נָקִי *innocent,* נְקִיִּים *innocents;* פָּקוֹד *to be visiting, caring for,* פּוֹקְדִים (plural); פָּקוּד *to be visited, cared for,* פְּקוּדִים (plural); etc.

Examples of the feminine plural.

מַלְכָּה *queen,* מַלְכוֹת *queens;* אֵם *mother,* אִמּוֹת *mothers;* צְדִיקָה *just one,* צְדִיקוֹת *just ones;* פּוֹקְדָה or פּוֹקֶרֶת *to be visiting, caring for,* פּוֹקְדוֹת (plural); פְּקוּדָה *to be visited, cared for,* פְּקוּדוֹת (plural); etc.

Examples of the dual.

שַׁד *breast,* שָׁדַיִם *both breasts;* יָרֵךְ *thigh,* יְרֵכַיִם *both thighs;* שָׂפָה *lip,* שְׂפָתַיִם *both lips;* מֵי *water,* מַיִם *the waters;* שְׁמֵי *heaven* (singular obsolete), שָׁמַיִם *the heavens;* יָד *hand,* יָדַיִם *both hands;* etc.

It can be observed in these examples that the final character י is sometimes preserved in the plural as in נָקִי *innocent,* נְקִיִּים *innocents;* or in אֲרִי *lion,* אֲרָיִים *lions;* but it is, however, more customary for this final character י, to become lost or amalgamated with the plural, as in יְהוּדִי *a Jew,* יְהוּדִים *the Jews.*

It can also be observed that feminine nouns which terminate in ה in the singular, lose this character in taking the plural, and that those which take the dual number, change this same character to ת, as in שָׂפָה *lip,* שְׂפָתַיִם *both lips;* חוֹמָה *wall,* חֹמָתַיִם *both walls.*

Sometimes the plural number of the masculine in ים, is changed into ין, after the Chaldaic manner, and one finds quite frequently אַחֵר *other,* אַחֲרִין *others;* בֵּן *son,* בְּנִין *sons,* etc.

Sometimes also the feminine plural in וֹת, loses its essential character and preserves only the character ת, preceded thus by the vowel point *ḥolem* as in תּוֹלְדֹת *the symbol of generations* (genealogical tree): צִדְקֹת *righteous acts,* etc. This is also an abuse born of the Chaldaic punctuation, and proves what I have said with regard to the facultatives. The rabbis are so averse to the suppression of this important sign ו in the feminine plural, that they frequently join to it the sign of manifestation י, to give it more force; writing אוֹת *sign, symbol, character,* and אוֹתִיוֹת *signs, symbols,* etc.

One finds in Hebrew, as in other tongues, nouns which are always used in the singular and others which are always in the plural. Among the former one observes proper names, names of metals, of liquors, of virtues, of vices, etc. Among the latter, the names of ages, and of conditions relative to men.

One finds equally masculine or feminine nouns in the singular which take, in the plural, the feminine or masculine termination inconsistent with their gender; as אָב *father*, אָבוֹת *fathers;* עִיר *city,* עָרִים *cities;* etc. One also finds the gender called common or epicene, which takes indifferently the masculine or feminine plural, as I have already remarked; as הֵיכָל *palace,* הֵיכָלִים or הֵיכָלוֹת *palaces.* But these are anomalies which the grammar of an unspoken tongue can only indicate, leaving to the dictionary the care of noting them in detail.

§ V.

MOVEMENT

I call *Movement,* in the Hebraic nouns, that accidental modification which they undergo by the articles of which I have spoken in the second section of chapter IV.

In the tongues where this Movement takes place by means of the terminations of the nouns themselves, the grammarians have treated it under the denomination of *case;* a denomination applicable to those tongues, but which can only be applied to a tongue so rich in articles as the Hebrew, by an abuse of terms and in accordance with a scholastic routine wholly ridiculous.

I say that the denomination of *case* was applicable to those tongues, the nouns of which experience changes of termination to express their respective modifications; for, as Court de Gébelin has already remarked, these cases are only articles added to nouns, and which have finally amalgamated with them.[1] But the grammarians of the past centuries, always restricted to the Latin or Greek forms, saw only the material in those tongues, and never even suspected that there might have been something beyond. The time has come to seek for another principle in speech and to examine carefully its influence.

As I have dilated sufficiently upon the signification of each article in particular, as well as upon those of the corresponding prepositions, I now pass on without other preamble to the kind of modification which they bring in the nouns and which I call *Movement.*

Now, movement is inflicted in Hebraic nouns according to the number of the articles. We can, therefore, admit seven kinds of movements in the tongue of Moses, including the designative movement which is formed by

[1] Gramm. univers., p. 379.

means of the designative preposition אֶת and without including the enunciative which is expressed without an article.

I shall call this series of movements *Inflection,* and by this term I replace that of declension which should not be used here.

Example of nominal inflection.

MOVEMENT
{
enunciative	דָּבָר	word, a word.
determinative	הַדָּבָר	the word, lo the word!
directive	לַדָּבָר	to the word; of, for or concerning the word.
extractive	מִדָּבָר	from the word; out of or by the word.
mediative	בְּדָבָר	in the word; by means of the word.
assimilative	כְּדָבָר	as the word; like the word; according to the word.
conjunctive	וְדָבָר	and the word.
designative	אֶת־דָּבָר	the selfsameness of the word, the w o r d itself; that which concerns the word.

The first remark to make with regard to this nominal inflection is, that the articles which constitute it, being of every gender and every number, are applied to the masculine as to the feminine, to the singular as to the plural or dual.

The second is, that they are often supplied by the corresponding prepositions of which I have spoken, and therefore, that the movement through them acquires greater force; for example, if it is a question of direct movement, the prepositions עַל־, אֱלִי־, אֶל־, which correspond with the article לְ, have an energy, drawing nearer, imminent: it is the same with the prepositions מָמֶנִּי, מֶנִּי, מִן, which correspond with the extractive article מ: with the prepositions בְּמוֹ, בְּדִי, בְּ, analogous to the mediative article בְּ: the prepositions כְּמוֹ, כֹּה, כְּ, which correspond with the assimilative article כְּ: all of these augment in the same manner, the force of the movement to which they belong.

The third remark to make is, that the vague vowel which I have indicated by the Chaldaic punctuation, beneath each article, is the one which is found the most commonly used, but not the one which is always encountered. It must be remembered that as this punctuation is only a sort of vocal note applied to the vulgar pronunciation, nothing is more arbitrary than its course. All those Hebraists who are engrossed in the task of determining its variations by fixed rules, are lost in an inextricable labyrinth. I beg the reader who knows how much French or English deviates from the written language by the pronunciation, to consider what a formidable labour it would be, if it were necessary to mark with small accents the sound of each word, often so opposed to the orthography.

Without doubt there are occupations more useful, particularly for the extinct tongues.

The vague vowel, I cannot refrain from repeating, is of no consequence in any way to the meaning of the words of the Hebraic tongue, since one does not wish to speak this tongue. It is to the *sign* that one should give attention: it is its *signification* which must be presented. Considered here as article, it is invariable: it is always ה, ל, מ, ב, כ, or ו, which strikes the eye. What matters it to the ear, whether these characters are followed or not, by a *kamez*, a *patah* or a *zere*, that is to say, the indistinct vowels a, o, e? It is neither the *zere,* nor the *patah* nor the *kamez* which makes them what they are, but their nature as article. The vague vowel is there only for the compass of the voice. Upon seeing it written, it should be pronounced as it is pronounced in the modern tongues without giving it further attention, and if one insists on writing Hebrew from memory, which is, however, quite useless, one should learn to put it down as one learns the orthography, often very arbitrary, of French and English, by dint of copying the words in the manner in which they are written.

The meaning of the article in itself is already sufficiently difficult without still tormenting oneself as to how one shall place a fly speck.

Asiatic idioms in general, and Hebrew in particular, are far from affecting the stiffness of our European idioms. The nearer a word is to its root, the richer it is in pith, so to speak, and the more it can, without ceasing to be itself, develop various significations. The more distant it is, the less it becomes fitting to furnish new ramifications. Also one should guard against believing that an Hebraic word, whatever it may be, can be accurately grasped and rendered in all its acceptations by a modern word. This is not possible. All that can be done is to interpret the acceptation which it presents at the time when it is used. Here, for example, is the word דָּבָר, which I have used in the nominal inflection; I have rendered it by *word;* but in this circumstance where nothing has bound me as to the sense, I might have translated it quite as well by *discourse, precept, commandment, order, sermon, oration;* or by *thing, object, thought, meditation;* or by *term, elocution, expression;* or by the consecrated word *verb*, in Greek λόγος. All these significations and many others that I could add, feel the effects of the root דר, which, formed from the signs of natural abundance, and of active principle, develops the general idea of *effusion;* of the *course* given to anything whatsoever. This root being united by contraction with the root בר, all *creation* of being, offers in the compound דָּבָר, all the means of giving *course* to its ideas, of producing them, of distinguishing them, of creating them exteriorly, to make them known to others.

This diversity of acceptations which must be observed in the words of the Mosaic tongue, must also be observed in the different movements of the nominal inflection. These movements are not, in Hebrew, circumscribed in the limits that I have been obliged to give them. To make them felt in their full extent, it would be necessary to enter into irksome details. I shall give a few examples.

Let us remark first that the article ה, is placed, not only at the head of words as determinative, or at the end as emphatic, but that it becomes also redundant by resting at either place, whereas the other articles act. Thus, one finds הַשָׁמַיִם, *the heavens,* שָׁמַיְמָה *heavens,* הַשָׁמַיְמָה *o heavens!* לְהַשָׁמַיִם *to the heavens, toward the heavens,* אֶת־הַשָׁמַיְמָה *the heavens themselves, that which constitutes the heavens.*

Such are the most common acceptations of this article: but the Hebraic genius by the extension which it gives them, finds the means of adding still a local, intensive, generative, vocative, interrogative and even relative force. Here are some examples.

Locative Force.

הָעִיר : הַפְּלִשְׁתִּים :   in the city; toward Palestine.
הָאֹהֱלָה שָׂרָה אִמּוֹ :   in the tent of Sarah his mother.
אַרְצָה : שָׁמַיְמָה :   on earth; in heaven.
צָפוֹנָה וָנֶגְבָּה וָקֵדְמָה וָיָמָּה :   toward the north and toward the south, and the east and the west.

Intensive Force.

נַחְלָה : עֲפָתָה :   a rapid torrent: a profound obscurity.

אֵימָתָה : הַמּוֹתָה : an extreme terror; a violent death.

Generative Force.

אֶת־הָאָרֶץ : selfsameness of the earth: that which constitutes it.
הַמִּזְבַּח הַנְּחֹשֶׁת : the altars of brass.
הַמַּמְלְכוֹת הָאָרֶץ : the kingdoms of the earth.
הַמִּסְגְּרוֹת הַגּוֹיִם : the abomination of the peoples.

Vocative Force.

הַיָּם הֶהָרִים : o waters! o mountains!
הַבַּת יְרוּשָׁלַיִם : o daughters of Jerusalem!
בֹּאִי הָרוּחַ : הַיּשְׁבִי : come, o spirit, o thou who dwellest!

Interrogative Force.

הַכְּתֹנֶת בִּנְךָ הוּא : is that the tunic of thy son?
הַיֵּיטַב : הֲרְאִיתֶם : was it good? did you see?
הָאֱמֶת : הָעֵת : הָאָנֹכִי : is it the truth? is it the time? is it I?

Relative Force.

בֶּן־הַנֵּכָר הַנִּלְוָה : the son of the stranger who was come.
הַנּוֹלַד־לוֹ : he who was born to him.
הָרֹפֵא : הַגּוֹאֵל : he who is healing; he who is redeeming.

The other articles without having so extended a use, have nevertheless their various acceptations. I give here a few examples of each of the movements which they express.

MOVEMENT

Directive Movement.

מִזְמוֹר לְדָוִד :	the canticle of David.
לְמֶלֶךְ : לְהָעָם : לְהַמִּזְבֵּחַ :	for the king: for the people: for the altar.
לָנֶצַח : לְעַד : לְשֹׂבַע :	forever: for eternity: to satiety.
אֶל־הַשָּׁמַיִם : עַל־הָאָרֶץ :	toward the heavens: upon the earth.
לְמִינֵהוּ :	according to his kind.

Extractive Movement.

מֵרֹב : מִכֹּהֵן :	among the multitude: among the priesthood.
מֵיְהֹוָה : מִלְאֹם :	by Yahweh: by the nation.
מִגְּבוּרָתָם : מִלִּבּוֹ :	by means of their power: from the depths of his heart.
מֵעָצְבְּךָ וּמֵרָגְזְךָ :	with thy pain and thine emotion.
לְמִבָּרִאשׁוֹנָה :	as it was from the beginning.
מִן־הָאָרֶץ :	beyond the land.
מִימֵי רָע : מִקְצֵה הָאָרֶץ :	from the days of evil: from the end of the earth.

Mediative Movement.

בְּשֵׁבֶט בַּרְזֶל :	by means of a rod of iron.
בִּנְעָרֵינוּ וּבִזְקֵנֵנוּ .	with our young men and with our old men.
בֶּחֳדָשִׁים :	in the festivals of the new moon.
בַּהַשָּׁמַיִם : בַּהַדֶּרֶךְ :	to the heavens: on the way.

Assimilative Movement.

כְּעָם ׃ כַּכֹּהֵן ׃ כְּעֶבֶד ׃	like the p e o p l e : like the priest : like the servant.
כְּהֶחָכָם ׃ כְּהַיּוֹם ׃	like the wise man : the same as to-day.
כְּהַחַלֹּנוֹת ׃ כְּאַלְפַּיִם ׃	like the windows : about two thousand.
כַּגֵּר כָּאֶזְרָח ׃	stranger as well as native.

Conjunctive Movement.

חָכְמָה וְדַעַת ׃	wisdom and knowledge.
וְרֶכֶב וסוּס ׃	the chariot and the horse.
עַם גָּדוֹל וְרַב וָרָם ׃	the great nation both numerous and powerful.

Designative Movement.

אֶת־הַשָּׁמַיִם וְאֶת־הָאָרֶץ ׃	the sameness of the heavens and the sameness of the earth.
אֶת־הַדָּבָר הַזֶּה ׃	the e s s e n c e of that same thing.
אֶת־נֹחַ ׃	with Noah.
אֶת־שֵׁם וְאֶת־חָם וְאֶת־יָפֶת ׃	Shem himself, and Ham himself, and Japheth himself.

These examples few in number, are sufficient to awaken the attention; but understanding can only be obtained by study.

§ VI.

CONSTRUCT STATE

Hebraic nouns, being classed in the rhetorical sentence according to the rank which they should occupy in developing the thought in its entirety, undergo quite commonly a slight alteration in the final character; now this is what I designate by the name of *construct state*.

In several of the derivative tongues, such as Greek and Latin, this accidental alteration is seen in the termination of the governed noun; it is quite the opposite in Hebrew. The governed noun remains nearly always unchanged, whereas the governing noun experiences quite commonly the terminative alteration of which we are speaking. I call the noun thus modified *construct,* because it determines the construction.

Here in a few words are the elements of this modification.

Masculine or feminine nouns in the singular, terminated by a character other than ה, undergo no other alteration in becoming constructs; when the Hebraic genius wishes, however, to make the construct state felt, it connects them with the noun which follows with a hyphen.

פֶּתַח־הָאֹהֶל׃ the door of the tent.

תָּם־לְבָבִי׃ the integrity of my heart.

This hyphen very frequently takes the place of the construct, even when the latter itself could be used.

סְאָה־סֹלֶת׃ a measure of meal.

עֲלֵה־זַיִת׃ a branch of the olive tree.

One recognizes, nevertheless, three masculine substantives which form their construct singular, by the addition of the character י: these are אָב *father*, אָח *brother*, and חָם *father-in-law;* one finds:

אֲבִי כְנַעַן: the father of Canaan.

אֲחִי יָפֶת: חָמִיהָ: the brother of Japheth; father-in-law of her.

But these three substantives are rarely constructed in this manner except with proper nouns, or with the nominal relations called *affixes,* of which I shall speak in the chapter following.

Feminine nouns terminating in ה, and masculine nouns which have received this final character as emphatic article, change it generally into ת.

יְפַת מַרְאֶה: beautiful of form.

עֲשֶׂרֶת הַדְּבָרִים: the ten commandments.

עֲצַת גּוֹיִם: the counsel of the peoples.

Masculine nouns in the plural lose the final character ם, in becoming constructs; feminine nouns add to their plural the character י, and lose in the dual the character ם, as do the masculine. But feminine constructs in the plural are only used with *affixes.* Masculine constructs, in the plural and in the dual, like feminine constructs in the dual, are, on the contrary, constantly employed in the oratorical phrase, as can be judged by the following examples.

תּוֹרֵי זָהָב: the ornaments of gold.

מֵי הַמַּבּוּל: דְּגֵי הַיָּם: the waters of the deluge: the fish of the sea.

כְּלֵי בֵית־יְהוָֹה: the vessels of the house of Yahweh.

יְמֵי שְׁנֵי־חַיֵּי אַבְרָהָם: the days (or luminous periods) of the years (or temporal mutations) of the lives of Abraham.

It is easy to see in these examples that all the plurals terminating in ים, as שָׁנִים, יָמִים, כֵּלִים, דָּגִים, מַיִם, תּוֹרִים, חַיִּים, have lost their final character in the construct state.

I refrain from enlarging my Grammar on this subject, for I shall have occasion to refer again to the construct state in speaking of the affixes which join themselves only to nominal and verbal constructs.

§ VII.

SIGNIFICATION

The Signification of nouns results wholly from the principles which I have laid down. If these principles have been developed with enough clarity and simplicity for an observant reader to grasp the *ensemble*, the signification of nouns should be no longer an inexplicable mystery whose origin he can, like Hobbes or his adherents, attribute only to chance. He must feel that this *signification,* so called from the primordial *signs* where it is in germ, begins to appear under a vague form and is developed under general ideas in the roots composed of these signs; that it is restrained or is fixed by aid of the secondary and successive signs which apply to these roots; finally, that it acquires its whole force by the transformation of these same roots into nouns, and by the kind of movement which the signs again impart to them, appearing for the third time under the denomination of articles.

CHAPTER VI.

NOMINAL RELATIONS.

§ I.

Absolute Pronouns.

I have designated the nominal relations under the name of *pronouns,* so as not to create needlessly new terms.

I divide the pronouns of the Hebraic tongue into two classes; each subdivided into two kinds. The first class is that of the *absolute pronouns,* or pronouns, properly so-called; the second is that of the *affixes,* which are derivatives, whose use I shall explain later.

The pronouns, properly so-called, are relative to persons or things; those relative to persons are called *personal;* those relative to things are named simply *relative.*

The affixes indicate the action of persons or things themselves upon things, and then I name them *nominal affixes;* or they can express the action of the verb upon persons or things and then I give them the name of *verbal affixes.* Below, is the list of the personal and relative pronouns.

Personal Pronouns.

	Singular			Plural	
1 {*mas.* / *fem.*}	אֲנִי or אָנֹכִי	I	1 {*mas.* / *fem.*}	אֲנַחְנוּ or נַחְנוּ	we
2 {*mas.* *fem.*}	אַתָּה / אַתְּ } thou		2 {*mas.* / *fem.*}	אַתֶּם / אַתֶּן }	ye
3 {*mas.* *fem.*}	הוּא he / הִיא or הוּא she		3 {*mas.* / *fem.*}	הֵם / הֵן }	they

Relative Pronouns.

Of every Gender and of every Number.

אֵל or אֵלֶה this, that, these, those.

אֲשֶׁר who, which, whom, whose, that which; what.

דָּא, דִּי or דָּן this, that, these, those. (*Chaldaic.*)

זֶה, זוּ or זֹאת this, that, these, those.

הָא this, that, these, those; lo! behold!

הֵן, הִנֵּה lo! behold! is there?

הֲל is it ? (interrogation sign).

מִי who? מָה what?

פֶּה that thing there, that place there. (*Egyptian.*)

I have a few remarks to make concerning this class of pronouns. The first is, that I present the table according to the modern usage, which gives the first rank to the pronoun *I* or *me*; and that in this, I differ from the ideas of the rabbis, who, after a false etymology given to the verb, have judged that the rank belonged to the pronoun *he* or *him*. It is not that I am unaware of the mystical reasons which lead certain of them to think that the preëminence belongs to the pronoun of the third person הוּא, *he* or *him*, as forming the basis of the Sacred Name given to the Divinity. What I have said in my notes explaining the Hebraic names אֱלֹהִים and יְהֹוָה proves it adequately; but these reasons, very strong as they appear to them, have not determined me in the least to take away from the personal pronoun אֲנִי or אָנֹכִי *I* or *me*, a rank which belongs to its nature. It is sufficient, in order to feel this rank, to put it into the mouth of the Divinity Itself, as Moses has frequently done : אָנֹכִי יְהֹוָה אֱלֹהֶיךָ, *I am* YAHWEH (*the Being-Eternal*), ÆLOHIM (HE-*the-Gods*) *thine*. It is also sufficient to remember that one finds אֶהְוֶה written in the first person, and that therefore, this name has a greater force than YAHWEH.

ABSOLUTE PRONOUNS

The second remark that I have to make is, that all these pronouns, personal as well as relative when they are used in an absolute manner, always involve the idea of the verb *to be,* in its three tenses, following the meaning of the phrase, and without the need of expressing it, as in the greater part of the modern idioms. Thus אֲנִי, אַתָה, הוּא, etc., signifies literally: *I-being,* or *I am, I was, I shall be: thou-being,* or *thou art, thou wast, thou shalt be: he-being,* or *he is, he was, he shall be;* etc. It is the same with all the others indiscriminately.

The third remark finally, concerns the etymology of these pronouns: an etymology worthy of great attention, as it is derived from my principles and confirms them.

Let us content ourselves with examining the first three persons אֲנִי, אַתָה and הוּא, so as not to increase the examples too much, besides leaving something for the reader to do, who is eager to learn.

Now, what is the root of the first of these pronouns? It is אן, where the united signs of power and of produced being, indicate sufficiently a sphere of activity, an individual existence, acting from the centre to the circumference. This root, modified by the sign of potential manifestation י, which we shall presently see become the affix of possession, designates the *I,* active, manifested and possessed.

The root of the second pronoun אַתָה, is not less expressive. One sees here as in the first, the sign of power א, but which, united now to that of the reciprocity of things ת, characterizes a mutual power, a coexistent being. One associates with this idea, that of veneration, in joining to the root את, the emphatic and determinative article ה.

But neither the pronoun of the first person, nor that of the second, is equal in energy to that of the third הוּא particularly when it is used in an absolute manner: I must acknowledge it, notwithstanding what I have said concerning the grammatical rank that ought to be accorded the pronoun אֲנִי. This energy is such that uttered in an universal sense, it has become throughout the Orient, one of the sacred names of the Divinity. The Arabs and all the peoples who profess Islamism, pronounce it even in this day, with the greatest respect. One can still remember the righteous indignation of the Turkish ambassador, when this sacred name was profaned in our theatre in the farce of *le Bourgeois-Gentilhomme,* and travestied in the ridiculous syllable *hou! hou!*

Here is its composition. The sign of power א, which as we have seen, appears in the first two pronouns, אֲנִי and אַתָּה, forms also the basis of this one. As long as this sign is governed only by the determinative article ה, it is limited to presenting the idea of a determined being, as is proved by the relative הא: even though the convertible sign ו, adds to it a verbal action, it is still only the pronoun of the third person; a person, considered as acting beyond us, without reciprocity, and that we designate by a root which depicts splendour and elevation, *he* or *him:* but when the character ה, instead of being taken as a simple article, is considered in its state of the sign of universal life, then this same pronoun הוא, leaving its determination, becomes the image of the All-Powerful: that which can be attributed only to GOD!

§ II.

Affixes.

Those of the affixes which I have called *nominal*, are joined without intermediary to the construct noun, to express dependence and possession in the three pronominal persons; for the Hebraic tongue knows not the use of the pronouns called by our grammarians, *possessive*.

Verbal affixes are those which are joined without intermediaries to verbs, whatever their modifications may be, and express the actual action either upon persons or upon things: for neither do the Hebrews know the pronouns that our grammarians call *conjunctive*.

Without further delay, I now give a list of the nominal and verbal affixes.

Nominal.

Singular

$$\begin{cases} 1 \begin{cases} m. \\ f. \end{cases} & \text{י or נִי} \quad \text{my, mine} \\ 2 \begin{cases} m. \;\; ךָ \text{ or } כָה \\ f. \;\;\; ךְ \text{ or } כִי \end{cases} & \text{thy, thine} \\ 3 \begin{cases} m. \;\; וֹ, וּ, הוּ \quad \text{his, his} \\ f. \;\; הָ \text{ or } נָה \quad \text{her, hers} \end{cases} \end{cases}$$

Plural

$$\begin{cases} 1 \begin{cases} m. \\ f. \end{cases} & \text{נוּ} \quad \text{our, ours} \\ 2 \begin{cases} m. \;\; כֶם \\ f. \;\; כֶן \end{cases} & \text{your, yours} \\ 3 \begin{cases} m. \;\; הֶם, ם\, \text{ or } מוֹ \\ f. \;\; הֶן, ן \end{cases} & \text{their, theirs} \end{cases}$$

Verbal.

Singular

1 { m. / f. } נִי or יְ   of me

2 { m. כָה or ךָ / f. כִי or ךְ } of thee

3 { m. הוּ, וּ, or וֹ   of him / f. הָ or הָ   of her }

Plural

1 { m. / f. } נוּ   of us

2 { m. כֶם / f. כֶן } of you

3 { m. מוֹ, ם, or כה / f. הֶן or ן } of them

It can be seen, in comparing these two lists, that the nominal and verbal affixes in the Hebraic tongue differ not in the least as to form, but only as to sense. However I must mention that one finds the simplest of these pronouns such as יְ, ךְ, וֹ, etc., used quite generally as nominal affixes, and the most composite such as הוּ, כָה, נִי, as verbal affixes, but it is not an invariable rule.

When the personal pronouns אֲנִי *I*, אַתָּה *thou*, הוּא *he*, etc., are subject to the inflection of the articles, it is the nominal affixes which are used in determining the different movements as is shown in the following example:

AFFIXES

Example of the Pronominal Inflection.
Singular

MOVEMENT	Enunciative	אֲנִי	I
	Determinative	הָאנֹכִי	it is I !
	Directive	לִי	to me
	Extractive	מֶנִּי : מִמֶּנִּי	from me
	Mediative	בִּי : כְּדִי	in me, with me
	Assimilative	כִּי : כָּמוֹנִי	as I
	Conjunctive	וַאֲנִי	and I
	Designative	אוֹתִי : אוֹתָנִי	myself, me

Plural

נַחְנוּ we

הָאֲנַחְנוּ us! it is us!

לָנוּ to us

מֶנּוּ : מִמֶּנּוּ from us

בָּנוּ in us, with us

כָּנוּ : כָּמוֹנוּ as we

וְנַחְנוּ and we

אוֹתָנוּ ourselves

I have chosen, in giving this example, the pronoun of the first person, which will suffice to give an idea of all the others. It will be noticed that I have added to the preposition אֵת of the designative movement, the sign וֹ, because the Hebraic genius affects it in this case and in some others, as giving more importance to this movement.

The designative relations which I have made known under the name of prepositions, are joined to the nominal affixes in the same manner as the articles. Here are some examples of this liaison.

אֵלַי : אֵלֶיךָ : אֲלֵיהֶם :   unto me, unto thee, **unto** them.

אֶצְלוֹ : אִתּוֹ :   beside him; with him.

בַּעֲדוֹ : בַּעֲדֵיהֶם :   for him; for them.

עָלַי : תַּחְתַּי : עָדַי :   upon me; under me; **as far as** me.

עִמִּי : עִמְּךָ : עִמּוֹ :   with me; with thee; with him.

Relative pronouns are inflected with articles and with prepositions in the same manner as nouns. I shall not stop to give any particular examples of this inflection which has nothing very remarkable. I prefer to illustrate it by the following phrases:

אֵלֶּה תוֹלְדוֹת :   these are the symbols of the generations.

אֲשֶׁר עָשָׂה :   that which he had done.

אָנֹכִי יְהוָֹה אֱלֹהֶיךָ אֲשֶׁר....   I am Yahweh, He-the-Gods thine, who....

וְכָל אֲשֶׁר.....   and all that which...

מַה־זֹּאת עָשִׂיתָ :   why hast thou done that?

מִי־אַתְּ : מִי־אֵלֶּה :   who art thou? who are those?

מִי־שְׁמֶךָ : מֶה קוֹל :   what is thy name? what is this voice?

מֶה מִשְׁפַּט הָאִישׁ :   what is the fashion of this man?

מַה־טּוֹב וּמַה־נָּעִים :   how good it is! how pleasing!

מֶה־הָיָה לוֹ :   what has happened to him?

בַּת־מִי אַתְּ :   the daughter of whom **art** thou?

AFFIXES

לְמִי הַנַּעֲרָה הַזֹּאת׃	to whom belongs the young woman there?
לָמָּה לִי׃ עַל־מֶה׃	why mine? upon what?
עַל־מֶה שָׁוְא׃	upon what futility?
הִנֵּנִי׃ הִנְנוּ׃ כֻּלָּנוּ׃ כֻּלְּכֶם׃	here am I: behold us: both: them all.
כָּזֶה׃ כָּהֵנָה׃	like this one; like that one.
כָּזֶה וּכָזֶה׃	like this and like that.
בָּזֶה׃ כָּאֵלֶּה׃	in this one: in that one.

The relative אֲשֶׁר whose use I have just shown in several examples, has this peculiarity, that it furnishes a sort of pronominal article which is quite commonly employed.

This article, the only one of its kind, is reduced to the character שׁ, and comprises in this state all the properties of the sign which it represents. Placed at the head of nouns or verbs, it implies all the force of relative movement. Sometimes in uniting itself to the directive article ל, it forms the pronominal preposition שֶׁל, which then participates in the two ideas of relation and direction contained in the two signs of which it is composed.

It is most important in studying Hebrew, to have the foregoing articles ever present in the mind, as well as those which I give below; for the Hebraists, unceasingly confusing them with the nouns that they inflect, have singularly corrupted the meaning of several passages. Here are a few examples which can facilitate understanding the prenominal articles in question.

עַד שַׁקַּמְתִּי׃	as much as I was opposed, so much was I strengthened.
שֶׁהָיָה לָנוּ׃ שֶׁלִּי׃	who was for us? who, for me?
שֶׁאַתָּה׃ שֶׁהוּא׃ שֶׁיְהוָֹה׃	for whom thou: for whom he: for whom YAHWEH.

שֶׁכָּבָה : בְּשָׁגָּם :	whose fellow-creature? in what also?
שַׁלָמָה :	what therefore? What is the why (the cause).
שֶׁאָהֲבָה ..... שִׁירֵד	that which she loved... That which descends...
שעכרתי	that which I passed over...
כְּנַף־הַמְּעִיל־שֶׁל־שָׁאוּל :	the border of the tunic which was Saul's.
מִשֶׁלָּנוּ :	of that which is ours.
כְּשֶׁלְמִי הָרָעָה :	in that which is the why (the cause) of evil.

§ III.

Use of the Affixes.

Let us examine now, the use of nominal affixes with nouns: later on we shall examine that of verbal affixes with verbs. These affixes are placed, as I have already stated, without intermediary after the nouns, to express dependence or possession in the three pronominal persons. It is essential to recall here what I said in speaking of the construct state; for it is the affix which makes a construct of every noun.

Thus, among the masculine nouns which do not terminate with ה, three only take the character י, in the construct singular, that is: אבי *father*, אחי *brother*, and חמי *father-in-law*, the others remain inflexible.

Thus, among the masculine and feminine nouns, all those which terminate in ה, or which have received this character as an emphatic article, change this character in the singular, to ת.

Thus, all of the masculine nouns terminating in the plural with םי, lose the character ם in becoming constructs; it is the same with the dual for both genders.

Thus, generally, but in a manner less irresistible, the feminine whose plural is formed with ות, adds י to this final syllable in taking the nominal affix.

This understood, I pass now to the examples.

Mas. Sing. { enunciative / construct } דָּבָר the word

SING. PERS.
1 { mas. / fem. } דְּבָרִי my word
2 { mas. דְּבָרְךָ / fem. דְּבָרֵךְ } thy word
3 { mas. דְּבָרוֹ his / fem. דְּבָרָהּ her } word

PLU. PERS.
1 { mas. / fem. } דְּבָרֵנוּ our word
2 { mas. דְּבַרְכֶם / fem. דְּבַרְכֶן } your word
3 { mas. דְּבָרָם / fem. דְּבָרָן } their word

Mas. Plu. { enunciative דְּבָרִים / construct דִּבְרֵי } the words

SING. PERS.
1 { mas. / fem. } דְּבָרַי my words
2 { mas. דְּבָרֶיךָ / fem. דְּבָרַיִךְ } thy words
3 { mas. דְּבָרָיו his / fem. דְּבָרֶיהָ her } words

USE OF AFFIXES

PLU. PERS.
- 1 { mas. / fem. } דְּבָרֵינוּ — our words
- 2 { mas. דִּבְרֵיכֶם / fem. דִּבְרֵיכֶן } your words
- 3 { mas. דִּבְרֵיהֶם / fem. דִּבְרֵיהֶן } their words

Fem. Sing. { enunciative צָרָה / construct צָרַת } the distress

SING. PERS.
- 1 { mas. / fem. } צָרָתִי — my distress
- 2 { mas. צָרָתְךָ / fem. צָרָתֵךְ } thy distress
- 3 { mas. צָרָתוֹ his / fem. צָרָתָהּ her } distress

PLU. PERS.
- 1 { mas. / fem. } צָרָתֵנוּ — our distress
- 2 { mas. צָרַתְכֶם / fem. צָרַתְכֶן } your distress
- 3 { mas. צָרָתָם / fem. צָרָתָן } their distress

Fem. Plu.	{ enunciative	צָרוֹת	} the distresses
	{ construct	צָרוֹתֵי	

SING. PERS.
- 1 { mas. / fem. } צָרוֹתַי my distresses
- 2 { mas. צָרוֹתֶיךָ / fem. צָרוֹתַיִךְ } thy distresses
- 3 { mas. צָרוֹתָיו his, / fem. צָרוֹתֶיהָ her } distresses

PLU. PERS.
- 1 { mas. / fem. } צָרוֹתֵינוּ our distresses
- 2 { mas. צָרוֹתֵיכֶם / fem. צָרוֹתֵיכֶן } your distresses
- 3 { mas. צָרוֹתֵיהֶם / fem. צָרוֹתֵיהֶן } their distresses

Mas. or fem. dual	{ enunciative	עֵינַיִם	} the eyes
	{ construct	עֵינֵי	

SING. PERS.
- 1 { mas. / fem. } עֵינַי my eyes
- 2 { mas. עֵינֶיךָ / fem. עֵינַיִךְ } thine eyes
- 3 { mas. עֵינָיו his / fem. עֵינֶיהָ her } eyes

USE OF AFFIXES

PLU. PERS.
1 { mas. / fem. } עֵינֵינוּ our eyes
2 { mas. עֵינֵיכֶם / fem. עֵינֵיכֶן } your eyes
3 { mas. עֵינֵיהֶם / fem. עֵינֵיהֶן } their eyes

Nouns, whether masculine or feminine, which take the common or dual number, follow in the singular, one of the preceding examples according to their gender.

The anomalies relative to the vague vowel marked by the Chaldaic punctuation are still considerable: but they have no effect, and should not delay us. The only important remark to make is, that often the affix of the third person masculine of the singular, is found to be הוּ or מוֹ in place of וֹ and again in the plural מוֹ in place of ם, or of הם: so that one might find דְּבָרהוּ or דְּבָרמוֹ *his word*, and דְּבָרִימוֹ *his words* or *their words;* or צָרָתמוֹ or צָרָתהוּ *his distress,* and צָרוֹתִימוֹ *his distresses* or *their distresses*. Besides it seems that the affix הוּ, may be applied to the emphatic style, and the affix מוֹ, to poetry.

CHAPTER VII.

THE VERB

§ I.

Absolute Verb and Particular Verbs.

If in the course of this Grammar I have been compelled, in order to be understood, to speak often of the plural verbs, it must not be thought for this reason, that I have forgotten my fundamental principle, namely, that there exists but one sole Verb: a principle which I believe fixed. The plural verbs, of which I have spoken, should only be understood as nouns *verbalized* as it were, by the unique Verb הוה *to be-being,* in which it develops its influence with more or less force and intensity. Let us forget therefore, the false ideas which we have kept through habit, of a mass of verbs existing by themselves, and return to our principle.

There is but one Verb.

The words to which one has ordinarily given the name of verbs, are only substantives animated by this single verb, and determined toward the end peculiar to them: for now we can see that the verb, in communicating to nouns the verbal life which they possess, changes in no respect their inner nature, but only makes them living with the life whose principles they held concealed within themselves. Thus the flame, communicated to all combustible substance, burns not only as flame but as enflamed substance, good or evil, according to its intrinsic quality.

The unique Verb of which I speak is formed in Hebrew, in a manner meriting the attention of the reader. Its principle is light, represented by the intellectual sign ו; its substance is life universal and absolute, represented by the root הה. This root, as I have before stated, never leaves the noun: for when it is a question of designating life proper, or, to express it better, *existence*,—which men ought never to confuse with *life*, the Hebraic tongue employs the root חי, in which the character ח, carries the idea of some sort of effort causing equilibrium between two opposed powers. It is by means of intellectual light, characterized by the sign ו, that this unique Verb dispenses its verbal force to nouns, and transforms them into particular verbs.

The verb in itself is immutable. It knows neither number nor gender; it has no kind of inflection. It is foreign to forms, to movement and to time, as long as it does not leave its absolute essence and as long as the thought conceives it independent of all substance. הוה *to be-being*, belongs to the masculine as well as to the feminine, to the singular as to the plural, to active movement as to passive movement; it exercises the same influence upon the past as upon the future; it fulfills the present; it is the image of a duration without beginning and without end: הוה *to be-being* fulfills all, comprehends all, animates all.

But in this state of absolute immutability and of universality, it is incomprehensible for man. When it acts independently of substance man cannot grasp it. It is only because of the substance which it assumes, that it is sentient. In this new state it loses its immutability. The substance which it assumes transmits to it nearly all its forms; but these same forms that it influences, acquire particular modifications through which an experienced eye can still distinguish its inflexible unity.

These details may appear extraordinary to the grammarians but little accustomed to find these sorts of speculations in their works; but I have forewarned them that it is upon the Hebraic grammar that I am writing and not

ABSOLUTE VERB AND PARTICULAR VERBS 169

upon any from their domain. If they consider my method applicable, as I think it is, they may adopt it; if they do not, nothing hinders them from following their own routine.

Let us continue. As the verb הוה becomes manifest only because of the substance which it has assumed, it participates in its forms. Therefore, every time that it appears in speech, it is with the attributes of a particular verb, and subject to the same modifications. Now, these modifications in particular verbs, or rather in facultative nouns verbalized, are four in number, namely, Form, Movement, Time and Person.

I shall explain later what these modifications are and in what manner they act upon the verbs; it is essential to examine first of all, how these verbs issue from the primitive roots or derivative nouns, subject to the unique Verb which animates them.

If we consider the unique Verb הוה, *to be-being*, as a particular verb, we shall see clearly that what constitutes it as such, is the intellectual sign ו, in which the verbal *esprit* appears wholly to reside. The root הה, by itself, is only a vague exclamation, a sort of expiration, which, when it signifies something, as in the Chinese tongue, for example, is limited to depicting the breath, its exhalation, its warmth, and sometimes the life that this warmth infers; but then the vocal sound *o* is soon manifest, as can be seen in *ho, houo, hoe*, Chinese roots, which express all ideas of warmth, of fire, of life, of action and of being.

The sign ו, being constituted, according to the genius of the Hebraic tongue, symbol of the universal verb, it is evident that in transferring it into a root or into any compound whatsoever of this tongue, this root or this compound will partake instantly of the verbal nature: for this invariably happens.

We have seen in treating particularly of the sign, that the one in question is presented under two distinct

170   THE HEBRAIC TONGUE RESTORED

modifications, first, as the universal convertible sign ו, and second, as the luminous sign וֹ: these two modifications are employed equally in the formation of verbs. I have already spoken of this in dealing with the facultatives in the Second section of the Fifth chapter. Here it is only a matter of verbs.

The facultative by which the Hebraic genius brings out the verbal action, is the finished facultative. It is in this manner.

This facultative is formed from roots by the insertion of the sign ו, between the two characters which compose it, as שׁוּם *to be placed*, גוּל *to be exhausted;* and from compound nouns by the insertion of this same sign between the last two characters of these nouns, as רגוּן *to be moved*, מָלוּךְ *to be ruled*.

Now if we take the finished facultative coming from the root, it will be sufficient, by a simple abstraction of thought, to make a verb of it, in that sort of original state which the grammarians call *infinitive*, though I cannot very well see why, and which I call, *nominal*, because it is governed by the articles and is subject to the nominal inflection. And as to the finished facultative coming from the compounds, we make a nominal verb of it by enlightening the sign ו that is to say, replacing it with the sign וֹ, as the following example illustrates:

root	קם:	every idea of substance and of material establishment
finished facultative	קוּם:	to be established
nominal verb	קוֹם:	the action of establishing
compound	רֶגֶן:	physical or moral movement; an emotion
finished facultative	רָגוּן:	to be moved
nominal verb	רָגוֹן:	the action of moving

It is well to observe that sometimes ו is enlightened in order to form the verb from the root, as in מוֹס *to waver,* and in some others. As to the nominal verbs coming from compounds, the rule is without exception in this respect. If the Chaldaic punctuation replaces this sign by the points *holem* or *kamez* these points have then the same value and that suffices. This abuse due to the indolence of the copyists was inevitable.

§ II.

Three kinds of Particular Verbs.

There is no need I think of calling attention to the effect of the convertible sign, which, insinuating itself into the heart of the primitive roots, makes them pass from the state of noun to that of verb, and which being enlightened or extinguished by turn, and changing its position in the compound substantives, produces the sentiment of an action, continued or finished, and as it were, fixes the verbal life by the successive formation of the two facultatives and the nominal verb. I believe that there is none of my readers who, having reached this point of my Grammar, and being impressed by this admirable development does not disdainfully reject any system tending to make of speech a mechanical art or an arbitrary institution.

Indeed! if speech were a mechanical art or an arbitrary institution as has been advanced by Hobbes, and before him by Gorgias and the sophists of his school, could it, I ask, have these profound roots which, being derived from a small quantity of signs and being blended not only with the very elements of nature, but also producing those immense ramifications which, coloured with all the fires of genius, take possession of the domain of thought and seem to reach to the limits of infinity? Does one see anything similar in games of chance? Do human institutions, however perfect they may be, ever have this progressive course of aggrandizement and force? Where is the mechanical work from the hand of man, that can compare with this lofty tree whose trunk, now laden with branches, slept not long since buried in an imperceptible germ? Does not one perceive that this mighty tree, which at first, weak blade of grass, pierced with difficulty the ground which concealed its principles, can in nowise be considered as the production of a blind and capricious force, but on the contrary, as that of wisdom enlightened and steadfast in its designs? Now speech is like this majestic tree; it has its germ, it spreads its roots gradually in a fertile nature whose elements are unknown, it breaks its bonds and rises upward escaping from terrestrial darkness and bursts forth into new regions where, breathing a purer element, watered by a divine light, it spreads its branches and covers them with flowers and fruit.

But perhaps the objection will be made that this comparison which could not be questioned for Hebrew, whose successive developments I have amply demonstrated, is limited to this tongue, and that it would be in vain for me to attempt the same labour for another. I reply, that this objection, to have any force must be as affirmative as is my proof, instead of being negative; that is to say, that instead of saying to me that I have not done it, it is still to be done; he must demonstrate to me, for example, that French, Latin or Greek are so constituted that they can not be brought back to their principles, or what amounts to the same thing, to the primordial signs upon which the mass of words which compose them rest; a matter which I deny absolutely. The difficulty of the analysis of these idioms, I am convinced, is due to their complexity and remoteness from their origin; however, the analysis is by no means impossible. That of Hebrew, which now appears easy owing to the method I have followed, was none the less before this test, the stumbling-block of all etymologists. This tongue is very simple; its material offers advantageous results; but what would it be if the reasons which have led me to chose Hebrew had also inclined me toward Chinese! what a mine to exploit! what food for thought!

I return to the formation of the Hebraic verbs. I have shown in the preceding section that it was by the intermediary of the facultatives that the convertible sign וֹ, raised the noun to the dignity of the verb. It is essential that we examine what the idiomatic genius adds to this creation.

This genius affects particularly the words composed of three consonant characters; that is to say, words which come from a primitive root governed by a sign, or from two roots contracted and forming two syllables. It is this which has caused the superficial etymologists and those who receive things without examination, to believe that the tongue of the Hebrews was essentially dissyllabic and that its roots could consist only of three characters. Ridiculous error, which veiling the origin of the words, and confounding the auxiliary sign and even the article, with the root itself, has finally corrupted the primitive meaning and brought forth in Hebrew, a sort of jargon, wholly different from the Hebrew itself.

Primitive roots are, in all known tongues, monosyllabic. I cannot repeat this truth too strongly. The idiomatic genius can indeed, as in Hebrew, add to this syllable, either to modify its meaning or to reinforce its expression; but it can never denature it. When by the aid of the convertible sign וֹ, the nominal verb is formed, as I have said, it is formed either of the root, as can be seen in שׂוּם *to constitute, to put up, to decree;* or of the compound substantive מְלוֹךְ *to rule*: but one feels the primitive root always, even in the nominal מְלוֹךְ, when he is intellectually capable of feeling it, or when he is not fettered by grammatical prejudices. If the reader is curious to know what this root is, I will tell him that it is אָךְ, and that the expansive sign ל, governs jointly with that of exterior and local action, מ. Now לָאָךְ, develops all idea of legation, of function to which one is linked: of vicariate, of mission, etc., thus the word מֶלֶךְ *a king*, the origin of which is Ethiopic, signifies properly, a delegate, an envoy absolute; a minister charged with representing the divinity on earth. This word has had in

THREE KINDS OF PARTICULAR VERBS 175

its origin, the same meaning as מַלְאָךְ, of which we have adopted the Greek translation ἄγγελος, *an angel.* The primitive root αγ, which forms the basis of the Greek word ἄγγελος, is precisely the same as the Hebraic root אך, and like it develops ideas of attachment and of legation. This root belongs to the tongue of the Celts as well as to that of the Ethiopians and the Hebrews. It has become, through nasalization, our idiomatic root *ang,* from which the Latins and all modern peoples generally, have received derivatives.

Taking up again the thread of my ideas, which this etymological digression has for a moment suspended, I repeat, that the Hebraic genius which is singularly partial to words of two syllables, rarely allows the verb to be formed of the root without adding a character which modifies the meaning or reinforces the expression. Now it is in the following manner that the adjunction is made and the characters especially consecrated to this use.

This adjunction is initial or terminative; that is to say, that the character added is placed at the beginning or the end of the word. When the adjunction is initial, the character added at the head of the root is י or נ; when it is terminative it is simply the final character which is doubled.

Let us take for example the verb שׁוֹם that I have already cited. This verb will become, by means of the initial adjunction יְשׁוֹם, or נְשׁוֹם, and by means of the terminative adjunction, שׁוֹמֵם: but then, not only will the meaning vary considerably and receive acceptations very different from the primitive meaning, but the conjugation also will appear irregular, on account of the characters having been added after the formation of the verb, and the root will not always be in evidence. The result of this confusion of ideas is that the Hebraists, devoid of all etymological science, take roots sometimes for radical verbs, relative to the new meaning which they offer, and sometimes for irregular verbs, relative to the anomalies that they experience in their modifications.

But the truth is, that these verbs are neither radical verbs nor irregular verbs: these are verbs of a kind, distinct and peculiar to the Hebraic tongue; verbs of which it is necessary to understand the origin and development, so as to distinguish them in speech and assign them a rank in grammar. I shall name them *compound radical* verbs, as holding a mean between those which come directly from the root and those which are formed from the derivative substantives.

I classify verbs in three kinds, with regard to conjugation, namely: the radical, the derivative and the compound radical. By the first, I mean those which are derived from the root and which remain monosyllables, such as גול, בול, שום etc. By the second, those which are derived from a substantive already compound, and which are always dissyllables such as מָלוֹךְ, רָגֹז, פָּקוֹד etc. By the third, those which are formed by the adjunction of an initial or terminative character to the root, and which appear in the course of the conjugation sometimes monosyllabic and sometime dissyllabic, such as יָשׂוּם, שׁוֹמֵם, נָשׂוּם etc.

§ III.

Analysis of Nominal Verbs: Verbal Inflection.

The signification of radical verbs depends always upon the idea attached to their root. When the etymologist has this root firmly in his memory, it is hardly possible for him to err in the meaning of the verb which is developed. If he knows well, for example, that the root שׁם contains the general idea of a thing, upright, straight, remarkable; of a monument, a name, a sign, a place, a fixed and determined time; he will know well that the verb שׁום, which is formed from it, must express the action of instituting, enacting, noting, naming, designating, placing, putting up, etc. according to the meaning of the context.

The compound radical verbs offer, it is true, a few more difficulties, for it is necessary to join to the etymological understanding of the root, that of the initial or terminative adjunction; but this is not impossible. The first step, after finding the root, is to conceive clearly the sort of influence that this same root and the character which is joined to it, exercise upon each other; for their action in this respect is reciprocal: here lies the only difficulty. The signification of the joined characters is not in the least perplexing. One must know that the characters י and נ express, in their qualities as sign, the first, a potential manifestation, an intellectual duration, and the second, an existence, produced, dependent and passive. So that one can admit as a general underlying idea, that the adjunction י, will give to the verbal action, an exterior force, more energetic and more durable, a movement more apparent and more determined; whereas the adjunction נ, on the contrary, will render this same action more interior and more involved, by bringing it back to itself.

As to the terminative adjunction, since it depends upon the duplication of the final sign, it also draws all its expression from this same sign whose activity it doubles.

But let us take as an example of these three modifications, the root שם, which we already know as radical verb, and let us consider it as compound radical verb. In taking this verb שם, in the sense of *setting up*, which is its simplest acceptation, we shall find that the initial adjunction manifesting its action, gives it in שׁים, the sense of *exposing*, of *placing in sight*, of *putting in a prominent place:* but if this verb is presented in a more figurative sense as that of *elevating*, we shall see that the initial adjunction נ, bringing back its action in itself, makes it signify, *to elevate the soul, to be inspired, to be animated; to assume,* as it were, *the spirit of the loftiest and most radiant parts of universal spirituality.* These are the two initial adjunctions.

The terminative adjunction being formed by the duplication of the final character, it is expedient to examine this character in the root שם. Now, this character, considered as the sign of exterior action, is used here in its quality of collective sign. But this sign which already tends very much to extension, and which develops the being in infinite space as much as its nature permits, can not be doubled without reaching that limit where extremes meet. Therefore, the extension, of which it is the image, is changed to a dislocation, a sort of annihilation of being, caused by the very excess of its expansive action. Also the radical verb שום, which is limited to signifying the occupation of a distinguished, eminent place, presents in the compound radical שׁמם, only the action of *extending* in the void, of *wandering* in space, of *depriving of stability* of *making deserted,* of *being delirious,* etc.

In this manner should the radical and the compound radical verbs be analyzed. As to the derivative verbs, their analysis is no more difficult; for, as they come for

VERBAL INFLECTION 179

the most part from a triliteral substantive, they receive from it verbal expression. I shall have many occasions for examining these sorts of verbs in the course of my notes upon the *Cosmogony of Moses*, so that I shall dispense with doing so here: nevertheless, in order to leave nothing to be desired, in this respect, for the reader who follows me closely, I shall give two examples.

Let us take two verbs of great importance. בָּרוֹא *to create* and אָמוֹר *to speak, to say, to declare*. The first thing to do is to bring them both back to the substantives from which they are derived: this is simply done, by taking away the sign ו, which verbalizes them. The former presents to me in ברא, the idea of an emanated production, since בר signifies *a son, an exterior fruit;* the latter, in אמר, *a declaration, a thing upon which light is thrown,* since מאר signifies a *luminous focus, a torch*. In the first, the character א is a sign of stability; in the second, it is only a transposition from the middle of the word to the beginning to give more energy. Let us take the first.

The word בר, considered as primitive root, signifies not only *a son*, but develops the general idea of every production emanated from a generative being. Its elements are worthy of the closest attention. It is on the other hand, the sign of movement proper ר, united to that of interior action ב. The first of these signs, when it is simply vocalized by the mother vowel א as in אר, is applied to the elementary principle, whatever it may be, and under whatever form it may be conceived; ethereal, igneous, aerial, aqueous or terrestrial principle. The second of these signs is preëminently the paternal symbol. Therefore the elementary principle, whatever it may be, moved by an interior, generative force, constitutes the root באר whence is formed the compound substantive בָּרָא and the verb that I am analyzing, ברוא : that is to say, *to draw from an unknown element; to make pass from the principle to the essence; to make same that which was other;*

to bring from the centre to the circumference; in short, *to create.*

Now let us see the word מאר. This word is supported likewise by the elementary root אר, but this root being enlightened by the intellectual sign ו, has become אוֹר *the light.* In this state it assumes, not the paternal sign ב, as in the word ברא, that I have just examined, but the maternal sign מ, image of exterior action, so as to constitute the substantive מֵאֹר or מָאוֹר: also, it is no longer an interior and creative action, but an action exterior and propagating, a *reflection;* that is to say, a luminous focus, a torch diffusing light from which it has received the principle.

Such is the image of speech. Such at least is the etymology of the Hebraic verb אָמוֹר, which is to say, *to spread abroad its light; to declare its thought, its will; to speak,* etc.

I have now shown how verbs are formed and analyzed; let us see how they are inflected with the aid of the designative relations which I have called articles. This inflection will prove that these verbs are really nominal, partaking, on the one hand, of the name from which they are derived by their substance, and on the other, of the absolute verb from which they receive the verbal life.

MOVEMENT.	*enunciative*	מְלוֹךְ	the action of ruling
	determinative	הַמְלוֹךְ	of the action of ruling
	directive	לַמְלוֹךְ	to the action of ruling
	extractive	מִמְלוֹךְ	from the action of ruling
	mediative	בִּמְלוֹךְ	in the action of ruling
	assimilative	כִּמְלוֹךְ	conformable to the action of ruling
	conjunctive	וּמְלוֹךְ	and the action of ruling
	designative	אֶת־מָלוֹךְ	that which constitutes the action of ruling

VERBAL INFLECTION

I have a very important observation to make concerning this verbal inflection. It is with regard to the conjunctive article וֹ. This article which, placed in front of the nominal verb, expresses only the conjunctive movement as in the above example, takes all the force of the convertible sign, before the future or past tense of this same verb, and changes their temporal modification in such a way that the future tense becomes past and the past tense takes all the character of the future. Thus for example the future יִהְיֶה *it shall be,* changes abruptly the signification in receiving the conjunctive article וֹ, and becomes the past וַיְהִי *and it was*: thus the past הָיָה *it was,* loses too its original meaning in taking the same article וֹ, and becomes the future וְהָיָה *and it shall be.*

It is impossible to explain in a satisfactory manner this idiomatic Hebraism without admitting the intrinsic force of the universal, convertible sign וֹ and without acknowledging its influence in this case.

Besides, we have an adverbial relation in our own tongue, that exercises an action almost similar, upon a past tense, which it makes a future. I do not recall having seen this singular idiomatism pointed out by any grammarian. It is the adverbial relation *if.* I am giving this example to the reader that he may see in what manner a past can become a future, without the mind being disturbed by the boldness of the ellipsis and without it even striking the attention. *They were* is assuredly of the past; it becomes future in this phrase: if *they were* in ten years at the end of their labours they would be happy!

The nominal verb participating, as I have said, in two natures, adopts equally the nominal and verbal affixes. One finds מְלוֹכִי and מַלְכֵנִי *the action of ruling, mine* (my rule) : מְלוֹכוֹ and מַלְכֵהוּ *the action of ruling, his* (his rule) : etc.

One perceives that it is only the sense of the sentence which can indicate whether the affix added here is nominal or verbal. It is an amphibology that Hebrew writers would have been able to evade easily, by distinguishing the nominal affixes from the verbal.

Here is an example of the verbal and nominal affixes united to the nominal verb. I have followed the Chaldaic punctuation, which, always submissive to the vulgar pronunciation, replaces the verbal sign ו, on this occasion, by the weak vowel point, named *shewa*.

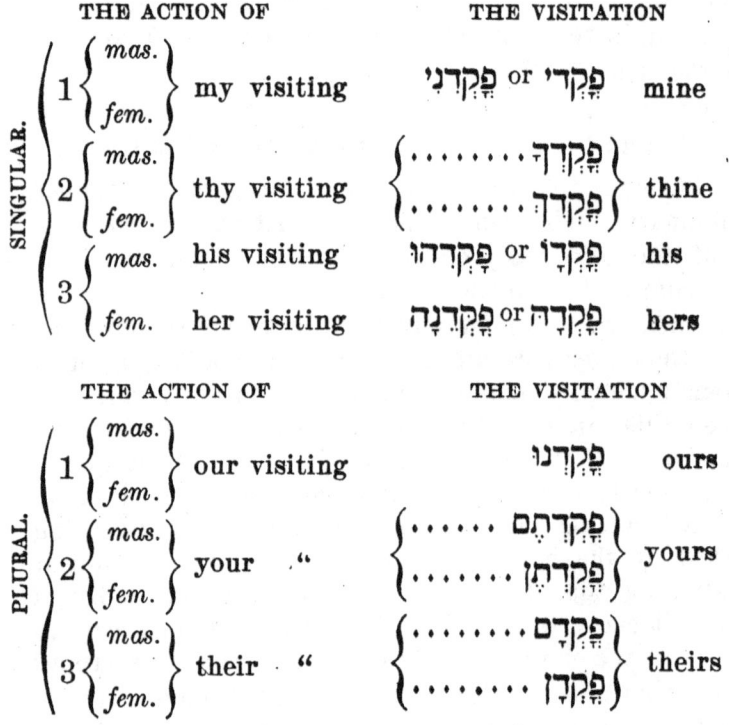

CHAPTER VIII.

MODIFICATIONS OF THE VERB.

§ I.

Form and Movement.

In the preceding chapter I have spoken of the absolute verb, of the particular verbs which emanate from it, and of the various kinds of these verbs. I have stated that these verbs were subject to four modifications: form, movement, time and person. I am about to make known the nature of these modifications; afterward, I shall give models of the conjugations for all the kinds of verbs of the Hebraic tongue: for I conceive as many conjugations as I have kinds of verbs, namely: radical, derivative and compound radical conjugations. I do not know why the Hebraists have treated as irregular, the first and third of these conjugations, when it is obvious that one of them, the radical, is the type of all the others and particularly of the derivative, which they have chosen for their model in consequence of an absurd error which placed the triliteral verb in the first etymological rank.

I am beginning with an explanation of what ought to be understood by the *form* of the verb, and its *movement* which is here inseparable.

I call verbal form, that sort of modification by means of which the Hebraic verbs display an expression more or less forceful, more or less direct, more or less simple or compound. I recognize four verbal forms: positive, intensive, excitative and reflexive or reciprocal form.

The movement is active or passive. It is inherent in the form; for under whatever modification the verb may appear, it is indispensable that it present an active or passive action; that is to say, an action which exercises itself from within outwardly by an agent upon an object, or an action which exercises itself from without inwardly, by an object upon an agent. *One loves* or *one is loved; one sees* or *one is seen*, etc.

The verbs to which modern grammarians have given the somewhat vague name of *neuter verbs* and which appear indeed to be neither active nor passive, such as *to sleep, to walk, to fall,* etc., are verbs, not which unite the two movements, as Harris[1] believed because this definition agrees only with the reflexive form; but verbs wherein the verbal action itself seizes the agent and suspends it between the two movements, making it object without taking from it any of its faculty of agent. Thus, when I say: *I sleep, I walk, I fall;* it is as if one said: *I devote myself to the action of sleeping, of walking, of falling, which now exercises itself upon me.* Far from having called these verbs *neuter*, that is to say, foreign to active and passive movement, the grammarians should have named them *superactives;* for they dominate the active movement, even as one has proof in considering that there is not a single active verb which, by an abstraction of thought, being taken in a general sense independent of any object, cannot take the character of the verbs in question. When one says, for example, *man loves, hates, wills, thinks*, etc., the verbs *to love, to hate, to will, to think* are in reality *superactives;* that is to say, that the verbal action which they express, dominates the agent and suspends in it the active movement, without in any manner rendering it passive.

But let us leave modern grammar which is not my domain and enter that of the Hebrews, to which I would confine myself. It is useless to speak of the superactive movement, which all verbs can take, which all can leave and which besides, differs in nothing from the active movement in its characteristic course. Let us limit ourselves to the two movements of which I have first spoken

[1] *Hermes*, L. I. c. 9.

FORM AND MOVEMENT

and see how they are characterized according to their inherent form.

I call *positive,* the first of the four forms of Hebraic verbs. In this form the verbal action, active or passive, is announced simply and in accordance with its original nature. The passive movement is distinguished from the active by means of the two characters נ and ה ; the first, which is the sign of produced being, governs the continued facultative; the second, which is that of life, governs the nominal verb. Therefore one finds for the active movement, קוֹם or קָם, *to be establishing,* קוֹם, *the action of establishing;* and for the passive movement נָקוֹם, *being established,* הָקוֹם, *the action of being established.*

The second form is what I name *intensive,* on account of the intensity which it adds to the verbal action. Our modern tongues which are deprived of this form, supply the deficiency by the aid of modificatives. This form, which a speaker can use with great force, since the accent of the voice is able to give energetic expression, is very difficult to distinguish today in writing, particularly, since the Chaldaic punctuation has substituted for the mother vowel ', placed after the first character of the verb, the imperceptible point called *hirek*. The only means which remains to recognize this form, is the redoubling of the second verbal character, which being marked unfortunately again by the insertion of the interior point, is hardly more striking than the point *hirek*. The rabbis having recognized this difficulty have assumed the very wise part of giving to the mother vowel ', the place which has been taken from it by this last mentioned point. It would perhaps be prudent to imitate them, for this form which is of the highest importance in the books of Moses, has scarcely ever been perceived by his translators. The active and passive facultative is governed by the character מ, sign of exterior action, and the second character is likewise doubled in both movements; but in the active movement, the nominal verb adopts the mother vowel י, or the point *hirek* after the first character; in the passive movement it takes the mother vowel וּ, or the point *kibbuz*. For the active movement, one finds מְפַקֵּד, *to be visiting, inspecting with diligence*: פִּיקֵּד or פַּקֵּד *the action of visiting*, etc.; for the passive movement מְפֻקָּד, *being visited, inspected with diligence*: פּוּקוֹד or פֻּקּוֹד, *the action of being visited*, etc.

I qualify the third form by the name of *excitative*, in order to make understood as much as possible, by one single word, the kind of excitation that it causes in the verbal action, transporting this action beyond the subject which acts, upon another which it is a question of making act. This form is of great effect in the tongue of Moses. Happily it has a character that the Chaldaic point has never been able to supply and which makes it easily recognized: it is the sign of life ה, which governs the nominal verb in the two movements. For the active movement מְקִים *to be establishing;* הָקֵם or הָקִים *the action of establishing*: and for passive movement מוּקָם *being established;* הוּקַם *the action of being established.*

The fourth form is that which I name *reciprocal* or *reflexive,* because it makes the verbal action reciprocal or because it reflects it upon the very subject which is acting. It is easily recognized by means of the characteristic syllable הת composed of the united signs of life and of reciprocity. The second character of the verb, is doubled in this form as in the intensive, thus conserving all the energy of the latter. The two movements are also here united in a single one, to indicate that the agent which makes the action, becomes the object of its own action. One finds for the continued facultative מִתְפַּקֵּד *visiting each other;* הִתְפַּקֵּד *the action of visiting each other.*

I shall now enter into some new details regarding these four forms in giving models of the conjugations.

§ II.

Tense.

Thus Hebraic verbs are modified with respect to form and movement. I hope that the attentive reader has not failed to observe with what prolific richness the principles, which I have declared to be those of the tongue of Moses in particular, and those of all tongues in general, are developed, and I hope it will not be seen without some interest, that the sign, after having furnished the material of the noun, becomes the very substance of the verb and influences its modifications. For, let him examine carefully what is about to be explained—two movements being united to four forms. One of these movements is passive, and from its origin, is distinguished from the active, by the sign of produced being. The form, if intensive, is the sign of the duration and the manifestation which constitutes it: if it is excitative, it is the same sign united to that of life: if it is reflexive, it is the sign of that which is reciprocal and mutual, which is presented. There is such a continuous chain of regularity that I cannot believe it is the result of chance.

Now, let us pass on to the different modifications of Hebraic verbs under the relation of Tense. If, before seeing what these modifications are, I should wish to examine, as Harris[1] and some other grammarians, the nature of this incomprehensible being which causes them,—Time, what trouble would I not experience in order to develop unknown ideas; ideas that I would be unable to sustain with anything sentient! for how can Time affect our material organs since *the past* is no more; since *the future* is not; since *the present* is contained in an indivisible in-

[1] *Hermes*, L. I. ch. 7.

stant? Time is an indecipherable enigma for whatever is contained within the circle of the sensations, and nevertheless the sensations alone give it a relative existence. If they did not exist, what would it be?

It is measure of life. Change life and you will change Time. Give another movement to matter and you will have another space. Space and Time are analogous things. There, it is matter which is changed; here, it is life. Man, intelligent and sentient being, understands matter through his corporeal organs, but not through those of his intelligence; he has the intellectual sentiment of life, but he grasps it not. This is why Space and Time which appear so near, remain unknown to him. In order to understand them, man must needs awaken a third faculty within him, which being supported at the same time both by sensations and by sentiment, and enlightening at the same time the physical and mental qualities, unites in them the separated faculties. Then a new universe would be unveiled before his eyes; then he would fathom the depths of space, he would grasp the fugitive essence of Time; it would be known in its double nature.

Still if one asks me if this third faculty exists, or even if it can exist, I shall state that it is what Socrates called *divine inspiration* and to which he attributed the power of virtue.

But whatever Time may be, I have not dwelt a moment upon its nature, I have only tried to make its profound obscurity felt, in order that it be understood, that all peoples, not having considered it in the same manner, could not have experienced the same effects. Also it is very necessary in all idioms, that verbs conform to the tenses, and especially that the idiomatic genius should assign them the same limits.

The modern tongues of Europe are very rich in this respect, but they owe this richness, first, to the great number of idioms whose *débris* they have collected and of which they were insensibly composed; afterward, with the progress of the mind of man whose ideas, accumulating with the centuries, are refined and polished more and more, and are developed into a state of perfection. It is a matter worthy of notice, and which holds very closely to the history of mankind, that the tongues of the North of Europe, those whence are derived the idioms so rich today in temporal modifications, had in their origin only two simple tenses, the *present* and the *past*: they lacked the future; whereas the tongues of Occidental Asia, which appear of African origin, lacked the present, having likewise only two simple tenses, the *past* and the *future*.

Modern grammarians who have broached the delicate question of the number of tenses possessed by the French tongue, one of the most varied of Europe, and of the world in this regard, have been very far from being in accord. Some have wished to recognize only five, counting as real tenses, only the simplest ones, such as *I love, I loved, I was loving, I shall love, I should love;* considering the others as but temporal gradations. Abbé Girard has enumerated eight; Harris, twelve; Beauzée, twenty. These writers instead of throwing light upon this matter have obscured it more and more. They are like painters who, with a palette charged with colours, instead of instructing themselves or instructing others concerning their usage and the best manner of mixing them, amuse themselves disputing over their number and their rank.

There are three principal colours in light, as there are three principal tenses in the verb. The art of painting consists in knowing how to distinguish these principal colours, *blue, red* and *yellow;* the median colours *violet, orange* and *green;* and those median colours of infinite shades which can arise from their blending. Speech is a means of painting thought. The tenses of the verb are the coloured lights of the picture. The more the palette is rich in shades, the more a people gives flight to its imagination. Each writer makes use of this palette according to his genius. It is in the delicate manner of composing the shades and of mixing them, that painters and writers are alike distinguished.

It is well known that ancient painters were ignorant of the shades and half-tones. They used the primary colours without mixing them. A picture composed of four colours was regarded as a miracle of art. The colours of speech were not more varied. These shades of verbal light which we call compound tenses were unknown. The Hebrews were not poorer in this respect, than the Ethiopians and the Egyptians, renowned for their wisdom; the Assyrians, famous for their power; the Phœnicians, recognized for their vast discoveries and their colonies; the Arabs finally, whose high antiquity can not be contested: all of these had, properly speaking, only two verbal tenses: the *future* and the *past*.

But one must not think that in these ancient tongues, and particularly in the Hebrew, these two tenses were so determined, so decisive, as they have since become in our modern idioms, or that they signified precisely that which was, or that which must be, as we understand by *it has been, it shall be;* the temporal modifications הָיָה, and יְהִיָה, express in Hebrew, not a rupture, a break in temporal continuity, but a continued duration, uniting, without the slightest interruption, the most extreme point of the past to the indivisible instant of the present, and this indivisible instant to the most extreme point of the future. So that it was sufficient by a single restriction of thought, by a simple inflection of the voice, to fix upon this temporal line, any point whatever from the past to the present, or from the present to the future, and to obtain thus by the aid of the two words הָיָה and יְהִיָה, the same differences which modern tongues acquire with difficulty, through the following combinations: *I was, I have been, I had been, I shall be, I should be, I may have been, I might have been, I ought to be, I would be, I have to be, I had to be, I am about to be, I was about to be.*

I have purposely omitted from this list of tenses the indivisible instant *I am*, which makes the fourteenth, because this instant is never expressed in Hebrew except by the pronoun alone, or by the continued facultative, as in אָנֹכִי יְהוֹה, *I am* YAHWEH: הִנְנִי מֵבִיא *behold me leading;* etc.

It is on this account that one should be careful in a correct translation, not always to express the Hebraic past or future, which are vague tenses, by the definite tenses. One must first examine the intention of the writer, and the respective condition of things. Thus, to give an example, although, in the French and English *word-for-word* translation, conforming to custom, I have rendered the verb בָּרָא, of the first verse of the Cosmogony of Moses, by *he created*, I have clearly felt that this verb signified there, *he had created;* as I have expressed it in the correct translation; for this antecedent nuance is irresistibly determined by the verb הָיְתָה, *it existed*, in speaking of the earth an evident object of an anterior creation.

Besides the two tenses of which I have just spoken, there exists still a third tense in Hebrew, which I call *transitive,* because it serves to transport the action of the past to the future, and because it thus participates in both tenses by serving them as common bond. Modern grammarians have improperly named it *imperative.* This name would be suitable if used only to express commands; but as one employs it as often in examining, desiring, demanding and even entreating, I do not see why one should refuse it a name which would be applicable to all these ideas and which would show its transitive action.

§ III.

Formation of Verbal Tenses by Means of Pronominal Persons.

After having thus made clear the modification of Hebraic verbs relative to tense, there remains only for me to say how they are formed. But before everything else it is essential to remember what should be understood by the three Pronominal Persons.

When I treated of nominal relations, known under the denomination of Personal and Relative pronouns, I did not stop to explain what should be understood by the three Pronominal Persons, deeming that it was in speaking of the verb that these details would be more suitably placed, so much the more as my plan was to consider *person,* as one of the four modifications of the verb.

Person and tense are as inseparable as form and movement; never can the one appear without the other; for it is no more possible to conceive person without tense, than verbal form without active or passive movement.

At the time when I conceived the bold plan of bringing back the Hebraic tongue to its constitutive principles by deriving it wholly from the *sign,* I saw that the sign had three natural elements: *voice, gesture* and *traced characters.* Now by adhering to the traced characters to develop the power of the sign, I think I have made it clearly understood, that I consider them not as any figures whatever, denuded of life and purely material, but as symbolic and living images of the generative ideas of language, expressed at first by the sundry inflections which the voice received from the organs of man. Therefore these characters have always represented to me, the voice, by means of the verbal inflections whose symbols they are; they have also represented to me, the gesture with which each inflection is necessarily accompanied, and when the sign has developed the three parts of speech, the noun, the relation and the verb, although there may not be a single one of these parts where the three elements of speech do not act together, I have been able to distinguish, nevertheless, that part where each of them acts more particularly. The voice, for example, appears to me to be the dominant factor in the verb; the vocal accent or the character in the noun, and the gesture finally in the relation. So that if man making use of speech follows the sentiment of nature he must raise the voice in the verb, accentuate more the noun and place the gesture upon the relation. It seems even as though experience confirms this grammatical remark especially in what concerns the gesture. The article and the prepositions which are designative relations, the pronouns of any kind which are nominal relations, the adverbs which are adverbial relations, always involve a gesture expressed or understood. Harris had already observed this coincidence of the gesture and had not hesitated to place in it the source of all pronouns, following in this the doctrine of the ancients, related by Apollonius and Priscian.[1]

Harris was right in this. It is the gesture which, always accompanying the nominal relations, has given birth to the distinction of the three persons, showing itself by turn identical, mutual, other or relative. The identical gesture produces the first person *I*, or *me*, אֲנִי: this is a being which manifests itself; the mutual gesture produces the second person, *thou* or *thee* אַתָּה: this is a mutual being; the other, or relative gesture, produces the third per-

---

[1] *Hermes.* Liv. I. Chap. 5 Apoll. de *Synt.*, Liv. II, Chap 5. Prisc. Liv. XII.

194   THE HEBRAIC TONGUE RESTORED

son, *he* or *him*, הוּא: this is another being, sometimes relative, as in the English pronoun, sometimes absolute, as in the Hebraic pronoun.

These personal pronouns whose origin I here explain, are like the substantive nouns which they replace in speech, subject to gender, number and inflection of the articles. I have explained them under these different relations and now we can see how in Hebrew, they determine the tense of the verbs. It is a matter worthy of attention and it has not escaped the sagacity of Court de Gébelin.[2] After being contracted in such a manner as not to be confused with the verbal affixes, the personal pronouns are placed before the nominal verb, when it is a question of forming the future, and to form the past, they are placed after the verb so as to express by this, that the action is already done.

By this simple yet energetic manner of showing verbal tenses, the Hebraic genius adds another which is none the less forceful and which proceeds from the power of the sign. It allows the luminous sign וֹ, which constitutes the nominal verb, to stand in the future; and not content with making it appear וֹ, in the finished facultative, makes it disappear wholly in the past; so that the third person of this tense, which is found without the masculine pronoun, is exactly the same as the root, or the compound whence the verb is derived. This apparent simplicity is the reason why the Hebraists have taken generally the third person of the past, for the root of the Hebraic verb and why they have given it this rank in all the dictionaries. Their error is having confounded the moment when it finishes, with that in which it begins, and not having had enough discernment to see that if the nominal verb

[2] *Grammaire Univ.* page 245. Court de Gébelin has put some obscurity into his explanation; but although he may be mistaken in respect to the tenses, it is plainly seen that what he said is exactly what I say.

FORMATION OF VERBAL TENSES

did not claim priority over all the tenses, this priority would belong to the transitive as the most simple of all.

Here is the new character which the personal pronouns take in order to form verbal tenses.

The affixes of the future placed before the verb, with the terminations which follow them.

SINGULAR.
1 { mas. / fem. } ....א I
2 { mas. ....ת / fem. ת....י } thou
3 { mas. ......י he / fem. ....ת she }

PLURAL.
1 { mas. / fem. } ......נ we
2 { mas. ת..ו / fem. ת..נה } ye
3 { mas. י..ו / fem. ת..נה } they

Affixes of the past placed after the verb.

SINGULAR.
1 { mas. / fem. } ...תי I
2 { mas. ....תָ / fem. ....ת } thou
3 { mas. ...... he / fem. ....הָ she }

PLURAL.
1 { mas. / fem. } ....נו we
2 { mas. ...תם / fem. ....תן } ye
3 { mas. / fem. } .....ו they

I do not speak of the affixes of the transitive, because this tense, which holds a sort of mean between the future and the past, has no affixes properly speaking, but has terminations which it borrows from both tenses.

Hebraic words moreover, do not recognize what we call verbal moods, by means of which we represent in our modern idioms, the state of the will relative to the verbal action, whether that will is influential or resolute, as in *I am doing, I have done, I shall do;* whether it is dubitative or irresolute, as in *I might have done, I should have done, I would do;* or whether it is influenced or constrained, as in *I must do, that I may do; I was obliged to do, that I might have done; I shall be obliged to do; I should be obliged to do;* the modern tongue is of an inexhaustible richness in this respect. It colours with the most delicate shades all the volitive and temporal modifications of verbs. The nominal verb and also the transitive show this fine shading of the meaning. *To do,* for example, is an indefinite nominal, but *I have just done, I am doing, I am going to do,* show the same nominal expression of the past, the present and the future. The transitive *do,* conveys visibly the action from one tense to the other, but if I say *may have done, may have to do,* this change marks first a past in a future, and afterward a future in a future.

After this data I now pass on to the models of the three verbal conjugations, according to their forms and their movements, supporting them with certain remarks concerning the most striking anomalies which can be found.

CHAPTER IX.

CONJUGATIONS.

§ I.

Radical Conjugation.

POSITIVE FORM.

ACTIVE MOVEMENT.
CONTINUED FACULTATIVE

mas. קוֹם or קָם } to be
fem. קוֹמָה } establishing

PASSIVE MOVEMENT.
CONTINUED FACULTATIVE

mas. נָקוֹם } being
fem. נְקוֹמָה } established

FINISHED.

mas. קוּם } to be established
fem. קוּמָה }

NOMINAL VERB.

absol. קוּם } to establish: action
constr. קוּם } of establishing

absol. } הקוּם { action of being
constr. } established

TEMPORAL VERB. FUTURE.

SINGULAR	1 { m. / f. }	אָקוּם	I shall or will establish
	2 { m.	תָּקוּם	thou shalt establish
	{ f.	תָּקוּמִי	
	3 { m.	יָקוּם	he shall establish
	{ f.	תָּקוּם	she " "
PLURAL	1 { m. / f. }	נָקוּם	we shall or will establish
	2 { m.	תָּקוּמוּ	you shall establish
	{ f.	תְּקוּמֶנָה	
	3 { m.	יָקוּמוּ	they shall establish
	{ f.	תְּקוּמֶנָה	
SINGULAR	1 { m. / f. }	אֶקּוֹם	I shall or will be established
	2 { m.	תִּקּוֹם	thou shalt be established
	{ f.	תִּקּוֹמִי	
	3 { m.	יִקּוֹם	he shall be established
	{ f.	תִּקּוֹם	she " " "
PLURAL	1 { m. / f. }	נִקּוֹם	we shall or will be established
	2 { m.	תִּקּוֹמוּ	you shall be established
	{ f.	תִּקּוֹמֶנָה	
	3 { m.	יִקּוֹמוּ	they shall be established
	{ f.	תִּקּוֹמֶנָה	

CONJUGATIONS

TRANSITIVE.

SING. 2 { m. / f. } קוּם / קוּמִי } establish

PLU. 2 { m. / f. } קוּמוּ / קוּמְנָה } establish

SING. 2 { m. / f. } הִקּוֹם / הִקּוֹמִי } be established

PLU. 2 { m. / f. } הִקּוֹמוּ / הִקּוֹמְנָה } be established

PAST.

SINGULAR.
1 { m. / f. } קַמְתִּי I established
2 { m. / f. } קַמְתָּ / קַמְתְּ } thou established
3 { m. } קָם he established
3 { f. } קָמָה she "

PLURAL.
1 { m. / f. } קַמְנוּ we established
2 { m. / f. } קַמְתֶּם / קַמְתֶּן } you established
3 { m. / f. } קָמוּ they established

SINGULAR.
1 {m. / f.} נְקוּמוֹתִי {I was / established}
2 {m. / f.} נְקוּמוֹתָ / נְקוּמוֹתְ {thou wast / established}
3 {m. / f.} נָקוֹם / נָקוֹמָה {he was established / she " "}

PLURAL.
1 {m. / f.} נְקוּמוֹנוּ {we were / established}
2 {m. / f.} נְקוּמוֹתֶם / נְקוּמוֹתֶן {you were / established}
3 {m. / f.} נָקוֹמוּ {they were / established}

INTENSIVE FORM.

ACTIVE MOVEMENT.   PASSIVE MOVEMENT.

FACULTATIVE.

CONTINUED.   CONTINUED.

mas. מְקוֹמֵם   mas. מְקוֹמָם

fem. מְקוֹמְמָה   fem. מְקוֹמְמָה

FINISHED.

mas. ....
fem. .... } like the passive

NOMINAL VERB.

absol. }   absol. }
        קוֹמֵם   קוֹמֵם
constr.}   constr.}

CONJUGATIONS

TEMPORAL VERB. FUTURE.

SINGULAR.	1	m./f.	אָקוּמֶם	SINGULAR.	1 m./f.	אֲקוֹמֵם
	2	m.	תְּקוּמֶם		2 m.	תְּקוֹמֵם
		f.	תְּקוּמְמִי		f.	תְּקוֹמְמִי
	3	m.	יְקוּמֶם		3 m.	יְקוֹמֵם
		f.	תְּקוּמֶם		f.	תְּקוֹמֵם
PLURAL.	1	m./f.	נְקוּמֶם	PLURAL.	1 m./f.	נְקוֹמֵם
	2	m.	תְּקוּמְמוּ		2 m.	תְּקוֹמְמוּ
		f.	תְּקוּמֶמְנָה		f.	תְּקוֹמַמְנָה
	3	m.	יְקוּמְמוּ		3 m.	יְקוֹמְמוּ
		f.	תְּקוּמֶמְנָה		f.	תְּקוֹמַמְנָה

TRANSITIVE.

SING.	2	m.	קוּמֶם	SING.	2 m.	......
		f.	קוּמְמִי		f.	......
PLU.	2	m.	קוּמְמוּ	PLU.	2 m.	......
		f.	קוּמֵמְנָה		f.	......

} wanting

PAST.

SINGULAR.	1	m./f.	קוֹמַמְתִּי	SINGULAR.	1 m./f.	קוֹמַמְתִּי
	2	m.	קוֹמַמְתָּ		2 m.	קוֹמַמְתָּ
		f.	קוֹמַמְתְּ		f.	קוֹמַמְתְּ
	3	m.	קוֹמֵם		3 m.	קוֹמֵם
		f.	קוֹמְמָה		f.	קוֹמְמָה

PLURAL.	1	m. f.	קוֹמַמְנוּ	PLURAL.	1	m. f.	קוֹמַמְנוּ
	2	m.	קוֹמַמְתֶּם		2	m.	קוֹמַמְתֶּם
		f.	קוֹמַמְתֶּן			f.	קוֹמַמְתֶּן
	3	m. f.	קוֹמְמוּ		3	m. f.	קוֹמְמוּ

EXCITATIVE FORM.

ACTIVE MOVEMENT.　　　　**PASSIVE MOVEMENT.**

FACULTATIVE.

CONTINUED.　　　　　　CONTINUED.

mas. מֵקִים　　　　*mas.* מוּקָם

fem. מְקִימָה　　　　*fem.* מוּקָמָה

FINISHED.

mas. . . . . }
fem. . . . . } like the passive

NOMINAL VERB.

absol. הָקֵם　　　*absol.* }
constr. הָקִים　　*constr.* } הוּקַם

CONJUGATIONS

TEMPORAL VERB.

FUTURE.

SINGULAR.	1	m. f.	אָקִים	SINGULAR.	1	m. f.	אוּקַם
	2	m. f.	תָּקִים תָּקִימִי		2	m. f.	תּוּקַם תּוּקְמִי
	3	m. f.	יָקִים תָּקִים		3	m. f.	יוּקַם תּוּקַם
PLURAL.	1	m. f.	נָקִים	PLURAL.	1	m. f.	נוּקַם
	2	m. f.	תָּקִימִי תְּקִימֶינָה		2	m. f.	תּוּקְמוּ תּוּקַמְנָה
	3	m. f.	יָקִימוּ תָּקִימְנָה		3	m. f.	יוּקְמוּ תּוּקַמְנָה

TRANSITIVE.

SING.	2	m. f.	הָקֵם הָקִימִי	SING.	2	m. . . . . . . f.	
PLU.	2	m. f.	הָקִימוּ הָקֵמְנָה	PLU.	2	m. . . . . . . f.	} wanting

PAST.

SINGULAR	1	m. f.	הֲקִימוֹתִי	1	m. f.	הוּקַמְתִּי
	2	m.	הֲקִימוֹתָ	2	m.	הוּקַמְתָּ
		f.	הֲקִימוֹתְ		f.	הוּקַמְתְּ
	3	m.	הֵקִים	3	m.	הוּקַם
		f.	הֵקִימָה		f.	הוּקְמָה
PLURAL	1	m. f.	הֲקִימוֹנוּ	1	m. f.	הוּקַמְנוּ
	2	m.	הֲקִימוֹתֶם	2	m.	הוּקַמְתֶּם
		f.	הֲקִימוֹתֶן		f.	הוּקַמְתֶּן
	3	m. f.	הֵקִימוּ	3	m. f.	הוּקְמוּ

REFLEXIVE FORM.

ACTIVE AND PASSIVE MOVEMENT UNITED.

FACULTATIVE.

CONTIN. { *mas.* מִתְקוֹמֵם
{ *fem.* מִתְקוֹמְמָה

FINISH. { *mas.* .... } wanting
{ *fem.* .... }

CONJUGATIONS

NOMINAL VERB.

FUTURE.

absol.
constr. } הִתְקוֹמֵם

TEMPORAL VERB.

FUTURE.

SINGULAR.
- 1 { mas. / fem. } אֶתְקוֹמֵם
- 2 mas. תִּתְקוֹמֵם
- 2 fem. תִּתְקוֹמְמִי
- 3 mas. יִתְקוֹמֵם
- 3 fem. תִּתְקוֹמֵם

PLURAL.
- 1 { mas. / fem. } נִתְקוֹמֵם
- 2 mas. תִּתְקוֹמְמוּ
- 2 fem. תִּתְקוֹמֵמְנָה
- 3 mas. יִתְקוֹמְמוּ
- 3 fem. תִּתְקוֹמֵמְנָה

TRANSITIVE

		mas.	הִתְקוֹמֵם
SING.	2	fem.	הִתְקוֹמְמִי
PLU.	2	mas.	הִתְקוֹמְמוּ
		fem.	הִתְקוֹמֵמְנָה

PAST.

SINGULAR	1	mas. / fem.	הִתְקוֹמַמְתִּי
	2	mas.	הִתְקוֹמַמְתָּ
		fem.	הִתְקוֹמַמְתְּ
	3	mas.	הִתְקוֹמֵם
		fem.	הִתְקוֹמְמָה
PLURAL	1	mas. / fem.	הִתְקוֹמַמְנוּ
	2	mas.	הִתְקוֹמַמְתֶּם
		fem.	הִתְקוֹמַמְתֶּן
	3	mas. / fem.	הִתְקוֹמְמוּ

Remarks upon the Radical Conjugation.

I have already clearly shown why the conjugation which the Hebraists treat as irregular, should be considered as the first of all. The verbs which depend upon it are those which are formed directly from the root. The one that I have chosen as type is the same as that which the Hebraists have ordinarily chosen. As to the meaning, it is one of the most difficult of all the Hebraic tongue. The Latin *surgere* expresses only the least of its acceptations. As I shall often have occasion to speak of it in my notes, I am limiting myself to one simple analysis.

The sign ק is, as we know, the sign of agglomerative or repressive force, the image of material existence, the means of the forms. Now this sign offers a different expression according as it begins or terminates the root. If it terminates it as in חק, for example, it characterizes that which is finished, definite, bound, arrested, cut, shaped upon a model, designed: if it begins it, as in קו, קה or קי, it designates that which is indefinite, vague, indeterminate, unformed. In the first case it is matter put in action; in the second, it is matter appropriate to be put in action. This last root, bearing in the word קום or קים, the collective sign, represents *substance* in general; employed as verb it expresses all the ideas which spring from substance and from its modifications: such as, *to substantialize, to spread out, to rise into space; to exist in substance, to subsist, to consist, to resist; to clothe in form and in substance, to establish, to constitute, to strengthen, to make firm,* etc. One must feel after this example, how difficult and dangerous it is to confine the Hebraic verbs to a fixed and determined expression; for this expression results always from the meaning of the phrase and the intention of the writer.

As to the four forms to which I here submit the verb קום, I must explicitly state, not only as regards this conjugation but also for those which follow, that all verbs do not receive them indifferently; that some affect one form more than another, and finally, that there are some which one never finds under the positive form. But once again, what matter these variations? It is not a question of writing but of understanding Hebrew.

Positive Form.

Active movement. Although the modern Hebraists, with an unprecedented whimsicality, have taken the third person of the past for the theme of all verbs, they are forced to agree that in this conjugation, this third person is not in the least thematic: one also finds in dictionaries, the nominal קוֹם presented as theme: and this ought to be, not only for all radical verbs such as this one, but for all kinds of verbs.

The continued facultative is often marked by the luminous, sign וֹ, as can be seen in אוֹר *to be shining*. The Chaldaic punctuation is not consistent in the manner of replacing this sign: Instead of the point *kamez* which is found here in קָם, one meets the *zere*, in עֵר *to be watching, vigilant,* and in some others. I state here once more, that the feminine facultative, in the continued active and passive, as well as in the finished, changes the character הָ into ת, and that one finds equally קוֹמָה or קוֹמֶת; נְקוֹמָה or נָקוֹמֶת; קוּמָה or קוּמֶת. I have already mentioned this variation in chapter V. § 3, in treating of gender. I do not mention the plural of the facultatives, since its formation offers no difficulties.

The future has sometimes the emphatic article ה, as well as the transitive. One finds אָקוֹמָה, *I shall establish, I shall raise up.* שׁוּבָה, *come! arise! return to thy first state,* etc.

The past, which, by its nature, ought to lose the luminous sign, conserves it, however, in certain verbs where it is identical; such as אוֹר, *it shone;* בּוֹשׁ, *it reddened,* etc. One also finds the *zere* substituted by the *kamez* in מָת *he died.* I observe at this point, that all verbs in general which terminate with ת, do not double this character, either in the first or second person of the past, but receive the interior point only as duplicative accent. One finds therefore מַתִּי *I was dying,* מַתָּ *thou wast dying,* מַתֶּם *you were dying,* etc.

Passive movement. The inadequate denomination which the Hebraists had given to the facultatives in considering them as *present* or *past* participles, had always prevented them from distinguishing the continued facultative of the passive movement, from the finished facultative belonging to the two movements. It was impossible in fact, after their explanations to perceive the delicate difference which exists in Hebrew between נָקוֹם *that which became, becomes* or *will become established,* and קוּם, *that which was, is* or *will be established.* When, for example, it was a matter of explaining how the verb הָיָה or הֱיוֹת *the action of being, of living,* could have a passive facultative, they are lost in ridiculous interpretations. They perceived not that the difference of these three facultatives הוֹיָה, נְהָיָה and הָיוֹה was in the continued or finished movement: as we would say *a being being, living; a thing being effected; a being realized, a thing effected.*

It is easy to see, moreover, in the inspection of the passive movement alone, that the Chaldaic punctuation has altered it much less than the other. The verbal sign is almost invariably found in its original strength.

Intensive Form.

Radical verbs take this form by redoubling the final character; so that its signification depends always upon the signification of this character as sign. In the case in question, the final character being considered as collective sign, its redoubling expresses a sudden and general usurpation. Thus the verb קוֹמֵם, can be translated, according to the circumstance, by the action of *extending indefinitely, of existing in substance in an universal manner; of establishing, of establishing strongly, with energy; of resisting, of opposing vigorously,* etc.

In this state this verb is easily confused with a derivative verb, if the verbal sign, instead of being placed after the first character, as it is, was placed after the second, as is seen in פָּקוֹד *to visit*: notwithstanding this difference, the rabbis, not finding this form sufficiently characterized, have substituted for it the hyphen of the Chaldaic, some examples of which, one finds moreover, in the Sepher of the Hebrews. This form consists in substituting the sign of manifestation and duration, for that of light, and in saying, without doubling the final character, קִים instead of קוֹמֵם ; חִית instead of חוֹבֵב, etc.

Sometimes too, not content with doubling the last character of the root as in קוֹמֵם, the entire root is doubled, as in כִּלְכֵּל *to achieve, to consummate wholly;* but these sorts of verbs belong to the second conjugation and follow the intensive form of the derivative verbs.

The passive movement has nothing remarkable in itself except the very great difficulty of distinguishing it from the active movement, which causes it to be little used.

Excitative Form.

This form perfectly characterized, as much in the passive movement as in the active, is of great usefulness in the tongue of Moses. I have already spoken of its effects and of its construction. It can be observed in this example that the convertible sign ו, which constitutes the radical verb קוֹם, is changed into י, in the active movement, and is transposed in the passive movement, before the initial character.

The only comment I have to make is, that the Chaldaic punctuation sometimes substitutes the point *zere* for the mother vowel ׳, of the active movement, and the point *kibbuz* for the sign ו of the passive movement. So that one finds the continued facultative מַפֵּר *making angry;* the future תָּשֵׁב, *thou shalt bring back,* and even the past הֻקַם, *he was aroused to establish himself;* etc.

Reflexive Form.

This form differs from the intensive in its construction, only by the addition of the characteristic syllable הת; as can be seen in the nominal התקומם. For the rest, the two movements are united in a single one.

All that is essential to observe, is relative to this syllable הת. Now it undergoes what the Hebraists call *syncope* and *metathesis*.

The syncope takes place when one of the two characters is effaced as in the facultative מִתְקוֹמֵם, and in the future אֶתְקוֹמֵם, where the character ה is found replaced by מ or א; or when, to avoid inconsonance, one supresses the character ת, before a verb commencing with ט, which takes its place with the interior point; as in תִּטָּהֵר *to be purified*.

The metathesis takes place when the first character of a verb is one of the four following: ז, ס, צ, שׁ. Then the ת of the characteristic syllable הת, is transposed after this initial character, by being changed into ד after ז, and into ט after צ; as can be seen in the derivative verbs cited in the examples.

שָׁבוֹהַ	to praise, to exhalt	הִשְׁתַּבִּיהַ	to be praised
צָדוֹק	to be just	הִצְטַדִּיק	to be justified
סָגוֹר	to close	הִסְתַּגִּיר	to be closed
זָמוֹן	to prepare	הִזְדַּמִּין	to be prepared

§ II.

DERIVATIVE CONJUGATION	POSITIVE FORM
ACTIVE MOVEMENT	PASSIVE MOVEMENT

FACULTATIVE

	CONTINUED.			CONTINUED.	
	mas.	פּוֹקָד		mas.	נִפְקָד
	fem.	פּוֹקְדָה		fem.	נִפְקָדָה

FINISHED.

	mas.	פָּקוּד		fem.	פָּקוּדה

NOMINAL VERB

	absol.	פָּקוֹד		absol.	הִפָּקֵד
	constr.	פְּקֹד		constr.	

TEMPORAL VERB
FUTURE.

SINGULAR
- 1 { m. / f. }   אֶפְקוֹד
- 2 { m. }   תִּפְקוֹד
- 2 { f. }   תִּפְקוֹדִי
- 3 { m. }   יִפְקוֹד
- 3 { f. }   תִּפְקוֹד

PLURAL
- 1 { m. / f. }   נִפְקוֹד
- 2 { m. }   תִּפְקְדוּ
- 2 { f. }   תִּפְקוֹדְנָה
- 3 { m. }   יִפְקְדוּ
- 3 { f. }   תִּפְקוֹדְנָה

SINGULAR
- 1 { m. / f. }   אֶפָּקֵד
- 2 { m. }   תִּפָּקֵד
- 2 { f. }   תִּפָּקְדִי
- 3 { m. }   יִפָּקֵד
- 3 { f. }   תִּפָּקֵד

PLURAL
- 1 { m. / f. }   נִפָּקֵד
- 2 { m. }   תִּפָּקְדוּ
- 2 { f. }   תִּפָּקַדְנָה
- 3 { m. }   יִפָּקְדוּ
- 3 { f. }   תִּפָּקַדְנָה

CONJUGATIONS

TRANSITIVE

SING.	2	mas.	פְּקוֹד	SING.	2	mas.	הִפָּקֵד
		fem.	פִּקְדִי			fem.	הִפָּקְדִי
PLU.	2	mas.	פִּקְדוּ	PLU.	2	mas.	הִפָּקְדוּ
		fem.	פְּקוֹדְנָה			fem.	הִפָּקֵדְנָה

PAST

SINGULAR.	1	mas./fem.	פָּקַדְתִּי	SINGULAR.	1	mas./fem.	נִפְקַדְתִּי
	2	mas.	פָּקַדְתָּ		2	mas.	נִפְקַדְתָּ
		fem.	פָּקַדְתְּ			fem.	נִפְקַדְתְּ
	3	mas.	פָּקַד		3	mas.	נִפְקַד
		fem.	פָּקְדָה			fem.	נִפְקְדָה
PLURAL.	1	mas./fem.	פָּקַדְנוּ	PLURAL.	1	mas./fem.	נִפְקַדְנוּ
	2	mas.	פְּקַדְתֶּם		2	mas.	נִפְקַדְתֶּם
		fem.	פְּקַדְתֶּן			fem.	נִפְקַדְתֶּן
	3	mas./fem.	פָּקְדוּ		3	mas./fem.	נִפְקְדוּ

INTENSIVE FORM

ACTIVE MOVEMENT		PASSIVE MOVEMENT	

FACULTATIVE.

CONTINUED

mas.	מְפַקֵּד	mas.	מְפֻקָּד
fem.	מְפַקְּדָה	fem.	מְפֻקָּדָה

FINISHED

mas.	פֻּקַּד	fem.	פֻּקְּדָה

NOMINAL VERB

absol. ⎫ constr. ⎭	פֻּקֵּד	absol. ⎫ constr. ⎭	פָּקוּד

TEMPORAL VERB

FUTURE.

SINGULAR
1 {m. / f.}	אֲפַקֵּד	1 {m. / f.}	אֲפֻקַּד
2 {m.}	תְּפַקֵּד	2 {m.}	תְּפֻקַּד
{f.}	תְּפַקְּדִי	{f.}	תְּפֻקְּדִי
3 {m.}	יְפַקֵּד	3 {m.}	יְפֻקַּד
{f.}	תְּפַקֵּד	{f.}	תְּפֻקַּד

PLURAL
1 {m. / f.}	נְפַקֵּד	1 {m. / f.}	נְפֻקַּד
2 {m.}	תְּפַקְּדוּ	2 {m.}	תְּפֻקְּדוּ
{f.}	תְּפַקֵּדְנָה	{f.}	תְּפֻקַּדְנָה
3 {m.}	יְפַקְּדוּ	3 {m.}	יְפֻקְּדוּ
{f.}	תְּפַקֵּדְנָה	{f.}	תְּפֻקַּדְנָה

CONJUGATIONS

TRANSITIVE

SING. 2	mas.	פְּקֹד		SING. 2	mas.	
	fem.	פִּקְדִי			fem.	wanting
PLU. 2	mas.	פִּקְדוּ		PLU. 2	mas.	
	fem.	פְּקֹדְנָה			fem.	

PAST

SINGULAR 1	mas.	פָּקַדְתִּי		SINGULAR 1	mas.	פֻּקַדְתִּ
	fem.				fem.	
2	mas.	פָּקַדְתָּ		2	mas.	פֻּקַדְתָּ
	fem.	פָּקַדְתְּ			fem.	פֻּקַדְתְּ
3	mas.	פָּקַד		3	mas.	פֻּקַד
	fem.	פָּקְדָה			fem.	פֻּקְדָה
PLURAL 1	mas.	פָּקַדְנוּ		PLURAL 1	mas.	פֻּקַדְנוּ
	fem.				fem.	
2	mas.	פְּקַדְתֶּם		2	mas.	פֻּקַדְתֶּם
	fem.	פְּקַדְתֶּן			fem.	פֻּקַדְתֶּן
3	mas.	פָּקְדוּ		3	mas.	פֻּקְדוּ
	fem.				fem.	

EXCITATIVE FORM

ACTIVE MOVEMENT		PASSIVE MOVEMENT	

FACULTATIVE

	CONTINUED		CONTINUED
mas.	מַפְקִיד	mas.	מְפְקָד
fem.	מַפְקִידָה	fem.	מְפְקָדָה

FINISHED

mas. ..... } like the passive
fem. ..... }

NOMINAL VERB

| absol. | הַפְקַד | absol. | } הָפְקֵד |
| constr. | הַפְקִיד | constr. | } |

TEMPORAL VERB

FUTURE

SINGULAR	1	mas.	אַפְקִיד		SINGULAR	1	mas.	אָפְקַד
		fem.					fem.	
	2	mas.	תַּפְקִיד			2	mas.	תָּפְקַד
		fem.	תַּפְקִידִי				fem.	תָּפְקְדִי
	3	mas.	יַפְקִיד			3	mas.	יָפְקַד
		fem.	תַּפְקִיד				fem.	תָּפְקַד
PLURAL	1	mas.	נַפְקִיד		PLURAL	1	mas.	נָפְקַד
		fem.					fem.	
	2	mas.	תַּפְקִידוּ			2	mas.	תָּפְקְדוּ
		fem.	תַּפְקֵדְנָה				fem.	תָּפְקַדְנָה
	3	mas.	יַפְקִידוּ			3	mas.	יָפְקְדוּ
		fem.	תַּפְקֵדְנָה				fem.	תָּפְקַדְנָה

CONJUGATIONS 217

TRANSITIVE

SING. 2 { mas.   הַפְקֵד
         fem.   הַפְקִידִי
PLU. 2 { mas.   הַפְקִידוּ
         fem.   הַפְקֵדְנָה

SING. 2 { mas. ......
         fem. ......
PLU. 2 { mas. ......   } wanting
         fem. ......

PAST

SINGULAR
1 { mas. / fem. }   הִפְקַדְתִּי
2 { mas. }   הִפְקַדְתָּ
   { fem. }   הִפְקַדְתְּ
3 { mas. }   הִפְקִיד
   { fem. }   הִפְקִידָה

SINGULAR
1 { mas. / fem. }   הָפְקַדְתִּי
2 { mas. }   הָפְקַדְתָּ
   { fem. }   הָפְקַדְתְּ
3 { mas. }   הָפְקַד
   { fem. }   הָפְקְדָה

PLURAL
1 { mas. / fem. }   הִפְקַדְנוּ
2 { mas. }   הִפְקַדְתֶּם
   { fem. }   הִפְקַדְתֶּן
3 { mas. / fem. }   הִפְקִידוּ

PLURAL
1 { mas. / fem. }   הָפְקַדְנוּ
2 { mas. }   הָפְקַדְתֶּם
   { fem. }   הָפְקַדְתֶּן
3 { mas. / fem. }   הָפְקְדוּ

REFLEXIVE FORM

| ACTIVE MOVEMENT | PASSIVE MOVEMENT |

FACULTATIVE

CONTIN. { *mas.* מִתְפַּקֵּד
{ *fem.* מִתְפַּקְּדָה

FINISH. { *mas.* ..... } wanting
{ *fem.* ..... }

NOMINAL VERB

absol. } הִתְפַּקֵּד
constr. }

TEMPORAL VERB

FUTURE

SINGULAR
1 { *mas.* } אֶתְפַּקֵּד
  { *fem.* }
2 { *mas.* } תִּתְפַּקֵּד
  { *fem.* } תִּתְפַּקְּדִי
3 { *mas.* } יִתְפַּקֵּד
  { *fem.* } תִּתְפַּקֵּד

PLURAL
1 { *mas.* } נִתְפַּקֵּד
  { *fem.* }
2 { *mas.* } תִּתְפַּקְּדוּ
  { *fem.* } תִּתְפַּקֵּדְנָה
3 { *mas.* } יִתְפַּקְּדוּ
  { *fem.* } תִּתְפַּקֵּדְנָה

CONJUGATIONS

TRANSITIVE

SING. 2 { mas.　הִתְפַּקֵּד
　　　　 fem.　הִתְפַּקְדִי

PLU. 2 { mas.　הִתְפַּקְדוּ
　　　　 fem.　הִתְפַּקֵּדְנָה

PAST

SINGULAR
1 { mas. / fem. }　הִתְפַּקַּדְתִּי
2 { mas.　הִתְפַּקַּדְתָּ
　　 fem.　הִתְפַּקַּדְתְּ
3 { mas.　הִתְפַּקֵּד
　　 fem.　הִתְפַּקְדָה

PLURAL
1 { mas. / fem. }　הִתְפַּקַּדְנוּ
2 { mas.　הִתְפַּקַּדְתֶּם
　　 fem.　הִתְפַּקַּדְתֶּן
3 { mas. / fem. }　הִתְפַּקְדוּ

Remarks upon the Derivative Conjugation.

I have not judged it necessary to change the typical verb which the Hebraists give as theme for this conjugation, because this verb lends itself to the four forms. I am going to present only its etymological meaning.

The primitive root פוּק from which it is derived, contains the general idea of an alternating movement from one place to another, such as one would see, for example, in a pendulum. This idea coming out more distinctly in the verbalized root, signifies *to pass from one place to another, to be carried here and there, to go and come.* Here is clearly observed the opposed action of the two signs פ and ק, of which the one opens the centre and the other cuts and designs the circumference. This root is joined, in order to compose the word of which we are speaking, to the root אד or יד, no less expressive, which, relating properly to the forefinger of the hand, signifies figuratively any object distinct or alone; an extract from abundance born of division: for this abundance is expressed in Hebrew by the same root considered under the contrary relation די.

Thus these two roots contracted in the compound פָּקַד, develop the idea of a movement which is carried alternately from one object to another: it is an *examination,* an *exploration,* an *inspection,* a *visit,* a *census,* etc; from this results the facultative פְּקֹד, *to be inspecting, examining, visiting;* and the nominal verb פָּקוֹד, *to visit, to examine, to inspect,* etc.

Positive Form.

Active movement. It must be remembered that the Chaldaic punctuation, following all the inflection of the vulgar pronunciation, corrupts very often the etymology. Thus it suppresses the verbal sign וּ of the continued fac-

CONJUGATIONS

ultative, and substitutes either the *holem* or the *kamez* as in כֹּפֶר *appeasing, expiating;* אָבֵל *grieving, mourning, sorrowing.*

Sometimes one finds this same facultative terminated by the character י, to form a kind of qualificative, as in אֹסְרִי, *linking, enchaining, subjugating.*

I shall speak no further of the feminine changing the final character ה to ת, because it is a general rule.

The nominal assumes quite voluntarily the emphatic article ה, particularly when it becomes construct; then the Chaldaic punctuation again suppresses the verbal sign ו, as in לְמָשְׁחָה, *to annoint, according to the action of annointing, to coat over, to oil, to paint,* etc. I must state here, that this emphatic article can be added to nearly all the verbal modifications, but chiefly to both facultatives, to the nominal and the transitive. It can be found even in the future and the past, as one sees it in אֶשְׁמְרָה, *I shall guard;* בָּגַדְתָּה, *he lied.*

When the nominal verb begins with the mother vowel א, this vowel blends with the affix of the first person future, disappears sometimes in the second, and has in the third, the point *holem;* thus אֱסוֹף *to gather,* makes אֶסֹף *I shall gather;* תְסֹף or תֶּאֱסֹף *thou shalt gather;* יֶאֱסֹף, *he shall gather:* thus, אָכוֹל *to feed oneself,* makes אֹכַל *I shall feed myself;* thus אֱמוֹר *to say,* makes אֹמַר *I shall say;* תֹּאמַר, *thou shalt say;* יֹאמַר, *he shall say;* etc. Some Hebraists have made of this slight anomaly an irregular conjugation that they call *Quiescent Pe 'Aleph.*

These same Hebraists ready to multiply the difficulties, have also made an irregular conjugation of the verbs whose final character נ or ת, is not doubled in receiving the future ending נָה, or the affixes of the past תִּי, תָּ, תְּ, תֶּן, תֶּם, נוּ; but is blended with the ending of the affix, being supplied with the interior point: as one remarks it in כָּרוֹת

to suppress, which makes כָּרַתִּי, *I suppressed*, כָּרַתָּ *thou suppressed;* etc., or in שְׁכוֹן, *to inhabit*, which makes תִּשְׁכֹּנָה, *you shall inhabit* (fem); *they shall inhabit;* שְׁכֹנָה, *inhabit* (fem.); שָׁכַבְנוּ, *we shall inhabit;* etc. There is nothing perplexing in this. The only real difficulty results from the change of the character נ into ת, in the verb נָתוֹן, *to give,* which makes נָתַתִּי, *I gave,* נָתַתָּ, *thou gavest;* etc., I have already spoken of this anomaly in treating of the radical conjugation.

There exists a more considerable irregularity when the verb terminates with א or ה, and concerning which it is necessary to speak more fully. But as this anomaly is seen in the three conjugations I shall await the end of this chapter to take up the subject.

Passive Movement. The Chaldaic punctuation sometimes substitutes the *zere* for the *hirek* in the passive nominal, as can be seen in הֵאָסֵף *the action of being gathered;* or in הֵאָכֹל, *the action of being consummated.* One observes in this last example the appearance even of the *holem.* It is useless to dwell upon a thing which follows step by step the vulgar pronunciation and which yields to all its caprices. The characteristic sign and the mother vowel, these, are what should be examined with attention. One ought to be concerned with the point, only when there is no other means of discovering the meaning of a word.

Moreover, it is necessary to remark that the passive movement can become reciprocal and even superactive when the verb is not used in the active movement. Thus one finds נִשְׁמַר *he took care of himself;* נִשְׁבַּע *he swore; he bore witness,* etc.

Intensive Form.

Ever since the Chaldaic punctuation has, as I have said, suppressed the mother vowels י and ו, which are placed after the first verbal character, the one in the ac-

CONJUGATIONS

tive movement and the other in the passive, there remains, in order to recognize this interesting form, whose force supplies the adverbial relation very rare in Hebrew, only the interior point of the second character. Therefore the utmost attention must be given.

All derivative verbs of two roots uncontracted as כִּלְכֵּל, *to achieve wholly,* כִּרְכֵּר, *to rise rapidly in the air,* etc.; in short, all verbs that the Hebraists name quadriliteral, because they are, in effect, composed of four letters in the nominal without including the verbal sign וֹ, belong to this form and follow it in its modifications.

Sometimes the point *hirek* which accompanies the first character of the verb in the intensive past, is replaced by the *zere* as in בֵּרֵךְ *he blessed fervently.*

The intensive form takes place in the active movement with as much method as without; sometimes it gives a contrary meaning to the positive verb: thus הַטּוֹא *the action of sinning,* makes חָטָא *he sinned;* and חִטֵּא *he is purged from sin;* thus שָׁרוֹשׁ, *the action of taking root,* makes שָׁרַשׁ, *it took root;* and שֵׁרֵשׁ, *it was rooted up;* etc. The passive movement follows nearly the same modifications.

Excitative Form.

I have spoken sufficiently of the utility and usage of this form. It is characterized clearly enough to be readily recognized. One knows that its principal purpose is to transport the verbal action into another subject which it is a question of making act; however, it must be noticed that when the positive form does not exist, which sometimes happens, then it becomes simply declarative, according to the active or passive movement, with or without method. It is thus that one finds הִצְדִּיק, *he was declared just, he was justified:* הִרְשִׁיעַ *he was declared impious;* הֵקִיץ, *he awakened, he was aroused, he made re-*

pose cease; הִשְׁלִיךְ, *he projected;* הִשְׁלַךְ *he was projected;* etc.

Reflexive Form.

Besides this form being reciprocal at the same time as reflexive, that is to say, that the nominal הִתְפַּקֵּד, can signify alike, *to visit oneself, to visit each other,* or *to be aroused to visit;* it can also, according to circumstances, become simulatory, frequentative and even intensive, returning thus to its proper source; for, as I have said, this form is no other than the intensive, to which was added the characteristic syllable הת. One finds under these different acceptations: הִתְהַלֵּךְ, *he went about, he walked up and down, he went without stopping;* הִתְפַּלֵּל, *he offered himself to administer justice, to be magistrate;* etc.

I have spoken of the syncope and metathesis which substitute the syllable הת, for the article of the radical conjugation. Its repetition is unnecessary. It is also unnecessary for me to repeat that the emphatic article ה is placed indifferently for all the verbal modifications, and that the Chaldaic punctuation varies.

CONJUGATIONS 225

§. III.

Compound Radical Conjugation with the Initial Adjunction וֹ

POSITIVE FORM

ACTIVE MOVEMENT   PASSIVE MOVEMENT

FACULTATIVE

	CONTINUED		CONTINUED
mas.	יוֹשֵׁב	*mas.*	נוֹשָׁב
fem.	יוֹשְׁבָה	*fem.*	נוֹשָׁבָה

FINISHED

	mas.	יָשׁוּב
	fem.	יְשׁוּבָה

NOMINAL VERB

| *absol.* | יָשׁוּב | *absol.* | } הוּשֵׁב |
| *constr.* | שֶׁבֶת | *constr.* | } |

TEMPORAL VERB

FUTURE

SINGULAR $\begin{cases} 1 \begin{cases} m. \\ f. \end{cases} & \text{אֵשֵׁב} \\ 2 \begin{cases} m. \\ f. \end{cases} & \begin{matrix}\text{תֵּשֵׁב}\\\text{תֵּשְׁבִי}\end{matrix} \\ 3 \begin{cases} m. \\ f. \end{cases} & \begin{matrix}\text{יֵשֵׁב}\\\text{תֵּשֵׁב}\end{matrix} \end{cases}$ SINGULAR $\begin{cases} 1 \begin{cases} m. \\ f. \end{cases} & \text{אוּשַׁב} \\ 2 \begin{cases} m. \\ f. \end{cases} & \begin{matrix}\text{תּוּשַׁב}\\\text{תּוּשְׁבִי}\end{matrix} \\ 3 \begin{cases} m. \\ f. \end{cases} & \begin{matrix}\text{יוּשַׁב}\\\text{תּוּשַׁב}\end{matrix} \end{cases}$

FUTURE

PLURAL	1	m. f.	נֵשֵׁב	1	m. f.	נִוָּשֵׁב
	2	m.	תֵּשְׁבוּ	2	m.	תִּוָּשְׁבוּ
		f.	תֵּשֵׁבְנָה		f.	תִּוָּשֵׁבְנָה
	3	m.	יֵשְׁבוּ	3	m.	יִוָּשְׁבוּ
		f.	תֵּשֵׁבְנָה		f.	תִּוָּשֵׁבְנָה

TRANSITIVE

SING.	2	mas.	שֵׁב	2	mas.	הִוָּשֵׁב
		fem.	שְׁבִי		fem.	הִוָּשְׁבִי
PLU.	2	mas.	שְׁבוּ	2	mas.	הִוָּשְׁבוּ
		fem.	שֵׁבְנָה		fem.	הִוָּשֵׁבְנָה

PAST

SINGULAR	1	m. f.	יָשַׁבְתִּי	1	m. f.	נוֹשַׁבְתִּ
	2	m.	יָשַׁבְתָּ	2	m.	נוֹשַׁבְתָּ
		f.	יָשַׁבְתְּ		f.	נוֹשַׁבְתְּ
	3	m.	יָשַׁב	3	m.	נוֹשַׁב
		f.	יָשְׁבָה		f.	נוֹשְׁבָה
PLURAL	1	m. f.	יָשַׁבְנוּ	1	m. f.	נוֹשַׁבְנוּ
	2	m.	יְשַׁבְתֶּם	2	m.	נוֹשַׁבְתֶּם
		f.	יְשַׁבְתֶּן		f.	נוֹשַׁבְתֶּן
	3	m. f.	יָשְׁבוּ	3	m. f.	נוֹשְׁבוּ

CONJUGATIONS

Intensive Form

ACTIVE MOVEMENT **PASSIVE MOVEMENT**

FACULTATIVE

	CONTINUED		CONTINUED
mas.	מְיַשֵּׁב	mas.	מְיֻשָּׁב
fem.	מְיַשְּׁבָה	fem.	מְיֻשָּׁבָה

FINISHED

mas. ...... } wanting
fem. ...... }

NOMINAL VERB

| absol. } | יַשֵּׁב | absol. } | יֻשַּׁב |
| constr. } | | constr. } | |

TEMPORAL VERB

FUTURE

| mas. } | אֲיַשֵּׁב | mas. } | אֲיֻשַּׁב |
| fem. } | | fem. } | |

TRANSITIVE

| mas. } | יַשֵּׁב | mas. } | wanting |
| fem. } | יַשְּׁבִי | fem. } | |

PAST

| mas. } | יִשַּׁבְתִּי | mas. } | יֻשַּׁבְתִּי |
| fem. } | | fem. } | |

EXCITATIVE FORM

FACULTATIVE

	CONTINUED		CONTINUED
mas.	מוֹשִׁיב	*mas.*	מוּשָׁב
fem.	מוֹשִׁיבָה	*fem.*	מוּשָׁבָה

FINISHED

mas. .....
fem. ..... } like the passive

NOMINAL VERB

| *absol.* | הוֹשִׁיב | *absol.* | } הוֹשֵׁב |
| *constr.* | הוֹשֵׁב | *constr.* | |

TEMPORAL VERB

FUTURE

| *mas.* | } אוֹשִׁיב | *mas.* | } אוּשַׁב |
| *fem.* | | *fem.* | |

TRANSITIVE

| *mas.* | הוֹשֵׁב | *mas.* ..... | } wanting |
| *fem.* | הוֹשִׁיבִי | *fem.* ..... | |

PAST

| *mas.* | } הוֹשַׁבְתִּי | *mas.* | } הוּשַׁבְתִּי |
| *fem.* | | *fem.* | |

CONJUGATIONS

REFLEXIVE FORM

ACTIVE AND PASSIVE MOVEMENT UNITED

FACULTATIVE

CONTIN. { *mas.* מִתְיַשֵּׁב
{ *fem.* מִתְיַשְּׁבָה

FINISH. { *mas.* .....
{ *fem.* ..... } wanting

NOMINAL VERB

absol. }
constr. } הִתְיַשֵּׁב

TEMPORAL VERB

FUTURE

mas. }
fem. } אֶתְיַשֵּׁב

TRANSITIVE

mas. הִתְיַשֵּׁב
fem. הִתְיַשְּׁבִי

PAST

mas. }
fem. } הִתְיַשַּׁבְתִּי

REMARKS ON THE COMPOUND RADICAL CONJUGATION.

Initial Adjunction יְ

The verb presented here as model is יְשׁוֹב. I am about to proceed with its analysis. The root שׁוֹב contains the idea of a return to a place, to a time, to a condition or an action, from which one had departed. It is the sign of the relative movement שׁ, which is united to that of interior, central and generative action בּ. This return, being determined and manifested by the initial adjunction יְ, becomes a real sojourn, a taking possession of, an occupation, a habitation. Thus the compound radical verb יָשׁוֹב can signify, according to circumstances, the action *of dwelling, of inhabiting, of sojourning, of taking possession;* etc.

Positive Form.

Active Movement. The initial adjunction יְ remains constant in the two facultatives, in the absolute nominal as well as in the past tense; but it disappears in the construct nominal, in the transitive and in the future. It seems indeed, that in this case the mother vowel יְ, ought to be placed between the first and second character of the verbal root, and that one should say שִׁיבָת, *the action of occupying;* אֲשִׁיב, *I shall occupy;* שִׁיב, *occupy;* etc. But the Chaldaic punctuation having prevailed, has supplied it with the *segol* or the *zere*.

The simplicity of the transitive tense in this conjugation has made many savants, and notably Court de Gébelin, think that it should be regarded as the first of the verbal tenses. Already Leibnitz who felt keenly the need of etymological researches, had seen that in reality the transitive is, in the Teutonic idioms, the simplest of the tenses. President Desbrosses had spoken loudly in favour of this opinion, and abbé Bergier limited the whole compass of

Hebraic verbs to it. This opinion, which is not in the least to be held in contempt, finds support in what Du Halde said pertaining to the tongue of the Manchu Tartars whose verbs appear to originate from the transitive. But it is evident through the examination of the radical conjugation, that the nominal and the transitive of the verb, are *au fond* the same thing in Hebrew, and that the latter differs not from the former except by a modification purely mental. The Hebrews said קוֹם *the action of establishing* and קֹם *establish*. The purpose of the speaker, the accent which accompanied it could alone feel the difference. The nominal יָשׁוּב differs here from the transitive שָׁב, only because the initial adjunction ' is unable to resist the influence of the modification. In the verbs where this mother vowel is not a simple adjunction but a sign, the transitive does not differ from the nominal. One finds, for example, יָרֹשׁ *possess*, and יְרוֹשׁ, *the action of possessing*.

Verbs similiar to the one just cited, where the sign is not an adjunction, belong to the derivative conjugation. It is only a matter of a good dictionary to distinguish them carefully. A grammar suffices to declare their existence.

Passive movement. The initial adjunctiton ', being replaced in this movement by the mother vowel וּ, varies no further, and gives to this conjugation all the strength of the derivative conjugation.

Intensive Form.

This form is little used in this conjugation, for the reason that the positive form itself is only a sort of intensity given to the radical verb by means of the initial adjunction '. When by chance, it is found employed, one sees that this adjunction has taken all the force of a sign and remains with the verb to which it is united

Excitative Form.

The initial adjunction ׳, is replaced in the active movement by the intellectual sign ו֫, and in the passive movement by the convertible sign וּ. This change made, the compound radical verb varies no more, and follows the course of the derivative verbs as it has followed it in the preceding form. If it sometimes happens that this change is not affected as in הֵיטִיב *to do good*, the verb remains none the less indivisible. This changes nothing in its conjugation.

Reflexive Form.

The compound radical verb continues under this new form to demonstrate all the strength of a derivative verb. The only remark, somewhat important, that I have to make, is relative to the three verbs following, which replace their initial adjunction ׳, by the convertible sign וּ, become consonant.

יָדֹעַ	to understand	הִתְוַדֵּעַ	to be understood
יָכֹחַ	to prove, to argue	הִתְוַכֵּחַ	to be proven
יָסֹר	to correct, to instruct	הִתְוַסֵּר	to be corrected

CONJUGATIONS

§ IV.
Compound Radical Conjugation.
with the Initial Adjunction נ
POSITIVE FORM

	ACTIVE MOVEMENT		PASSIVE MOVEMENT
	FACULTATIVE		
	CONTINUED		CONTINUED
mas.	נוֹגֵשׁ	*mas.*	נִגָּשׁ
fem.	נוֹגְשָׁה	*fem.*	נִגָּשָׁה
	FINISHED		
mas.	נָגוּשׁ	*fem.*	נְגוּשָׁה

NOMINAL VERB

| *absol.* | נָגוֹשׁ | *absol.* | הִנָּגֵשׁ |
| *constr.* | גֶּשֶׁת | *constr.* | |

TEMPORAL VERB
FUTURE

SINGULAR	1 {m. / f.}	אֶגַּשׁ	SINGULAR	1 {m. / f.}	אֶנָּגֵשׁ
	2 {m.	תִּגַּשׁ		2 {m.	תִּנָּגֵשׁ
	2 {f.	תִּגְּשִׁי		2 {f.	תִּנָּגְשִׁי
	3 {m.	יִגַּשׁ		3 {m.	יִנָּגֵשׁ
	3 {f.	תִּגַּשׁ		3 {f.	תִּנָּגֵשׁ
PLURAL	1 {m. / f.}	נִגַּשׁ	PLURAL	1 {m. / f.}	נִנָּגֵשׁ
	2 {m.	תִּגְּשׁוּ		2 {m.	תִּנָּגְשׁוּ
	2 {f.	תִּגַּשְׁנָה		2 {f.	תִּנָּגַשְׁנָה
	3 {m.	יִגְּשׁוּ		3 {m.	יִנָּגְשׁוּ
	3 {f.	תִּגַּשְׁנָה		3 {f.	תִּנָּגַשְׁנָה

TRANSITIVE

SING. 2	m.	גַּשׁ	SING. 2	m.	הַנָּגֵשׁ
	f.	גְּשִׁי		f.	הַנָּגְשִׁי
PLU. 2	m.	גְּשׁוּ	PLU. 2	m.	הַנָּגְשׁוּ
	f.	גְשְׁנָה		f.	הַנָּגֵשְׁנָה

PAST

SINGULAR 1	m. / f.	נָגַשְׁתִּי	SINGULAR 1	m. / f.	נִגַּשְׁתִּי
2	m.	נָגַשְׁתָּ	2	m.	נִגַּשְׁתָּ
	f.	נָגַשְׁתְּ		f.	נִגַּשְׁתְּ
3	m.	נָגַשׁ	3	m.	נִגַּשׁ
	f.	נָגְשָׁה		f.	נִגְּשָׁה
PLURAL 1	m. / f.	נָגַשְׁנוּ	PLURAL 1	m. / f.	נִגַּשְׁנוּ
2	m.	נְגַשְׁתֶּם	2	m.	נִגַּשְׁתֶּם
	f.	נְגַשְׁתֶּן		f.	נִגַּשְׁתֶּן
3	m. / f.	נָגְשׁוּ	3	m. / f.	נִגְּשׁוּ

CONJUGATIONS 235

Intensive Form

| ACTIVE MOVEMENT | PASSIVE MOVEMENT |

FACULTATIVE

CONTINUED	CONTINUED
mas. מְנַגֵּשׁ	mas. מְנֻגָּשׁ
fem. מְנַגְּשָׁה	fem. מְנֻגָּשָׁה

FINISHED

mas. ....
fem. .... } like the passive

NOMINAL VERB.

| absol. } נַגֵּשׁ | absol. } נֻגּוֹשׁ |
| constr. } | constr. } |

TEMPORAL VERB

FUTURE

| mas. } אֲנַגֵּשׁ | mas. } אֲנֻגָּשׁ |
| fem. } | fem. } |

TRANSITIVE

| mas. } נַגְּשִׁי | mas. .... } wanting |
| fem. } | fem. .... } |

PAST

| mas. } נִגַּשְׁתִּי | mas. } נֻגַּשְׁתִּי |
| fem. } | fem. } |

Excitative Form

ACTIVE MOVEMENT **PASSIVE MOVEMENT**

FACULTATIVE

CONTINUED

	ACTIVE		PASSIVE
mas.	מַגִּישׁ	mas.	מֻגָּשׁ
fem.	מַגִּישָׁה	fem.	מֻגָּשָׁה

FINISHED

mas. .... ⎫
fem. .... ⎬ like the passive

NOMINAL VERB

	ACTIVE		PASSIVE
absol.	הַגִּישׁ	absol. ⎫	הֻגַּשׁ
constr.	הַגֵּשׁ	constr. ⎬	

TEMPORAL VERB

FUTURE

mas. ⎫		mas. ⎫	
fem. ⎬	אַגִּישׁ	fem. ⎬	אֻגַּשׁ

TRANSITIVE

mas. ⎫		mas. ⎫	
fem. ⎬	הִגַּשְׁתִּי	fem. ⎬	הֻגַּשְׁתִּי

PAST

mas.	הַגֵּשׁ	mas. ⎫	
fem.	הַגִּישִׁי	fem. ⎬	wanting

CONJUGATIONS 237

Reflexive Form

ACTIVE MOVEMENT   **PASSIVE MOVEMENT**

FACULTATIVE

CONTIN. { *mas.*   מִתְנַגֵּשׁ
{ *fem.*   מִתְנַגְּשָׁה

FINISH. { *mas.*
{ *fem.* ...... } wanting

NOMINAL VERB

absol. }
constr. } הִתְנַגֵּשׁ

TEMPORAL VERB

FUTURE

mas. }
fem. } אֶתְנַגֵּשׁ

TRANSITIVE

mas.   הִתְנַגֵּשׁ
fem.   הִתְנַגְּשִׁי

PAST

mas. }
fem. } הִתְנַגַּשְׁתִּי

REMARKS ON THE COMPOUND RADICAL CONJUGATION.

Initial Adjunction נ.

Here is the somewhat difficult etymology of the verb נָגוֹשׁ, which I give as type, thus following the usage of the Hebraists, from which I never digress without the strongest reasons.

The root גו or גוֹה, offers the general idea of some sort of detachment, destined to contain something in itself, as a sheath; or to pass through, as a channel. This root united to the sign of relative movement, offers in the word גוּשׁ, the most restrained idea of a local detachment, of a letting go. This detachment being arrested and brought back upon itself by the initial adjunction נ, will signify an approaching, a nearness; and the compound radical verb נָגוֹשׁ, will express the action of drawing near, of joining, of meeting, of approaching, etc.

Positive Form.

Active movement. The initial adjunction נ, disappears in the construct nominal, in the future and transitive, as I have already remarked concerning the initial adjunction י; it remains the same in the two facultatives, in the absolute nominal and in the past. I infer that in the original tongue of Moses and before the Chaldaic punctuation had been adopted, it was the sign וֹ which was placed between the first and second character of the verbal root, and which read נְוֹשֶׁת, *the action of approaching,* אֶגְוֹשׁ *I shall approach,* גוֹשׁ *approach.* This mother vowel has been replaced by the point *patah*. A thing which makes this inference very believable, is that one still finds it in several verbs belonging to this conjugation, which preserve this sign in the future, such as יָכוֹל *he shall fail,* etc.

CONJUGATIONS

It must be observed that in the verb נָקוֹה, *to take, to draw to oneself*, the nominal sometimes takes the character ל in place of the initial adjunction נ, and follows the course of the compound radical conjugation, of which I have given the example; so that one finds very often לָקַח, or קַחַת *the action of taking,* אֶקַּח *I shall take,* קַח *take,* etc.

Passive movement. The Chaldaic punctuation having suppressed the mother vowel, which should characterize this movement, has made it very difficult to distinguish the active movement, especially in the past. It can only be distinguished in this tense by the meaning of the phrase.

INTENSIVE FORM.

This form is but little used. When it is however, it should be observed that the initial adjunction נ, takes the force of a sign and is no longer separated from its verb. It acts in the same manner as the initial adjunction י, of which I have spoken. The compound radical conjugation therefore, does not differ from the derivative conjugation.

EXCITATIVE FORM.

This form is remarkable in both movements, because the adjunctive character נ, disappears wholly and is only supplied by the interior point placed in the first character of the root. It is obvious that in the origin of the Hebraic tongue, the compound radical conjugation differed here from the radical conjugation, only by the interior point of which I have spoken, and that the mother vowel י, was placed between the two radical characters in the active movement; whereas the convertible sign ו, was shown in front of the first radical character in the passive movement. One should say אַגִּישׁ, *I shall make approach;* as one finds הַגִּישׁ *to make approach,* אוּגַּשׁ *I shall be excited to approach;* as one finds הוּגַּשׁ, *the action of being excited to approach;* but almost invariably the Chaldaic punctuation has replaced these mother vowels by the *hirek* or the *zere*, in the active movement, and by the *kibbuz* in the passive movement.

REFLEXIVE FORM

The initial adjunction נ, never being separated from the root, reappearing in this form, gives it the character of a derivative verb.

CONJUGATIONS

§ V.

Compound Radical Conjugation with the Terminative Adjunction

POSITIVE FORM

ACTIVE MOVEMENT   **PASSIVE MOVEMENT**

FACULTATIVE

CONTINUED	CONTINUED
סוֹבֵב	נָסָב
סוֹבְבָה	נְסַבָּה

FINISHED

mas.	סָבוּב	*fem.*	סְבוּבָה	

NOMINAL VERB

absol.	סוֹב	*absol.*	}	הִסּוֹב
constr.	סְבוֹב	*constr.*	}	

TEMPORAL VERB

FUTURE

SINGULAR 1 {m. f.} אָסוֹב   SINGULAR 1 {m. f.} אֶסַּב

2 {m.} תָּסוֹב   2 {m.} תִּסַּב

  {f.} תָּסוֹבִי   {f.} תִּסַּבִּי

3 {m.} יָסוֹב   3 {m.} יִסַּב

  {f.} תָּסוֹב   {f.} תִּסַּב

242 THE HEBRAIC TONGUE RESTORED

TEMPORAL VERB. FUTURE

PLURAL	1	m. f.	נָסוֹב	PLURAL	1	m. f.	נָסֵב
	2	m.	תָּסוֹבּוּ		2	m.	תִּסְבּוּ
		f.	תְּסֻבֶּינָה			f.	תִּסְבֶּינָה
	3	m.	יָסֹבּוּ		3	m.	יִסְבּוּ
		f.	תְּסֻבֶּינָה			f.	תִּסְבֶּינָה

TRANSITIVE

SING.	2	mas.	סוֹב	SING.	2	mas.	הָסֵב
		fem.	סוֹבִי			fem.	הָסֵבִּי
PLU.	2	mas.	סֹבּוּ	PLU.	2	mas.	הָסֵבּוּ
		fem.	סֻבֶּינָה			fem.	הַסְבֶּינָה

PAST

SINGULAR	1	m. f.	סַבּוֹתִי	SINGULAR	1	m. f.	נְסִבּוֹתִי
	2	m.	סַבּוֹתָ		2	m.	נְסִבּוֹתָ
		f.	סַבּוֹתְ			f.	נְסִבּוֹתְ
	3	m.	סָב		3	m.	נָסֵב
		f.	סָבָּה			f.	נָסֵבָּה

PLURAL	1	m. f.	סַבּוֹנוּ	PLURAL	1	m. f.	נְסִבּוֹנוּ
	2	m.	סַבּוֹתֶם		2	m.	נְסִבּוֹתֶם
		f.	סַבּוֹתֶן			f.	נְסִבּוֹתֶן
	3	m. f.	סַבּוּ		3	m. f.	נָסֵבּוּ

CONJUGATIONS 243

INTENSIVE FORM

ACTIVE MOVEMENT **PASSIVE MOVEMENT**

FACULTATIVE

CONTINUED

	ACTIVE		PASSIVE
mas.	מְסוֹבֵב	*mas.*	מְסוֹבָב
fem.	מְסוֹבְבָה	*fem.*	מְסוֹבָבָה

FINISHED

mas. .....
fem. ..... } like the passive

NOMINAL VERB

absol.		*absol.*	
constr. }	סוֹבֵב	*constr.* }	סוֹבָב

TEMPORAL VERB

FINISHED

mas. }		*mas.* }	
fem. }	אֲסוֹבֵב	*fem.* }	אֲסוֹבָב

TRANSITIVE

mas.	סוֹבֵב	*mas.*	
fem.	סוֹבְבִי	*fem.*	} wanting

PAST

mas. }		*mas.* }	
fem. }	סוֹבַבְתִּי	*fem.* }	סוֹבַּבְתִּי

EXCITATIVE FORM

ACTIVE MOVEMENT		PASSIVE MOVEMENT	

FACULTATIVE

CONTINUED

mas.	מֵסֵב	*mas.*	מוּסָב
fem.	מְסִבָּה	*fem.*	מוּסָבָּה

FINISHED

mas. ...... ⎫
fem. ...... ⎬ like the passive

NOMINAL VERB

absol. ⎫
constr. ⎭ הָסֵב

absol. ⎫
constr. ⎭ הוּסָב

TEMPORAL VERB

FUTURE

mas. ⎫
fem. ⎭ אָסֵב

mas. ⎫
fem. ⎭ אוּסָב

TRANSITIVE

| *mas.* | הָסֵב | *mas.* ...... ⎫ |
| *fem.* | וְסִבִי | *fem.* ...... ⎬ wanting |

PAST

mas. ⎫
fem. ⎭ הֲסִכּוֹתִי

mas. ⎫
fem. ⎭ הוּסַבּוֹתִי

CONJUGATIONS 245

REFLEXIVE FORM

ACTIVE AND PASSIVE MOVEMENT UNITED

FACULTATIVE

CONTIN. { *mas.* מִסְתּוֹכֵב
{ *fem.* מִסְתּוֹכְבָה

FINISH. { *mas.* ..... } wanting
{ *fem.* ..... }

NOMINAL VERB

absol. } הִסְתּוֹכֵב
constr. }

TEMPORAL VERB

FUTURE

mas. } אֶסְתּוֹכֵב
fem. }

TRANSITIVE

mas. הִסְתּוֹכֵב
fem. הִסְתּוֹכְבִי

PAST

mas. } הִסְתּוֹכַבְתִּי
fem. }

REMARKS ON THE COMPOUND RADICAL CONJUGATION

Terminative Adjunction

This conjugation is, in general, only a modification of the radical conjugation. It seems also that this may be the intensive form represented by the verb קוֹמֵם, for example, which has been given as positive form, so that the following forms may have greater energy.

The root סב, from which is derived the compound radical verb סוֹבֵב, which I give here as type following the Hebraists, being formed from the sign of interior and central action ב, and from the sign of circular movement ס expresses necessarily any kind of movement which operates around a centre. The duplication of the last character ב, in giving more force to the central point, tends to bring back the circumference ס, and consequently to intensify the action of turning, of closing in turning, of enveloping, of *surrounding* in fact, expressed by the verb in question.

Positive Form

Active movement. The final character ב, which has been doubled to form the compound radical verb סוֹבֵב, is only found in the two facultatives. It disappears in all the rest of the conjugation, which is, in substance, only the radical conjugation according to the intensive form, with a few slight differences brought about by the Chaldaic punctuation. The sole mark by which one can distinguish it, is the interior point placed in the second character of the verbal root, to indicate the prolonged accent which resulted no doubt from the double consonant.

Passive movement. This movement experiences a great variation in the vowel point. The facultatives and the nominals are often found marked by the *zere*, as in נמֵס, *becoming dissolved, falling into dissolution;* הֵמֵס

to be dissolved, liquified; הֵחֵל *to be profaned, divulged;* etc. It is necessary in general, to be distrustful of the punctuation and to devote oneself to the meaning.

Intensive Form

This form differs from the intensive radical only in this; that the Chaldaic punctuation has replaced almost uniformly the sign וֹ, by the point *holem*. Care must be taken, before giving it a signification, to examine well the final character which is doubled; for it is upon it alone that this signification depends.

Excitative Form

Again here the excitative radical form, (exception being made of the sign י,) is replaced in the active movement by the point *zere*. The passive movement is found a little more characterized by the mother vowel וֹ, which one finds added to the verbal root in some persons of the past.

Reflexive Form

The characteristic syllable הת, is simply added to the intensive form, as we have already remarked in the radical conjugation; but here it undergoes metathesis: that is to say, when placed before a verb which begins with the character ס, the ת must be transferred to follow this same character, in the same manner as one sees it in the nominal, where instead of reading הִתְסוֹבֵב one reads הִסְתוֹבֵב.

§ VI.

Irregularities in the Three Conjugations

I have already spoken of the trifling anomalies which are found in verbs beginning with the character א, or ending with the characters נ or ת.

Verbs of the three conjugations can be terminated

with the mother vowels א or ה, and in this case they undergo some variations in their course.

When it is the vowel א, which constitutes the final character of any verb whatever, as in the radical בוא *to come;* the compound ברוא, *to create;* the compound radical יצא, *to appear;* or נשׂא, *to raise;* this vowel becomes ordinarily mute as to pronunciation, and is not marked with the Chaldaic point. Nevertheless, as it remains in the different verbal forms, the irregularity which results from its lack of pronunciation is not perceptible, and should be no obstacle to the one who studies Hebrew only to understand and to translate it. The rabbis alone, who still cantillate this extinct tongue, make a particular conjugation of this irregularity.

There is no difficulty for us to know that the radical בוא, *the action of coming,* follows the radical conjugation,

אָבוֹא	I shall come	בָּאתִי	I came
תָּבוֹא	thou wilt come	בָּאתָ	thou camest
יָבוֹא	he will come	בָּא	he came
etc.		*etc.*	

or that the compound בְּרוֹא, or בְּראת, *the action of creating,* is conjugated in a like manner.

אֶבְרָא or אֶבְרוֹא	I shall create	בָּרָאתִי	I created
תִּבְרָא	thou wilt create	בָּרָאתָ	thou createdst
יִבְרָא	he will create	בָּרָא	he created
etc.		*etc.*	

But when it is the vowel ה which constitutes the final character of the verb, then the difficulty becomes considerable, for this reason. This vowel not only remains mute, but disappears or is sometimes changed to another vowel; so that it would be impossible to recognize the verb, if one had not a model to which it might be related. Therefore I shall present here this model, taking for type the nominal גלוֹה or גלוֹת, and giving the etymological analysis.

This verb belongs to the root גּוֹ, of which I spoke in the case of the compound radical verb נָגוֹשׁ, and which contains the idea of some sort of detachment. This root, united to the sign of expansive movement ל, expresses as verb, the action of being released from a place, or from a veil, a vestment, a covering; the action of being shown uncovered, revealed, released; being set at liberty; etc.

It must be observed that the greater part of the verbs belonging to the three regular conjugations also receive modifications from what I call the irregular conjugation, according as they are terminated with the character ה, either as radical, derivative or compound radical verbs.

Nevertheless there are some verbs which terminate in this same character הּ, (marked with the interior point to distinguish it,) which are regular; that is to say, which follow the derivative conjugation to which they belong. These verbs are the four following:

  נָבֹהּ the action of excelling, of surpassing, of exalting
  כָּמֹהּ the action of languidly desiring, of languishing
  נָגֹהּ the action of emitting, or of reflecting light
  תָּמֹהּ the action of being astonished by its *éclat*, of being dazzled.

§ VI.
Irregular Conjugations
Positive Form

	ACTIVE MOVEMENT		PASSIVE MOVEMENT

FACULTATIVE

	CONTINUED		CONTINUED
mas.	גוֹלֶה	*mas.*	נִגְלֶה
fem.	גוֹלְה	*fem.*	נִגְלָה

FINISHED

mas.	גָלוּי
fem.	גְלוּיָה

NOMINAL VERB

| *absol.* | גָלוֹה | *absol.* | הִגָלוֹה |
| *constr.* | גְלוֹת | *constr.* | הִגָלוֹת |

TEMPORAL VERB
FUTURE

		ACTIVE			PASSIVE
SINGULAR	1 {m./f.}	אֶגְלֶה	SINGULAR	1 {m./f.}	אֶנָּלֶה
	2 {m.}	תִּגְלֶה		2 {m.}	תִּגָּלֶה
	2 {f.}	תִּגְלִי		2 {f.}	תִּגָּלִי
	3 {m.}	יִגְלֶה		3 {m.}	יִגָּלֶה
	3 {f.}	תִּגְלֶה		3 {f.}	תִּגָּלֶה
PLURAL	1 {m./f.}	נִגְלֶה	PLURAL	1 {m./f.}	נִגָּלֶה
	2 {m.}	תִּגְלוּ		2 {m.}	תִּגָּלוּ
	2 {f.}	תִּגְלֶינָה		2 {f.}	תִּגָּלֶינָה
	3 {m.}	יִגְלוּ		3 {m.}	יִגָּלוּ
	3 {f.}	תִּגְלֶינָה		3 {f.}	תִּגָּלֶינָה

CONJUGATIONS

TRANSITIVE

SING. 2	mas.	גְּלֵה	SING. 2	mas.	הִגָּלֵה
	fem.	גְּלִי		fem.	הִגָּלִי
PLU. 2	mas.	גְּלוּ		mas.	הִגָּלוּ
	fem.	גְּלֶינָה		fem.	הִגָּלֶינָה

PAST

SINGULAR 1	m. f.	גָּלִיתִי	SINGULAR 1	m. f.	נִגְלֵיתִי
2	m.	גָּלִיתָ	2	m.	נִגְלֵיתָ
	f.	גָּלִית		f.	נִגְלֵית
3	m.	גָּלָה	3	m.	נִגְלָה
	f.	גָּלְתָה		f.	נִגְלְתָה
PLURAL 1	m. f.	גָּלִינוּ	PLURAL 1	m. f.	נִגְלֵינוּ
2	m.	גְּלִיתֶם	2	m.	נִגְלֵיתֶם
	f.	גְּלִיתֶן		f.	נִגְלֵיתֶן
3	m. f.	גָּלוּ	3	m. f.	נִגְלוּ

THE HEBRAIC TONGUE RESTORED

INTENSIVE FORM

| ACTIVE MOVEMENT | PASSIVE MOVEMENT |

FACULTATIVE

CONTINUED

	ACTIVE		PASSIVE
mas.	מְגַלֶּה	mas.	מְגֻלֶּה
fem.	מְגַלָּה	fem.	מְגֻלָּה

FINISHED

mas. ..... }
fem. ..... } like the passive

NOMINAL VERB

absol.	גַּלֵּה	absol.	גֻּלֵּה
constr.	גַּלּוֹה	constr.	גֻּלּוֹת

TEMPORAL VERB

FUTURE

| mas. } | | mas. } | |
| fem. } | אֲגַלֶּה | fem. } | אֲגֻלֶּה |

TRANSITIVE

| mas. | גַּלֵּה | mas. ..... } | |
| fem. | גַּלִּי | fem. ..... } | wanting |

PAST

| mas. } | | mas. } | |
| fem. } | גִּלִּיתִי | fem. } | גֻּלֵּיתִי |

CONJUGATIONS

EXCITATIVE FORM

ACTIVE MOVEMENT   **PASSIVE MOVEMENT**

FACULTATIVE

	CONTINUED			CONTINUED
mas.	מַגְלֶה		*mas.*	מָגְלֶה
fem.	מַגְלָה		*fem.*	מָגְלָה

FINISHED

mas. ......⎫
fem. ......⎭ like the **passive**

NOMINAL VERB

absol.	הַגְלֵה		*absol.*	הָגְלֵה
constr.	הַגְלוֹת		*constr.*	הָגְלוֹת

TEMPORAL VERB

FUTURE

mas. ⎫	אַגְלֶה		*mas.* ⎫	אָגְלֶה
fem. ⎭			*fem.* ⎭	

TRANSITIVE

mas.	הַגְלֵה		*mas.* ...... ⎫	wanting
fem.	הַגְלִי		*fem.* ...... ⎭	

PAST

mas. ⎫	הִגְלֵיתִי		*mas.* ⎫	הָגְלֵיתִי
fem. ⎭			*fem.* ⎭	

253

REFLEXIVE FORM

ACTIVE AND PASSIVE MOVEMENT UNITED

FACULTATIVE

CONTIN. { mas. מִתְגַלֶה
{ fem. מִתְגַלָה

FINISH. { mas. ....} wanting.
{ fem. ....}

NOMINAL VERB

absol. } הִתְגַלוּת
constr. }

TEMPORAL VERB

FUTURE

mas. } אֶתְגַלֶה
fem. }

TRANSITIVE

mas. } הִתְגַלֶה
fem. } הִתְגַלִי

PAST

mas. } הִתְגַלִיתִי
fem. }

CHAPTER X.

CONSTRUCTION OF VERBS: ADVERBIAL RELATIONS: PARAGOGIC CHARACTERS: CONCLUSION

§ I.

UNION OF VERBS WITH VERBAL AFFIXES

I call the Construction of Verbs, their union with the verbal affixes. I have already shown the manner in which the nominal affixes are united to nouns. It remains for me to indicate here the laws which follow the verbal affixes when united to verbs.

These laws, if we omit the petty variations of the vowel points, can be reduced to this sole rule, namely; every time that any verbal modification whatsoever, receives an affix, it receives it by being constructed with it: that is to say, that if this modification, whatever it may be, has a construct, it employs it in this case.

Now let us glance rapidly over all the verbal modifications according to the rank that they occupy in the table of conjugations.

FACULTATIVES

The facultatives belong to nouns with which they form a distinct class. When they receive the verbal affix it is after the manner of nouns.

פוֹקְדֵנִי	visiting me	(him)
פוֹקְדַי	" "	(them, *m.*)
פוֹקַדְתִי	" "	(her)
פוֹקְדוֹתַי	" "	(them, *f.*)
פוֹקְדֵנוּ	" "	(him)
פוֹקְדֵינוּ	" "	(them, *m.*)
פוֹקַדְתְנוּ	" "	(her)
פוֹקְדוֹתֵינוּ	" "	(them, *f.*)

256 THE HEBRAIC TONGUE RESTORED

Those facultatives of the irregular conjugation which terminate in the character ה, lose it in the construct state.

עֹשֵׂנִי making me (him)

רֹאִי or רֹאֲנִי seeing me (him)

מְלַמֶּדְךָ teaching thee (him)

רֹדֵם domineering them, *m.* (him)

רֹדֵן   "   them, *f.* (him)

מְלַמְּדִי teaching me (them)

Nominal Verb

I have already given the nominal verb united to the nominal and verbal affixes. I have been careful, in giving the table of the different conjugations, to indicate always the nominal construct, when this construct is distinguished from the absolute nominal. So that one might with a little attention recognize easily any verb whatsoever, by the nominal when it has the affix. Here are, besides, some examples to fix the ideas in this respect and to accustom the reader to the varieties of the punctuation.

קוֹמִי or קָמִי the action of establishing myself; my establishment

תֻּמִּי the action of perfecting myself; my perfection

שׁוּבְנִי the action of restoring myself; my return, resurrection

פָּקְדִי the action of visiting myself; of examining myself; my examination

הִפָּקְדוֹ the action of being visited by another; his visit

פַּקְדֵנִי the action of visiting myself, of inspecting myself diligently

CONSTRUCTION OF VERBS 257

הַפְקִידָהּ   the action of making her visit, of arousing her to visit

שָׁבְתוֹ   the action of occupying, of inhabiting, of dwelling

לְדִתָּהּ   the action of bringing forth (*fem*)

גִּשְׁתְּךָ   the action of thy approaching (*mas*); thy approach

תִּתִּי   the action of giving myself

The emphatic article ה, when added to a nominal, is changed to ת, following the rules of the construct state.

אַהֲבָתוֹ   the action of loving him greatly

קָרְבָתָם   the action of pressing them closely

מָשְׁחָתִי   the action of consecrating me, of anointing me with holy oil

The irregular conjugation loses sometimes the character ה but more often changes it to ת.

TEMPORAL VERB

FUTURE

The sign וֹ which is in the greater part of the verbal modifications of the future, is lost in the construct state. The final character does not change in the three regular conjugations. I shall now present in its entirety, one of the persons of the future, united to the verbal affixes, taking my example from the derivative conjugation as the most used.

SINGULAR AFFIXES	mas.	יִפְקְדֵנִי	he will visit me
	fem.	יִפְקְדִי	
	mas.	יִפְקָדְךָ	he will visit thee
	fem.	יִפְקְדֵךְ	
	mas.	יִפְקְדֵנוּ or יִפְקְדוֹ	he will visit him
	fem.	יִפְקְדֶנָּה or יִפְקְדָהּ	he will visit her
PLURAL AFFIXES	mas.	יִפְקְדֵנוּ	he will visit us
	fem.		
	mas.	יִפְקָדְכֶם	he will visit you
	fem.	יִפְקָדְכֶן	
	mas.	יִפְקְדֵם	he will visit them
	fem.	יִפְקְדֵן	

It must be observed that the affix וֹ is changed quite frequently to הוּ, and usually one finds יִפְקְדֵהוּ instead of יִפְקְדֵנוּ or יִפְקְדוֹ.

In the irregular conjugation, the temporal modifications of the future which terminate in the character ה, lose this character in being constructed. Here are some examples, in which I have compared designedly these irregularities and some others of little importance.

CONSTRUCTION OF VERBS

יְסָבֶּנּוּ	he will surround him
תְּסוֹבְכֵנִי	thou wilt surround me
תְּקִמֵנִי	thou wilt establish me
יְרָאַנִי	he will see me
יֶאֱהָבַנִי	he will love me
יְשַׁבִּיעֵנִי	he will crown me with blessings
יַבְדִּילֵנִי	he will separate me with care
יְסָבֵּנוּ	he will make us surrounded
יְבָרְכֶנְהוּ	he will bless him fervently
יִרְאָנוּ	he will see us
תִּרְאַנִי	she will see me
יְכָנֵנוּ	he will fashion us
יוֹשִׁיבֵנוּ	he will make me dwell
אֲבָרְכֵם	I will bless them

TRANSITIVE

The transitive modifications are very similar to those of the future: that is to say that the verbal sign ו disappears in the construct state. The final character remains mute.

פָּקְדֵנִי	visit me (*mas.*)	פָּקְדוּנוּ	visit us
פָּקְדִינִי	visit me (*fem.*)	שְׁאָלוּנוּ	ask us
שְׁמָעֵנִי	hear me	תְּנֵם	give them
שַׂמְּחֵנִי	gladden me well	דָּעֵן	know them
חָנֵּנִי	accord me grace	הֲקִימֵנוּ	make us established
נְחֵנִי	lead me	קַבְּצֵנוּ	gather us
קָבְנוּ	curse him	חָקְדֵם	consider them

Past

In the temporal modifications of the past, the first person singular and plural, the second and third person masculine singular, and the third person of the plural, change only the vowel point in being constructed with the affixes: but the second and third person of the feminine singular, and the second of the masculine and feminine plural, change the final character; as:

			absol.	*constr.*	
SINGULAR	1	{ mas. / fem. }	פָּקַדְתִּי	פְּקַדְתִּי	I visited
	2	{ mas.	פָּקַדְתָּ	פְּקַדְתָּ	} thou "
		fem.	פָּקַדְתְּ	פְּקַדְתִּי	
	3	{ mas.	פָּקַד	פְּקַד	he "
		fem.	פָּקְדָה	פָּקְדָת	she "
PLURAL	1	{ mas. / fem. }	פָּקַדְנוּ	פְּקַדְנוּ	we "
	2	{ mas.	פְּקַדְתֶּם	פְּקַדְתּוּ	} you "
		fem.	פְּקַדְתֶּן		
	3	{ mas. / fem. }	פָּקְדוּ	פָּקְדוּ	they "

with affix

פְּקַדְתִּיךָ I visited thee   פְּקָדַתּוֹ she visited him

פְּקַדְתַּנִי } thou " me   פְּקָדְנוּם we " them
פְּקַדְתִּינִי

    פְּקָדָהּ he " her   פְּקַדְתּוּנִי you " us

                                  פְּקָדוּן they " them

CONSTRUCTION OF VERBS

It is needless for me to dwell upon each of these modifications in particular. I shall conclude by giving some examples taken from different forms and from different conjugations.

פְּקָדוֹ	he visited him diligently
אֲרָרָהּ	he cursed her violently
גִּלְגַּלְתִּיךָ	I encircled thee well
צִוִּיתִיךָ	I confirm thee much
הוֹרַדְתָּנוּ	thou madest us descend
הֶעֱלִיתָנוּ	thou madest us rise
הֵפִיצָךְ	he made himself scattered
הוֹדְעָךְ	he made himself known
הִדְמָנוּ	he made us silent
הֱשִׁיבוּם	he made them return
שָׂמְךָ	he placed thee
שָׂמַתְהוּ	she placed him
שָׂמוּךָ	they were placed
קְרָאוֹ	he called him
עָשָׂהוּ	he made him
גִּלִּיתוֹ	thou revealedst him
יְכָלְתִּיו	I subdued him
מְצָאתָהּ	thou foundedst her
שׁוֹבַכְתָּךְ	she perverted thee
חֲזִיתִיךָ	I perceived thee

etc.

§ II.

ADVERBIAL RELATIONS

In Chapter IV of this Grammar, I have stated that the Relation ought to be considered under three connections, according to the part of speech with which it preserves the most analogy. I have called *designative relation*, that which appears to me to belong most expressly to the sign, and I have treated it under the name of *article:* I have then named *nominal relation*, that which has appeared to me to replace more especially the noun and to act in its absence, and I have called it *pronoun:* now this latter is what I qualify by the name of *adverbial relation*, because it seems to form a sort of bond between the noun and the verb, and without being either the one or the other, to participate equally in both. I shall treat of this last kind of relation under the name of *adverb*.

I beg my reader to remember that I do not confound the adverb with the modificative. The latter modifies the verbal action and gives it the colour of the noun by means of the qualificative: the adverb directs it and indicates its use. Thus, *gently, strongly, obediently* are modificatives; they indicate that the action is done in a manner, gentle, strong, obedient: *above, below, before, after,* are adverbs: they show the direction of the action relative to things, persons, time, place, number or measure.

When the modern grammarians have said, in speaking of adverbs such as those just cited, that they were *indeclinable,* I fear that following Latin forms, they may be mistaken in this as in many other things. I know well that the designative relation, for example, the article which inflects the noun, could not be inflected, unless there existed a new article for this use; I know well that the modificative could not be inflected either, since it contains an implied action which can only be developed by the verb; but I also know that an adverbial relation, a veritable relation becoming a noun by a simple deduction of thought, must be subject to inflection. I can go

ADVERBIAL RELATIONS

further. I say that a designative relation, **an article, if it is made absolute**, will experience a sort of inflection. Consider the adverbs *below, above, before, after, today, tomorrow*, etc., all these are capable of being inflected to a certain point. Does not one say: *bring that from below above;* place yourself *before;* speak only *after your opinion;* consider the usages *of today;* think *of tomorrow*, etc., etc.?

Nearly all the adverbial relations of the Hebraic tongue receive the articles and lend themselves to their movements. Many even have number and gender, as can be noticed among those here cited.

Adverbs of Place

אִי : אַיֵה :	where? where
אֵיפֹה : אֵיפוֹא :	where? wherein
פֹּא : פֹּה :	here, in this place
שָׁם :	there, in that place
מִפּוֹ : מִפֹּה : מִשָּׁם :	hence, whence
חוּץ :	outside
מִבַּיִת : בְּתוֹךְ :	inside, within
עֵבֶר : מֵעֵבֶר :	beyond
בֵּין : בֵּינַיִם :	between, among
עַל : מַעְלָה :	upon, on high
פְּנֵי : פָּנִים : לִפְנֵי :	in front of, facing
מַטָּה :	down, beneath
תַּחַת : מִתַּחַת :	below, from under
אַחַר : אַחֲרֵי :	after, behind
סָבִיב :	round about
הָלְאָה :	afar off etc.

Of Time

מָתַי : עַד־מָה :	when, how long
עַד :	until
אָז : אֲזָי :	then
עַתָּה :	now
עוֹד :	again
תָּמִיד :	continually
טֶרֶם :	before
יוֹםָ :	today
מָחָר : תְּמוֹל :	tomorrow, yesterday
מִלְפָנִים	from before
מְהֵרָה :	quickly
	etc.

Of Number

אַף־כִּי :	how much more?	שֵׁשׁ :	six
אֶחָד :	one, first	שֶׁבַע :	seven
שְׁנֵי : שְׁנַיִם :	two, second	שְׁמֹנָה :	eight
שָׁלֹשׁ :	three	תֵּשַׁע :	nine
אַרְבַּע :	four	עֶשֶׂר :	ten
חָמֵשׁ :	five		etc.

Of Measure

אֵיךְ :	how?	מְאֹד :	very much
כֵּן : אָכֵן :	thus	שָׁוְא :	in vain
רַב :	enough	בְּלִי : מִבְּלִי :	nothing
מְעַט :	a little		etc.

ADVERBIAL RELATIONS

Affirmative Adverbs

אָמֵן ׃ אָמְנָם amen, verily   אַךְ ׃ wholly

כֹּה ׃ כֵּן ׃ thus, so   etc.

Suspensive and Interrogative

אוּלַי ׃ perhaps   אִם ׃ הַאִם ׃ is it?

לָמָה ׃ why   פֶּן ׃ lest

לְמִן ׃ because   מַדּוּעַ ׃ therefore

לְמַעַן ׃ on account of   etc.

Negatives

אַל ׃ not, no more   אַיִן ׃ אֵינִי ׃ nothing

לֹא ׃ no, not   רֵיקָם ׃ empty

בַּל ׃ בְּלֹא ׃ no, not   etc.

It is easy to see in glancing through these adverbial relations that their purpose is, as I have said, to show the employment of the action, its direction, its measure, its presence or its absence; and not to modify it. The action is modified by the modificative nouns. In the tongues where few nouns exist as in Hebrew for example, then the verbal form assists. This form which I have called intensive, lends itself to the intention of the writer, receives the movement of the sentence and gives to the verb the colour of the circumstance. This is what an intelligent translator ought never to lose sight of in the idioms of the Orient.

The reader who follows with close attention the progress of my grammatical ideas, should perceive that after having traversed the circle of the developments of speech, under the different modifications of the noun and the verb, we return to the sign from which we started: for the adverbial relation with which we are at the moment occupied, differs little from the designative relation and even mingles with it in many common expressions. I have already indicated this analogy, so that one **can observe**, when the time comes, the point where the **circle of speech** returning to itself, unites its elements.

This point merits attention. It exists between the affirmative and negative adverb; between *yes* and *no*, אך and אל or כה and לא: the substance and the verb: it can have nothing beyond. Whoever would reflect well upon the force of these two expressions, would see that they contain not alone the essence of speech but that of the universe, and that it is only by affirming or denying, wishing or not wishing, passing from nothingness to being or from being to nothingness, that the sign is modified, that speech is born, that intelligence is unfolded, that nature, that the universe moves toward its eternal goal.

I shall not dwell upon such speculations. I feel that to limit every tongue to two elementary expressions, would be too great a boldness in the state of our **present grammatical knowledge**. The mind encumbered **with a multitude** of words would hardly conceive a truth of this nature and would vainly attempt to bring back to elements so simple, a thing which appears to it so complicated.

But it can, however, be understood that the adverbial affirmation exists by itself in an absolute, independent manner, contained in the verb whose essence it constitutes: for every verb is affirmative: the negation is only its absence or its opposition. This is why, in any tongue whatsoever, to announce a verb is to affirm: to destroy it is to deny.

Sometimes without entirely destroying the verb one suspends the effect: then he interrogates. The Hebrew possesses two adverbial relations to illustrate this modification of speech: אם and האם: it could be rendered by *is it?* but its usage is quite rare. The interrogation appears to have occurred most commonly in the tongue of Moses, as it still occurs among most of the meridional peoples: that is to say, by means of the accent of the voice.

ADVERBIAL RELATIONS

It indicates the meaning of the phrase. Sometimes, as I have said, the determinative article ה, takes an interrogative force.

The negation is expressed by means of the many adverbial relations that I have already given. Those most in use are לא and אֵין. The former expresses cessation, opposition, defense: the latter, absence and nothingness. These merit very particular attention.

Besides, all the adverbial relations without exception, are connected with the nominal and verbal affixes, and often form with them ellipses of great force. I am about to give some of these Hebraisms interpreting word-for-word when necessary.

אַיוֹ : אַיָּם :	where-of-him? where-of-them? (where is he, where are they?)
אַחֲרֶיךָ :	behind-thee
תַּחְתִּי :	under me (in my power)
בֵּינֵינוּ : וּבֵינֶיךָ : בֵּינַיִם :	between us and between thee: between them
לְפָנַי : לְפָנֶיךָ : לְפָנֵינוּ :	before me, before thee, before us
בַּעֲדִי : בַּעֲדִיכֶם : בַּעֲדֵיהֶם :	around me, around you, around them
עוֹדֵינוּ : הַעוֹדָם :	again us (we are again) what! again them? (are they again?)
אִישׁ־הַבֵּנַיִם :	a man between (wavering between two parts)
אֶל־בִּינוֹת : לַגַלְגַּל :	toward the midst of the deep (toward the centre of ethereal spaces, of celestial spheres, of worlds)

מִבֵּינוֹת לַכְּרֻבִים: from between the cherubims (from the midst of that which represents the manifold forces)

INTERROGATION

מָה הוּא־לָהּ: what him-to her? (what did he say to her?)

מֶה חַטָּאתִי: what sin—mine? (what is my sin?)

אֶת־שׁוֹר מִי לָקַחְתִּי: of whom the ox I have taken? (whose is the ox that I have taken?)

בִּשְׁאוֹל מִי יוֹרֶה־לָךְ: in Sheol who will point out to thee? (who will show thee?)

וּבֶן־אָדָם כִּי תִפְקְדֶנּוּ: and-the-son-of Adam thus shalt thou-visit-him? (shalt thou visit him thus, the son of Adam?)

מִי אָדוֹן לָנוּ: who is the Lord of us?

אֶשָּׂא עֵינַי אֶל־הֶהָרִים: shall I lift mine eyes unto these hills?

מֵאַיִן יָבוֹא עֶזְרִי: whence will come help to me?

אִם עֲוֹנוֹת תִּשְׁמָר־יָהּ: dost thou consider the iniquities, Jah!

NEGATION

אַל־תּוֹסֵף: thou shalt add no more

אַל־תָּצַר: thou shalt act no more vindictively

אַל־יֵרָא: he shall not see

ADVERBIAL RELATIONS

צִוִּיתִיךָ לְבִלְי אֲכָל׃	I commanded thee not to eat
בִּבְלִי אֲשֶׁר׃ עַל־בְּלִי׃	of nothing which... because not
לֹא מָצָא עֵזֶר׃	he found no help
לֹא־יִהְיֶה לְךָ אֱלֹהִים אֲחֵרִים׃	not shall-there-be-for-thee other Gods (there shall exist no other Gods for thee.)
לֹא תַעֲשֶׂה לְךָ פֶסֶל׃	thou shalt not make for thee any image
וְלֹא־יִהְיֶה עוֹד הַמַּיִם לְמַבּוּל׃	and-there shall not be again the waters of deluge. (the waters of deluge shall no more be raised)
לְבִלְתִּי הַכּוֹת אֹתוֹ׃	not to wound him
לֹא יָדַעְתִּי׃	I knew it not
וְאֵינֶנּוּ׃	and he is not
וְאֵינְךָ׃ וְאֵינֵימוֹ׃	and thou art not: and they are not
אֵין־יֵשׁ־רוּחַ בְּפִיהֶם׃	nothing being spirit in the-mouth-to-them (there was nothing spiritual in their mouth)
כִּי־אֵין הַמֶּלֶךְ יוּכַל אֶתְכֶם דָּבָר׃	for nothing of the king being able with you thing. (for there is nothing of the king which may be something with you)
וְאֵין רֹאֶה וְאֵין יוֹדֵעַ וְאֵין מֵקִיץ׃	and nothing seeing, and nothing knowing and nothing watching (he saw and he knew and he watched nothing)

| כִּי אֵין בַּמָּוֶת זִכְרֶךָ: | for nothing in death to remember thee (there is no memory in death of thou who survives) |
| יְהֹוָה אַל־בְּאַפְּךָ תוֹכִיחֵנִי׃ | Yahweh no more in the wrath thine shalt thou chastise me (chastise me no more in thy wrath) |

---

§ III.

Paragogic Characters

The thinkers of the last centuries in their innumerable labours concerning the tongue of the Hebrews, many of which are not without merit, must have seen that the Hebraic characters had nearly all an intrinsic value, which gave force to the words to which they were added. Although the majority of these savants were very far from going back to the origin of the sign, and although nearly all of them discerned that the meaning attached to these characters was arbitrary, they could nevertheless, detect it. Some, considering more particularly those characters which appear at the beginning or the end of words to modify the signification, have chosen six: א, ה, י, מ, נ and ת: and taking the sound which results from their union, have designated them by the barbarous name of *héémanthes*. Others, selecting only those which chance appears to insert in certain words or to add them without evident reason, have named them *paragogics;* that is to say, *happened*. These characters, likewise six in number are: א, ה, י, ו, נ and ת. The only difference which exists between the *héémanthes* and the *paragogics*, is in the latter, where the vowel ו is substituted for the consonant מ.

I might omit further discussion of these characters since I have already considered them under the relation of signs; but in order to leave nothing to be desired, I shall state concisely what the Hebraists have thought of them.

א In considering this character as belonging to the *héémanthes*, the Hebraists have seen that it expressed force, stability, duration of substance, denomination. As *paragogic*, they have taught that it was found without motives, added to certain verbal tenses which terminate in וֹ, as in the following examples:

הָלְכוּא they went   נָשׂוּא they raised

בוּא they wished   etc.

This addition is a sort of redundancy in imitation of the Arabs. It expresses the force and duration of the action.

ה Whether this character is ranked among the *héémanthes*, or among the *paragogics* it is useless for me to add anything more to what I have said, either as sign, or as determinative or emphatic article. We know now that it can begin or terminate all kinds of words, nouns, verbs or relations.

ו It is not a question here of its astonishing power of changing the temporal modifications of the verbs, by carrying to the past those which are of the future, and to the future those which are of the past. When the Hebraists called it *paragogic*, they considered it simply as added to certain words without other reasons than of joining them together.

וְחַיְתוֹ־אֶרֶץ׃ the terrestrial animality (the animal kingdom)

בְּנוֹ־בְעוֹר׃ the son of Beor

לְמַעְיְנוֹ־מָיִם׃ the source of the waters

י The Hebraists who have considered this character as *héémanthe*, have attributed to it the same qualities as the vowel א, but more moral and bearing more upon mind than upon matter. Those who have treated it as *paragogic* have said that it was found sometimes inserted in words and oftener placed at the end, particularly in the feminine. They have not given the cause of this insertion or this addition, which results very certainly from the faculty that

PARAGOGIC CHARACTERS   273

it has as sign, of expressing the manifestation and the imminence of actions. For example:

לִדְרוֹשׁ׃ with a view to being informed, being instructed; to inquire

תִּעָשֶׂה׃ מֵיאָתִי׃ it will be done without interruption: by myself, openly

רַבָּתִיעָם׃ הַחֵצִי׃ an immense crowd of people: a swift arrow

מְקִימִי׃ establishing him with glory

אֹיְבְתִי׃ hostile with boldness

מ This character placed among the *héémanthes* by the Hebraists is found equally at the beginning and the end of words. When it is at the beginning it becomes, according to them, local and instrumental; it forms the names of actions, passions and objects. When it is at the end it expresses that which is collective, comprehensive, generic, or more intense and more assured. It is very singular that with these ideas, these savants have been able so often to misunderstand this sign whose usage is so frequent in the tongue of Moses. What has caused their error is the readiness with which they have confused it with the verbal affix ם. I shall produce in my notes upon the Cosmogony of Moses, several examples wherein this confusion has caused the strangest mistranslation. Here for instance, are some examples without comment.

אָמְנָם׃ a truth universal; a faith immutable

יוֹמָם׃ שְׁמָם׃ all the day; a name collective, generic, universal

אֵתָם׃ the whole; the collective self-sameness; the ipseity

עוֹלָם׃ the universality of time, space, duration, ages

נָחַם׃ he ceased entirely; he rested wholly

בְּשׁוּם׃ in the general action of declining, of being lost

מַשְׁחִיתָם: to degrade, to destroy, to ruin entirely

נ Among the *héémanthes*, this character expresses either passive action and turns back to itself when it appears at the beginning of words; or, unfoldment and augmentation when it is placed at the end. Among the *paragogics*. it is added without reason, say the Hebraists, to the verbal modifications terminated by the vowels ו or י: or is inserted in certain words to soften the pronunciation. It is evident that even in this case it retains its character as can be judged by the following examples.

יָדְעוּן: they knew at full length
תַּעֲשִׂין: thou shalt do without neglecting
לִתִּתֵּן: so as to give generously
יְסֹבְבֶנְהוּ: he surrounded it well
יִצְּרֶנְהוּ: he closed it carefully
יֶשְׁנוֹ: behold his manner of being (his being)
יָגוֹן: torment of the soul, sorrow, entire disorganization
זִכְרוֹן: steadfast remembrance, very extended
בִּצָּרוֹן: well-stored provisions

ת The Hebraists who have included this character among the *héémanthes,* have attributed to it the property that it has as sign, of expressing the continuity of things and their reciprocity. Those who have made it a *paragogic* have only remarked the great propensity that it has for being substituted for the character ה; propensity of which I have spoken sufficiently. Here are some examples relative to its reciprocity as sign:

תּוּגָה: reciprocal sorrow
תְּנוּאָה: mutual estrangement, aversion
תָּאַב: he desired mutually and continually
תְּנוּמָה: sympathetic sleep
תַּגְמוּל: mutual retribution, contribution

§ IV.

Conclusion.

This is about all that the vulgar Hebraists have understood of the effects of the sign. Their knowledge would have been greater if they had known how to apply it. But I do not see one who has done so. It is true that in the difficulties which they found in the triliteral and dissyllabic roots, they applied, with a sort of devotion to the Hebraic tongue, this application which already very difficult in itself, obtained no results.

I venture to entertain the hope that the reader who has followed me with consistent attention, having reached this point in my Grammar, will no longer see in the tongues of men so many arbitrary institutions, and in speech, a fortuitous production due to the mechanism of the organs alone. Nothing arbitrary, nothing fortuitous moves with this regularity, or is developed with this constancy. It is very true that without organs man would not speak; but the principle of speech exists none the less independently, ever ready to be modified when the organs are suspectible of this modification. Both the principle and the organs are equally given, but the former, exists immutable, eternal, in the divine essence; the latter, more or less perfect according to the temporal state of the substance from which they are drawn, present to this principle, points of concentration more or less homogeneous and reflect it with more or less purity. Thus the light strikes the crystal which is to receive it and is refracted with an energy analogous to the polish of its surface. The purer the crystal the more brilliant it appears. A surface unpolished, sullied or blackened, gives only an uncertain dull reflection or none at all. The light remains immutable although its refracted rays may be infinitely varied. In this manner is the principle of speech developed. Ever the same *au fond*, it indicates nevertheless, in its effects the organic state of man. The more this state acquires perfection, and it acquires it unceasingly, the more speech gives facility to display its beauties.

According as the centuries advance, everything advances toward its perfection. Tongues experience in this respect, the vicissitudes of all things. Dependent upon the organs as to form, they are independent as to principle. Now this principle tends toward the unity from which it emanates. The multiplicity of idioms is a reflection upon the imperfection of the organs since it is opposed to this unity. If man were perfect, if his organs had acquired all the perfection of which they were susceptible, one single tongue would extend and be spoken from one extremity of the earth to the other.

I feel that this idea, quite true as it is, will appear paradoxical; but I cannot reject the truth.

From the several simple tongues I have chosen the Hebrew to follow its developments and make them perceived. I have endeavoured to reveal the material of this ancient idiom, and to show that my principal aim has been to make its genius understood and to induce the reader to apply this same genius to other studies; for the sign upon which I have raised my grammatical edifice is the unique basis upon which repose all the tongues of the world.

The sign comes directly from the eternal principle of speech, emanated from the Divinity, and if it is not presented everywhere under the same form and with the same attributes, it is because the organs, charged with producing it exteriorly, not only are not the same among all peoples, in all ages and under all climates, but also because they receive an impulse which the human mind modifies according to its temporal state.

The sign is limited to the simple inflections of the voice. There are as many signs possible as inflections. These inflections are few in number. The people who have distinguished them from their different combinations, representing them by characters susceptible of being linked together, as one sees it in the literal alphabet which we possess, have hastened the perfecting of the language with respect to the exterior forms; those who, blending them with these same combinations have applied them to an indefinite series of compound characters, as one sees among the Chinese, have perfected its interior images. The Egyptians who possessed at once the literal sign and the hieroglyphic combination, became, as they certainly were in the temporal state of things, the most enlightened people of the world.

The different combinations of signs constitute the roots. All roots are monosyllabic. Their number is limited; for it can never be raised beyond the combinations possible between two consonant signs and one vocal at the most. In their origin they presented only a vague and generic idea applied to all things of the same form, of the same species, of the same nature. It is always by a restriction of thought that they are particularized. Plato who considered general ideas as preëxistent, anterior to particular ideas, was right even in reference to the formation of the words which express them. Vegetation is conceived before the vegetable, the vegetable before the tree, the tree before the oak, the oak before all the particular kinds. One sees animality before the animal, the animal before the quadruped, the quadruped before the wolf, the wolf before the fox or the dog and their diverse races.

At the very moment when the sign produces the root, it produces also the relation.

Particular ideas which are distinguished from general ideas, are assembled about the primitive roots which thenceforth become idiomatic, receive the modifications of the sign, combine together and form that mass of words which the different idioms possess.

Nevertheless the unique verb until then implied, appropriates a form analogous to its essence and appears in speech. At this epoch a brilliant revolution takes place in speech. As soon as the mind of man feels it, he is penetrated by it. The substance is illumined. The verbal life circulates. Thousands of nouns which it animates become particular verbs.

Thus speech is divided into substance and verb. The substance is distinguished by gender and by number, by quality and by movement. The verb is subject to movement and form, tense and person. It expresses the different affections of the will. The sign, which transmits all its force to the relation, binds these two parts of speech, directs them in their movements and constructs them.

Afterward all depends upon the temporal state of things. At first a thousand idioms prevail in a thousand places on the earth. All have their local physiognomy. All have their particular genius. But nature obeying the unique impulse which it receives from the Being of beings, moves on to unity. Peoples, pushed toward one another like waves of the ocean, rush and mingle together, losing the identity of their natal idiom. A tongue more extended is formed. This tongue becomes enriched, is coloured and propagated. The sounds become softened by contact and use. The expressions are numerous, elegant, forceful. Thought is developed with facility. Genius finds a docile instrument. But one, two or three rival tongues are equally formed; the movement which leads to unity continues. Only, instead of some weak tribes clashing, there are entire nations whose waves now surge, spreading from the north to the south and from the Orient to the Occident. Tongues are broken like political existences. Their fusion takes place. Upon their common *débris* rise other nations and other tongues more and more extended, until at last one sole nation prevails whose tongue enriched by all the discoveries of the past ages, child and just inheritor of all the idioms of the world, is propagated more and more, and takes possession of the earth.

O France! O my Country! art thou destined to so great glory? Thy tongue, sacred to all men, has it received from heaven enough force to bring them back to unity of Speech? It is the secret of Providence.

PREFATORY NOTE

After all that I have said in my Grammar, both concerning the force of the sign and the manner in which it gives rise to the root, there remains but little to be added. The strongest argument that I can give in favour of the truths that I have announced upon this subject, is undoubtedly the Vocabulary which now follows. I venture to say that the attentive and wisely impartial reader will see with an astonishment mingled with pleasure, some four or five hundred primitive roots, all monosyllables resulting easily from the twenty-two signs, by twos, according to their vocal or consonantal nature, developing all universal and productive ideas and presenting a means of composition as simple as inexhaustible. For as I have already said, and as I shall often prove in my notes, there exists not a single word of more than one syllable, which is not a compound derived from a primitive root, either by the amalgamation of a mother vowel, the adjunction of one or several signs, the union of the roots themselves, the fusion of one in the other, or their contraction.

This great simplicity in the principles, this uniformity and this surety in the course, this prodigious richness of invention in the developments, had caused the ancient sages of Greece, those capable of understanding and appreciating the remains of the sacred dialect of Egypt, to think that this dialect had been the work of the priests themselves who had fashioned it for their own use; not perceiving, from the irregular turn pursued by the Greek idiom and even the vulgar idiom then in use in Lower Egypt, that any tongue whatsoever, given its own full sway, might attain to this degree of perfection. Their error was to a certain point excusable. They could not know, deprived as they were of means of comparison, the enormous difference which exists between a real mother tongue and one which is not. The merit of the Egyptian priests was not, as has been supposed, in having invented the ancient idiom, which they used instead of the sacred dialect, but in having fathomed the genius, in having well understood its elements, and in having been instructed to employ them in a manner conformable with their nature.

The reader will discern, in glancing through the Vocabulary which I give and which I have restored with the utmost care possible, to what degree of force, clarity and richness, the tongue whose basis it formed, could attain; he will also perceive its usefulness in the hands of the wise and studious man, eager to go back to the origin of speech and to sound the mystery, hitherto generally unknown, of the formation of language.

The universal principle is not for man. All that falls beneath his senses, all that of which he can acquire a real and positive understanding is diverse. God alone is one. The principle which presides at the formation of the Hebrew is not therefore universally the same as that which presides at the formation of Chinese, Sanskrit or any other similar tongue. Although issued from a common source which is Speech, the constitutive principles of the tongues differ. Because a primitive root formed of such or such sign, contains such a general idea in Hebrew, it is not said for that reason that it ought to contain it in Celtic. Very close attention must be given here. This same root can, on the contrary, develop an opposite idea; and this occurs nearly always when the spirit of a people is found in contradiction with that of another people concerning the sentiment which is the cause of the idea. If a person, reading my Vocabulary, seeing the most extended developments follow the simplest premises, and discovering at first glance irresistible relations in Hebrew with his own language and the ancient or modern tongues which he knows, ventures to believe that Hebrew is the primitive tongue from which all the others descend, he would be mistaken. He would imitate those numberless systematic scholars who, not understanding the vast plan upon which nature works have always wished to restrict it to the narrow sphere of their understanding.

It is not enough to have grasped the outline of one single figure to understand the arrangement of a picture. There is nothing so false, from whatever viewpoint one considers it, as that impassioned sentence which has become a philosophic axiom: *ab uno disce omnes*. It is in following this idea that man has built so many heterogeneous edifices upon sciences of every sort.

The Radical Vocabulary which I give is that of Hebrew; it is therefore good primarily for the Hebrew; secondarily, for the tongues which belong to the same stock, such as Arabic, Coptic, Syriac, etc; but it is only in the third place and in an indirect manner that it can be of use in establishing the etymologies of Greek or Latin, because these two tongues having received their first roots from the ancient Celtic, have with Hebrew only coincidental relations given them by the universal principle of speech, or the fortuitous mixture of peoples: for the Celtic, similar to Hebrew, Sanskrit and Chinese in all that comes from the universal principle of speech, differs essentially in the particular principle of its formation.

The French, sprung from the Celtic in its deepest roots, modified by a mass of dialects, fashioned by Latin and Greek, inundated by Gothic, mixed with Frank and Teutonic, refashioned by Latin, repolished by Greek, in continual struggle with all the neighbouring idioms; the French is perhaps, of all the tongues extant today upon the face of the earth, the one whose etymology is most difficult. One cannot act with too much circumspection in this matter. This tongue is beautiful but its beauty lies not in its simplicity: on the contrary, there is nothing so complicated. It is in proportion as one is enlightened concerning the elements which compose it, that the difficulty of its analysis will be felt and that unknown resources will be discovered. Much time and labour is necessary before a good etymological dictionary of this tongue can be produced. Three tongues well understood, Hebrew, Sanskrit and Chinese can, as I have said, lead one to the origin of speech; but to penetrate into the etymological details of

French, it would be necessary to know also the Celtic, and to understand thoroughly all the idioms which are derived therefrom and which directly or indirectly have furnished expressions to that of the Gauls, our ancestors, of the Romans, our masters, or of the Franks, their conquerors. I say to understand thoroughly, for grammars and vocabularies ranged in a library do not constitute real knowledge. I cannot prove better this assertion than by citing the example of Court de Gébelin. This studious man understood Greek and Latin well, he possessed a slight knowledge of the oriental tongues as much as was possible in his time; but as he was ignorant of the tongues of the north of Europe or at least as their genius was unfamiliar to him, this defect always prevented his grasping in their real light, French etymologies. The first step which he took in this course, was an absurd error which might have brought entire discredit upon him if there had been anyone capable of detecting his mistake. He said, for example, that the French word *abandon* was a kind of elliptical and figurative phrase composed of three words *a-ban-don;* and that it signified a gift made to the people, taking the word *ban* for the people, the public. Besides it is not true that the word *ban* may signify *people* or *public* in the sense in which he takes it, since its etymology proves that it has signified *common* or *general*,[1] it was not necessary to imagine an ellipsis of that force to explain *abandon*. It is only necessary to know that in Teutonic *band* is a

---

[1] We still say *banal* to express that which is *common*. It is worthy of notice that the word *banal* goes back to the Gallic root *ban*, which in a restricted sense characterizes *a woman;* whereas its analogues *common* and *general* are attached, the one to the Celtic root *gwym*, *cwym* or *kum*, and the other to the Greek root Γυν, which is derived from it; now these two roots characterize alike, *a woman*, and all that which is *joined*, *united*, *communicated*, or *generated*, *produced*. *Cym* in Gallic-Celtic, Συν or Συμ in Greek, *cum* in Latin, serves equally the designative or adverbial relation, to express *with*. The Greek word γαμεῖν signifies to be *united*, to *marry*, to *take wife*, and the word *gemein* which, in modern German holds to the same root, is applied to all that is *common*, *general*.

root expressing all that is *linked, retained, guarded,* and that the word *ohn* or *ohne,* analogous to the Hebrew אִין is a negation which being added to words, expresses absence. So that the compound *band-ohne* or *aband-ohn,* with the redundant vowel, is the exact synonym of our expressions *abandon* or *abandoment.*

Court de Gébelin made a graver mistake when he wrote that the French word *vérité* is derived from a so-called primitive root *var,* or *ver,* which according to him signified *water* and all that which is limpid and transparent as that element: for how could he forget that in the Celtic and in all the dialects of the north of Europe the root *war, wer, wir,* or *wahr, ward,* develops the ideas of being, in general, and of man in particular, and signifies, according to the dialect, that which *is,* that which *was,* and even becomes a sort of auxiliary verb to express that which *will be?* It is hardly conceivable.

Now if a savant so worthy of commendation has been able to go astray upon this point in treating of French etymologies, I leave to the imagination what those who lack his acquired knowledge would do in this pursuit.

Doubtless there is nothing so useful as etymological science, nothing which opens to the meditation a field so vast, which lends to the history of peoples so sure a link; but also, nothing is so difficult and nothing which demands such long and varied preparatory studies. In the past century when a writer joined to Latin, certain words of Greek and of bad Hebrew, he believed himself a capable etymologist. Court de Gébelin was the first to foresee the immensity of the undertaking. If he has not traversed the route he has at least had the glory of showing the way. Notwithstanding his mistakes and his inadvertencies which I have disclosed with an impartial freedom, he is still the only guide that one can follow, so far as general maxims are concerned, and the laws to be observed in the exploration of tongues. I cannot conceive how a writer who appears to unite so much positive learning as the one who has just published a book in German full of excellent views upon the tongue and science of the Indians[1] can have misunderstood the first rules of etymology to the point of giving constantly for roots of Sanskrit, words of two, three and four syllables; not knowing or feigning not to know that every root is monosyllabic; still less can I conceive how he has not seen that, in the comparison of tongues, it is never the compound which proves an original analogy, but the root. Sanskrit has without doubt deep connection with ancient Celtic and consequently with Teutonic, one of its dialects; but it is not by analyzing about thirty compound words of modern German that these connections are proved. To do this one must go back to the primitive roots of the two tongues, show their affinity, and in compounds, inevitably diverse, distinguish their different genius and give thus to the philosopher and historian, materials for penetrating the *esprit* of these two peoples and noting their moral and physical revolutions.

In this Prefatory Note, my only object has been to show the difficulty of the etymological science and to warn the overzealous reader as much as possible, against the wrong applications that he might make in generalizing particular principles, and against the errors into which too much impetuosity might lead him.

[1] *Ueber die Sprache und Weisheit der Indier*... I vol. in-8 Heidelberg. 1808.

The
Hebraic Tongue Restored

HEBRAIC ROOTS.

RADICAL VOCABULARY

OR

SERIES OF HEBRAIC ROOTS.

א A. First character of the alphabet in nearly all known idioms. As symbolic image it represents universal man, mankind, the ruling being of the earth. In its hieroglyphic acceptation, it characterizes unity, the central point, the abstract principle of a thing. As sign, it expresses power, stability, continuity. Some grammarians make it express a kind of superlative as in Arabic; but this is only a result of its power as sign. On some rare occasions it takes the place of the emphatic article ה either at the beginning or at the end of words. The rabbis use it as a sort of article. It is often added at the head of words as redundant vowel, to make them more sonorous and to add to their expression.

Its arithmetical number is 1.

אב AB. The potential sign united to that of interior activity produces a root whence come all ideas of productive cause, efficient will, determining movement, generative force. In many ancient idioms and particularly in the Persian اب, this root is applied especially to the aqueous element as principle of universal fructification.

אב All ideas of *paternity.* Desire *to have*: a *father*: *fruit.* In reflecting upon these different significations, which appear at first incongruous, one will perceive that they come from one another and are produced mutually.

The Arabic اب contains all the significations of the Hebraic root. As noun, it is *father* and *paternity, fruit* and *fructification;* that which is producer and produced; that which germinates and comes forth as verdure upon the earth. As verb[1] it is the action *of tending toward* a desired end, *proceeding, returning*, etc.

אָב or אבב (*intensive*) That which *grows, is propagated*: *vegetation, germination*.

אהב (*compound*) All ideas of *love, sympathy, inclination, kindness*. It is the sign of life ה which gives to the idea of *desire to have*, contained in the root אָב, the movement of expansion which transforms it into that of *love*. It is, according to the etymological sense, that which seeks to spread out.

אוב (*comp.*) This is, in a broader sense, *the Universal Mystery, the Matrix of the Universe, the Orphic Egg, the World, the Vessel of Isis, the Pythonic Mind*: in a more restricted sense, *belly; leather bottle, cavity, vase*, etc.

אג AG. This root, which is only used in composition, characterizes in its primitive acceptation, an acting thing which tends to be augmented. The Arabic اج expresses *ignition, acrimony, intense excitation*.

אג The Chaldaic אג signifies a *lofty, spreading tree*: the Hebrew אגוז *a walnut tree*: the Arabic اوج contains every idea of magnitude, physically as well as morally.

[1] In order to conceive this root اب according to its verbal form, we must consider the last character ب doubled. It is thus that the radical verbs in Arabic are formed. These verbs are not considered as radical by the Arabic grammarians; but on the contrary, as defective and for this reason are called *surd verbs*. These grammarians regard only as radical, the verbs formed of three characters according to the verb فعل *to do*, which they give as verbal type. It is therefore from this false supposition, that every verbal root must possess three characters, that the Hebraist grammarians misunderstood the true roots of the Hebraic tongue.

אד AD. This root, composed of the signs of power and of physical divisibility, indicates every distinct, single object, taken from the many.

The Arabic اذ conceived in an abstract manner and as adverbial relation, expresses a temporal point, a determined epoch: *when, whilst, whereas.*

אד That which *emanates* from a thing: *the power of division, relative unity, an emanation; a smoking fire brand.*

אוד (*comp.*) That which is done *because of* or *on occasion of* another thing: *an affair, a thing, an occurrence.*

איד (*comp.*) Every idea of *force, power, necessity*: see יד.

אה AH. Vocal principle. Interjective root to which is attached all passionate movements of the soul, those which are born of joy and pleasure as well as those which emanate from sorrow and pain. It is the origin of all interjective relations called *interjections* by the grammarians. Interjections, says Court de Gébelin, varying but slightly as to sound, vary infinitely according to the degree of force with which they are pronounced. Suggested by nature and supplied by the vocal instrument, they are of all times, all places, all peoples; they form an universal language. It is needless to enter into the detail of their various modifications.

אה The potential sign united to that of life, forms a root in which resides the idea most abstract and most difficult to conceive,—that of *the will;* not however, that of determined or manifested will, but of will in potentiality and considered independent of every object. It is *volition* or *the faculty of willing.*

אוה Determined will: action of *willing, desiring, tending toward* an object. See או.

איה or אהי Manifested will: *place* of the desire, *ob-*

ject of the will, represented by the adverbial relation *where*. See אִי.

אָהַב׃ (*comp.*) Action of *desiring, loving, willing.* See אִי.

אהל (*comp.*) A raised, fixed *place, where* one dwells by choice, *a tent.* See אל.

או   AO. The potential sign united to the universal convertible sign, image of the mysterious link which joins nothingness to being, constitutes one of the most difficult roots to conceive which the Hebraic tongue can offer. In proportion as the sense is generalized, one sees appear all ideas of appetence, concupiscible passion, vague desire: in proportion as it is restricted, one discerns only a sentiment of incertitude, of doubt, which becomes extinct in the prepositive relation *or*.

The Arabic او has exactly the same meaning.

אוּב (*comp.*) *Desire* acting interiorly. See אָב.

אוּד (*comp.*) *Desire* acting exteriorly. See אד.

אוה (*comp.*) Action of *longing ardently, desiring, inclining with passion.* See אה.

אוּל (*comp.*) *Desire* projected into space, represented by the adverbial relation *perhaps*. See אל.

און (*comp.*) *Desire* vanishing, being lost in *space* in *nothingness.* See אן.

אוּף (*comp.*) Action of *drawing* into one's will. See אף.

אוּץ (*comp.*) Action of *hastening, pressing* toward a desired end. See אץ.

אור (*comp.*) *Desire* given over to its own movement, producing *ardour, fire;* that which *burns,* in its literal as well as its figurative sense. See אר.

אות (*comp.*) Action of *having the same desire, the same will; agreeing, being of the same opinion.* See את.

אָז AZ. This root, but little used in Hebrew, designates a fixed point in space or duration; a measured distance. It is expressed in a restricted sense by the adverbial relations *there* or *then*.

The Arabic اذ characterizes a sort of locomotion, agitation, pulsation, bubbling, generative movement. As verb it has the sense of *giving a principle; of founding*. The Chaldaic אזא expresses a movement of ascension according to which a thing is placed above another in consequence of its specific gravity. The Ethiopic ЗНН (*azz*) develops all ideas of *command, ordination, subordination*.

אָז This is, properly speaking, the action of *gas* which is exhaled and seeks its point of equilibrium: figuratively, it is the movement of the ascension of fire, ether, gaseous fluids in general.

אָה AH. The potential sign united to that of elementary existence ה, image of the travail of nature, produces a root whence result all ideas of equilibrium, equality, identity, fraternity. When the sign ה characterizes principally an effort, the root אה takes the meaning of its analogues אג, אך, and represents a somewhat violent action. It furnishes then all ideas of excitation and becomes the name of the place where the fire is lighted, *the hearth*.

אָח Brother, kinsman, associate, neighbour: *the common hearth* where all assemble.

The Arabic اخ contains all the meanings attributed to the Hebrew אח.

אח and אחד One: *first*: all ideas attached to *identity*, to *unity*.

אחו All ideas of *junction, adjunction, union, reconciliation*. Bulrush, reed, sedge.

אחז (*comp.*) All ideas of *adhesion, apprehension, agglomeration, union, possession, heritage*.

אחר (comp.) That which is *other, following, posterior;* those who *come after*, who remain *behind; descendants*, etc.

אם AT. This root is scarcely used in Hebrew except to describe a sound, or a slow, silent movement. The Arabic اب expresses any kind of murmuring noise.

אם *A magic murmur; witchcraft, enchantment.*

אי AI. Power accompanied by manifestation, forms a root whose meaning, akin to that which we have found in the root או, expresses the same idea of desire, but less vague and more determined. It is no longer sentiment, passion without object, which falls into incertitude: it is the very object of this sentiment, the centre toward which the will tends, the place where it is fixed. A remarkable thing is, that if the root או is represented in its most abstract acceptation by the prepositive relation *or*, the root אי is represented, in the same acceptation, by the adverbial relation *where*.

The Arabic اي expresses the same assent of the will, being restricted to the adverbial relation *yes*. As pronominal relation, اي distinguishes things from one another; when this root is employed as verb it expresses in اي or اوي the action of *being fixed* in a determined place, choosing an abode, being united voluntarily to a thing; etc.

אי Every centre of activity, every place distinct, separate from another place. *An isle, a country, a region; where* one is, *where* one acts.

איב (comp.) Every idea of *antipathy, enmity, animadversion*. It is an effect of the movement of contraction upon the volitive centre אי by the sign of interior activity ב.

איד (comp.) A *vapour, an exhalation, a contagion*: that which *is spread* without. See יד.

אי and איה Every exact centre of activity: in a restricted sense, *a vulture, a crow*: in an abstract sense, *where, there where*.

איך (comp.) The restriction of place, of mode; *where* and *in what fashion* a thing acts, represented by the adverbial relations *wherefore? how? thus?* See אך.

איל (comp.) *A ram, a deer*; the idea of force united to that of desire. See אל.

אים (comp.) Every formidable object, every being leaving its nature; *a monster, a giant*. It is the root אי, considered as expressing any centre of activity whatsoever, which assumes the collective sign ם, to express a disordered will, a thing capable of inspiring terror.

אין Absence of all reality. See אן

איש (comp.) Intellectual principle constituting *man*. I shall explain in the notes how the root אי, united to the root אש, has formed the *compound* root איש which has become the symbol of intellectual man.

אית (comp.) Every idea of *constancy, tenacity of will*: that which is *rude, harsh, rough, obstinate*.

אך ACH. This root, composed of the signs of power and of assimilation, produces the idea of every compression, every effort that the being makes upon himself or upon another, to fix him or to be fixed. It is a tendency to make compact, to centralize. In the literal acceptation it is the action of restraining, of accepting. In the figurative and hieroglyphic sense it is the symbol of concentric movement tending to draw near. The contrary movement is expressed by the opposed root הל or אל.

It must be observed as a matter worthy of the greatest attention, that in an abstract sense the root אך represents the adverbial relation *yes*, and the root אל the adverbial relation *no*. The root אָךְ expresses again in the same sense, *but, however, certainly*.

The Arabic اَلْ contains, as the Hebrew אָךְ, all ideas of pressure, compression, vehemence.

אוּךְ   The Arabic اوْك signifies *anger, malice, hateful passion*. The Syriac ܐܘܟܐ is a name of the devil.

אִיךְ   Every idea of intrinsic *quality, mode*, etc.

אַל   AL. This root springs from the united signs of power and of extensive movement. The ideas which it develops are those of elevation, force, power, extent. The Hebrews and Arabs have drawn from it the name of GOD.

אֶל   Hieroglyphically, this is the symbol of excentric force. In a restricted sense, it is that which tends toward an end, represented by the designative or adverbial relations *to, toward, for, by, against, upon, beneath*, etc.

The Arabic اَلْ is employed as the universal designative relation *the, of the, to the*, etc. As verb, it expresses in the ancient idiom, the action of *moving quickly*, going with promptness from one place to another: in the modern idiom it signifies literally, to *be wearied* by too much movement.

אַל and אָלַל (*intens.*) In its excess of extension, it is that which *passes away*, which is *empty, vain;* expressed by the adverbial relations *no, not, not so, nought, nothing;* etc.

אֹהֶל   A raised dwelling, *a tent*.

אוּל   Action of *rising, extending, vanishing, filling* time or space.

אִיל   All ideas of *virtue, courage* or *vigour*, of physical and moral *faculties;* of extensive and vegetative *force: an oak, a ram, a chief, a prince; the door posts, threshold;* etc.

אָם AM. The potential sign united to that of exterior activity; as collective sign it produces a root which develops all ideas of passive and conditional casuality, plastic force, formative faculty, maternity.

אָם Mother, origin, source, metropolis, nation, family, rule, measure, matrix. In an abstract sense it is conditional possibility expressed by the relation *if*. But when the mother vowel א, gives place to the sign of material nature ע, then the root עָם loses its conditional dubitative expression and takes the positive sense expressed by *with*.

The Arabic اٰم contains all the significations of the Hebraic root. As noun it is *mother, rule, principle, origin;* in a broader sense it is *maternity*, the cause from which all emanates, the *matrix* which contains all; as verb, it is the action of *serving as example, as model;* action of *ruling, establishing in principle, serving as cause;* as adverbial relation it is a sort of dubitative, conditional interrogation exactly like the Hebrew אָם; but what is quite remarkable is, that the Arabic root اٰم, in order to express the adverbial relation *with*, does not take the sign of material nature ע before that of exterior activity מ, it takes it after; so that the Arabic instead of saying עָם, says in an inverse manner مَع. This difference proves that the two idioms although having the same roots have not been identical in their developments. It also shows that it is to Phœnician or to Hebrew that the Latin origins must be brought back, since the word *cum* (with) is derived obviously from עָם, and not from مَع.

אִם This modification, not used in Hebrew, signifies in Chaldaic *the basis of things*.

אִים See א.

אָן AN. An onomatopoetic root which depicts the agonies of the soul; pain, sorrow, anhelation.

The Arabic اٰن used as verb, signifies *to sigh, to complain.*

און Every idea of *pain, sorrow, trouble, calamity.*

אן The signs which compose this root are those of power and of individual existence. They determine together the seity, sameness, selfsameness, or *the me* of the being, and limit the extent of its circumscription.

אן In a broader sense, it is the *sphere of moral activity;* in a restricted sense, it is *the body* of the being. One says in Hebrew, אנּי *I;* as if one said *my sameness,* that which constitutes the sum of my faculties, *my circumscription.*

The Arabic اٰن develops in general the same ideas as the Hebrew אן. In a restricted sense this root expresses, moreover, the actual time, *the present;* as adverbial relation it is represented by, *that, but, provided that.*

און When the root אן has received the universal convertible sign, it becomes the symbol of being, in general. In this state it develops the most opposed ideas. It expresses *all* and *nothing, being* and *nothingness, strength* and *weakness, virtue* and *vice, riches* and *poverty;* according to the manner in which the being is conceived and the idea that one attaches to the spirit or matter which constitutes its essence. One can, in the purity of the Hebraic tongue, make these oppositions felt to a certain point, by enlightening or obscuring the mother vowel ו in this manner:

אי the being $\begin{cases} \text{אוֹן } virtue, strength \\ \text{אוּן } vice, weakness \end{cases}$ etc.

אין When the sign of manifestation replaces the convertible sign in the root אן, it specifies the sense; but in a fashion nevertheless, of presenting always the contrary of what is announced as real: so that wherever the word אין is presented it expresses absence.

אִס AS. Root but little used in Hebrew where it is ordinarily replaced by אִשׁ. The Arabic اس presents all ideas deduced from that of *basis*. In several of the ancient idioms the very name of the earth has been drawn from this root, as being the basis of things; thence is also derived the name of *Asia,* that part of the earth which, long considered as the entire earth, has preserved, notwithstanding all its revolutions, this absolute denomination.

The Chaldaic אִסִי has signified in a restricted sense *a physician;* no doubt because of the health whose basis he established. The Syriac, Samaritan and Ethiopic follow in this, the Chaldaic.

אַע AH. Root not used in Hebrew. It is an onomatopoetic sound in the Arabic اٰ, *ah! alas!* used in defending something. The Chaldaic אַע, characterizes vegetable matter.

The Arabic expression واع as a defense, a rejection, gives rise to the compound word اغيه which signifies *an ironical hyperbole.*

אַף APH. Sign of power united to that of speech, constitutes a root, which characterizes in a broad sense, that which leads to a goal, to any end whatsoever; *a final cause.* Hieroglyphically, this root was symbolized by the image of a *wheel.* Figuratively, one deduced all ideas of impulse, transport, envelopment in a sort of vortex, etc.

The Arabic اف is an onomatopoetic root, developing all ideas of disgust, ennui, indignation. In the ancient language it was received in the same sense as the Hebrew אַף, and represented the adverbial relation *why.*

אַף That part of the mind called *apprehension,* or

comprehension. In a very restricted sense, *the nose:* figuratively, *wrath*.

אוף   Action *of conducting to an end, of involving, enveloping* in a movement of rotation; action of *seizing* with the understanding; action of *being impassioned, excited*, etc.

אץ   ATZ. Every idea of bounds, limits; of repressing force, term, end.

The Arabic اص expresses in general, that which is closed and restricted; the central point of things. The Chaldaic אץ contains every idea of pressure and compression. The analogous Arabic root اض in the modern idiom, signifies every kind of doubling, reiteration. In conceiving the root اض as representing the centre, substance, depth of things, one finds, in its redoubling اضاض a very secret, very hidden place; *a shelter, a refuge*.

אוץ Action of *hastening, drawing near, pushing toward* an end.

אק   ACQ. Every idea of vacuity. Root little used in Hebrew except in composition.

The Hebrew word איק signifies literally, *a wild goat;* the Arabic اف as verb, designates that which is nauseous.

אר   AR. This root and the one which follows are very important for the understanding of the Hebraic text. The signs which constitute the one in question here, are those of power and of movement proper. Together they are the symbol of the elementary principle, whatever it may be, and of all which pertains to that element or to nature in general. Hieroglyphically אר was represented by the straight line, and אש by the circular line. אר,

conceived as elementary principle, indicated direct movement, rectilinear; אש relative movement, curvilinear, gyratory.

אר   That which belongs to the elementary principle, that which is *strong, vigorous, productive*.

The Arabic ار offers the same sense as the Hebrew. It is ardour, impulse in general: in a restricted sense, amorous ardour; action of giving oneself to this ardour; union of the sexes.

אר or יאר   That which flows, that which is fluid: *a river*. The Chaldaic אר or איר signfies *air*.

אור   *Fire, heat;* action of *burning*.

אור   *Light;* action of *enlightening, instructing. Life, joy, felicity, grace;* etc.

ארר   (*intens.*) In its excessive force, this root develops the ideas *of cursing, of malediction*.

ארג   (*comp.*) *Tapestry, woven material.*

ארה   (*comp.*) *A gathering, a mass.*

ארז   (*comp.*) *A cedar.*

ארך   (*comp.*) Every *prolongation, extension, slackness.*

ארץ or in Chaldaic ארק (*comp.*) *The earth.*

אש ASH. This root, as the preceding one, is symbol of the elementary principle whatever it may be. It is to the root אר, what the circular line is to the straight line. The signs which constitute it are those of power and of relative movement. In a very broad sense it is every active principle, every centre unfolding a circumference, every relative force. In a more restricted sense it is *fire* considered in the absence of every substance.

אש   The Hebraic genius confounds this root with the root אם, and considers in it all that which is of *the basis* and *foundation* of things; that which is hidden in its principle; that which is *absolute, strong, unalterable;* as the appearance of *fire*.

The Arabic اسٔ designates that which moves with *agility*, vehemence. This idea ensues necessarily from that attached to the mobility of fire אֵשׁ.

אוּשׁ   Action of *founding, making solid, giving force* and *vigour*.

אחשׁ   (comp.) *Power, majesty, splendour.*

אִישׁ   (comp.) *Man.* See אִ.

אֵת ATH. The potential sign united to that of sympathy and of reciprocity, constitutes a root which develops the relations of things to themselves, their mutual tie, their sameness or selfsameness relative to the universal soul, their very substance. This root differs from the root אֶן in what the former designates as the active existence of being, *I*, and what the latter designates as the passive or relative existence, *thee*. אֶן is *the subject*, following the definition of the Kantist philosophers; אֵת is *the object*.

אֵת   That which serves as *character, type, symbol, sign, mark*, etc.

אוּת or אִית   The being, distinguished or manifested by its sign; that which is real, substantial, material, consistent. In the Chaldaic, אִית signifies *that which is*, and לֵית *that which is not*.

The Arabic اتٔ or اتَ indicates as noun, an irresistible argument, supernatural sign, proof; as verb, it is the action of convincing by supernatural signs or irresistible arguments.

ב B. BH. This character, as consonant, belongs to the labial sound. As symbolic image it represents the mouth of man, his dwelling, his interior. As grammatical sign, it is the paternal and virile sign, that of interior and active action. In Hebrew, it is the integral and indicative article expressing in nouns or actions, as I have explained in my Grammar, almost the same movement as the extractive article מ, but with more force and without any extraction or division of parts.

Its arithmetical number is 2.

בא BA. The sign of interior action united to that of power, image of continuity, forms a root, whence is drawn all ideas of progression, gradual going, coming; of passage from one place to another; of locomotion.

The Arabic بٰ indicates in the ancient idiom, a movement of return.

בוא Action of *coming, becoming, happening, bringing to pass;* action of *proceeding, going ahead, entering,* etc.

באר (comp.) That which is *put in evidence, is manifested,* etc.; in its literal sense *a fountain.* See בר.

באש (comp.) That which becomes *stagnant,* which is *corrupt.* See בש.

בב BB. Every idea of interior void, of exterior swelling.

בב *Pupil of the eye.* In Chaldaic, *an opening, a door.*

The Arabic بٜ has the same sense.

בוב Action of being interiorly *void, empty;* every image of *inanity, vacuity.*

בג BG. That which nourishes; that is to say, that which acts upon the interior; for it is here a compound of the root אג united to the sign ב.

The Arabic جٜ expresses in general an inflation, an evacuation; it is in a restricted sense in لٜج, the action of *permitting, letting go.* As onomatopoetic root جٜ characterizes the indistinct cry of a raucous voice.

בד BD. The root אד, which characterizes every object distinct and alone, being contracted with the sign of interior activity, composes this root whence issue ideas of separation, isolation, solitude, individuality, particular existence.

From the idea of *separation* comes that of *opening;* thence that of *opening the mouth* which is attached to this root in several idioms, and in consequence, that of *chattering, babbling, jesting, boasting, lying,* etc.

The Arabic ﺑﻮ signifies literally *middle, between.* As verb, this root characterizes the action of *dispersing.*

בה BH. Onomatopoetic root which depicts the noise made by a thing being opened, and which, representing it *yawning,* offers to the imagination the idea of *a chasm, an abyss,* etc.

בהו *An abyss,* a thing whose depth cannot be fathomed, physically as well as morally. See הה.

The Arabic ﺑﻮ, as onomatopoetic root characterizes astonishment, surprise. The Arabic word ﺑﻬﻮ which is formed from it, designates that which is astonishing, surprising; that which causes admiration. ﺑﻬﺎ signifies to be *resplendent,* and ﺑﻬﻲ *glorious.*

בהט (comp.) *Marble;* because of its weight. See הט.

בהל (comp.) A rapid movement which *exalts,* which *transports,* which *carries one beyond self: frightful terror.* See הל.

בהמ (comp.) Everything which is raised, extended, in any sense; as *a noise, a tumult; a corps, a troop:* it is literally *a quadruped.* See הם.

בהן (comp.) Every *guiding* object; literally *the finger.*

בז BZ. The root אז, which depicts the movement of that which rises to seek its point of equilibrium, being contracted with the sign of interior activity, furnishes all ideas which spring from the preëminence that one assumes over others, of pride, presumption, etc.

The Arabic بَذَ signifies literally, the action of *growing, sprouting, putting forth shoots*.

בּוּז Action of *rising* above others, *despising* them, *humiliating* them: every idea of *disdain*, every object of *scorn*.

בּזז (*intens.*) In its greatest intensity, this root signifies *to deprive* others of their rights, of their property; to appropriate them: thence every idea of *plunder*.

The Arabic بَزَّ has the same sense. The word بَاز signifies a bird of prey, *a vulture*.

בּח BH. This root is used in Hebrew only in composition. The Ethiopic ባሐ (*baha*) signifies every kind of acid, of ferment.

The Arabic بَخ signifies in the modern idiom, *to blow water between the lips*.

בּחל (*comp.*) Fruit which *begins to mature*, which is still *sour*; an *early* fruit; metaphorically, a thing which *annoys*, which *fatigues*.

בּחן (*comp.*) The *test* of a fruit to judge if it is ripe; metaphorically, any kind of *experiment*.

בּחר (*comp.*) *An examination, a proof*; in consequence, that which is *examined, proved, elected*.

בּט BT. The root אט, which depicts a sort of dull noise, of murmuring, being contracted with the sign of interior activity, characterizes that which sparkles, glistens: it is a vapid and thoughtless locution, futile discourse.

The Arabic بَت indicates that which cuts off physically as well as morally. The onomatopoeia بَط, characterizes that which falls and is broken.

בטט (intens.) *A flash of wit; a spark.*

בהר (comp.) *Crystal.* That which throws out brightness, sparks. *An emerald, marble,* etc.

בי BI. Root analogous to the roots בו, בה, בא, which characterize the movement of a thing which advances, appears evident, comes, opens, etc. This applies chiefly to the desire that one has to see a thing appear, an event occur, and that one expresses by *would to God!*

בין (comp.) See ין.

ביר (comp.) See בר.

בית (comp.) See בת.

בֹּךְ BCH. The root אָךְ which develops all ideas of compression, being united to the sign of interior activity, forms the root בֹּךְ, whose literal meaning is *liquefaction, fluxion,* resulting from a somewhat forceful grasp, as expressed by the Arabic بك. Thence בֹּךְ, the action of *flowing, dissolving in tears, weeping.* Every fluid accruing from *contraction,* from *contrition: an overflowing, a torrent, tears,* etc.

The Arabic بك has exactly the same meaning.

בוּךְ State of being afflicted by pain, saddened to tears.

בל BL. This root should be conceived according to its two ways of composition: by the first, the root אל, which designates elevation, power, etc., is united to the sign of interior activity בּ: by the second, it is the sign of extensive movement ל, which is contracted with the root בא, whose use is, as we have seen, to develop all ideas of progression, gradual advance, etc.: so that it is, in the first case, a dilating force, which acting from the centre to the circumference, augments the volume of things, causing a kind of bubbling, swelling; whereas in the second it is the thing itself which is transported or which is overthrown without augmenting in volume.

בל Every idea of *distention, profusion, abundance;* every idea of *expansion, extension, tenuity, gentleness.* In a figurative sense, *spirituality, the human soul, the universal soul, the All,* GOD.

The Arabic بل characterizes in a restricted sense, that which humectates, moistens, lenifies, dampens, and makes fertile the earth, etc.

בלל (*intens.*) From excess of extension springs the idea of *lack, want, neglect, weakness, nothingness:* it is everything which is *null, vain, illusory:* NOTHING.

The Arabic بل is restricted to the same sense as the Hebrew, and is represented by the adverbial relation *without.*

בהל (*comp.*) *An interior emotion, trouble, confusion, extraordinary perturbation.* See בה.

בול Action of *dilating, swelling, boiling, spreading* on all sides: *a flux, an intumescence, a diffusion; an inundation, a general swelling.*

בם BM. The union of the signs of interior and exterior activity, of active and passive principles, constitutes a root little used and very difficult to conceive. Hieroglyphically, it is the universality of things: figuratively or literally, it is every elevated place, every sublime, sacred, revered thing; *a temple, an altar,* etc.

The Arabic بم signifies in a restricted sense the fundamental sound of the musical system called in Greek ὑπάτη. See קב.

בן BN. If one conceives the root בא, which contains all ideas of progression, growth, birth, as vested with the extensive sign ן, to form the root בן, this root will develop the idea of generative extension, of production analogous to the producing being, of *an emanation;* if one considers this same root בֶּן, as result of the contraction of the sign of interior activity בּ with the root אן which characterizes the circumscriptive extent of being, then it would be the symbol of every active production proceeding from potentiality in action, from every manifestation of generative action, from the *me.*

בֶּן   In a figurative sense it is *an emanation*, intelligible or sentient; in a literal sense it is *a son, a formation, an embodiment, a construction.*

The Arabic بن has exactly the same acceptations as the Hebrew.

בָּן   Action of *conceiving,* of *exercising one's conceptive, intellectual faculties;* action of *thinking, having ideas, forming a plan, meditating;* etc.

בִּין   *Intelligence;* that which elects interiorly and prepares the elements for the *edification of the soul.* That which is interior. See ין.

בס   BS. That which belongs to the earth, expressed by the root אס; that which is at the base.

The Arabic بس indicates that which suffices, and is represented by the adverbial relation *enough.*

בוּס   Action of *throwing down, crushing, treading upon, pressing against the ground.*

The Arabic بس signifies the action of *pounding* and of *mixing;* باس contains every idea of force, violence, compulsion.

בע   BHO. Every idea of precipitate, harsh, inordinate movement. It is the root בא, in which the mother vowel has degenerated toward the material sense.

The Arabic بع is an onomatopoetic root which expresses the bleating, bellowing of animals.

בעה An anxious inquiry, a search; a turgescence, a boiling; action of boiling, etc.

The Arabic باع signifies in a restricted sense, *to sell* and *to buy*, to make a negotiation; بع *to interfere* for another, and *to prompt* him in what he should say. The word باع which springs from the primitive root בע, contains all ideas of iniquity and of injustice.

בעט (*comp.*) Action of *kicking*.

בעל (*comp.*) Every idea of domination, power, pride: *a lord, master, absolute superior; the Supreme Being.*

בער (*comp.*) Every idea of *devastation* by fire, *annihilation, conflagration, combustion, consuming heat:* that which *destroys, ravages;* that which makes *desert* and *arid*, speaking of the earth; *brutish* and *stupid*, speaking of men. It is the root ער, governed by the sign of interior activity ב.

בעת (*comp.*) Action of *frightening, striking with terror, seizing suddenly.*

בץ BTZ. Onomatopoetic and idiomatic root which represents the noise that one makes walking in *the mud:* literally, it is *a miry place, a slough.*

The Arabic بص does not belong to the onomatopoetic root בץ; it is a primitive root which possesses all the force of the signs of which it is composed. In a general sense, it characterizes every kind of luminous ray being carried from the centre to the circumference. In a restricted sense it expresses the action of *gleaming, shining;* of *glaring at*. As noun, it denotes *embers*. The Chaldaic בץ, which has the same elements, signifies *to examine, scrutinize, make a search.*

בעץ Action of *wading through* the mud. It is the name given to *flax* on account of its preparation in water.

בַּק BCQ. Every idea of evacuation, of draining. It is the root אק united to the sign of interior action ב.

בּוק Action of *evacuating, dissipating, making scarce*.

The Arabic بَاق signifies *eternal;* بَنى *to eternize.*

בַּר BR. This root is composed either of the elementary root אר, united to the sign of interior activity ב, or of the sign of movement proper ר, contracted with the root בא; thence, first, every active production with power, every conception, every potential emanation; second, every innate movement tending to manifest exteriorly the creative force of being.

בר Hieroglyphically, it is the *radius of the circle* which produces the circumference and of which it is the measure: figuratively, *a potential creation:* that is to say a *fruit* of some sort, whose germ contains in potentiality, the same being which has carried it: in the literal sense, *a son.*

The Arabic بر signifies in a restricted sense, *a continent;* and in a more extended sense, that which is upright.

בּרר (*intens.*) Every extracting, separating, elaborating, purifying movement: that which *prepares* or *is prepared;* that which *purges, purifies,* or which is itself *purged, purified*. Every kind of metal.

The Arabic بر raised to the potentiality of verb, develops the action of *justifying*, of *purifying*.

בּאר (*comp.*) Every idea of *manifestation, explanation:* that which brings to light, that which explores, that which produces exteriorly. In a very restricted sense, *a fountain, a well.*

בּהר (*comp.*) Every idea of *lucidity, clarity.* That which is *candid; resplendent.*

בּוֹר (comp.) Every idea of *distinction, éclat, purity.* In a restricted sense, *wheat.*

בִּיר or בּוֹר (comp.) In a broad sense, *an excavation;* in a restricted sense, *a well;* in a figurative sense, *an edifice, citadel, palace.*

בּשׁ BSH. This root, considered as being derived from the sign of interior activity בּ, united to the root אשׁ which characterizes fire, expresses every idea of heat and brightness: but if it is considered as formed of the root בּא which denotes every progression, and of the sign of relative movement שׁ, then it indicates a sort of delay in the course of proceeding.

The Arabic بس or بش has also these two acceptations. The word باس which belongs to the first, signifies *a violence;* بش, which belongs to the second, signifies *void.*

בּוּשׁ Action of *blushing:* experiencing an inner sentiment of modesty or shame: action of *delaying, diverting one's self,* turning instead of advancing.

בּאשׁ (comp.) That which is *corrupted.* Thence the Chaldaic בּאשׁ, בּוּשׁ or בּישׁא, that which is *bad.*

בּת BTH. Every idea of inside space, place, container, proper dwelling, receptacle, lodge, habitation, etc.

The Arabic بت characterizes a thing detached, cut, pruned, distributed in parts. By بط is understood a sort of *gushing forth;* by بث *a brusque exit, a clashing.*

בּוּת Action of *dwelling, inhabiting, passing the night, lodging, retiring at home;* etc.

בּית A separate and particular place; *a lodge, a habitation;* that which composes *the interior, the family:* that which is *internal, intrinsic, proper, local,* etc.

310   THE HEBRAIC TONGUE RESTORED

גּ G. GH. This character as consonant, belongs to the guttural sound. The one by which I translate it, is quite a modern invention and responds to it rather imperfectly. Plutarch tells us that a certain Carvilius who, having opened a school at Rome, first invented or introduced the letter G, to distinguish the double sound of the C. As symbolic image the Hebraic גּ indicates the throat of man, any conduit, any canal, any deep hollow object. As grammatical sign, it expresses organic development and produces all ideas originating from the corporeal organs and from their action.

Its arithmetical number is 3.

גַא GA. The organic sign ג united to the potential sign א, constitutes a root which is attached to all ideas of aggrandizement, growth, organic development, augmentation, magnitude.

The Arabic ﺟ signifies literally *to come*.

גאה That which *augments, becomes wider, is raised, slackens, increases*, literally as well as figuratively. *Grandeur* of height, *eminence* of objects, *exaltation* of thought, *pride* of the soul, *ostentation;* etc.

גאל (*comp.*) Every idea of *liberation, redemption, release, loosening of bonds:* figuratively, *vengeance* for an offense; metaphorically, the idea of remissness, *defilement, pollution*.

גב GB. The organic sign united by contraction to the root אב, symbol of every fructification, develops, in general, the idea of a thing placed or coming under another thing.

גב *A boss, an excrescence, a protuberance; a knoll, an eminence; the back;* everything convex.

גב or גוב *A grasshopper.* See גו.

גבב (*intens.*) The sign of interior activity being doubled, changes the effect of the positive root and presents the inverse sense. It is therefore every concavity; *a trench, a recess, a furrow:* action of digging a trench, of hollowing; etc.

The Arabic جب presents the same sense as the Hebrew. As verb it is the action of *cutting,* of *castrating.*

גג GG. Every idea of elasticity; that which stretches and expands without being disunited.

The Arabic جّ contains the same ideas of extension.

גג or גוג *The roof* of a tent; that which extends to cover, to envelop.

גד GD. The root גא, symbol of that which augments and extends, united to the sign of abundance born of division, produces the root גד whose use is to depict that which acts in masses, which flocks, agitates tumultuously, assails in troops.

The Arabic جد signifies literally *to make an effort.* In a more general sense جد characterizes that which is important, according to its nature; as adverbial relation this root is represented by *very, much, many.* The verb جاد signifies *to be liberal,* to give generously.

גד *An incursion, an irruption,* literally and figuratively. *An incision* in anything whatsoever, *a furrow;* metaphorically, in the restricted sense, *a kid:* the sign of Capricorn; etc.

גיד *A nerve, a tendon;* everything that can be stretched for action.

גה, גו and גי GHE, GOU and GHI. The organic sign united either to that of life, or to that of universal convertible force, or to that of manifestation, constitutes a root which becomes the symbol of every organization. This root which possesses the same faculties of extension and aggrandizement that we have observed in the root נא, contains ideas apparently opposed to envelopment and development, according to the point of view under which one considers the organization.

The Arabic جَ indicates universal envelopment, *space, atmosphere;* جَ characterizes that which protects.

גהה That which *organizes;* that which gives life to the organs: *health,* and metaphorically, *medicine.*

גוה Every kind of *organ* dilated to give passage to the vital spirits, or closed to retain them: every *expansion,* every *conclusion:* that which serves as *tegument; the body,* in general; *the middle* of things: that which *preserves* them as, *the sheath* of a sword; etc.

גוב (*comp.*) Action of *digging, ploughing.* In a restricted sense, *a scarab.*

גור (*comp.*) Action of making *an irruption.* See גר.

גז (*comp.*) Action of *mowing,* removing with a scythe. See גז.

גוח (*comp.*) Action of *ravishing,* taking by force. See גח.

גוי A political organization; a body of people; *a nation.*

גול (*comp.*) That which brings the organs to development. See גל.

גיל (*comp.*) An organic movement; *an evolution, a revolution.*

גוע (*comp.*) That which *disorganizes;* every *dissolution* of the organic system: action of *expiring,* of being distended beyond measure, of *bursting.*

גוף (*comp.*) Action of *closing.*

גור (*comp.*) Action of *prolonging,* of *continuing* a same movement, a same route; action of *voyaging;* action of living in a same place, dwelling there. See גר.

גּוּשׁ (intens.) See גֵּשׁ.

גַּז GZ. The root אַז, which indicates the movement of that which tends to take away, united to the organic sign, constitutes a root whose use is to characterize the action by which one suppresses, takes away, extracts every superfluity, every growth; thence גָּזַז, the action of *clipping wool, shaving the hair, mowing the grass; taking away* the tops of things, *polishing* roughness.

The Arabic جَزّ has the same meaning as the Hebrew. The verb جَازَ is applied in the modern idiom to that which is allowable and lawful.

גַּח GH. That which is carried with force toward a place, toward a point; that which inclines violently to a thing.

גּוֹחַ Action of *acting with haughtiness, making an irruption, rushing* into a place, *ravishing* a thing.

The Arabic root جَحّ has the same meaning in general; in particular, the verb جَحّ signifies *to swagger*.

גָּחַן (comp.) *An inclination, a defective propensity, a winding course.*

גַּט GT. This root is not used in Hebrew.

The Arabic جَطّ denotes a thing which repulses the effort of the hand which pushes it.

גִּי GHI. Root analogous to the roots גָּה and גוּ.

גַּיְא *Valley, gorge, depth.*

The Arabic جِيَة indicates a place where water remains stagnant and becomes corrupt through standing.

גִּיד (comp.) *A nerve.* See גַּד.

גִּיל (comp.) See גָּה and גַּל.

גִּיר (comp.) That which makes things *endure*, and

preserves them in good condition: in a restricted sense *lime*.

גֵךְ GCH. This root is not used in Hebrew nor in Arabic.

גל GL. This root can be conceived according to its two ways of composition: by the first, it is the root גו, symbol of all organic extension, united to the sign of directive movement ל; by the second, it is the organic sign ג, which is contracted with the root אל, symbol of elevation and expansive force. In the first case it is a thing which is displayed in space by unfolding itself; which is developed, produced, according to its nature, unveiled; in the second, it is a thing, on the contrary, which coils, rolls, complicates, accumulates, heaps up, envelops. Here, one can recognize the double meaning which is always attached to the sign ג under the double relation of organic development and envelopment.

גל That which moves with a light and undulating movement; which manifests joy, grace, and ease in its movements. The revolution of celestial spheres. The orbit of the planets. *A wheel; a circumstance, an occasion*.

That which *is revealed*, that which *appears*, is *uncovered*.

That which *piles up* by rolling: the movement of the waves, *the swell; the volume* of anything whatsoever, *a heap, a pile; the circuit* or *contour* of an object or a place: *its confines*.

The Arabic جل presents the same ideas of unfoldment and aggrandizement, as much in the physical as in the moral: it is also the unfolding of the sail of a ship, as well as that of a faculty of the soul. جل expresses at the same time *the majesty* of a king, *the eminence* of a virtue, *the extent* of anything whatsoever.

גל or גלל (*intens.*) Excessive deployment shown in the idea of *emigration, transmigration, deportation; abandonment* by a tribe of its country, whether voluntarily or by force.

גאל (*comp.*) A *relaxation*, either in the literal or figurative sense. See גא.

גול Action of *unfolding* or of *turning*. Every *evolution* or *revolution*.

גיל An *appearance* caused by the revelation of the object; effect of a mirror; *resemblance*.

גם GM. Every idea of accumulation, agglomeration, complement, height; expressed in an abstract sense by the relations *also, same, again.*

The Arabic جم develops, as does the Hebraic root, all ideas of abundance and accumulation. As verb, it is the action of *abounding, multiplying;* as noun, and in a restricted sense, جام signifies a precious stone, in Latin *gemma.*

גן GN. The organic sign united by contraction to the root אן or און, forms a root from which come all ideas of circuit, cloture, protective walls, sphere, organic selfsameness.

גן That which *encloses, surrounds* or *covers* all parts; that which forms *the enclosure* of a thing; *limits* this thing and *protects it;* in the same fashion that a sheath encloses, limits and protects its blade.

The Arabic جن has all the acceptations of the Hebraic root. It is, in general, everything which covers or which surrounds another; it is, in particular, a protecting *shade, a darkness,* as much physically as morally; *a tomb.* As verb, this word expresses the action of enveloping with darkness, making night, obscuring the mind, rendering foolish, covering with a veil, enclosing with walls, etc. In the ancient idiom جن has signified *a demon, a devil, a dragon;* جنان *a shield;* جنون *bewilderment* of mind; جنين *an embryo* enveloped in the womb of its mother; جنه *a cuirass,* and every kind of *armour;* etc. In the modern idiom, this word is restricted to signify *an enclosure, a garden.*

גס GS. Root not used in Hebrew. The Chaldaic draws from it the idea of that which is puffed up, swollen, become fat. גוס or גיס signifies *a treasure.*

The Arabic جس designates an exploration, a studious research. As verb it is the action of *feeling, groping, sounding.*

גע GH. Root analogous to the root גו, but presenting the organism under its material view point.

The Arabic جع signifies in the modern idiom *to be hungry.* In the ancient idiom one finds جعه for a sort of *beer* or other fermented liquour.

גע Onomatopoetic and idiomatic root which represents the bellowing of an ox.

געה Action of opening the jaw, of *bellowing;* every *clamour,* every *vociferation.*

גוע (*comp.*) Action of *bursting.* See גו.

געל (*comp.*) Action of rejecting from the mouth; every idea of *disgust.*

גער (*comp.*) Every kind of noise, fracas, murmuring.

געש (*comp.*) Action of *troubling, frightening* by clamours and vociferations.

גף GPH. All ideas of conservation, protection, guarantee: in a restricted sense, *a body.*

The Arabic جف develops the idea of dryness and of that which becomes dry. The verb جاف signifies literally, *to withdraw from*.

גוף Action of *enclosing, incorporating, embodying, investing* with a body; that which serves for defense, for conservation.

גץ GTZ. Root not used in Hebrew. The Ethiopic ጋጽ (*gatz*) characterizes the form, the corporeal figure, the face of things. The Arabic جصص signifies *to coat with plaster*, or *to glaze* the interior of structures.

גק GCQ. Root not used in Hebrew. The Arabic جق indicates *excrement*.

גר GR. The sign of movement proper ר, united by contraction to the root of organic extension גא, constitutes a root which presents the image of every iterative and continued movement, every action which brings back the being upon itself.

גר That which assembles in *hordes* to journey, or *to dwell* together; the place where one meets in the course of a journey. Every idea of *tour, detour; rumination; continuity* in movement or in action.

The Arabic جر presents the idea of violent and continued movement. It is literally, the action of *alluring, drawing to one's self, ravishing*. The verb جار signifies *to encroach, to usurp*.

גרר (*intens.*) Duplication of the sign ר, indicates the vehemence and continuity of the movement of which it is the symbol; thence, the analogous ideas of *incision, section, dissection;* of *fracture, hatching, engraving;* of *rumination, turning over in one's mind;* of *grinding*, etc.

גהר (comp.) Every extending movement of the body or of a member of the body. Action of reaching out full length.

גור Action of prolonging, continuing an action. See גנ.

גש GSH. This root represents the effect of things which approach, touch, contract.

גוש Action of *being contracted*, made corporeal, dense and palpable; figuratively, *matter* and that which is obvious to the senses: metaphorically, *ordure, filth*.

The Arabic جش denotes every kind of fracture and broken thing.

גת GTH. That which exercises a force extensive and reciprocally increasing; גת, in a restricted sense, *a vice, a press*.

The Arabic جث expresses the action of *squeezing, pressing in the hand*, etc.

ד D. This character as consonant belongs to the dental sound. It appears that in its hieroglyphic acceptation, it was the emblem of the universal quaternary; that is to say, of the source of all physical existence. As symbolic image it represents the breast, and every nourishing and abundant object. As grammatical sign, it expresses in general, abundance born of division: it is the sign of divisible and divided nature. The Hebrew does not employ it as article, but it enjoys that prerogative in Chaldaic, Samaritan and Syriac, where it fulfills the functions of a kind of distinctive article.

Its arithmetical number is 4.

דא DA. This root which is only used in Hebrew in composition, is the analogue of the root די, which bears the real character of the sign of natural abundance and of division. In Chaldaic it has an abstract sense represented by the relations *of, of which, this, that, of what.*

The Arabic داؤا characterizes a movement which is propagated without effort and without noise.

דאה (*onom.*) Action of *flying with rapidity;* of *swooping down* on something: thence דאה *a kite;* דיה *a vulture.*

דאב (*comp.*) See דב.

דאג (*comp.*) See דג.

דב DB. The sign of natural abundance united by contraction to the root אב, symbol of all generative propagation, constitutes a root whence are developed all ideas of effluence and influence; of emanation, communication, transmission, insinuation.

דב That which *is propagated* and *is communicated* by degrees; *sound, murmur, rumour, discourse; fermentation,* literally and figuratively; *vapour;* that which proceeds slowly and noiselessly: *calumny, secret plot, contagion.*

The Arabic دب develops in general the idea of that which crawls, insinuates itself, goes creeping along.

דאב In a figurative sense, *a dull pain, an uneasiness concerning the future.*

דוב In a restricted sense, *a bear,* on account of its slow and silent gait.

דג DGH. The sign of natural abundance joined to that of organic development, produces a root whose use is to characterize that which is fruitful and multiplies abundantly.

דג It is literally, *the fish* and that which is akin.

דאג (*comp.*) In considering this root as composed of the sign ד, united by contraction to the root אג which represents an acting thing which tends to augment, one finds that it expresses, figuratively, every kind of *solicitude, anxiety, anguish*.

דך DD. Every idea of abundance and division; of propagation, effusion and influence; of sufficient reason, affinity and sympathy.

דד That which is divided in order to be propagated; that which acts by sympathy, affinity, influence: literally *breast, mammal*.

The Arabic جد indicates a pleasing thing, game, or amusement.

דוד Action of *acting by sympathy* and *by affinity;* action of *attracting, pleasing, loving; sufficing mutually*. In a broader sense, *a chosen vessel,* a place, an object toward which one is attracted; every sympathetic and electrifying purpose. In a more restricted sense, *a friend, a lover; friendship, love;* every kind of flower and particularly *the mandragora* and *the violet*.

דה and דו DHE and DOU. See the root ד׳ of which these are the analogues and which bear the real character of the sign ד.

דו DOU. Onomatopoetic and idiomatic root which expresses a sentiment of pain, trouble, sorrow.

דוה Action of *suffering, lamenting, languishing, being weak*.

The Arabic ده, دو, دا offers as onomatopoetic root, the same sense as the Hebraic דו. Thence, in Hebrew as well as in Syriac, Ethiopic and Arabic, a mass of words which depict pain, anguish, affliction; that which is infirm and calamitous. Thence, in ancient Celtic, the words *dol* (mourning), *dull* (lugubrious); in Latin, *dolor* (pain), *dolere* (to feel pain); in the modern tongues, their numberless derivatives.

דהם (*comp.*) That which overwhelms with astonishment; every *sudden calamity,* astounding and stupifying.

דוי and דות *Pain, languor, debility.*

דוי Metaphorically, that which is *sombre, lugubrious, funereal, gloomy; mourning.*

דח DH. Every idea of forced influence, impulsion, constraint.

The Arabic دح contains the same meaning in general.

In particular دحْ is a sort of exclamation to command secrecy or to impose silence upon someone: *hush!*

דחה or דוח Action of *forcing, necessitating, constraining;* action of *expulsion, evacuation;* etc.

דוח That which *constrains.*

דחי *Separation, violent impulsion.*

דחף (*comp.*) Every idea of *excitement.*

דחק (*comp.*) An *impression,* an *extreme oppression.*

דט DT. This root is not used in Hebrew.

The Arabic دط contains the idea of *rejection* and *expulsion.*

די DI. The sign of natural abundance united to that of manifestation, constitutes the true root characteristic of this sign. This root develops all ideas of sufficiency and of sufficient reason; of abundant cause and of elementary divisibility.

דה or די That which is *fecund, fertile, abundant, sufficient;* that which *contents, satisfies, suffices.*

The Arabic دي or ذي indicates, in general, the distribution of things, and helps to distinguish them. In particular, the roots دي, ده or دّ and ذي are represented by the pronominal demonstrative relations *this, that;* etc. The root دو which preserves a greater conformity with the Hebraic root ד׳, signifies literally *possession*.

דִין (*comp.*) That which *satisfies everybody;* that which makes a difference cease; *a judgment*.

דִיק (*comp.*) That which *divides,* that which reduces to pieces. See דק.

דִישׁ (*comp.*) Every kind of *trituration*. See דש.

דַךְ DCH. The sign of natural abundance contracted with the root אך, symbol of concentric movement and of every restriction and exception, composes a root infinitely expressive whose object is to depict need, necessity, poverty and all ideas proceeding therefrom.

The Arabic دق or دك constitutes an onomatopoetic and idiomatic root which expresses the noise made in striking, beating, knocking; which consequently, develops all ideas which are attached to the action of *striking,* as those of *killing, breaking, splitting,* etc. In a restricted sense دق signifies *to pillage;* دك *to ram* a gun; ذق *to push* with the hand.

דַךְ That which is *needy, contrite, sad, poor, injurious, calamitous, vexatious;* etc.

דוּךְ Action of *depriving, vexing* by privation, *oppressing, beating unmercifully;* etc.

דַל DL. This root, conceived as the union of the sign of natural abundance or of divisibility, with the root אל symbol of elevation, produces the idea of every extraction, every removal; as for example, when one draws water from a well, when one takes away the life of a plant; from this idea, proceeds necessarily the accessory ideas of exhaustion and weakness.

RADICAL VOCABULARY

The Arabic دل contains the same sense in general; but in particular, this root is attached more exclusively to the idea of distinguishing, designating, conducting someone toward a distinct object. When it is weakened in ذل it expresses no more than a distinction of *scorn; disdain, degradation.*

דל That which *extracts; to draw* or *to attract* above; that which *takes away, drains;* that which *attenuates, consumes, enfeebles:* every kind of *division, disjunction; emptiness* effected by *extraction;* any kind of *removal.* In a very restricted sense, *a seal;* a vessel for drawing water.

דם DM. The roots which, by means of any sign whatever, arise from the roots אב or אם, symbols of active or passive principles, are all very difficult to determine and to grasp, on account of the extent of meaning which they present, and the contrary ideas which they produce. These particularly demand close attention. It is, at first glance, universalized sympathy; that is to say, a homogeneous thing formed by affinity of similar parts, and holding to the universal organization of being.

דם In a broader sense, it is that which is *identical;* in a more restricted sense, it is *blood,* assimilative bond between soul and body, according to the profound thought of Moses, which I shall develop in my notes. It is that which *assimilates,* which becomes *homogeneous; mingles with* another thing: thence the general idea of that which is no longer distinguishable, which ceases to be different; that which renounces its seity, its individuality, *is identified* with the whole, *is calm, quiet, silent, asleep.*

The Arabic دم has developed in the ancient language the same general ideas; but in the modern idiom this root has received acceptations somewhat different. دم expresses in general a glutinous, sticky fluid. In particular, as noun, it is *blood;* as verb, it is the action of *covering with a glutinous glaze.* From the latter meaning results, in the analogue دَمَ, that of *contaminating, calumniating, covering with blame.*

דוּם State of *universalized being,* that is, having only the life of the universe; *sleeping, being silent, calm;* metaphorically, *taciturn, melancholy.* Action of *assimilating to one's self,* that is, *thinking, imagining, conceiving;* etc.

דן DN. The sign of sympathetic divisibility united to the root אן, symbol of the circumscriptive activity of being, constitutes a root whose purpose is to characterize, in a physical sense, every kind of *chemical parting* in elementary nature; and to express, in a moral sense, every contradictory judgment, resting upon litigious things.

The Arabic دن offers the same sense in general. In particular, ذن expresses a mucous excretion. One understands by دان the action *of judging.*

דוּן Every idea of *dissension;* literally as well as figuratively; every idea of *debate, bestowal, judgment.*

דין A *cause, a right, a judgment, a sentence.*

דם DS. Root not used in Hebrew.

The Arabic دس designates that which is hidden, concealed; which acts in a secret, clandestine manner.

דע DH. Every thing which seeks to expose itself, to appear. This root is not used in Hebrew except in composition. The Arabic ذع characterizes that which pushes, that which puts in motion.

דע or דעה Perception of things, consequently, *understanding, knowledge.*

RADICAL VOCABULARY 325

רֵעַךְ (*comp.*) The root רע united by contraction to the root אך symbol of restriction, expresses that which is no more sentient, that is *extinct, obscure, ignorant.*

דף DPH. Root not used in Hebrew. The Arabic دن or دفا expresses a sort of rubbing by means of which one drives away cold, and is warmed. دف is also in Arabic, an onomatopoetic and idiomatic root, formed by imitation of the noise that is made by a stretched skin when rubbed or struck. The Hebrew renders this root by the analogue תף. We represent it by the words *drum, tympanum; to beat a drum;* etc. In the modern Arabic دف signifies *a tambourine*, and also *a base drum*.

The Chaldaic signifies a thing which is smooth as a board, a table. One finds in Hebrew דפי for *scandal, evil report, shame.*

דץ DTZ. Every idea of joy and hilarity.
The Arabic دس characterizes the action of shaking a sieve.

דוץ Action of living in abundance; transported with joy.

דק DCQ. Every idea of division by break, fracture; that which is made small, slender or thin, by division: extreme subtlety. This root is confounded often with the root רק.

The Arabic دق develops the same ideas.

דור Action of *making slender, subtle;* etc.

דר DR. This root, composed of the sign of abundance born of division, united to the elementary root אר, characterizes the temporal state of things, the age, cycle, order, generation, time. Thence דר, every idea of cycle, period, life, customs, epoch, generation, abode.

דוֹד   Action of *ordering* a thing, *disposing* of it following a certain order; *resting* in any sphere whatsoever; *dwelling* in a place; *living* in an age: that which *circulates*, that which *exists* according to a movement and a regulated order. *An orb, universe, world, circuit; a city.*

דרר   (*intens.*) The broad and generalized idea of circulating without obstacle, of following a natural movement, brings forth the idea of *liberty*, the state of *being free*, the action of *acting without constraint*.

The Arabic در has lost almost all the general and universal acceptations of the Hebrew; this ancient root has preserved in the modern idiom only the idea of a fluxion, of yielding plentifully, particularly in the action of milking.

דש   DSH. Every idea of germination, vegetation, elementary propagation.

דוּשׁ   In a broad sense, action of *giving the seed;* and in a more restricted sense that of *thrashing the grain, triturating.*

The Arabic دش has the same meaning as the Hebrew דוּשׁ.

דת   DTH. Everything issued for the purpose of sufficing, satisfying, serving as sufficient reason.

דת   *A law, an edict, an ordinance.*

In the modern idiom, the Arabic دث is limited to signifying a *shower; a humid, abundant emission: broth.*

ה   E. HE. This character is the symbol of universal life. It represents the breath of man, air, spirit, soul; that which is animating, vivifying. As grammatical sign, it expresses life and the abstract idea of being. It is, in the Hebraic tongue, of great use as article. One can see what I have said in my Grammar under the double relation of determinative and emphatic article. It is needless to repeat these details.

Its arithmetical number is 5.

הא   HA. Every evident, demonstrated and determined existence. Every demonstrative movement expressed in an abstract sense by the relations *here, there; this, that.*

The Arabic ها expresses only an exclamation.

הב   HB. Every idea of fructification and of production. It is the root אב of which the sign of life ה spiritualizes the sense.

הוב   It is again the root אוב, but which, considered now according to the symbolic sense, offers the image of being or nothingness, truth or error. In a restricted sense, it is an exhalation, a vapoury-rising, an illusion, a phantom, a simple appearance; etc.

The Arabic هب characterizes in general, a rising, a spontaneous movement, an ignition. As verb, هب signifies *to be inflamed.*

הג   HEG. Every idea of mental activity, movement of the mind, warmth, fervour. It is easy to recognize here the root אג, which the sign of life spiritualizes.

הג   Every *interior agitation;* that which *moves, stirs, excites; eloquence, speech, discourse; an oratorical piece.*

The Arabic هج conserves of the Hebraic root, only the general idea of an interior agitation. As noun, it is literally *a dislocation:* as verb, it is the action of changing of place, of *expatriation.*

הד HED. Like the root אד, of which it is only a modification, it is attached to all ideas of spiritual emanation, the diffusion of a thing *absolute* in its nature, as the effect of *sound, light, voice, echo.*

The Hebraic root is found in the Arabic هود which is applied to every kind of sound, murmur, noise; but by natural deviation the Arabic root having become onomatopoetic and idiomatic, the verb هد signifies *to demolish, cast down, overthrow,* by similitude of the noise made by the things which are demolished.

הוד Every idea of *éclat, glory, splendour, majesty, harmony,* etc.

הה HEH. This is that double root of life of which I have spoken at length in my Grammar and of which I shall still have occasion to speak often in my notes. This root, which develops the idea of Absolute Being, is the only one whose meaning can never be either materialized or restricted.

הוא In a broad sense, *the Being,* the one who *is;* in a particular sense, *a being;* the one of whom one speaks, represented by the pronominal relations *he, that one, this.*

The Arabic هو has the same meaning.

הוה Preëminently, the verbal root, the unique verb *To be-being.* In an universal sense, it is the *Life of life.*

הוה This root materialized expresses *a nothingness, an abyss of evils, a frightful calamity.*

היה This root, with the sign of manifestation י, replacing the intellectual sign ו, expresses the existence of things according to a particular mode of being. It is the absolute verb *to be-existing.*

היה Materialized and restricted, this same root designates *a disastrous accident, a misfortune.*

הוּ HOU. The sign of life united to the convertible sign, image of the knot which binds nothingness to being, constitutes one of the roots most difficult to conceive that any tongue can offer. It is the potential life, the power of being, the incomprehensible state of a thing which, not yet existing, is found, nevertheless, with *power of existing*. Refer to the notes.

The Arabic roots هي, هه, هو, ها having lost nearly all the general and universal ideas developed by the analogous Hebraic roots, and conserving nothing of the intellectual, with the sole exception of the pronominal relation هو in which some traces are still discoverable, are restricted to the particular acceptations of the root היה, of which I have spoken above; so that they have received for the most part a baleful character. Thus هوه has designated that which is cowardly, weak and pusillanimous; هوي that which is unstable, ruinous; the verb هوي has signified *to pass on, to die, to cease being*. The word هوا which designated originally potential existence, designates only *air, wind, void;* and this same existence, degraded and materialized more and more in هواه has been the synonym of *hell*.

הוּם (comp.) This is the *abyss of existence*, the potential power of being, universally conceived.

The Arabic هو having retained only the material sense of the Hebraic root designates a deep place, an abyss; aerial immensity.

הוֹן (comp.) *Substance, existence; the faculties* which hold to life, to being.

חֵז HEZ. Movement of ascension and exaltation expressed by the root אז, being spiritualized in this one, becomes a sort of mental delirium, *a dream, a sympathetic somnambulism.*

The Arabic مر restricted to the material sense signifies *to shake, to move to and fro, to wag the head;* etc.

הה HEH. Root not used in Hebrew. The Arabic مج indicates only an exclamation.

הט HET. Root not used in Hebrew.

The Arabic هت or هط indicates, according to the value of the signs which compose this root, any force whatsoever acting against a resisting thing. In a restricted sense هت signifies *to menace;* هط *to persevere* in labour; هطا *to struggle;* هطي *struggle.* See אט.

הי HEI. Root analogous to the vital root הה whose properties it manifests.

The Arabic هي represents the pronominal relation *she, that, this.* As verb, this root develops in هيو or هي the action of *arranging,* of *preparing* things and giving them an agreeable form.

היא. See הוא of which this is the feminine: *she, that, this.*

הי Onomatopoetic root expressing all painful and sorrowful affections.

הוי Interjective relation, represented by *oh! alas! ah! woe!*

הך HECH. See the root אך of which this is but a modification.

The Arabic هق expresses a rapid movement in marching; هك indicates, as onomatopoetic root, the noise of the sabre when it cleaves the air. These two words characterize a vigorous action.

הִיךְ See אִיךְ.

הֵל HEL. The sign of life, united by contraction to the root אַל, image of force and of elevation, gives it a new expression and spiritualizes the sense. Hieroglyphically, the root הל is the symbol of excentric movement, of distance; in opposition to the root הך, which is that of concentric movement, of nearness: figuratively, it characterizes a sentiment of cheerfulness and felicity, an exaltation; literally, it expresses that which is distant, ulterior, placed beyond.

The Arabic هل develops in general, the same ideas as the Hebrew. As verb, it is, in particular, the action of *appearing,* of beginning to shine, in speaking of the moon. As adverbial relation it is, in a restricted sense, the interrogative particle.

הל or היל That which is *exalted, resplendent, elevated, glorified, worthy of praise;* that which is *illustrious, celebrated,* etc.

הל and הלל (*intens.*) That which *attains* the desired end, which recovers or gives *health,* which arrives in or conducts to *safety.*

הם HEM. Universalized life: the vital power of the universe. See הו.

הם Onomatopoetic and idiomatic root, which indicates every kind of tumultuous noise, commotion, fracas.

The Arabic هم characterizes, in general, that which is heavy, painful, agonizing. It is literally *a burden, care, perplexity.* As verb, هم expresses the action of *being disturbed,* of *interfering,* of bustling about to do a thing.

הום Action of *exciting a tumult, making a noise,*

disturbing with clamour, with an unexpected crash; every *perturbation, consternation, trembling,* etc.

הן HEN. The sign of life united to that of individual and produced existence, constitutes a root which characterizes existences and things in general; an object, a place; the present time; that which falls beneath the senses, that which is conceived as real and actually exciting.

הן That which is before the eyes and whose existence is indicated by means of the relations, *here, behold,* in this place; *then,* in that time.

The Arabic هن has in general the same ideas as the Hebrew. It is any thing distinct from others; a small part of anything whatsoever. As onomatopoetic and idiomatic root هن expresses the action of *lulling,* literally as well as figuratively.

הון Every idea of actual and present existence: state of *being there,* present and ready for something: *realities, effects of all sorts, riches.*

הם HES. Onomatopoetic and idiomatic root which depicts silence. The Arabic هس seems to indicate a sort of dull murmur, as when a herd grazes in the calm of night.

הע HEH. Root not used in Hebrew. The Arabic هع indicates a violent movement; a sudden irruption.

הף HEPH. This root, which the Hebraic genius employs only in composition, constitutes in the Arabic هف an onomatopoeia which depicts a breath that escapes quickly and lightly. As verb, it is the action of *grazing,* touching slightly, slipping off, etc. See אף.

RADICAL VOCABULARY 333

חֵץ HETZ. The Chaldaic הוּץ signifies *a branch*, and the Arabic هص a thing composed of several others united by contraction.

This root expresses also in the verb هص the action of *gleaming in the darkness,* in speaking of the eyes of a wolf.

חֵק HECQ. The Arabic هق indicates an extraordinary movement in anything whatsoever; an impetuous march, a vehement discourse; a delirium, a transport.

חֵר HER. The sign of life united by contraction to the elementary root אר, constitutes a root which develops all ideas of conception, generation and increase, literally as well as figuratively.

As onomatopoetic root, the Arabic هر depicts a noise which frightens suddenly, which startles. It is literally, the action of *crumbling,* or of *causing to crumble.*

הֹר Conception, thought; pregnancy; a swelling, intumescence, inflation; a hill, a mountain; etc.

חֵשׁ HESH. Root not used in Hebrew. The Arabic هش signifies literally *to soften, to become tender.* As onomatopoetic root, هش indicates a tumultuous concourse of any kind whatsoever.

חֵת HETH. Every occult, profound, unknown existence.

הוּת Action of *conspiring* in the darkness, of *scheming,* of *plotting.*

The Arabic هث expresses the accumulation of clouds and the darkness which results.

ו O. OU. W. This character has two very distinct vocal acceptations, and a third as consonant. Following the first of these vocal acceptations, it represents the eye of man, and becomes the symbol of light; following the second, it represents the ear, and becomes the symbol of sound, air, wind: as consonant it is the emblem of water and represents taste and covetous desire. If one considers this character as grammatical sign, one discovers in it, as I have already said, the image of the most profound, the most inconceivable mystery, the image of the knot which unites, or the point which separates nothingness and being. In its luminous vocal acceptation וֹ, it is the sign of intellectual sense, the verbal sign *par excellence,* as I have already explained at length in my Grammar: in its ethereal verbal acceptation וּ, it is the universal convertible sign, which makes a thing pass from one nature to another; communicating on one side with the sign of intellectual sense וֹ, which is only itself more elevated, and on the other, with that of material sense ע, which is only itself more abased: it is finally, in its aqueous consonantal acceptation, the link of all things, the conjunctive sign. It is in this last acceptation that it is employed more particularly as article. I refer to my Grammar for all the details into which I cannot enter without repeating what I have already said. I shall only add here, as a matter worthy of the greatest attention, that the character ו, except its proper name וו, does not begin any word of the Hebraic tongue, and consequently does not furnish any root. This important observation, corroborating all that I have said upon the nature of the Hebraic signs, proves the high antiquity of this tongue and the regularity of its course. Because if the character ו is really the universal convertible sign and the conjunctive article, it should never be found at the head of a root to constitute it. Now it must not appear, and indeed it never does appear, except in the heart of nouns to modify them, or

RADICAL VOCABULARY 335

between them for the purpose of joining them, **or in front of the verbal tenses to change them.**

The arithmetical number of this character is 6.

The Arabic, Ethiopic, Syriac and Chaldaic, which are not so scrupulous and which admit the character ו at the head of a great number of words, prove by this that they are all more modern, and that they have long since corrupted the purity of the principles upon which stood the primitive idiom from which they descend; this idiom preserved by the Egyptian priests, was delivered as I have said, to Moses who taught it to the Hebrews.

In order to leave nothing to be desired by the amateurs of etymological science, I shall state briefly the most important roots which begin with this character, in the dialects which possess them and which are nearly all onomatopoetic and idiomatic.

וא OUA. Onomatopoetic root which, in the Syriac ܘܐܘܐ expresses the action of *barking*. Thence the Arabic واغ signifies *a hungry dog*.

וב OUB. Every idea of sympathetic production, of emanation, of contagion. The Arabic وبا signifies in a particular sense, to *communicate a plague* or any other contagious malady.

וג OUG. *Aromatic cane.* The Arabic, which possesses this root, is derived from وجل action of *striking*, of *amputating;* of *castrating* animals.

וד OUD. In Arabic ود every idea of *love, friendship, inclination.* It is the sympathetic root דוד.

In the modern idiom ود signifies to *cultivate friendship for some one,* to give evidence of kindness.

וֹה   OUH. In Chaldaic and in Arabic, it is an onomatopoetic root which expresses a violent condition of the soul; واه is applied to a cry of extreme pain; وهوه denotes the roaring of a lion. The verb وهي characterizes that which is torn, lacerated, put to rout.

וֹו   WOU. Is the name itself of the character ו in a broad sense it is *every conversion, every conjunction;* in a restricted sense, *a nail.*

וֹז   OUZ. The Syriac ܐܘܙ signifies literally *a goose.*

The Arabic وز is an onomatopoetic root which represents every kind of excitation. Thence the verbs وز and وهز which signify *to excite,* to act with violence, *to trample under foot,* etc.

יֿח   OUH. Onomatopoetic root which depicts in the Arabic وحوح a *hoarseness of the voice.* The Ethiopic root ወሂ (*whi*) characterizes a sudden emission of light, a manifestation. It is the Hebraic root חוה.

וֹט   OUT. *The sound of a voice, clear and shrill, a cry of terror;* the kind of *pressure which brings forth this cry:* in Arabic وط and وطط.

וֹי   WI. Onomatopoetic root which expresses *disdain, disgust,* in Chaldaic, Syriac and Ethiopic: it is the same sentiment expressed by the interjective relation *fi!*

The Arabic وي has the same sense. In the Ethiopic idiom ወይን (*win*) signifies *wine;* in ancient Arabic وين is found to designate a kind of raisin.

וָךְ   OUCH. Every agglomeration, every movement given in order to concentrate; in Arabic وك

RADICAL VOCABULARY   337

The compound وكوك, signifies properly *a roll*.

וּל OUL. Onomatopoetic root which depicts a drawling and plaintive sound of the voice; in Arabic ولول; in Syriac ܘܠܠܘ. Thence the Arabic وله every idea of sorrow, anxiety of mind. The word وهل which expresses that which holds to *intention, opinion*, is derived from the root אל.

וּם OUM. Every kind of *consent, assent, conformity*.

The Arabic وام signifies *to form, make similar to a model*. It is the root אם.

The verb وما signifies *to make a sign*.

וּן OUN. Every kind of delicacy, corporeal softness, indolence. The Arabic وني signifies *to languish, to become enervated*. The Ethiopic ቶኡፕ (*thouni*) signifies *to be corrupted through pleasures*.

וּס OUS. Onomatopoetic root representing the noise that one makes speaking in the ear: thence, the Arabic وسوس *an insinuation, a suggestion*. When this word is written عوص then it signifies *a temptation of the devil*.

וּע OUH. Onomatopoetic root representing the noise of a violent fire, conflagration; thence, the Ethiopic ⴍሂፕ (*wohi*), action of *inflaming*; the Arabic وع or وعوع *howling; crackling of a furnace; a clamour*, etc.

וּף OUPH. Onomatopoetic root which expresses

a sentiment of pride on the part of one who sees himself raised to dignity, decoration, power. Thence, the Arabic وهف every idea of *exterior ornament, dress, assumed power*.

וץ OUTZ. Every idea of firmness, solidity, consistence, persistence: thence, the Arabic وض which signifies in general, that which resists, and in particular *necessity*.

The verb ض signifies *to vanquish* resistance; also, to make expiation; a religious ablution.

וק OUCQ. Onomatopoetic root to express literally the voice of birds, in Arabic وق and وقرنه : figuratively, that which is made *manifest to the hearing*.

ור OUR. Onomatopoetic root which depicting the noise of the air and the wind, denotes figuratively, that which *is fanned, puffed with wind, vain*. In Arabic وره.

The verb ورور which appears to be attached to the root אר, characterizes the state of that which is sharp, which cleaves the air with rapidity.

וש OUSH. Onomatopoetic root which expresses the confused noise of several things acting at the same time: it is *confusion, diffusion, disordered movement*, in Arabic وشوش .

The verb وشي expresses the action of tinting with many colours, of *painting*.

ות OUTH. Onomatopoetic root which depicts the difficulty of being moved and the moaning which follows this difficulty: thence, in Arabic وث , ونا and وني , all idea of *lesion* in the limbs, *numbness, decrepitude, affliction,* etc.

ז Z. This character as consonant, belongs to the hissing sound, and is applied as onomatopoetic means, to all hissing noises, to all objects which cleave the air. As symbol, it is represented by the javelin, dart, arrow; that which tends to an end: as grammatical sign, it is the demonstrative sign, abstract image of the link which unites things. The Hebrew does not employ it as article; but in Ethiopic it fulfills the functions of the demonstrative article.

Its arithmetical number is 7.

זא ZA. Every idea of movement and of direction; noise, the terror which results therefrom: *a dart; a luminous ray; an arrow, a flash.*

The Arabic زاز indicates, as onomatopoetic root the state of being shaken in the air, the noise made by the thing shaken.

זאב *A wolf*, on account of the luminous darts which flash from its eyes in the darkness.

זאת Demonstrative relation expressed by *this, that*. See זה.

זב ZB. The idea of reflected movement contained in the root זא united by contraction to that of all generating propagation, represented by the root אב, forms a root whose object is to depict every swarming, tumultuous movement, as that of insects; or every effervescent movement as that of water which is evaporated by fire.

The Arabic زب develops the same ideas as the Hebrew. As verb, this root expresses in the ancient idiom, the action of throwing out any excretion, as scum, slime, etc. In the modern idiom it signifies simply *to be dried,* in speaking of raisins.

זוב Action of *swarming as insects; of boiling, seething,* as water.

זג ZG. That which shows itself, acts exteriorly; such as *the bark* of a tree, *the shell* of an egg, etc.

The Arabic زج designates the butt-end of a lance. As onomatopoetic root زهج characterizes a quick, easy movement; زهج, the neighing of a horse.

זד ZD. That which causes effervescence, excites the evaporation of a thing; every idea of arrogance, pride.

זוד Action of *boiling*, literally; of *being swollen, puffed up with pride*, figuratively, *to act haughtily*.

זה, זו, זוה ZHE, ZOU, ZO. Every demonstrative, manifesting, radiant movement: every objectivity expressed in an abstract sense by the pronominal relations *this, that, these, those.*

The Arabic زو expresses the action of shedding light, of shining.

זאת *This, that.*

זה That which *is shown, appears, shines, reflects the light;* in an abstract sense, *an object.*

זהב (*comp.*) *Gold,* on account of its innate brightness.

זהם (*comp.*) That which is loathsome.

זהר (*comp.*) That which *radiates communicates, manifests the light.* See אור.

זו Absolute idea of *objectivity;* everything from which light is reflected.

זוית (*comp.*) *A prism;* by extension, *the angle* of anything whatsoever.

זול (*comp.*) Action of *diverging;* by extension, *wasting, neglecting.* See זל.

זון (*comp.*) *Corporeal objectivity.* See זן.

זוע (*comp.*) See זע.

זור (*comp.*) Every idea of *dispersion.* See זר.

זז ZZ. Every movement of vibration, reverberation; every luminous refraction.

The Arabic زز as onomatopoetic root develops the same ideas. The verb زوزي denotes the conduct of an arrogant man.

זוז Action of *vibrating*, being *refracted* as the light, *shining*.

זיז *Splendour, reflection* of light, *luminous brightness*.

זח ZH. Every difficult movement made with effort; that which is done laboriously; a presumptuous, tenacious spirit.

The Arabic زح develops the same ideas. The verb زخ expresses in general a vehement action of any nature whatsoever; in particular to *rain in torrents*.

זט ZT. Root not used in Hebrew. The Arabic زط is an onomatopoetic root which depicts the noise made by insects when flying.

זחל (*comp.*) That which is difficult to put in movement, slow in being determined. That which *drags, creeps;* which is *heavy, timid,* etc.

זי ZI. Root analogous to roots לא, הי, וז; but whose sense is less abstract and more manifest. It is in general, that which is light, easy, agreeable; that which is sweet, gracious; that which shines and is reflected as light. Every idea of grace, of brightness.

The Arabic زي develops in general, all ideas which have relation with the intrinsic qualities of things. As noun زي characterizes the form, aspect, manner of being; as verb زيي expresses the action of assuming an aspect, of being clothed in form, of having quality, etc.

זִיו In Chaldaic, *splendour, glory, majesty, joy, beauty*: in Hebrew it is the name of the first month of spring.

זִיז (*comp.*) *An animal;* that is to say, a being which reflects the light of life. See זו.

זִין (*comp.*) *An armour:* that is to say a resplendent body. The Arabic زان signifies *to adorn*.

זִיק (*comp.*) *A flash of lightning, a quick, rapid flame, a spark,* etc.

זִית (*comp.*) *An olive tree, the olive* and *the oil* which it produces; that is to say, *the luminous essence*.

זָךְ ZCH. The demonstrative sign united by contraction to the root אָךְ, symbol of all restriction and exception, constitutes an expressive root whose purpose is to give the idea of that which has been pruned, cleaned, purged, disencumbered of all that might defile.

זָךְ Every *purification*, every refining test; that which is *clean, innocent*, etc.

The Arabic زك contains the same ideas. As noun زكي designates that which is pure, pious; as verb, زكا characterizes the state of that which abounds in virtues, in good works.

זָל ZL. The demonstrative sign united to the root אַל, symbol of every elevation, of every direction upward, forms a root whence are developed all ideas of elongation, prolongation; consequently, of attenuation, weakness; also of prodigality, looseness, baseness, etc.

זוּל Action of *wasting, profaning, relaxing;* of rendering *base, weak, feeble,* etc.

In a restricted sense the Arabic verb زل signifies *to stumble*, to make false steps.

זִם ZM. That which gives form, figure; that which binds many parts together to form a whole.

The Arabic زم contains the same ideas. As onomatopoetic and idiomatic root, it is in the Arabic زمزم a dull noise, a rumbling.

זִם *A system, a composition, a scheme*: every work of the understanding, good or bad: *a plot, a conspiracy*, etc.

זִן ZN. The demonstrative sign united to the root אִן, symbol of the moral or physical circumscription of the being, constitutes a root which develops two distinct meanings according as they are considered as mind or matter. From the view point of mind, it is a moral manifestation which makes the faculties of the being understood and determines the kind; from that of matter, it is a physical manifestation which delivers the body and abandons it to pleasure. Thence:

זִן Every classification by *sort* and by *kind* according to the faculties: every pleasure of the body for its *nourishment*: figuratively, all *lewdness, fornication, debauchery: a prostitute, a place of prostitution*, etc.

The Arabic زن expresses a sort of suspension of opinion in things of divers natures. As onomatopoetic root زن , describes a *murmuring*.

זוּן Action of *being nourished, feeding* the body; or metaphorically the action of enjoying, making abuse, *prostituting* one's self.

זִס ZS. Root not used in Hebrew nor in Arabic.

זִע ZH. This root, which is only the root זִה or זוּ, inclined toward the material sense, develops the idea of painful movement, of agitation, anxiety; of trouble caused by fear of the future.

In a restricted sense the Arabic زاغ signifies to act like a fox, to use round about ways.

זוע   Action of *being troubled, fearful, trembling* in expectation of misfortune. Action of *being tormented, disquieted.*

זעה   *Trouble, agitation of mind, fatigue;* that which is the consequence, *sweat.*

זעם   (*comp.*) *Violent* and *general* agitation; that which results, *foam*: figuratively, *rage indignation.*

זעף   (*comp.*) Tumult of irascible passions; *tempest, storm;* etc.

זעק   (*comp.*) Great visible commotion: *outburst of voices, clamour, loud calling.*

זער   (*comp.*) *Ebbing, waning*: *diminution, exiguity;* that which is *slender, moderate, small.*

זף   ZPH. That which is sticky, gluey; that which exercises a mutual action; literally, *pitch.*

It is, in the Arabic زف, an onomatopoetic root which denotes the effect of a puff of wind. The verb زفي expresses the action of being carried away by the wind.

זוף   Action of *being attached*, of experiencing a mutual, reciprocal sentiment.

זץ   ZTZ. Root not used in Hebrew nor in Arabic.

זק   ZCQ. Every idea of diffusion in time or space.

The Arabic زق as onomatopoetic root denotes the action of *pecking.*

זק   *A chain, suite, flux; a draught* of anything whatsoever. That which *spreads, glides, flows* in space or time. Thence, *years, old age,* and the veneration which is attached to it: *water* and the purity which ensues: *a chain* and the strength which attends it; *an arrow,* etc.

In a restricted sense, the Arabic زق signifies *a leather bottle* wherein one puts any kind of liquid. It is doubtless the Hebrew word שׂק or the Chaldaic סק, *a sack*.

זר ZR. The demonstrative sign united to that of movement proper, symbol of the straight line, constitutes a root which develops the idea of that which goes from the centre, spreads, disperses in every sense, radiates, leaves a sphere, or any enclosure whatsoever and becomes foreign.

זר Every *dispersion, dissemination, ventilation*: that which is abandoned to its own movement, which goes from the centre, *diverges*: in a broad sense, *a stranger, an adversary, a barbarian*: in a more restricted sense, *a fringe, a girdle*.

The Arabic زر having lost all the primitive ideas contained in this root, has preserved only those which are attached to the word *girdle* and is restricted to signifying the action of *girding, tying* a knot, *binding*, etc.

זור Action of being *disseminated, separated from* the centre, *abandoned* to its own impulsion; considered as *estranged, alienated, scorned, treated as enemy;* action of *sneezing*, etc.

זש ZSH. Root not used in Hebrew. The Arabic زوش signifies *a lout, a boorish fellow;* lacking manners and politeness.

זת ZTH. Every objective representation expressed by the pronominal relations *this, that, these, those*.
זעת *This, that*.

ח E. H. CH. This character can be considered under the double relation of vowel or consonant. As vocal sound it is the symbol of elementary existence and represents the principle of vital aspiration: as consonant it belongs to the guttural sound and represents the field of man, his labour, that which demands on his part any effort, care, fatigue. As grammatical sign it holds an intermediary rank between ה, life, absolute existence, and כ, life, relative and assimilated existence. It presents thus, the image of a sort of equilibrium and equality, and is attached to ideas of effort, labour, and of normal and legislative action.

Its arithmetical number is 8.

חא HA. Root is analogous with the root חו, which bears the real character of the sign ח. This is used more under its onomatopoetic relation, to denote the violence of an effort, a blow struck, an exclamatory cry.

חב HEB. The sign of elementary existence united to the root אב, symbol of all fructification, forms a root whose purpose is to describe that which is occult, hidden, mysterious, secret, enclosed, as a germ, as all elementary fructification: if the root אב is taken in its acceptation of desire to have, the root in question here, will develop the idea of an amorous relation, of fecundation.

This is why the Arabic حب taken in a restricted sense, signifies *to love;* whereas in a broader sense this root develops all ideas of grain, germ, semence, etc.

חב or חבב (*intens.*) *To hide mysteriously, to impregnate, to brood,* etc.

In a restricted sense, the Arabic حاب signifies *to become partial, to favour.* As onomatopoetic root حب suggests the noise of whetting a sabre.

חוב (*comp.*) One who hides, who keeps the property of another; *a debtor.*

חג HEG. Every hard and continued action; every turbulent movement: every transport of joy; joust, game, popular fête, tournament, carousal.

חג or חגג (*intens.*) Every idea of *fête,* of *solemnity,* where all the people are acting.

It is, in the Arabic ‎حج‎ , the action of visiting a holy place, going on a pilgrimage; in ‎خج‎ , that of *trotting.*

חוג Action of *whirling, dancing in a ring, devoting one's self to pleasure, celebrating the games.* Metaphorically, *an orbit, a circumference, a sphere of activity, the terrestrial globe.*

חד HED. The power of division, expressed by the root אד which, arrested by the effort which results from its contraction with the elementary sign ה, becomes the image of relative unity. It is literally, *a sharp thing, a point, a summit.*

The Arabic ‎حد‎ presents in general, the ideas of *terminating, determining, circumscribing, limiting.* It is, in a more restricted sense, *to grind;* metaphorically, *to punish.* This root being reinforced in the verb ‎خد‎ , expresses the action of breaking through and excavating the ground. As noun, ‎خد‎ signifies literally *the cheek.*

חד *The point* of anything whatever. Everything which *pricks,* everything which is *extreme, initial:* metaphorically, *a drop* of wine; *gaiety,* lively and piquant.

חוד Action of *speaking cleverly, uttering witticisms,* giving *enigmas.*

חיד *Enigma, parable.*

חה HEH. This root, analogue of the root הא, is little used. The characteristic root of the sign is הו.

חו HOU. Elementary existence in general; in particular, that which renders this existence manifest and obvious; that which declares it to the senses.

In the analogue ‎حو‎ , this root has not conserved the

intellectual ideas of the Hebrew; but being reinforced in خو , it has presented what is most profound in elementary existence, *chaos*.

חוה and חוי All ideas of *indication, elementary manifestation, declaration;* action of *uncovering* that which was hidden, etc.

    חוב (*comp.*) See חב.

    חוג (*comp.*) See חג.

    חוד (*comp.*) See חד.

    חוז (*comp.*) *The horizon.* See חז.

    חוח (*comp.*) Action of *hooking*. See חח.

    חוט (*comp.*) Action of *mending, sewing*. See חט.

    חול (*comp.*) See חל.

    חום (*comp.*) See חם.

    חום (*comp.*) Action of *sympathizing, condoling.* See חם.

חוץ (*comp.*) That which is *exterior*, or which *acts exteriorly;* that which leaves the ordinary limits and which, in an abstract sense is expressed by the relations *beyond, outside, extra, except,* etc.

    חור (*comp.*) See חר.

    חוש (*comp.*) See חש.

חז HEZ. The sign of elementary existence, united to that of demonstration, or of objective representation, forms a very expressive root whose purpose is to bring forth all ideas of vision, visual preception, contemplation.

The Arabic خ in losing all the intellectual acceptations of the Hebraic root, has conserved only the physical ideas which are attached to it as onomatopoetic root, and is limited to designating any kind of notch, incision; metaphorically, scrutiny, inspection. The verb خز signifies literally *to pierce*.

RADICAL VOCABULARY 349

זה   Action of *seeing, regarding, considering, contemplating;* the aspect of things; *a seer, a prophet, one who sees.*

חזה   (*intens.*) *A vision; a flash of lightning.*

חוז   Extent of the sight, *the horizon; boundaries, the limits* of a thing; *a region.*

חה   HEH. Every idea of effort applied to a thing, and of a thing making effort; *a hook, fish-hook, ring; a thorn-bush.*

חוה   That which is *pointed, hooked;* that which exercises any force whatever, as *pincers, hooks, forceps:* thence the Arabic verb حاق , *to penetrate, to go deeply into.*

חט   HET. The sign of effort united to that of resistance, constitutes a root whence come all ideas of frustrated hope; of failure, sin, error.

The Arabic حـ signifies properly *to cut in small morsels;* and حـط , *to pose, depose; place, replace: to lower, humble, reduce,* etc.

חט or חטט (*intens.*) That which *misses* the mark, which is *at fault,* which *sins* in any manner whatsoever.

חוט (*comp.*) The root חט, symbol of effort united to resistance, being considered from another viewpoint, furnishes the restricted idea of *spinning,* and in consequence, every kind of *thread,* and of *sewing;* so that from the sense of *sewing,* comes that of *mending;* metaphorically, that of *amendment, restoration:* whence it results that the word חטא, which signifies *a sin,* signifies also *an expiation.*

חי   HEI. Elementary life and all ideas thereunto attached. This root is the analogue of the root הי.

חיה   Action of *living* in the physical order, action of *existing:* that which *lives;* every kind of *animal, living being, beast.* Physical life, the *animality* of nature.

The Arabic ع develops every idea contained in the Hebraic root.

חיל (*comp.*) *Vital force;* that which maintains, procures, sustains existence: *elementary virtuality; the physical faculties,* literally as well as figuratively: *power* which results from force; *virtue* which is born of courage; *an army,* that which is *numerous, valorous, redoubtable; a fort, fortress, rampart; a multitude,* etc.

חֵךְ HECH. The sign of elementary existence united to that of assimilative and relative existence, forms a root which is related to all perceptions of judgment and which develops all interior ideas.

The Arabic root حك, having lost nearly every moral idea which comes from the primitive root and being confined to purely physical ideas, is limited to express as noun, *an itching, a friction;* and as verb, the analogous action of *itching, scratching.*

חֵךְ That which grasps forms inwardly and which fixes them, as the sense of *taste;* that which is *sapid; sensible to savours; the palate, throat:* that which *covets, desires, hopes,* etc.

חל HEL. This root, composed of the sign of elementary existence united to the root אל, symbol of extensive force and of every movement which bears upward, produces a mass of ideas which it is very difficult to fix accurately. It is, in general, a superior effort which causes a distention, extension, relaxation; it is an unknown force which breaks the bonds of bodies by stretching them, breaking them, reducing them to shreds, or by dissolving them, relaxing them to excess.

חל Every idea of *extension, effort* made upon a thing to *extend, develop, stretch* or *conduct* it to a point or end: *a twinge, a pain: a persevering movement; hope, expectation.*

The Arabic ﺣﻞ develops, in general, all the ideas contained in the Hebraic root. In a restricted sense it is the action of *loosening, relaxing, releasing, resolving, absolving*, etc. When this root receives the guttural reinforcement, it expresses in ﺧﻞ, the state of privation, indigence; that which lacks, which is wanting in any manner whatsoever.

חל and חלל (*intens.*) *Distention, distortion, contortion; endurance, solution of continuity; an opening, a wound: extreme relaxation, dissolution; profanation, pollution; weakness, infirmity, debility; vanity, effeminate dress, ornament; a flute; a dissolute dance, a frivolous amusement;* etc.

חול or חיל Action of *suffering* from the effect of a violent effort made upon one's self; action of *being twisted, stretched,* action of *being confined, bringing into the world; being carried* in thought or action *toward an end; producing* ideas: action of *tending, attending, hoping, placing faith in* something; action of *disengaging, resolving, dissolving, opening, milking, extracting,* etc.

חיל (*comp.*) *Elementary virtuality.* See 'ח.

חם HEM. The sign of elementary existence, symbol of every effort and every labour, united to the sign of exterior activity, and employed as collective and generalizing sign, forms an important root whose purpose is to signify, in a broad sense, a general envelopment and the warmth which results, considered as an effect of contractile movement.

חם Idea of that which is *obtuse; curved, hot, obscure; enveloping, striking; a curvature; dejection; a compressive force: natural heat, solar fire, torrefaction* and *the burnish* which follows; *blackness:* that which *heats,* literally or figuratively; *generative ardour, amorous passion, wrath,* etc.

The Arabic حم , having lost to a certain point, the intellectual ideas developed by the Hebraic root, is limited to expressing the particular ideas of warmth and heating; when reinforced by the guttural aspiration in خم , it signifies literally *to be corrupted, spoiled, putrefied.*

חום Action of *enveloping, seizing* by a contractile movement, *exercising* upon something *a compressive force; heating; rendering obscure.* In a restricted sense, *a wall,* because it *encloses;* a *girdle,* because it *envelops;* in general, every *curved, round* figure; *simulacrum of the sun,* etc.

חן HEN. The composition of this root is conceived in two ways, according to the first, the sign ח, which characterizes every effort, every difficult and painful action, being contracted with the onomatopoetic root אן, image of pain, expresses the idea of a prayer, a supplication, a grace to grant or granted: according to the second, the same sign, symbol of elementary existence, being united to that of individual and produced existence, becomes a sort of reinforcement of the root חן, and designates all proper and particular existences whether in time or space.

חן That which results from *prayer;* as *grace, a favour;* that which is *exorable,* which allows itself *to relent;* that which is *clement, merciful, full of pity:* that which is *easy, a good bargain,* etc.

The Arabic حن develops, as the Hebraic root, all ideas of kindness, mercy, tenderness, clemency. This root in reinforcing itself in خن designates separation, seclusion; it is, literally, a place for travellers, *a hostelry.* As onomatopoetic root, خن expresses the action of *speaking through the nose.*

חן Every separate intrenched place: *a cell, a hospice, a fort, a camp.* Action of *living apart,* having one's own residence, being *fixed, intrenched,* and consequetly *to besiege, to press* the enemy, etc.

חם HES. Every silent, secret action; that which is done with connivance; that which is confided, trusted or said secretly.

חום Action of *conniving* at a thing, of *sympathizing;* of *conspiring:* a place of refuge, *a shelter,* etc. It is also the action of making effort upon one's self, of experiencing an interior movement of *contrition.*

The diverse acceptations of the Hebraic root are divided in the analogous Arabic words خس , حص , حس and خص, in which they modify themselves in diverse manners. Considered as verb, حس signifies *to feel,* to have the sensation of some thing; حص *to act with celerity;* خس *to diminish* in volume, *to be contracted, shrunken;* خص *to particularize,* etc.

חע HEH. Root not used in Hebrew. The Arabic خوع indicates a grievous and painful sensation.

חף HEPH. Every idea of protective covering given to a thing; a guarantee, a surety.

The Arabic حف is an onomatopoetic and idiomatic root, which depicts that which acts upon the surface, which skims, passes lightly over a thing. The verb خف characterizes the condition of that which becomes light; خاف anything which shivers, shudders with fear, trembles with fright, etc.

חוף Action of *covering, protecting, brooding, coaxing. A roof, nest, shelter, port:* action of separating from that which *harms;* of *combing, appropriating,* etc.

חֵץ HETZ. Every idea of division, scission, gash, cut; that which acts from the exterior, as the adverbial relation חוּץ expresses, *outside*.

The Arabic حض signifies *to stimulate;* and خض *to keep stirring, to agitate.*

חץ That which divides by making irruption, passing without from within: *an arrow, an obstacle; a stone coming from the sling; an axe, a dart: a division* of troops; *a quarrel;* etc.

חֹק HECQ. Every idea of definition, impression of an object in the memory, description, narration; that which pertains to symbols, to characters of writing. In a broader sense matter used according to a determined mode.

חק The action of *defining, connecting, giving a dimension, deciding upon forms;* of *hewing, cutting* after a model; *to carve, to design:* a thing *appointed, enacted, decreed, constituted,* etc.

The Arabic حق develops, in general, the same ideas as the Hebraic root; but is applied more particularly to that which confirms, verifies, certifies; to that which is true, just, necessary.

חֵר HER. The sign of elementary existence united to that of movement proper, symbol of the straight line, constitutes a root which develops, in general, the idea of a central fire whose heat radiates. It is in particular, a consuming ardour, literally as well as figuratively.

The Arabic حر has exactly the same meaning. When this root is reinforced by the guttural aspiration in خر it is no longer applied to the expansion of heat, but to that of any fluid whatsoever. In a restricted sense خر signifies *to ooze.*

חר and חרר (*intens.*) That which *burns* and *consumes*, that which is *burned* and *consumed;* that which is *arid, desert, barren;* every kind of *residue, excrement: the mouth* of a furnace, *the entrance* of a cavern; etc.

חור Action of *consuming* by fire; *setting fire, irritating:* the ardour of *fever,* that of *wrath;* effect of *the flame,* its brilliancy; *the blush* which mounts to the face; *candour;* every *purification* by fire; etc.

חרע (*comp.*) That which is *sharp, cutting, acute, stinging, destructive.*

חש HESH. Every violent and disordered movement, every inner ardour seeking to extend itself; central fire; avaricious and covetous principle; that which is arid.

The Arabic حش develops in general, the same ideas as the Hebrew. As onomatopoetic root, حش expresses the action of *chopping, mowing;* when it is reinforced by the guttural aspiration, it signifies, in the verb خش , *to penetrate.*

חוש Action of *acting with vehemence* upon something; every *vivacity; avidity; aridity.* This root, taken in the latter sense of *aridity,* is applied metaphorically, to that which is *barren,* which produces nothing; to *mutes;* to those who do not speak, who keep *silent.*

חת HETH. This root contains all ideas of shock, terror, sympathetic movement which depresses and dismays. It is, in general, the reaction of useless effort; elementary existence driven back upon itself; in particular, it is a *shudder, consternation, terror; a sinking, a depression; a degradation,* etc.

The Arabic حث has not conserved the moral ideas developed by the Hebraic root. It is, as onomatopoetic root, an exciting, instigating, provocative movement.

ט T. This character, as consonant, belongs to the dental sound. As symbolic image it represents the shelter of man; the roof that he raises to protect him; his shield. As grammatical sign it is that of resistance and protection. It serves as link between ד and ת, and partakes of their properties, but in an inferior degree.

Its arithmetical number is 9.

טא TA. Every idea of resistance, repulsion, rejection, reflection; that which causes luminous refraction.

The Arabic طب develops the idea of every kind of bending, inflection. Thence the verb طبل, *to bow down*.

טאם. (*intens.*) Action of *repulsing* a dart, as from a shield; of *making hail rebound*, as from a roof; etc.

טב TB. The sign of resistance united to that of interior action, image of all generation, composes a root which is applied to all ideas of conservation and central integrity: it is the symbol of healthy fructification, and of a force capable of setting aside every corruption.

The Arabic نب or طب, has, in general, the same sense as the Hebrew. In a restricted sense, نب signifies *to amend;* طب , *to supply* the want, the lack of anything whatsoever; *to become well, to be healed,* etc.

טוב That which keeps a just mean; that which is *well, healthy;* that which defends itself and resists corruption; that which is *good*.

טג TG. Root not used in Hebrew. The Arabic طج indicates a violent shock, a warlike cry.

By نج is understood, that which declares force, audacity, pride. In a restricted sense تاج signifies *a crown, a mitre*.

RADICAL VOCABULARY 357

טד TD. Root not used in Hebrew. The Arabic طاد seems to indicate a thing strong and capable of resistance.

טה TEH. Root analogous to the root טא. It is only used in composition. The Arabic طه as interjection, inspires security.

In a restricted sense, the verb طبا or طهو signifies to *dispose of* and *prepare* a thing in such a way as to render it useful.

טהר (*comp.*) That which is *pure*. See טר.

טו TOU. That which arrests, which opposes resistance. See טא.

The Arabic طو is used as adverbial relation to impose silence upon someone. ڋ signifies literally *an hour*.

טוב (*comp.*) That which is *good*. See טב.

טוה Every kind of *thread*, of *spinning: a net*.

טוח Action of *placing in safety, guaranteeing, covering, inlaying: a covering, an inlay, a coat of plaster;* etc.

טול (*comp.*) Action of *projecting*, especially *the shadow*. See טל.

טור (*comp.*) Action of *disposing,* putting in order. See טר.

טוש (*comp.*) Action of *flying away, disappearing.* See טיש.

טז TZ. Root not used in Hebrew. Appears only in Arabic through wrong usage.

טח TEH. Every idea of a stroke hurled or repulsed; metaphorically, *a calumny, an accusation*.

The Arabic طح expresses as onomatopoetic root, the

action of repulsing with the foot. This root reinforced by the guttural aspiration, signifies in طَح to be obscured, made dense, thick; in طَح, to be lessened.

טַט TT. Root not used in Hebrew. The Chaldaic טַט, is sometimes taken to express the number *two*.

The Arabic طَى appears to designate putrid slime, offensive mire.

טִי TI. Root analogous to the root טָא, and which like it, expresses every kind of reflection as is indicated by the following:

טִיט (*intens.*) That which *gushes forth;* that which *splashes*, as *mud, slime, mire;* etc. Figuratively, *the earth*.

The Arabic طى signifies properly *to bend, to give way, to be soft*.

טַךְ TCH. Root not used in Hebrew. The Chaldaic is used to signify *a siege*.

As onomatopoetic root the Arabic طق depicts the noise of that which explodes.

טַל TL. The sign of resistance united by contraction to the root אַל, symbol of every elevation, composes a root whose object is to express the effect of a thing which raises itself above another thing, covers, veils, or puts it under shelter.

The Arabic طل contains in general, all the ideas developed by the Hebraic root.

טַל That which *casts a shadow*, that which *is projected* from above below; that which *varies, changes, moves* like a shadow: *a veil, a garment* with which one is covered; *a spot* which changes colour; *the dew* which forms a veil over plants; *an unweaned lamb* still under the shelter of its mother.

RADICAL VOCABULARY

The Arabic طل has many divers acceptations like the Hebrew, all of which can, however, be reduced to the primitive idea of a thing emanating from another, as *dew, shade;* metaphorically, *length, duration,* etc. In a restricted sense نل signifies *to raise up;* طل *to continue.*

טם TM. Every idea of contamination, of anathema; that which is impure and profane.

The Arabic طم has lost, in general, the primitive ideas contained in the Hebraic root. In a restricted sense, this word signifies simply *to throw dust.*

טום Action of *separating as impure,* of *anathematizing;* every kind of *impurity, pollution, vice, filthiness.*

טן TN. Everything woven in a manner to form a continuous whole, as a *screen, trellis, pannier, basket.*

As onomatopoetic and idiomatic root, the Arabic نن or طن denotes every kind of tinkling, resounding noise. It is from the idea of persistence developed by the Hebraic root, that is formed the Arabic verb ظن, *to presume, to believe,* to regard as certain.

טס TS. Root not used in Hebrew. The Chaldaic טס signifies *a plate* of any kind whatsoever: the Arabic طس denotes very nearly that sort of receptacle called *cup* or *bowl* in English.

As verb طس, signifies in the vulgar idiom *to put in a sack; to be settled, effaced.*

טע TOH. Every idea of obstinacy and persistence in an evil manner. This root is the analogue of the root טא, but more inclined toward the material sense.

טע The *tenacity,* the *hardness* of an evil character: *obstinacy.*

The Arabic طُعْ presents the same ideas as the Hebrew. The verb طَغَا signifies literally *to err, to behave badly.*

טַעַם (comp.) That which is attached to *sensuality of taste; to sensation, to the knowledge* which results: figuratively, a good or bad *habit, custom: reason, judgment.*

טַעַן (comp.) *To charge, to load* someone with *burdens; to fix* in a place, *to nail:* metaphorically *to overwhelm.*

טָף TPH. Everything which struggles, which stirs incessantly; which goes and comes without stopping; which persists in its movement.

The Arabic طَفّ develops in a broad sense the idea of that which is impending, which can happen, occur. In a very restricted sense, طَفّ signifies *to pour out,* as onomatopoetic root تَفّ, indicates the action of *spitting.*

טַף In a figurative sense, *a child;* anything whatsoever floating in the air or upon the water: *a swimmer; a palm branch,* etc.

טַע TOH. Root not used in Hebrew nor in Arabic.

טַק TCQ. Root not used in Hebrew. The Arabic طَقّ , is an onomatopoetic root which depicts the noise of stones crushed beneath the feet of horses, or that of frogs croaking upon the banks of pools, or that which produces a harsh, rough utterance.

טַר TR. The sign of resistance united by contraction to the elementary root אר, as image of fire, forms a root which develops all ideas of purification, consecration, ordination.

The Arabic طَرّ has lost nearly all the ideas developed by the Hebraic root; so that restricting it to physical forms, this root characterizes an abrupt, unexpected movement, a fortuitous thing, an incidence; etc.

טהר (*comp.*) That which is *pure, purified, purged* of its impurities.

טור (*comp.*) That which *is conducted* with *purity,* with *rectitude;* that which maintains *order; clarity.*

טש TSH. Root not used in Hebrew. The Chaldaic expresses a change of place; to hide and take away from sight.

The Arabic ط is an onomatopoetic root which depicts the noise of falling rain, the simmering of boiling oil, etc.

טת TTH. Root not used in Hebrew. The Arabic ط is an onomatopoetic root which depicts the noise of a top spinning; thence, the name of various games for children and several other related things.

י I. This character is the symbol of all manifested power. It represents the hand of man, the forefinger. As grammatical sign, it is that of potential manifestation, intellectual duration, eternity. This character, remarkable in its vocal nature, loses the greater part of its faculties in becoming consonant, where it signifies only a material duration, a refraction, a sort of link as ז, or of movement as ש.

Plato gave particular attention to this vowel which he considered as assigned to the female sex and designated consequently all that which is tender and delicate.

The Hebraist grammarians who rank this character among the *héémanthes,* attribute to it the virtue of expressing at the beginning of words, duration and strength; but it is only a result of its power as sign.

I have shown in my Grammar what use the idiomatic

genius of the Hebraic tongue made of the mother vowel י, in the composition of compound radical verbs as initial adjunction.

Its arithmetical number is 10.

יא **IA.** This root manifests the potential faculties of things.

The Arabic ﻴ expresses, as adverbial or interjective relation, all the movements of the soul which spring from admiration, astonishment, respect; *o! oh! ah!*

יאה That which is *suitable, worthy, conformable* with the nature of things, *specious, decent;* that which has *beauty, elegance,* etc.

יאב (*comp.*) That which desires ardently. See אב.

יאל (*comp.*) Every idea of proneness, inclination: that which aspires, tends toward an object. See אל.

יאור (*comp.*) *A river.* See אר.

יב **IB.** Onomatopoetic root which describes the yelping of a dog. Figuratively it is *a cry, howl, vociferation*. The Ethiopic ያበ (*ibbe*) signifies *jubilation*.

יג **IG.** Every idea of fatigue, languor, sadness, as result of long continued action. See אג.

The Arabic ﻴﻮج indicates an overwhelming, stifling heat.

יד **ID.** The sign of potential manifestation, united to the root אד, image of every emanation, of every divisional cause, forms a remarkable root, whose purpose is to produce ideas relative to the hand of man.

The Arabic ﺪ presents exactly the same ideas as the Hebrew.

יד In the literal and restricted sense, *the hand;* in the figurative and general sense, it is the *faculty, executive force, power of acting, dominion:* it is every kind of *aid, instrument, machine, work, term; administration, liberality, faith, protection:* it is the symbol of *relative unity,* and of the *power of division;* it is *the margin, boarder, edge;* the point by which one grasps things; it is *the place, the point* that one indicates, etc.

יאד (*comp.*) Every idea of power and of force: that which is irresistible in good as in evil: *fate, destiny, necessity.*

יד or ידד (*intens.*) Action of *throwing, hurling* with the hand; of *issuing, sending;* of *spreading, divulging,* etc.

יה IEH. Absolute life manifested, Eternity, the eternally living Being: GOD.

The Arabic به has lost all the intellectual ideas developed by the Hebraic root, but the Syriac ܗܘ and the Samaritan ᛞᛗ, signify alike *the Absolute Being.* By the word يَهِ is understood only a sort of call.

יהב (*comp.*) Action of being fruitful, manifesting fruits; *a litter, a burden.* Action of bearing, producing. See אב and הב.

יהוד (*comp.*) Divine emanation, *God-given:* it is the name of the Jewish people, or that of *Judah,* from which it is derived.

יו IO. Every luminous manifestation; everything intelligible.

This root no longer exists in Arabic in its primitive simplicity. It is found only in the Coptic word Ioh to designate *the moon;* it is rather remarkable that the same Arabic word بوح, designates *the sun.* This last word, in receiving the guttural aspiration in بوخ , signifies literally *the day,* and is used sometimes in place of يوم.

יום (*comp.*) The luminous, continued, universalized manifestation: *day.* See י׳.

The Arabic يَوْم has conserved none of the intellectual ideas contained in the Hebrew. As noun, it is, in a restricted sense, *a day*; as verb, *to fix a day, to adjourn*.

יון (*comp.*) The being, passing from power into action: *the manifested being*. See און. In a broader sense, *the generative faculty of nature, the plastic force*: in a more restricted sense, a thing indeterminate, tender, soft, easy, suitable to receive all forms; clayey, ductile land; *a mire*; etc.

יז IZ. Root not used in Hebrew nor in Arabic.

יזם (*comp.*) *To mediate, to think*. See זם, and also the other positive roots which receive the initial adjunction in large numbers.

יח IHE. Root not used in Hebrew nor in Arabic.

יחד (*comp.*) Manifestation of unity; action of *being united*, state of being *one, unique, solitary*. See חד.

יחל (*comp.*) Every idea of *tension, attention, expectation*; action of *suffering, having anxiety, hoping*, etc. See חל

יחם (*comp.*) Action of *being heated, burned*, literally and figuratively. See חם.

יחף (*comp.*) *To be barefooted*. See חף.

יחש (*comp.*) Every idea of *origin, source, race*. See חש. It is considered here as central principle.

יט IT. Root not used in Hebrew.

יי II. Manifestation of all spiritual power, of all intellectual duration. In a more restricted sense, the mind.

יי In Chaldaic, it is the name of the Eternal; that by which one finds translated the *Ineffable Name* יהוה the interpretation of which I have given in my notes. This name is often written in the Targum ייי, *the Spirit of Spirits, the Eternity of Eternities*.

RADICAL VOCABULARY 365

יּן֞ (*comp.*) *Incorporated spirit:* in a restricted sense, every spirituous liquor, *wine*.

יָךְ ICH. Manifestation of restriction; that is to say, the place wherein things are restricted, *the side*.

The Arabic does not rightfully possess this root; the Arabic words which are here attached are derived from the Persian یَك, which signifies *one*.

יל IL. Every idea of emission and of prolongation.

The Arabic يَل is applied only to teeth and to their different forms.

יֹל Action of *filling the air with cries; a lively song; a jubilation*.

יִם IM. The sign of manifestation united to that of exterior action as collective sign, composes a root whose purpose is to indicate universal manifestation and to develop all ideas of mass and accumulation.

The intellectual force of this root is weakened in Arabic, since this idiom has not conserved the characterization of the plurality of things as in Hebrew. It is the root יִן, whose expression is much less forceful, which has replaced it; also, the manner of forming the plurals of nouns with numberless anomalies and irregularities, has become one of the greatest difficulties of the Arabic tongue.

יָם In a literal and restricted sense, *the sea;* that is to say, the universal aqueous manifestation, the mass of waters.

As noun, the Arabic عَ, signifies *the sea*, and as verb, *to submerge*. This word is preserved in the Coptic ΦIOM, and appears not to be foreign to the Japanese *umi*.

יוֹם (*comp.*) *Day;* that is to say, *universal luminous manifestation*. See יּ.

יִן IN. The sign of manifestation united to that of individual and produced existence, composes a root whence are developed all ideas of particular manifestation and of individual being: thence the accessory ideas of particularity, individuality, property.

The Arabic بن has preserved scarcely any of the intellectual ideas developed by the Hebrew. This ancient root, however, still forms the plural of masculine nouns in Arabic, as in Chaldaic and Syriac, but it is often changed into ان following the usage of the Samaritans, and more often disappears entirely allowing this same plural to be formed in the most irregular manner.

יִן That which manifests *individual sentiment, existence proper, interest*: that which is relative to *a determined centre*, to *a particular point;* that which *draws to itself, appropriates, envelops, involves* in its vortex; *deprives, oppresses* others for its own interest: every *internal movement*, every *desire for growth*.

יוֹן (comp.) *Generative faculty* of nature, *plastic force:* in a restricted sense, *a dove,* symbol of fecundating warmth.

יִם IS. Root not used in Hebrew. The Arabic يس appears to indicate a movement of progression.

יִע IOH. Everything hollow, empty and fit to receive another, as *a vessel, a shovel,* etc.

The Arabic يع as onomatopoetic root, depicts the cry of one who wishes to catch something, or seize it with the hand.

יָעַד (comp.) Every kind of *convention, appointing* the day, place, time for *an assembly, a fête, a resolution*. See עַד.

יָעַז (comp.) That which is *rough, steep*. See עַז.

RADICAL VOCABULARY

יעט (comp.) That which *covers, envelops*, as a garment. See עט.

יהל (comp.) Every thing which *is raised;* which *grows, augments, profits.* See עט.

יעף (comp.) Every movement which *tires, fatigues.* See עף.

יעץ (comp.) Every kind of *consultation, deliberation*: every thing which tends to *fix upon a point, to determine.* See עץ.

יער (comp.) That which *surrounds, defends* a thing, as *the covering* of the kernel, *bark* of the tree, *skin* of the body: *a forest, a thicket of trees, to protect, to preserve a habitation,* etc. See ער.

יף IPH. The sign of manifestation united to that of speech, constitutes a root which is applied to all ideas of beauty, grace, charm, attraction.

The Arabic يف is only preserved in the composition of words as in طريف *beautiful,* طرينه *beauty,* etc.

יץ ITZ. Root not used in Hebrew; but it expresses every idea of progeny and propagation in the Arabic إضض which signifies *to grow,* in speaking of plants; in the Syriac مومرl it designates a tribe, a nation.

יק ICQ. Every idea of obedience and subjection.

The Arabic بق characterizes literally that which is white.

יר IR. Every idea of respect, of fear, of reverence, of veneration.

The Arabic ير signifies a thing which is polished, smooth, without roughness, but firm, as crystal. It is also a thing of igneous nature; but in this case the Arabic word يَعِرّ is applied to the root אוּר

יֵשׁ ISH. The sign of manifestation joined to that of relative movement, or by contraction with the elementary root אש, produces a root whence come all ideas of reality, substantiality: in general, it is the substantial, effective being; in particular, an old man. This root often expresses the state *of being, of appearing like,* of being manifested in substance.

This root is not preserved in Arabic in its original purity; it has become onomatopoetic and idiomatic like many others; the verb بَشّ has signified in a restricted sense, *to leap, gambol, give way to joy.*

יִת ITH. Root not used in Hebrew; but in Chaldaic, in the Syriac ܠ, in the Samaritan ࡀࡔࡎ, it expresses always the essence and objective nature of things. See אֵת.

כ CH. KH. This character as consonant, belongs to the guttural sound. As symbolic image it represents every hollow object, in general; in particular, the hand of man half closed. As grammatical sign, it is the assimilative sign, that of reflective and transient life: it is a sort of mould which receives and communicates indifferently all forms. This character is derived, as I have already said, from the aspiration ה, which comes from the vocal principle ה, image of absolute life; but here it joins the expression of organic character ג, of which it is a sort of reinforcement. In Hebrew, it is the assimilative and concomitant article. Its movement in nouns and actions is similitude and analogy. The Hebraist grammarians, since they have neither included it among the *héémanthes* nor among the *paragogics,* have committed the grossest errors;

they have merely regarded it as an inseparable article or an affix, and often have confused it with the word that it governs as article.

Its arithmetical number is 20.

כא CHA. Every idea of assimilated existence, of formation by contraction; that which is compact, tightened, condensed to take some sort of form.

The Arabic ك develops, in general, the same ideas as the Hebraic root. In a restricted sense, this root is represented in English by the adverbial relations *thus, the same, such as*, etc. It is remarkable that this character ك , as sign, fulfills in the Arabic idiom, the same functions as the Hebrew כ. As onomatopoetic root ك expresses the clucking of the hen; metaphorically, the action of *gathering together*, as a hen her chickens; or again, the state of being timid, chicken-hearted.

כאב (*comp.*) *A moral heaviness;* an interior repression; every pain which is caused by a restrained and *repressed desire.*

כאה (*comp.*) Action of being *repressed interiorly*, of leading *a sad life, restricted, afflicted, painful.*

כב CHB. Every idea of centralization; that which draws near the centre; which gravitates there.

The Arabic ك characterizes in general, that which carries from above below, precipitates, pours out, throws down, sinks, goes down. As onomatopoetic root قب signifies *to cut*. This root used in music designates the fundamental sound, the keynote.

כג CHG. Root not used in Hebrew. The Arabic ك seems to indicate a sort of movement executed upon itself in spiral line. In particular it is a certain game for children.

כד CHD. That which partakes of relative unity, isolation, division. In a restricted sense *a spark, a fragment*.

The Chaldaic כד is represented in a restricted sense, by the adverbial relation *when*. The Arabic كد signifies in general, to act in one's own interest, to work for self; in particular, *to be industrious, to intrigue, to be fatigued, tormented*.

כה CHE. Root analogous to the root כא, but whose expression is spiritualized and reinforced by the presence of the sign ה.

כה That which is conformable to a given model; that which coincides with a point of space or time, which can be conceived in an abstract sense, by the adverbial relations *yes, thus, like this; that; in that very place; at that very time*, etc.

The Arabic كه having lost all the ideas attached to the Hebraic root or having concentrated them in the primitive sign ك or ه , has become an onomatopoetic root depicting an oppressed respiration either by old age, by illness, or by excess of drinking.

כהה (*intens.*) From the idea of an excess of restriction, comes that of *fright, weakness, pusillanimity; contrition; dimming of the eyes; dizziness, faintness*, etc.

כהל (*comp.*) Every *value*. See הל.

כהן (*comp.*) Every administration, distinguished function; literally, *priesthood, pontificate; a priest*, a man raised in dignity to special supervision. See כן.

כו CHOU. Every assimilating, compressing, restraining force: the natural faculty which fetters the development of bodies and draws them back to their elements. Root analogous to the root כא, but modified by the presence of the convertible sign ו.

RADICAL VOCABULARY   371

The Arabic root كَ has certainly developed the same universal ideas in the ancient idiom; but in the modern, it is restricted to characterize a sort of cauterization. The idea of combustion, of burning is expressed in particular, by the root كِي , and by the word كَوِي is understood in general, that which is strong, vigorous, violent, extreme.

כֹּה Action of arresting the scope of vegetation; *repressing bodies*, *shrivelling* them by burning; *reducing them to ashes*.

כּוֹי or כּוִיה   *Combustion;* that which *roasts, burns; corrodes*.

כּוֹח (*comp.*) That which holds to *the central force;* that which depends upon *igneous power;* that which after being centralized is unbound like *a spring;* in general it is *the virtual faculty* of the earth.

כּוֹל (*comp.*) That which *seizes* and *agglomerates*. See אל.

כּוּן (*comp.*) See כן.

כּוּר (*comp.*) *A furnace*.

כּוּשׁ (*comp.*) See כשׁ.

כֹּז CHZ. Root not used in Hebrew. The Arabic كَزّ indicates everything which is contracted in itself, shrivelled.

In a restricted sense كَزّ signifies *to be disgusted*.

כֹּח CHEH. Root not used in Hebrew. In Syriac, ܟܗ is onomatopoetic, expressing the effort made in retaining one's breath.

The Arabic كَحّ , being the reinforcement of the root كَ , characterizes the state of an asthmatic person, or of one worn out with old age.

כחד (*comp.*) Action of *retaining* a thing, *hiding* it, *concealing* it carefully.

כחל (*comp.*) Action of *disguising* a thing, *smearing* it.

כחש (*comp.*) Action of *denying* a thing, *lying*.

כט CHT. Root not used in Hebrew. The Arabic كظ, expresses the action of *gorging with food* to the point of being unable to breathe. Figuratively, it is to fill beyond measure, to overpower with work. In the modern idiom كظ signifies *bushy hair*.

כי CHI. Manifestation of any assimilating, compressing force. See כא, כה, and כו.

The Arabic كي signifies in a restricted sense, *a burn*.

כי The force expressed by this root is represented in an abstract sense, by the relations *that, because, for, then, when,* etc.

כיד (*comp.*) Everything which compresses strongly, which *crowds*, which *presses*: literally, *armour; a scourge*.

כיל (*comp.*) That which is covetous, tenacious; *a miser*.

כיס (*comp.*) Constellation of the *Pleiades;* because of the manner in which the stars cluster.

כיס (*comp.*) A *purse* filled with money; *a casket*.

כיף (*comp.*) A *rock;* a thing hard and strong, of *compressed* substance.

כך CHKH. Root not used in Hebrew. The Chaldaic כך signifies nothing more than the Hebrew כה.

The Ethiopic ከሐ (*caćh*) is an onomatopoetic root which denotes the cry of a crow.

כל CHL. This root expresses all ideas of apprehension, shock, capacity, relative assimilation, consummation, totalization, achievement, perfection.

The Arabic كل develops in general, the same ideas of complement, totalization, as the Hebrew; but in leaving its source, it inclines rather toward the totalization of evil than toward that of good; so that in the Arabic idiom كل is taken figuratively, for excess of fatigue, height of misfortune, extreme poverty, etc. This root being reinforced by the guttural aspiration, offers in زلج, a meaning absolutely contrary to the primitive sense of accumulation, and designates the state of that which diminishes, which is lessened.

כֹּל That which is *integral, entire, absolute, perfect, total, universal*: that which *consumes, concludes, finishes, totalizes* a thing; that which renders it *complete, perfect, accomplished;* which *comprises, contains* it, in determining its *accomplishment: the universality* of things; their *assimilation, aggregation, perfection; the desire* of possessing; *possession; a prison: the consumption of foods,* their *assimilation* with the substance of the body, etc.

כֹּל Action of *totalizing, accomplishing, comprising, universalizing, consummating,* etc.

כֹּם CHM. Every tension, inclination, desire for assimilation. The Arabic كم signifies *how much*.

The root كم, as verb, signifies to know the quantity of some thing, or to fix that quantity.

כֵּן CHN. This root, wherein the assimilative sign is united to the root אן, image of all corporeal circumscription, is related to that which enjoys a central force energetic enough to become palpable, to form a body, to acquire solidity: it is in general, the base, the point upon which things rest.

The Arabic كن has not differed from the Hebraic root in its primitive origin; but its developments have been different. The intellectual root הוה *to be-being*, almost entirely lost in Arabic, has been replaced by the physical root כן ; so that in the Arabic idiom the word كون, which should designate only material, corporeal existence, *substance* in general, signifies *being*. This substitution of one root for another has had very grave consequences, and has served more than anything else to estrange Arabic from Hebrew.

כן That which holds to *physical reality, corporeal kind; stability, solidity, consistency;* a *fixed, constituted, naturalized* thing: in a restricted sense, *a plant:* in an abstract sense, it is the adverbial relatives, *yes, thus, that, then*, etc.

The Arabic كان, in consequence of the reasons explained above, characterizes the state of that which is, that which exists, or passes into action in nature. This root which, in Arabic, has usurped the place of the primitive root הוה, signifies literally *it existed*. It can be remarked that the Samaritan and Chaldaic follow the sense of the Hebraic root, whereas the Syriac and Ethiopic follow that of the Arabic.

כון Action of *constituting, disposing, fixing, grounding;* action of *strengthening, affirming, confirming;* action of *conforming, qualifying* for a thing, *producing* according to a certain mode, *designating* by a name, *naturalizing,* etc.

כס CHS. Every idea of accumulation, enumeration, sum.

כס *The top; the pinnacle* of an edifice; *a throne*.

The Arabic نص expresses in general, the action of removing the superficies of things; in particular, that of *clipping, cutting* with scissors. The onomatopoetic root كس

expresses the idea of utmost exertion, and the Arabic noun كس *pudendum muliebre.*

כוס Action of *numbering, calculating; accumulating, carrying to the top; filling up, covering,* etc.

כע CHOH. Root not used in Hebrew. The Chaldaic indicates in an onomatopoetic manner, the sound of spitting.

The Arabic كع develops only ideas of baseness, cowardice.

כעם (*comp.*) Action of being *indignant, vexed; provoking, irritating* another.

כף CHPH. Every idea of curvature, concavity, inflection; of a thing capable of containing, holding: in a restricted sense, palm of the hand, sole of the foot, talons, claws of an animal, a spoon; that which curves like a sleeve, a branch: that which has capacity, like a stove, a spatula, etc.

The Arabic كنف contains exactly the same ideas as the Hebraic root. As verb, and in a figurative sense, كنف signifies to *preserve, defend, keep.*

כוף Action of *bending, being inflected, made concave,* etc.

כץ CHTZ. Root not used in Hebrew. The Arabic كص appears to signify a sort of undulatory movement as that of water agitated.

This root being doubled in كصكص indicates a movement extremely accelerated.

כר CHR. The assimilative sign united to that of movement proper ר, or by contraction with the elementary root אר, constitutes a root related in general, to that which is apparent, conspicuous; which serves as monument, as distinctive mark: which engraves or serves to engrave; which hollows out, which preserves the memory of things in any manner whatsoever; finally, that which grows, rises, is noticeable.

The Arabic ک has certainly developed the same general sense as the Hebraic root, in its primitive acceptation; but in a less broad sense, the Arabic root is limited to expressing the action of *returning* on itself, on its steps; *reiterating* the same movement, *repeating* a speech, etc.

כר Every kind of *character, mark, engraving;* every distinctive object: leader of a flock, *a ram;* leader of an army, *a captain:* every kind of excavation; *a furrow, ditch, trench,* etc.

כיר A *round vessel, a measure.*

כש CHSH. This root is applied in general to the idea of a movement of vibration which agitates and expands the air.

The Arabic کش signifies literally to *shrivel up, to shrink* in speaking of the nerves: *to shorten.*

כוש (*comp.*) That which is of the nature of fire and communicates the same movement. Figuratively, that which is *spiritual, igneous.*

כת CHTH. Every idea of retrenchment, scission, suspension, cut, schism.

כות Action of *cutting, carving, retrenching, excluding, separating, making a schism,* etc.

The Arabic کت presents exactly the same sense in general. In particular, کت signifies *to shrink;* by کت is understood the action of *curling the hair.*

RADICAL VOCABULARY 377

ל L. This character as consonant, belongs to the lingual sound. As symbolic image it represents the arm of man, the wing of a bird, that which extends, raises and unfolds itself. As grammatical sign, it is expansive movement and is applied to all ideas of extension, elevation, occupation, possession. It is, in Hebrew, the directive article, as I have explained in my Grammar, expressing in nouns or actions, a movement of union, dependence, possession or coincidence.

Its arithmetical number is 30.

לא LA. This root is symbol of the line prolonged to infinity, of movement without term, of action whose duration is limitless: thence, the opposed ideas of being and nothingness, which it uses in developing the greater part of its compounds.

The Arabic ل develops the same ideas as the Hebraic root. In a restricted sense ل is represented by the negative adverbial relations *no, not*. The verb لل signifies literally to *shine, sparkle, glisten*.

לוֹא or לא It is in general, an indefinite expansion, an absence without term expressed in an abstract sense by the relations, *no, not, not at all*. Definite direction, that is to say, that which is restrained by means of the assimilative sign כ, is opposed to it. See כה or כן.

לאה It is in general, *an action without end;* in its literal sense, a labour which *fatigues, wearies, molests*.

לאט (*comp.*) Action of *covering, hiding*. See לט.

לאך (*comp.*) Action of *despatching, delegating*. See לך.

לאם (*comp.*) A nation. See לם.

לב LB. The expansive sign united by contraction to the root אב, image of every interior activity, every appetent, desirous, generative force, constitutes a root whence emanate all ideas of vitality, passion, vigour, courage, audacity: literally, it is *the heart,* and figuratively, all things which pertain to that centre of life; every quality, every faculty resulting from the unfolding of the vital principle.

לב *The heart,* the centre of everything whatsoever from which life radiates; all dependent faculties: *courage, force, passion, affection, desire, will; sense.*

The Arabic لـ participates in the same acceptations as the Hebraic root.

ליב Action of *showing force, developing vital faculties, moving with audacity, animating, making vigorous, germinating,* etc.

להב (comp.) *Ardour, flame, vital fire,* literally as well as figuratively.

לג LG. Every idea of liaison, of intimate, complicated thing; *of litigation.* The meaning of the Arabic جـ is similar and signifies literally *to insist, to contest.* The Hebrew לג presents in the figurative, symbolic style, the measure of extent, *space.*

לד LD. The expansive sign, joined to that of abundance born of division, or by contraction with the root אד, image of every emanation, composes a root whose purpose is to express every idea of propagation, of generation, of any extension whatsoever given to being.

The Arabic جد expresses in general the same ideas as the Hebraic root. In a restricted sense it is, to *make manifest, to put forward, to discuss.* The verb جد characterizes the state of that which is relaxed, put at ease; to enjoy one's self, to delight in, etc.

לד That which *is born, generated, propagated, bred:*

progeny, increase of family, race, lineage: confinement, childbirth, etc.

לה LEH. This root, analogue of the root לא contains the idea of a direction given to life, of a movement without term.

Thence the Arabic لَ which signifies properly GOD. In a more materialized sense, the word لَ designates that which is refined, softened, become beautiful, pure, elegant.

להה Every idea of indeterminate action, of insupportable fatigue; *frenzy.*

להב (*comp.*) Every desirous movement; every projection into vacuity: *a flame* of any sort whatsoever.

להג (*comp.*) Keen disposition to study, desire to learn: in a figurative sense, *a system, a doctrine.*

להט (*comp.*) That which *is inflamed, takes fire, burns* for something.

להם (*comp.*) To universalize an expansive movement, to render it sympathetic; *to electrify, inspire, propagate;* etc.

לו or לי LOU or LI. Every idea of liaison, cohesion, tendency of objects toward each other. The universal bond. The abstract line which *is conceived* going from one point to another and which is represented by the relations, *oh if! oh that! would to God that!*

The Arabic لَ has not preserved the ideas contained in the primitive root as those have which are represented by the adverbial relations *if, if not, though.* The verb لَ, which is attached to the root לה or لَ, signifies to make divine power shine forth, *to create;* to give vital movement to matter. It is to the sense of *radiating* which is contained in this root, that one applies the word لؤلؤ *a pearl*.

לוה Action of being *adherent, coherent,* united by *mutual ties,* by *sympathetic movement:* every *adjunction, liaison, copulation, conjunction, addition,* etc.

לוז (*comp.*) That which *cedes, gives way, bends.* See לז.

לוח (*comp.*) That which is *polished, shining.* See לח.

לוט (*comp.*) To *hide, envelop.* See לט.

לוי (*comp.*) *Addition, supplement.*

לוך (*comp.*) That which is *detached, disunited;* figuratively, that which *drags, is dirty, soiled.* See לך.

לון (*comp.*) See לן.

לוע (*comp.*) Action of *swallowing.* See לע.

לוץ (*comp.*) See לץ.

לוש (*comp.*) See לש.

לז LZ. Every movement directed toward an object to show it, and expressed in an abstract sense by the relations *this, that.*

The Arabic ل has preserved the physical developments more than the Hebraic root; for one finds there all the acceptations which have relation to things coming together, their collision, clashing, etc.

לח LH. Every movement directed toward elementary existence and making effort to produce itself, to make its appearance.

The Arabic ح develops in general, all ideas of cohesion, of contraction, and retains only the physical and material acceptations of the Hebraic root.

לח Natural vigour; innate movement of vegetation; *radical moisture:* that which is *verdant, young, moist, fresh;* that which is *glowing* with youth, beauty, freshness; that which is *smooth, soft* to the touch; etc.

לחך (*comp.*) Action of *licking, sucking, polishing.*

לחם (*comp.*) That which serves as *food* to elementary life: action of *subsisting,* of *being fed:* every idea of *alimentation; consumption* of anything whatsoever.

לחץ (*comp.*) A *hostile incursion, public misfortune, oppression.* See חץ.

לחש (*comp.*) A *magic incantation, an enchantment: a talisman.* See לש.

לט LT. The directive sign united to that of protective resistance, composes a root which contains all ideas of seclusion, envelopment, mystery, hiding place. See לאט and לוט.

The Arabic ل characterizes, in general, that which agglutinates, makes sticky, etc. The verb ل signifies properly *to knead,* and in the figurative sense, ل indicates the action of *sullying, compromising, contaminating.*

לי LI. Root analogous to roots לו, לה, לא.

The Arabic ل designates literally a pliant, flexible thing.

ליל (*comp.*) That which renders things adherent, binds, envelops them: *night.* See לל.

ליש (*comp.*) A *lion.* See לש.

לך LCH. The extensive sign united to the root אך, image of every restriction, constitutes a root whence is developed the idea of a restrained utterance, as a determined message; executing a mission; a legation, a vicarship.

The Arabic لاك has lost absolutely all the intellectual ideas developed by the Hebraic root and has preserved but few of its physical acceptations. In a restricted sense, the verb لاك signifies *to chew;* as onomatopoetic root لق depicts the *gurgle* of a bottle.

לאך Every kind of *legation, delegation, envoy,* to fulfill any *function* whatsoever.

לוּךְ (*comp.*) State of being *detached, delegated, loosened, released; without bond, lawless; impious, profane,* etc.

לל LL. The sign of extensive movement being opposed to itself, composes a root which gives the idea of circular movement: in the same manner as one sees in natural philosophy, this movement springs from two opposed forces, one drawing to the centre, and the other drawing away from it.

The Arabic ل is not preserved; but one recognizes the Hebraic root in the verb اول which expresses anxiety, despair of a person *tossed about.*

לוּל Action of *moving around, turning* alternately from one side to another; *rocking, winding, twisting.*

ליל (*comp.*) That which binds things and envelops them; *night.*

לם LM. A sympathetic, mutual bond; a movement directed toward universalization.

The Arabic م develops the same ideas as the Hebraic root but in a more physical sense. As verb, it is the action of *uniting together, assembling, gathering,* etc. When the word م signifies *no,* it is attached to the root ע or לא.

RADICAL VOCABULARY

לאם *A people;* that is to say, a more or less considerable number of men united by common bond.

לן LN. Root not used in Hebrew. The Arabic اون expresses every kind of colour, tint, reflection cast upon objects; that which varies, changes colour, flashes iridescent hues, etc.

In the modern idiom, the verb لن signifies literally *to soften.*

לון A reflected light, a *nocturnal lamp*: action of *watching* by lamp-light, of *passing the night,* of *taking rest.*

לס LS. Root not used in Hebrew. The Arabic لس indicates the action of *browsing*. By the word لص is understood *a thief, a robber.*

לע LOH. Root not used in Hebrew. The Arabic لوع appears to express in general, covetous desire, consuming ardour.

The root لع which appears to be idiomatic and onomatopoetic in Arabic, denotes the articulate or inarticulate sound emitted by the voice and modified by the tongue; thence the verb لغا which signifies *to speak* or *to bark,* according to whether it is a question of man or dog. The word لغة signifies literally, *a speech, an idiom,* etc.

לוע *A yawning jaw, an engulfing abyss;* that which *swallows, absorbs, devours.*

לף LPH. Every idea of reaction, of return to itself, of refraction.

The Arabic لف indicates a complication, an adjunction of several things. It is literally, the action of *enveloping*.

ליץ LTZ. Every kind of turn, *détour*, turning about, sinuosity, inflection.

The Arabic لص expresses in general, every kind of trickery, ruse, cheating. Literally *a thief*.

ליץ Action of *making light of, making a play on words; of laughing;* action of *turning* one tongue into another, of employing *an oratorical trope*, etc.

לק LCQ. In a literal sense, that which is seized by the tongue, that which is lapped, *licked*: figuratively, that which is seized by the mind, *a lesson, a lecture, an instruction*.

The Arabic لك signifies *to chew*, and لق, as onomatopoetic root denotes every kind of slapping, clapping, clicking.

להק From the idea of *instruction* springs that of *doctrine*; from that of *doctrine, doctor*. Thence, the idea of *academy*, of the gathering of savants, of sages, of elders, of *the senate*.

לר LR. Root not used in Hebrew nor in Arabic.

לש LSH. Every union *en masse*, every forming, composing.

The Arabic لش indicates the state of that which is agitated, shaken. The word لشلش characterizes one who is trembling, troubled, unsteady.

לוש That which tends *to soften, knead; to make ductile* a thing which is firm and divided.

לת LTH. Root not used in Hebrew. The Arabic لت indicates a mutual union, a sympathetic bond.

מ M. This character as consonant, belongs to the nasal sound. As symbolic image it represents woman, mother, companion of man; that which is productive, creative. As grammatical sign, it is the maternal and female sign of exterior and passive action; placed at the beginning of words it depicts that which is local and plastic; placed at the end, it becomes the collective sign, developing the being in infinitive space, as far as its nature permits, or uniting by abstraction, in one single being all those of the same kind. In Hebrew it is the extractive or partitive article, as I have explained in my Grammar, expressing in nouns or actions that sort of movement by which a name or an action, is taken for means or instrument, is divided in its essence, or is drawn from the midst of several other similar nouns or actions.

The Hebraist grammarians whilst considering this character as *héémanthe* have not ceased, nevertheless, to confound it with the words which it modifies as sign, as I shall show in several important examples in my notes.

Its arithmetical number is 40.

מא MA. That which tends to the aggrandizement of its being, to its entire development; that which serves as instrument of generative power and manifests it exteriorly.

The Arabic ما presents in its original sense the same ideas as the Hebraic root; but this root has acquired in Arabic a greater number of developments than it has in Hebrew; this is why it demands in both idioms all the attention of those who wish to go back to the essence of language. מא or ما, characterizes in general, passive matter, the thing of which, with which, and by means of which, all is made. It is in particular, in the Arabic idiom, *water;* anything whatsoever, *all* or *nothing*, according to the manner in which it is considered. This important root, conceived as pronominal relation designates the possibility of all things, and is represented by the analogues *what* and *which;* conceived, on the contrary, as adverbial relation, it is employed in Arabic to express the absence of every determined object and is rendered by the analogues *not, no.* As verb, the root ما or ملي signifies in general, *to go everywhere, to extend everywhere, to fill space,* etc.

מאה   This is, in general, that which is developed according to the extent of its faculties; in a more restricted sense it is the number *one hundred.*

מב   MB. Root not used in Hebrew. The Arabic ماب seems to indicate an idea of return, remittance; of honour rendered.

מג   MG. Root not used in Hebrew. The Arabic ماج expresses the idea of a thing which is sour, acrid, bitter, sharp; which irritates, troubles, torments.

In a restricted sense the verb مج signifies *to be repugnant.*

מד   MD. The sign of exterior action, being united to that of elementary division, constitutes that root whence come all ideas of measure, dimension, mensuration, commensurable extent, and in a metaphorical sense, those of custom, rule, condition.

The Arabic مد develops in general, the same ideas as the Hebrew. In particular, it is that which extends, lengthens, unfolds.

מאד   That which fills its measure, which has all the dimensions that it can have, which enjoys the whole extent of its faculties: in an abstract sense, *much, very, exceedingly,* etc.

מָה MEH. That which is essentially mobile, essentially passive and creative; the element from which everything draws its nourishment; that which the ancients regarded as the female principle of all generation, *water*, and which they opposed to the male principle, which they believed to be *fire*.

מָה׳ מוּ or מִי Every idea of *mobility, fluidity, passivity*; that which is tenuous and impassive, whose intimate essence remains unknown, whose faculties are relative to the active principles which develop them; in a literal and restricted sense, *water*, in an abstract sense *who? which? what is it? some one, something.*

The Arabic ما has lost all the intellectual ideas of the Hebraic root and has substituted the root له for all physical ideas. Today, by ماه, is understood only a vain futile, inane thing.

מָהָל (*comp.*) Every kind of *mixture*; the *fusion* of several things together.

מָהַר (*comp.*) That which *passes away* with rapidity, that which *changes, varies* easily and quickly. See מָר.

מוּ MOU. Analogue of the root מָה.
מוּ This is, in Hebrew, a passive syllable which is added to nearly all articles and to some pronouns, to give them more force and without bringing any change to their proper expression.

The Arabic مو is an onomatopoetic root which depicts in particular the mewing of a cat; by extension, every harsh, shrill sound. The Ethiopic ሞዋእ (*mowa*) characterizes, in general, the action of triumphing, and that of celebrating a triumph with a fanfare.

מוּג (*comp.*) Action of *liquifying, dissolving, melting.*

מוֹחַ (*comp.*) *Marrow.*

מוֹט (comp.) Every kind of *communicated movement*. See מט.

מוּךְ (comp.) Every idea of *attenuation, depression*. See מך.

מוּל (comp.) Action of *amputating, cutting off exuberance, circumcising*. See מל.

מוֹם (comp.) *Stain, vice.* See מם.

מוּן (comp.) *Image, representation, figure*: See מן.

מוּר (comp.) Every *variation*, every *permutation*. See מר.

מוּשׁ (comp.) That which is *contracted* and *rolled up* in itself: See מש.

מוּת (comp.) Passing into another life, *death*. See מת.

מז MZ. Every burning; combustion through the effect of refraction. Intense dazzling; reflection of the solar rays; incandescence, heat, sudden dryness.

The Arabic ﻣﺰ not having conserved the primitive sense of the Hebraic root, offers only particular consequences of the most general ideas, as those which spring from heat or from dryness; or from that which is sour or dried up, in speaking of liquids.

מח MH. Onomatopoetic root which depicts the noise that is made in clapping the hands: figuratively, action of applauding; state of being joyous, of having good appearance.

מח *Clapping, applause, fullness of the body; good humour*.

מח The sign of exterior and passive action united to that of elementary labour, or to the root אח, symbol of all equality, constitutes a root to which are attached the ideas of abolition, desuetude; of ravage carried on by time, by the action of the elements, or by man; thence,

מחה   Action of *effacing, depriving, taking away, destroying;* of *razing* a city, an edifice; of *washing, cleansing,* etc.

The Arabic ﻣﺢ presents the same general ideas as the Hebraic root מח. The particular ideas are developed in the modern idiom by the derivative root ﻣﺤﻰ.

מחץ   (comp.) Action of *hurting, striking violently, wounding.* See חץ.

מחק   (comp.) Action of *razing, scraping, taking away, removing* by force, *erasing,* etc.

מחר   (comp.) Every idea of *contingent* future, of *fatal, irresistible* thing: in a literal sense, it is the adverbial relation *tomorrow.*

מט   MT. This root, composed of the sign of exterior and passive action, united to that of resistance, develops all ideas of motion or emotion given to something; vacillation; stirring; a communicated movement especially downward.

The Arabic ﻣﻂ has the same sense. As verb, this root indicates the action of *drawing, stretching,* extending by pulling.

מוט   Action of *moving, rousing, budging, stirring, agitating; going, following, happening, arriving,* etc.

מי   MI. See מה.

The Chaldaic מי is an indefinite pronominal relation represented by *what?* The Ethiopic ማይ (*mai*) signifies properly *water.*

מים   *The waters:* that is to say, the mass of that which is eminently mobile, passive and suitable for elementary fecundation.

מך   MCH. The root אך, image of every restriction, every contraction, united to the sign of exterior and passive action, constitutes a root whence spring the ideas of attenuation, weakening, softening of a hard thing: its liquefaction; its submission.

מךְ   That which is *attenuated, debilitated, weakened; distilled; humiliated.* See מוּךְ.

The Arabic مك expresses in general, every idea of extenuation, absorption, consumption. By مخ, is understood *the brain.*

מל   ML. The sign of exterior and passive action united by contraction to the root אל, symbol of every elevation and every extent, composes a root to which is attached all ideas of continuity, plentitude, continued movement from the beginning to the end of a thing: thence, the accessory ideas of locution, elocution, eloquence, narration, etc.

The Arabic مل not having preserved the intellectual ideas developed by the Hebraic root is limited to recalling that sort of physical plentitude which constitutes lassitude, *ennui,* dislike to work and the negligence which follows. The particular ideas expressed by the Hebrew, are found again in part, in the Arabic words ملا ملو ملي.

מל   That which is *full, entirely formed;* that which has attained its *complement*: that which is *continued* without lacunas; every kind of *locution, narration, oration; a term, an expression.*

מלל   (*intens.*) From the excess of *plentitude* springs the idea of exuberance and the idea of that which is announced outwardly; in a figurative sense, *elocution, speech.*

מול   From the idea of *exuberance* comes that of *amputation;* thence, the action of *amputating, circumcising, taking away* that which is *superabundant, superfluous.*

מם   MM. Root not used in Hebrew. The Arabic

مس seems to indicate a thing livid, or which renders livid; a thing inanimate, and as dead. Literally *wax, a mummy;* figuratively, *solitude, a desert.*

מן MN. This root, composed of the sign of exterior and passive action, united by contraction to the root אן, symbol of the sphere of activity and of the circumscriptive extent of being, characterizes all specification, all classification by exterior forms; all figuration, determination, definition, qualification.

The Arabic من has not followed the same developments as the Hebrew, although they have come from an identical root in the two idioms, as is proved by the usage of this root as designative relation represented by *of, from,* etc. As noun the Arabic root من designates a thing emanated from another, *a gift;* as verb, it characterizes the state of that which is benign, beneficial; action of that which is deprived in order *to give, to distribute;* that which is weakened *to reinforce,* impoverished *to enrich,* etc.

מן The kind of things, their *exterior figure, mien, image,* that is conceived; *the idea* that is formed, *the definition* that is given to it; their proper *measure, number, quota.*

מנן Action of *figuring, defining, forming an idea, an image* of things: action of *imagining;* action of *measuring, numbering, qualifying,* etc.

מין *Form, aspect* of things; their *mien, figure,* etc.

מס MS. Every dissolution, literally as well as figuratively: that which enervates, which takes away from physical and moral strength.

The Arabic مس characterizes the state of that which is touched, that which is contiguous. By مص, is understood *to suck;* by مضى to be fatigued, to lose one's strength, to *be enervated.*

מַע MOH. That which circulates or which causes circulation.

מֵעָה Inmost part; the intestines, the viscera of the body: the finances of state, money; sand, gravel, etc.

The Arabic مع, which as I have already remarked in speaking of the root מא signifies literally *with*, contained primitively the same sense as the Hebraic root מה which is alluded to here; but its developments have been somewhat different. Thus, whereas the Chaldaic מִעָא designates a thing in circulation, as a piece of money, the Arabic مع characterizes that which is uniform, unaminous, simultaneous.

מְעַט (comp.) That which is *moderate, exiguous*, of little value, *common, poor.*

מָעַךְ (comp.) Action of *pressing, compressing, provoking.*

מָעַל (comp.) That which is *tortuous; distorted, deceitful;* a *transgression*, a *prevarication*.

מָף MPH. Root not used in Hebrew. The Chaldaic signifies a sort of carpet or cloth.

The Arabic verb منج signifies the condition of an idiot; a false or stupid mind.

מָץ MTZ. This root characterizes that which attains an end, a finish; which encounters, finds, obtains the desired object.

The Arabic مص signifies properly *to suck*.

מָצַץ (intens.) Action of *milking,* that is to say, of *obtaining* milk: thence, the idea of *pressure, expression; pressing* etc.

מק MCQ. That which is founded, literally as well as figuratively. The action of being melted, liquefied; growing faint, vanishing.

The Arabic ڡ expresses the state of that which experiences a sentiment of tenderness, which covers, shelters, loves, etc.

מר MR. The sign of exterior and passive action being united to that of movement proper, constitutes a root whose purpose is to characterize that which gives way to its impulsion, which extends itself, usurps or invades space; but when this same sign is linked by contraction to the root אר symbol of elementary principle, then the root which results is applied to all the modifications of this same element.

The Arabic مر contained primitively the same ideas as the Hebraic root. In the modern idiom this root is limited to two principal acceptations; the first is applied to the action of *passing, exceeding, going beyond;* the second, to the state of being bitter, strong, sturdy.

מר That which extending and rising, affects *the empire, the dominion;* as a *potentate*: that which exceeds the limits of one's authority; as *a tyrant, a rebel*: that which is attached to the idea of elementary principle, as *an atom, a drop.*

מרר (*intens.*) That which is *exaggerated* in its movement, in its quality: literally, that which is *sour, bitter, ferocious.*

מאר (*comp.*) That which *gnaws*, which *corrodes;* literally and figuratively.

מאר or מאור (*comp.*) That which *shines, lightens, heats.*

מהר (*comp.*) That which *changes, varies, passes, flows off* rapidly.

מור or יר (*comp.*) *Change, variation, mutation.*

מש **MSH.** From the union of the sign of exterior activity with that of relative movement, or by contraction with the elementary root אש springs a root whose purpose is to express that which is stirred by contractile movement.

The Arabic مش signifies properly *to feel, touch softly, brush lightly.*

מש Everything *palpable, compact, gathered*: every pile, as *a crop, a harvest.* That which is *drawn, extracted, shrunken,* as *silk* etc.

מת **MTH.** If one considers this root as composed of the sign of exterior action, united to that of reciprocity, or this same sign joined by contraction to the root את image of the ipseity, the selfsameness of things, it will express either a sympathetic movement, or a transition; a return to universal seity or sameness. Thence the idea of the passing of life; of death.

The Arabic مت or مث, has lost all the intellectual ideas contained in the Hebrew. Today it is only extension or physical expansion, a sort of flux of any thing whatever. مث indicates dissolution of being, and مت signifies *death.* The verb مات characterizes that which is dead, dissolved, deprived of existence proper.

מות Action of *passing away*, of *passing* into another life, of *dying*: state of *being dead; death.*

נ **N.** This character as consonant, belongs to the nasal sound; as symbolic image it represents the son of man, every produced and particular being. As grammatical sign, it is that of individual and produced existence. When it is placed at the end of words it becomes the augumentative sign ן, and gives to the being every extension of which it is individually susceptible. The Hebraist grammarians in placing this character among the *hééman-*

thes, had certainly observed that it expressed, at the beginning of words, passive action, folded within itself, and when it appeared at the end, unfoldment and augmentation: but they had profited little by this observation.

I shall not repeat here what I have said in my Grammar concerning the use that the idiomatic genius of the Hebraic tongue made of this character in the composition of compound radical verbs, as initial adjunction.

Its arithmetical number is 50.

נא NA. Every idea of youth, newness; every idea of freshness, grace, beauty; every idea springing from that which is formed of a new production, of a being young and graceful.

The Arabic لا although holding to the same primitive root as the Hebrew, has developed, however, ideas apparently opposed: this is the reason. That which is new, of recent birth, is graceful, fresh, pleasing; but it is also frail, weak, unsteady. Now, the Hebraic idiom is attached to the first idea; the Arabic idiom has followed and developed the second. Thence the verb لاَ , which indicates the state of that which is frail, feeble, impotent; the verb لَي, expresses the action *of letting go, being separated, abandoning* a thing, etc. What proves the identity of the root is that the compound verb نَالَ. signifies literally *to nurse* an infant.

נאה That which is *beautiful, lovable, new, young, fresh;* which is not worn out, fatigued, peevish; but, on the contrary, that which is *new, tender, pretty, comely.*

נוא From the idea of *youth* and *childhood* comes the idea of that which has not attained its point of perfection, which is *not sufficiently ripe,* in speaking of fruit; *not sufficiently cooked,* in speaking of meat; thence, the action of *acting abruptly,* without reflection, *contradicting* like a child, *leading without experience, being new, unaccustomed to something, acting impetuously.*

נֹאךְ (*comp.*) *A leather bottle,* for holding water, milk or any liquor whatsoever.

נאם (*comp.*) Action of *exposing the substance or source of something; speaking the truth, going back to the cause.* See אם.

נאף (*comp.*) Action of *giving way* to a passion, to an impulse; *to commit adultery; to apostatize, to worship strange gods.* See אף.

נאץ (*comp.*) Action of *passing the limits, going too far;* the action of *spitting.* See אץ.

נאת (*comp.*) Every idea of *clamour, lamentation.*

נאר (*comp.*) Action of being *execrable, abominable.* See ארר.

נב   NB. The mysterious root אוֹב being united by contraction to the sign of produced existence, gives rise to a new root, whence emanate all ideas of divine inspiration, theophany, prophecy; and in consequence, that of exaltation, ecstasy, rapture; perturbation, religious horror.

The Arabic ن indicates in general, *a shudder;* exterior movement caused by interior passion. As onomatopoetic and idiomatic root ن denotes the sudden cry of a man or animal keenly roused. Literally, *the bark* of a dog. Figuratively نا and ني express the action of one who announces the will of heaven, who prophecies.

The Hebrew word נביא, *prophet,* is formed of the root נב here alluded to, and the root יא, symbol of divine power.

נוּב Action of *speaking* by inspiration; *producing* exteriorly the spirit with which one is filled: in a literal and restricted sense, *divulgation, fructification, germination.*

In this last sense, it is the root אב, which is united simply to the sign נ employed as initial adjunction.

נג NG. This root is applied to every kind of reflected light, after the manner of a mirror; of solar refraction: thence, the ideas of opposition, of an object put on the opposite side.

The Arabic نج indicates every idea of liquid emission, watery emanation.

נהג Action of *leading* by taking possession of the will of some one; of *inducing, deducing, suggesting* ideas; action of giving or receiving *an impulse, opinion*, etc.

נד ND. From the union of the signs of produced existence and natural division, springs a root which develops all ideas of dispersion, uncertain movement, agitation, flight, exile, trouble, dissension.

The Arabic ند develops the idea of that which evaporates, is exhaled, escapes. This word is applied also in Arabic to the idea of equality, similitude; then it is compound and derived from the primitive יד, contracted with the sign of produced existence נ.

נוד That which *is moved, stirred*, by a principle of trouble and incertitude; that which is *wandering, agitated;* that which *goes away, flees, emigrates,* etc.

ניד An *agitation, a trembling, a disturbance* manifested by movement.

נה NHE. This root is the analogue of the root נא and as it, characterizes that which is fresh, young, recent: thence;

נוה State of being *young, alert, vigorous, pleasing*; in consequence, action of *forming a colony, founding a new habitation, establishing one's flock elsewhere*, etc.

נה Onomatopoetic root which describes the long moaning of a person who weeps, suffers, sobs.

The Arabic نه depicts every kind of noise, clamour.

נו NOU. The convertible sign ו image of the bond which unites being and nothingness, which communicates from one nature to another, being joined to that of produced existence, produces a root whose sense, entirely vague and indeterminate is fixed only by means of the terminative sign by which it is accompanied.

The Arabic نو is an onomatopoetic and idiomatic root which depicts the aversion that one experiences in doing a thing, the disgust that it inspires. As verb, it is the action of being *repugnant*, of *refusing*, of *being unwilling*.

נוה (*comp.*) Every idea of a *new dwelling*. See נה.

נוח (*comp.*) *The point of equilibrium* where an agitated thing finds *repose*: action of *resting, remaining tranquil, enjoying peace and calm.* See נח.

נוט (*comp.*) Every kind of *bond*.

נום (*comp.*) Action of *sleeping*.

נון (*comp.*) Every idea of *propagation* or *growth* of family. See נן.

נוס (*comp.*) Action of *wavering* in uncertainty, *erring, fleeing.* See נם.

נוע (*comp.*) That which *changes*, that which lacks constancy and force, literally as well as figuratively.

נוף (*comp.*) *Dispersion, aspersion, distillation*: action of *winnowing, scattering;* of *ventilating*, etc.

נוץ (*comp.*) Action of *flourishing*, that of *flying;* being *resplendent.* See נץ.

נוק (*comp.*) Every pure, beneficial, nourishing fluid; *milk;* action of *suckling, nursing* an infant.

נור (comp.) A luminous production, *éclat, splendour.* See נר.

נש (comp.) That which is *unstable, weak, infirm.*

נז NZ. This root characterizes that which overflows, spreads, disperses; that which makes its influence felt outwardly.

The Arabic نز has the same sense. It is literally, the action of *flowing, passing away.*

נז (intens.) From excess of dispersion springs the idea of *the breaking* of that which is solid; *the distillation* of that which is liquid.

נח NH. If one considers this root as formed of the united signs of produced existence and elementary existence, it implies a movement which leads toward an end: if one considers it as formed of the same sign of produced existence united by contraction to the root אח, image of all equilibratory force, it furnishes the idea of that perfect repose which results for a thing long time agitated contrarily, and the point of equilibrium which it attains where it dwells immobile. Thence,

נח In the first case, and in a restricted sense, *a guide*: in the second case, and in a general sense, *the repose of existence.* See נוח.

The Arabic نح is an onomatopoetic root which depicts a moan, a profound sigh; thence, all ideas of lamentation, of plaint. The intellectual ideas developed by the Hebraic root are nearly all lost in the Arabic. Nevertheless one still finds in the modern idiom the verb نح signifying *to stoop, to kneel.* The compound word نحابه, indicates sometimes *patience, tenacity.*

נחל (*comp.*) That which is *extended* with effort, which is *divided, separated*: *a valley* hollowed out by a torrent: *a share* of inheritance: *the sinuosity* of a running stream; *taking* possession, any *usurpation* whatsoever.

נחם (*comp.*) That which *ceases entirely, desists* from a sentiment, *renounces completely* a care, *surrenders* an opinion, *calms* a pain, *consoles*, etc.

נחץ (*comp.*) Every idea of *urgency, haste, importunity*. See חץ.

נחר (*comp.*) See חר.

נחש (*comp.*) See חש.

נחת (*comp.*) See חת.

נט NT. The sign of produced existence united to that of resistance and protection, forms a root whence emanate all ideas of nutation, inflection, inclination, liason, literally as well as figuratively, thence,

נט Every kind of *off-shoot, tendril, reed* suitable to *braid, tie, plait*: a thing which *twines, grows* upon another, is *bound, tied* to it; as *a twig, branch, stick; a sceptre; a mat, a bed*; etc. See טוב.

The Arabic ﻧﻂ has not preserved the ideas developed by the Hebrew, or rather the Arabic root being formed in another manner has expressed a different sense. In general, the verb ﻧﻂ characterizes that which makes effort to separate itself from the point at which it is arrested; in particular, it is *to jump, to escape, to be emancipated*. By ﻧﻂﻞ or ﻧﻂﺞ is understood the state of a thing suspended, separated from the point toward which it inclines. The Chaldaic נטה signifies properly *eccentric*.

ני NI. Root analogous to the roots נא נה and נו whose expression it manifests.

RADICAL VOCABULARY 401

The Arabic فى indicates the state of that which is raw.

נִין (*comp.*) *An offspring, a son.* See נִן.

נִיר (*comp.*) *Light manifested* in its production, *splendour.* See נר.

נךְ NCH. *That which is injurious to existence arrests, restrains, represses it.*

נךְ *A blow, a lesion; chastisement, torment*: action of *rebuking, chastising, treating harshly, punishing; bruising, striking, sacrificing;* etc.

The Arabic ذكا presents in general the same ideas as the Hebrew. Is it the same with the Syriac ܢܟܐ

נל NL. *Every idea of suite, series, sequence, consequence: every idea of abundant succession, of effusion holding to the same source.* The Arabic words نل, نال, نيل, all present the sense of succeeding, following in great number, furnishing, giving, rendering abundantly.

נם NM. *Individual existence represented by the sign* נ, *being universalized by the adjunction of the collective sign* ם, *forms a root whence is developed the idea of sleep.* This hieroglyphic composition is worthy of closest attention. One is inclined to believe that the natural philosophy of the ancient Egyptians regarded sleep as a sort of universalization of the particular being. See רום and נוס.

The Arabic نم only participates in the Hebraic root in the case where the verb نم signifies *to exhale, to spread out,* in speaking of odours; for when it expresses the action of *spreading rumours, cursing, calumniating,* it results from another formation. Besides it can be remarked that nearly all the roots which are composed of the sign נ are in the same case; and this, for the reason shown in the grammar, with regard to this sign when it has become initial adjunction.

בן NN. The sign of individual and produced existence, being united to itself as augmentative sign, constitutes a root whose use is to characterize the continuity of existence by generation. It is a new production which emanates from an older production to form a continuous chain of individuals of the same species.

The Arabic نّ has not preserved the ideas developed by the Hebraic root. It can only be remarked that نِي is one of the names which has been given to Venus, that is to say, to the generative faculty of nature.

בנן That which is *propagated abundantly*, that which *spreads* and *swarms;* in a restricted sense, the *specie of fish;* action of *abounding, increasing.*

בִּן Every *new progeny* added to the older, every extension of lineage, family, race. See בִּי.

נס NS. Every idea of vacillation, agitation, literally as well as figuratively: that which wavers, which renders uncertain, wavering.

נס In a restricted sense, *a flag, an ensign, the sail of a ship*: in a broader sense, a movement of *irresolution, uncertainty;* from the idea of *flag* develops that of *putting in evidence, raising*: from the idea of *irresolution,* that of *tempting, of temptation.*

The Arabic نس has only an onomatopoetic root which describes the noise of a thing floating, as water; consequently, characterizing literally, that which imitates the movement of waves; figuratively, that which is given over to such a movement.

נע NH. This root expresses the idea of everything weak, soft, feeble, without consistency. The Arabic نع

RADICAL VOCABULARY 403

signifies literally *an herb fresh and tender*. In a more extended sense, it is every idea of movement within oneself, vacillation, trepidation, oscillation.

נוע That which is *weak*, without strength; that which is *variable;* which *changes, vacillates, totters;* which goes from one side to another: it is, in a broader sense, *the impulse* given to a thing *to stir* and draw it from its torpor.

נעם (*comp.*) That which is *easy, pleasant, convenient, agreeable*.

נער (*comp.*) In a restricted sense, *a new born infant*: in a figurative sense, the primary impulse given to vital element.

נף NPH. Every idea of dispersion, ramification, effusion, inspiration; of movement operated inwardly from without, or outwardly from within: distillation if the object is liquid, a scattering if the object is solid. See נוף.

The Arabic نف has in general, the same ideas. In particular, it is, in the modern idiom, the action of *snuffing, blowing the nose*.

נץ NTZ. That which reaches its term, end, extreme point: that which is raised as high and spreads as far as it can be, according to its nature.

The Arabic نص does not differ from the Hebrew in the radical sense. In a restricted sense one understands by the verb نص, the action of *giving a theme,* furnishing authority, *confirming,* demonstrating by text, by argument, etc.

נץ The end of every germination, *the flower,* and the action of *blossoming;* the term of all organic effort, *the feather,* and the action of *flying;* the end of all desire; *splendour,* and the action of being *resplendent, gleaming, shining*. See נוץ.

נצץ (*intens.*) From the idea of attaining to the highest point, comes that of *flying;* from that of flying, that of *vulture* and every bird of prey; from this latter, taken in the figurative and intensive sense, that of *ravaging, devastating, wrangling* over plunder, *stealing, robbing;* etc.

נק NCQ. This root, which contains the idea of void, is applied metaphorically to that which is related to this idea: thence נק, every *hollow, cavernous* place; every *excavated* space: an *innocent* being, one without vice, without evil thought; that which is free from all stain, impurity; which is *purified, absolved; fair, white.* In a figurative and restricted sense, *milk;* the nursling which sucks, *an infant.* See נוק

The Arabic نق is an onomatopoetic root which depicts every kind of deep, raucous, sound, like the grunting of a pig, cawing of a crow, etc.

נר NR. The root אור, united by contraction to the sign of produced existence, constitutes a root whose purpose is to characterize that which propagates light, literally as well as figuratively: thence,

נר A *lamp, a beacon, a torch: a sage, a guide;* that which *enlightens, shines,* is *radiant*: metaphorically, *a public festivity, an extreme gladness.* See נור and ניר.

The Arabic نر signifies literally, *fire.*

נש NSH. This root which is applied to the idea of things temporal and transient, in general, expresses their instability, infirmity, decrepitude, caducity: it characterizes that which is feeble and weak, easy to seduce, variable, transitory; literally as well as figuratively.

The Arabic نش characterizes in particular, the absorption of water by the earth; in the modern idiom it signifies, *to whisk flies.*

RADICAL VOCABULARY 405

נשׁ Every idea of *mutation, permutation, subtraction, distraction, cheating, deception, weakness, wrong,* etc.

נת NTH. Every corporeal division. **In a restricted** sense, *a member.*

The Arabic ن characterizes extension given to anything whatsoever. The verb ن expresses literally, the action of oozing through, of perspiring.

נת *A morsel* of something, *a piece, a portion; a section*: action of *parcelling out,* of *dissecting,* etc.

ס S. This character as consonant, belongs to the sibilant sound, and is applied as onomatopœia to depicting all sibilant noises: certain observant writers among whom I include Bacon, have conceived this letter S, as the symbol of the consonantal principle, in the same manner that they conceived the letter ה, or the aspiration H, as that of the vocal principle. This character is, in Hebrew, the image of the bow whose cord hisses in the hands of man. As grammatical sign, it is that of circular movement in that which is related to the circumferential limit of any sphere.

Its arithmetical number is 60.

סא SA. Every idea of circumference, tour, circuit, rotundity.

סאה Every round thing suitable for containing anything; as *a sack, a bag.* In a figurative sense, it is the action of *emigrating,* changing the place, taking one's bag.

The Arabic سا or ساء, designates that which disturbs, harms.

סאן (*comp.*) Covering for the feet, *sandals.*

סב SB. When this root is conceived as the product of the circumferential sign united to that of **interior** action ב, it expresses every idea of occasional force, cause, reason: but when it is the root אב, image of every conceivable fructification, joined by contraction to this same sign, then this root is applied to that which surrounds, circumscribes, envelops.

The Arabic سب contains in general all the acceptations of the Hebraic root; but inclining toward those which are more particularized in a physical sense than in a moral one.

סב Every kind of *contour, circuit, girdle; a circumstance, an occasion, a cause.*

The Arabic سبب has the same sense; but the primitive root سب having deviated toward the physical, signifies *to distort* a thing, to take the wrong side; *to curse* someone, *to injure* him, etc.

סב and סבב (*intens.*) Action of *turning, going round, circuiting, enveloping, circumventing, warning, converting, perverting,* etc.

The Arabic صب signifies *to put* a thing *upside down; to pour out, upset.*

סג SG. The circumferential sign united to the organic sign, constitutes a root whose purpose is to depict the effect of the circumferential line opening more and more, and departing from the centre: thence,

סג All ideas of *extension, augmentation, growth: physical possibility.* See סגן and סיג.

The Arabic سج offers in general, the same sense as the Hebrew.

סד SD. This root whose effect is opposed to that of the preceding one, characterizes, on the contrary, the circumferential line entering upon itself, and approaching the centre: thence,

סר   All ideas of *repression, retention, closing.*

The Arabic سد has not separated from the Hebrew in the radical sense. As verb it is literally the action of closing. It must be remarked that the verb ساد which signifies *to master, to dominate,* is attached to the root יד, يد which indicates properly *the hand,* and the power of which it is the emblem.

סה   SEH. Root analogous to סא.

The Arabic سه indicates the circumference of the buttocks: *the rump.*

סהר   That which is round of form: *a tower, a dome; the moon; a necklace; bracelets,* etc.

סו   SOU. Root analogous to סא and סה.

The Arabic سو does not differ from the Hebrew as to the radical sense; but the developments of this root being applied in Arabic, to the idea of what is bent rather than to what is round, characterizes consequently, that which is bad rather than that which is good: thence the verbs ساء or سوء which express the state of what is bent, false, malicious, traitorous, depraved, corrupt, etc.

סוה   *A veil,* a garment which *surrounds, envelops, undulates.*

סוג   (*comp.*) Action of being *extended* by going away from the centre; *yielding;* offering *a facility, a possibility.*

סוד   (*comp.*) Action of *welding; closing, shutting;* that which is *secret, closed, covered.*

סוך   (*comp.*) Action of *anointing.* See סך.

סון   (*comp.*) That which *shines,* that which *renders joyous.* See סן.

סוס   (*comp.*) *A horse.* See סס.

סוֹף (comp.) That which *finishes* a thing; *makes an end* of it; *to sweep away; to fulfill.* See סָ.

סוּר (comp.) That which *turns around, bends, is perverted, changes sides, is made adverse;* that which is *audacious, independent;* that which is *raised, bred, trained, turned,* given a *proper outline, directed* etc. See סָר.

סוּת (comp.) Action of *working in the shadow* of something, of *being covered* with a veil, of *seducing, persuading,* etc. See סָת.

סָז SZ. Root not used in Hebrew nor in Arabic.

סָח SH. Root not used in Hebrew. The Arabic ســ expresses the action of being *dissolved* in water, of being *poured out, spread over,* etc. The Chaldaic סוּח signifies *to swim; to wash, to be purified* in water: the Syriac and Samaritan have the same sense.

סחה Action of *cleansing, washing.*

סחי Every idea of *cleansing.*

סחף (comp.) Every idea of *subversion, sweeping away; a torrent.*

סחר (comp.) Every idea of the *circulation* of produce, of merchandise; action of *negotiating, selling, buying,* etc.

סחש (comp.) That which *springs* from corruption: that which *swarms* from putrid water.

סָט ST. Root not used in Hebrew. The Arabic ســ characterizes in general, a vehement, illegal action. The compound verb ســ signifies literally *to command with arrogance, to act like a despot.*

סִי SI. Root analogous to סָה and סוֹ. The Arabic ســ coming from the radical idea taken in a good sense, characterizes that which is *regular, equal;* that which is

RADICAL VOCABULARY 409

made in accordance with its own nature: thus the **verb** سي. or سيا has reference to milk which flows without being drawn.

סִיג (comp.) *An extension*: a thing which has yielded, which has gone away from the centre. In a restricted sense, *scoria*. See סג.

סִיר (comp.) *Curvature*. See סר.

סָךְ SCH. The circumferential sign united by contraction of the root אך, image of every restriction and exception, forms a root whose use is to characterize a thing which is round, closed, fitting to contain, to cover; thence,

סך *A sack, veil, covering* of any sort: that which *envelops, covers, obstructs*. In a figurative sense, *the multitude* of men which cover the earth; *ointment* with which the skin is covered and which closes the pores. See סוּךְ.

The Arabic سك has preserved few of the expressions which hold to the radical sense. Its principle developments spring from the onomatopoetic root سك which depicts the effect of the effort that one makes in striking. Literally it is *striking* a thing to make it yield.

סָל SL. Every kind of movement which *raises, exalts, takes away, ravishes*.

The Arabic سل signifies in a restricted sense, *to draw to one's self*.

סל In a very restricted sense, *a leap, a gambol;* in a broad and figurative sense, the *esteem* or *value* that is put upon things. Also *a heap* of anything; a thing formed of many others raised one upon another, as *a mound* of earth, etc.

סם SM. The circumferential sign being universalized by the collective sign ם, becomes the symbol of the olfactory sphere, of every fragrant influence given to the air: thence,

סמ   Every kind of *aromatic*.

The Arabic سم appears to have preserved more of the developments and even more of the radical force than the Hebraic analogue. This root characterizes that which is penetrated with force whether good or evil. Thence, in the modern idiom the verb سم, which signifies *to bore* a hole, *to pierce*.

סן   SN. The circumferential sign having attained its greatest dimension by the addition of the augmentative sign, ן , becomes the symbol of the visual sphere and of all luminous influence: thence,

סן   Every kind of *light,* of *bright colour,* in general; in particular the colour *red,* as the most striking. This colour, taken in a bad sense, as being that of blood, has furnished the idea of *rage* and *rancour* in the Chaldaic סנא ; but the Syriac has only a luminous effect, as is proved by the word ܣܗܪ which signifies *the moon*. The Hebrew has drawn from it the name of the most brilliant month of the year, סיון the month of *May*. See סון .

The Arabic سن characterizes that which *illumines* things and gives them *form* by shaping, polishing them; in the modern idiom the verb سن signifies *to sharpen*.

סס   SS. The circumferential sign being added to itself, constitutes a root which denotes in an intensive manner every eccentric movement tending to increase a circle and give it a more extended diameter: thence, every idea of going away from the centre, of emigration, travel: thence,

סוס   A *horse;* that is to say an animal which aids in emigration, travel. See סא and סע .

RADICAL VOCABULARY 411

The Arabic ماس belongs evidently to the primitive root סס, and designates in general, a thing which is carried from the centre to the circumference, *to administer, to govern.*

סע SH. That which is rapid, audacious, vehement, fitted for the race; thence,

סעה *A courier, a thing which rushes;* figuratively *an arrogant person, a calumniator.*

The Syriac ܣܥܐ has the same sense as the Hebrew. The Arabic ع appears to have deviated much from the radical sense. It is literally, *a straw;* but figuratively, it is that which makes the subject of a deliberation.

סעד (*comp.*) That which serves for *support, prop, corroboration.* See סד.

סעף (*comp.*) That which is extended by branching out; *a genealogy; a series.*

סער (*comp.*) A violent, tumultuous movement; *a tempest, a storm.*

סף SPH. Every idea of summit, end, finish; anything which terminates, consummates, achieves.

סף *The extremity* of a thing, the point where it ceases; *its achievement, consummation, end: the defection, the want* of this thing: *the border, top, summit, threshold;* that which *commences* or *terminates* a thing; that which is *added* for *its perfection*: also, reiteration of the same action, *an addition, supplement;* the final thing where many others come to *an end*: a time involving many actions.

The Arabic سف has preserved of the radical sense only the idea of a thing reduced to powder, which is taken as medicine. The Syriac ܣܦ characterizes every kind of consummation, of reducing to powder by fire.

סףף (*intens.*) Action of *approaching, drawing near, touching* the threshold, *receiving* hospitality.

סץ STZ. Root not used in Hebrew nor in Arabic.

סק SCQ. Root not used in Hebrew. The Samaritan ꟺ, likewise the Syriac ܣܩ, indicate a movement of evasion, of leaving; of germination.

The Arabic سق is an onomatopoetic root which designates the action of striking.

סר SR. The circumferential sign joined to that of movement proper, constitutes a root whence issue all ideas of disorder, perversion, contortion, apostasy; also those of force, audacity, return, education, new direction, etc.

The Arabic سر offers in general, the same radical character as the Hebrew but its developments differ quite obviously. The verb سر signifies in particular, *to be diverted;* that is to say, turned from serious occupations.

סר and סרר (*comp.*) That which is *disordered, rebellious, refractory;* which leaves its sphere to cause *trouble, discord;* that which is *vehement, audacious, independent, strong*: that which *distorts, turns aside* takes another direction; *is corrected,* etc. See סור.

סש SSH. Root not used in Hebrew nor in Arabic.

סת STH. Every kind of mutual, sympathetic covering, every kind of veil, of darkness. The Arabic ست indicates the parts of the human body that must be veiled. The Hebrew, as well as the Chaldaic סתו, characterizes winter, the dark season when nature is covered with a veil. See סות.

ע   U.H.WH. This character should be considered under the double relation of vowel and consonant. Following its vocal acceptation, it represents the interior of the ear of man, and becomes the symbol of confused, dull, inappreciable noises; deep sounds without harmony. Following its consonantal acceptation, it belongs to the guttural sound and represents the cavity of the chest. Under both relations as grammatical sign, it is in general, that of material sense, image of void and nothingness. As vowel, it is the sign ו, considered in its purely physical relations: as consonant, it is the sign of that which is crooked, false, perverse and bad.

Its arithmetical number is 70.

עא   HA. Physical reality. This root is the analogue of the roots הע and עו.

עב   HB. The sign of material sense united by contraction to the root אב, symbol of all covetous desire and all fructification, constitutes a root which hieroglyphically characterizes the material centre: it is, in a less general sense, that which is condensed, thickened; which becomes heavy and dark.

The Arabic عب signifies properly to charge with *a burden;* by غب, is understood *to finish, to draw to an end, to become putrid.*

עב   Every idea of *density, darkness; a cloud, a thick vapour; a plank, a joist.*

עוב   Action of being *condensed, thickened,* of becoming *palpable, cloudy, sombre, opaque;* etc. See אוב of which עוב is the degeneration and intensifying.

עג   HG. Every kind or ardour, desire, vehement fire, which increases constantly; every active warmth, as much literally as figuratively.

The Arabic غ is an onomatopoetic and idiomatic root which characterizes a violent noise; the roaring of winds and waves. غ depicts also in an onomatopoetic manner the noise made by water when drunk or swallowed.

עֻג In a restricted sense, the action of *baking;* that which has been exposed to the heat of a hot oven, *a cake,* etc.

עד HD. The sign of material sense, contracted with the root אד, symbol of relative unity, image of every emanation and every division, constitutes a very important root which, hieroglyphically, develops the idea of *time,* and of all things temporal, sentient, transitory. Symbolically and figuratively it is worldly voluptuousness, sensual pleasure in opposition to spiritual pleasure; in a more restricted sense, every limited period, every periodic return.

The Arabic عد, which is related in general, to the radical sense of the Hebrew, signifies in particular, *to count, number, calculate,* etc.; the word غد, the time which follows the actual time; *tomorrow.*

עד *The actual time;* a fixed point in time or space expressed by the relations *to, until, near*: a same state continued, a temporal duration, expressed in like manner by, *now, while, still;* a periodic return as *a month;* a thing *constant, certain, evident, palpable,* by which one can give *testimony; a witness.*

עד or עדד (*intens.*) Continued time furnishes the idea of *eternity, stability, constancy;* thence, the action of *enacting, constituting, stating,* etc.

עוד Action of returning periodically furnishes the idea of *evidence, certitude;* action of returning unceasingly, furnishes the idea of *accumulation;* that of accumulation, the ideas of *riches, plunder, prey;* thence, the action of *despoiling*: now these latter ideas, being linked with those of sentient pleasures contained in the primitive idea of *time,* produce all those of *voluptuousness, sensuality, delights, beauty, grace, adornment,* etc.

עוּ, עָה HEH, HOU. That which is sentient in general; obvious to the senses: physical reality. Superficies, the exterior form of things. Their growth, material development.

The Arabic عو has not preserved the intellectual ideas developed by the Hebraic root. It is today, only an onomatopoetic root depicting a sentiment of self-sufficiency, pride. عو signifies literally *to bark.*

עוה Every *inflection,* every circumferential form; every kind of *curvature, inversion, circle, cycle;* everything *concave* or *convex.* In a figurative sense *perversion, iniquity;* state of being *perverse, iniquitous, deceitful, vicious.*

עוּז (comp.) Action of *fleeing for refuge* to any person or place.

עוּט (comp.) Action of making *an irruption.*

עוּל (comp.) To act with *duplicity, hypocrisy;* to be curved as a dais, a yoke, foliage, etc. See עַל.

עוּן (comp.) Action of *being joined corporeally; cohabiting.* See עַן.

עוּף (comp.) Action of *being raised,* sustained in the air, *flying;* as *vapour, winged fowl* or *bird,* etc. See עַף.

עוּץ (comp.) Action of *consolidating; strengthening.* See עַץ.

עוּק (comp.) Action of *compressing.* See עַק.

עוּר (comp.) Action of *impassioning, exciting, putting into movement:* action of *involving, blinding,* etc. See עַר.

עוּשׁ (comp.) Action of *assembling, composing, putting together.* See עַשׁ.

עוּת (comp.) Action of communicating a movement of perversion, of *perverting.* See עַת.

עז HUZ. Every idea of sentient, material force, of physical demonstration: that which is strong; corroborative auxiliary.

עז This is, in general, a thing which *is strengthened* by *being doubled*, by being added to itself. Every body which is *hard, rough, firm, persistent,* as *a stone, rock, fortress*: that which enjoys great, generative vigour, as *a goat;* that which is *vigorous, audacious;* that which serves as *prop, support, lining, substitute;* that which *corroborates, strengthens, encourages,* etc. See עוז.

The Arabic عز while diverted very slightly from the radical sense of the Hebraic root has, however, acquired a great number of developments which are foreign to the Hebrew. Thus the root عز characterizes that which is precious, dear, rare, worthy of honour; that which is cherished, honoured, sought after, etc. The verb عز signifies properly *to pierce*.

עח HUH. Root not used in Hebrew. The Samaritan ᾱ indicates in general, material substance, and in particular, *wood*.

עט HUTH. This root develops the idea of resistance overcome by physical means.

עט *A notch, a cut,* made upon a thing: *a stylus, a chisel* for inscribing, engraving; every kind of *incision, line, cleft.* See עיט.

The Arabic عط offers the same sense as the Hebrew. عط signifies *to wear out* in speaking of clothes; عط to *plunge* into the water.

עי HI. This root is the analogue of the roots עה and עו, whose physical expression it manifests. It is, in general, growth, material development; accumulation.

The Arabic غِي indicates an overwhelming burden, *a fatigue;* غُي signifies *to goad.*

עיט (*comp.*) Action of *cleaving* the air with rapidity, *swooping* down upon something: literally, *a bird of prey.*

עיח (*comp.*) That which tends *to be united, to amalgamate* strongly; a violent desire, keen sympathy; *thirst.* See עם.

עין (*comp.*) Corporeal manifestation; *the eye.* See ען.

עיה (*comp.*) That which manifests a thing which is *volatile, dry, inflammable, arid;* thence, that which *languishes* for lack of humidity. See עף.

עיר (*comp.*) That which manifests a physical impulsion, a general attraction; a common centre of activity, a supervision: as *a city, fort, rampart, body-guard.* See ער.

עך HUCH. Root not used in Hebrew. In composition it has the sense of the Arabic علك, which characterizes that which is held with effort, which delays, defers, etc.

In a restricted sense علك signifies *to soil, to stain.*

על HUL. The material sign ע considered under its vocal relation, being united to that of expansive movement, composes a root which characterizes, hieroglyphically and figuratively, primal matter, its extensive force, its vegetation, its development in space, its elementary energy: this same sign, considered as consonant changes the expression of the root which it constitutes, to the point of making it represent only ideas of crime, fraud, perversity.

The Arabic عل has lost nearly all the intellectual ideas characterized by the Hebraic root. In a restricted sense عل signifies to give up to physical relaxation, to grow weak, to become effeminate, to be made sick, and the verb غل, the formation of seed in the plant.

עַל   *Material extent;* its progression, its indefinite extension, expressed by the relations *toward, by, for, on account of, notwithstanding, according to,* etc. Its aggregative power, its growth by juxtaposition, expressed by *upon, over, above, along with, near, adjoining, about, overhead, beyond,* etc.

עַל or עָלַל (*intens.*) That which *grows, extends, rises, mounts;* that which is *high, eminent, superior;* the *aggregated, superficial* part of anything whatsoever: that which constitutes *the form, the factor, the exterior appearance; the labour of things; an extension, a heap;* etc.

עוּל   Every kind of material development; that which is raised above another thing: *a fœtus* in the womb of the mother, *an infant* at the breast; *a leaf* upon the tree; every manner of acting conformable to matter; every *appearance,* every *superficies* as much literally as figuratively; the state of being *double, false, hypocritical,* etc. See עוה.

עַם   HUM. Matter universalized by its faculties: tendency of its parts one toward another; the force which makes them gravitate toward the general mass, which brings them to aggregation, accumulation, conjunction; the force whose unknown cause is expressed, by the relations *with, toward, among, at.*

עַם   Every idea of union, junction, conjunction, nearness: *a bond, a people, a corporation.*

The Arabic عم presents in general the same sense as the Hebrew. As a verb, it is the action of generalizing, of making common. By غم is understood a painful condition, *a sorrow, an uneasiness,* etc.

עָמַם (*intens.*) Every union in great number; *a multitude*: action of *gathering, covering, hiding, obscuring, heating* by piling up. See עִים.

RADICAL VOCABULARY 419

עֻן HUN. Material void embodied, made heavy, obscure, dark. In considering here the root עֻ, image of every superficies, every inflection, united by contraction to the augmentative sign ן, one sees easily an entire inflection: if this inflection is convex, it is a circle, a globe; if it is a concave, it is a hole, a recess.

עֻן and עֻנן (*intens.*) *A space, a gloomy air, a thick vapour, a cloud.*

The Arabic عن signifies in general, *to appear,* to be obvious to the senses, to be shown under a material form. In an abstract sense, it is a designative relation represented by *from*.

עֻנן Action of *darkening, of thickening vapours, of gathering clouds;* action of *forming a body; of inhabiting, cohabiting;* the idea of *a corporation, troop, corps, people, association;* of *a temporal dwelling;* the idea of every *corruption* attached to the body and to bodily acts; *vice*: that which is *evil; that which afflicts, humiliates, affects;* in a restricted sense *a burden; a crushing occupation; poverty,* etc.

עִין From the idea attached to the manifestation of bodies, comes that of the eye, and of everything which is related thereunto. In a metaphorical sense, *a source, a fountain,* etc. See עֻן and עִין.

עֻן Onomatopoetic root expressing a deep breath, either in lamenting, groaning or crying; thence,

עֻן *A cry, clamour, evocation, response;* a keen tightness of breath, *suffocation, oppression,* literally as well as figuratively.

עֻם HUS. This root, little used, expresses the action of pressing, of trampling under foot.

The Arabic عس expresses the action of *feeling, groping;* also that of *roving, going about without a purpose,* etc.

עֻע HUH. Root not used in Hebrew. The Arabic عاه indicates everything which bends and turns.

עף HUPH. This root, considered as a compound of the sign of material sense, united to that of interior activity, has only the idea of obscurity and darkness; but its greatest usage is onomatopoetic to depict movements which are easy, agile, light, swift.

The Chaldaic עפף signifies properly *to blow the fire;* to light it and make it burn; the Arabic عف, with this idea, characterizes the state of that which has passed through the fire, which is pure, spotless, without vice, innocent; which abstains from all evil, etc.

עף (*onom.*) That which *rises, expands, opens out* into the air; that which *soars, flies,* etc. See עוף and עיף.

עץ HUTZ. Determined matter offered to the senses according to any mode of existence whatsoever.

עץ Hieroglyphically, *substance* in general; in the literal or figurative sense, *vegetable substance,* and the physical faculty of *vegetation*: in a very restricted sense, *wood, a tree*: that which is *consolidated* and *hardened,* which appears under a constant and determined form. See עוץ.

The Arabic عص characterizes, in general, the root of things, their radical origin. In a less extended sense it is that which serves as point of support; that which is solid, firm, valid. When this root is reinforced by the guttural inflection in غص, it is applied to that which is oppressive by nature; which molests, vexes, mystifies; it is, in a restricted sense, the action of *causing indigestion; an obstruction, a lump in the throat.* By عض is understood the action of *biting,* and by غض, that of *making defective.*

עק HUCH. Every idea of extreme condensation, of contraction with itself, of hardness; figuratively, anguish. See עוק.

The Arabic غقّ characterizes the idea of that which is refractory, that which being pushed, repels; that which disobeys, etc. As onomatopoetic root غقّ expresses the flight and cry of the crow, the noise made by waves breaking, etc.

ער HUR. This root should be carefully distinguished under two different relations. Under the first, it is the root עִ image of physical reality and symbol of the exterior form of things which is united to the sign of movement proper ר; under the second, it is the sign of material sense united by contraction to the root אוֹר, image of light, and forming with it a perfect contrast: thence, first:

ער *Passion,* in general; *an inner ardour, vehement, covetous; an irresistible impulse; a rage, disorder; an exciting fire* literally as well as figuratively. Secondly:

ער *Blindness, loss of light* or *intelligence,* literally as well as figuratively; *absolute want, destitution,* under all possible relations; *nakedness, sterility,* physically and morally. In a restricted sense, *the naked skin, the earth, arid and without verdure: a desert.*

The Arabic عر has preserved almost none of the intellectual ideas developed by the Hebraic root. One recognizes, however, the primitive sense of this important root even in the modern idiom, where عر signifies *to dishonour, contaminate, cover with dirt,* and غر, *to deceive* by false appearances, *to lead* into error, *to delude;* etc.

ערר (*intens.*) The highest degree of excitement in the fire of passions; the most complete privation of anything whatsoever.

עור Action of inflaming the fire of passions, depriving of physical and moral light. Here the primitive root ער, confounding its two relations by means of the convertible sign ו, presents a mass of mixed expressions. It is the action of *awaking, exciting, stirring; of renouncing. depriving one's self, being stripped naked, of watching, superintending, guarding; of drawing away, misleading*: it is *a nude body, a skin; a guard house, a dark cavern; a city*, etc. See עוּר and עִיר.

עָשׁ HUSH. Every idea of conformation by aggregation of parts, or in consequence of an intelligent movement, of combination or plan formed in advance by the will: thence,

עַשׂ *A work, a composition; a creation, a fiction, a labour* of any sort, *a thing;* action of *doing* in general. See עָשִׂיו.

The Arabic عش has lost the radical sense, and instead of a formation in general, is restricted to designating a particular formation, as that of a nest, garment, etc. غش signifies to commit fraud, falsification; to feign, dissimulate, etc.

עֵת HUTH. That which takes all forms, which has only relative existence, which is inflected by sympathy, reaction, reciprocity. The product of material sense, *time;* that is to say *the moment when one feels,* expressed by the adverbial relations *now, already, at once, incontinent, etc.*

The Arabic عت signifies literally *to prey upon, to wear out, to ruin;* which is a result of the lost radical meaning. عت or غث signifies that which preys upon the mind, as *care, sorrow, alarm, sad news,* etc.

פ P.PH. This character as consonant, belongs to the labial sound, and possesses two distinct articulations: by the first P, it is joined to the character בּ or B, of which it is a reinforcement; by the second PH, it is joined to the character ו become consonant and pronounced V or F.

As symbolic image it represents the mouth of man, whose most beautiful attribute it depicts, that of uttering his thoughts. As grammatical sign, it is that of speech, and of that which is related thereunto. The Hebrew does not employ it as article; but everything proves that many of the Egyptians used it in this way and thus confounded it with its analogue ב, by a peculiar affectation of the pronunciation. Perhaps also a certain dialect admitted it at the head of words as emphatic article in place of the relation פה; this appears all the more probable, since in Hebrew, a fairly large quantity of words exist where it remains such, as I shall remark in my notes.

Its arithmetical number is 80.

פא PHA. That which is the most apparent of a thing, the part which first strikes the sight.

פא *The face* of things in general; in a more restricted sense, *the mouth, the beak;* that of which one speaks with emphasis, that which is made noticeable.

In Arabic this root displays its force in فِ *mouth*, and in فه *to speak*. The verb فا characterizes literally, that which opens, separates, as the mouth.

פאר (*comp.*) Every kind of *ornament, glory, palms*. See פר.

פב PHB. Root not used in Hebrew nor in Arabic.

פג PHG. That which extends afar, which wanders, is extended, loses its strength, its heat.

The Arabic جِ has nearly the same sense. As noun, it is every kind of crudeness, unripeness; as verb, it is the action of *separating, opening, disjoining*, etc.

פוג Action of *being cool, freezing;* of losing movement.

פַּד   PHD. Every idea of enlargement, liberation, redemption. The Arabic ڢد signifies to raise the voice, to show one's self generous, magnificent, arrogant.

The meaning of the Hebraic root is found in the compound ڢدا which signifies literally *to deliver*.

פֶּה   PHEH. This root is the analogue of the root פא ; but in Hebrew particularly, it emphasizes the thing that one wishes to distinguish in time or in a fixed place; as in *that very place, right here, this, that, these*.

פה   In a literal sense, *mouth, breath, voice*, in a figurative sense, *speech, eloquence, oratorical inspiration*: that which presents *an opening*, as the mouth; which constitutes part of a thing, as *a mouthful;* which follows *a mode, a course*, as speech.

The Arabic ڢه has in general, the same sense as the Hebrew.

פוֹ   PHOU. This root is the analogue of the roots פא and פה: but its expression is more onomatopoetic in describing the breath which comes from the mouth.

The Arabic ڢو is not far removed from the radical sense of the Hebrew.

פוה   (*comp.*)   Action of *blowing.*   See פה.

פון   (*comp.*)   Action of *hesitating.*   See פן.

פוץ   (*comp.*)   Action of *spreading, dispersing, melting.*   See פץ.

פוק   (*comp.*)   Action of being moved by an alternating movement.   See פק.

פור   (*comp.*)   That which *bursts forth, shines out, appears.*   See פר.

פוש   (*comp.*)   That which *spreads* abundantly, which *overflows.*   See פש.

RADICAL VOCABULARY

פָּז PHZ. That which throws flashes, **gleams**, rays: which is sharply reflected: thence,

פָז *Purest gold; keenest joy; a topaz.*

The Arabic فّ characterizes the movement of that which rises quickly, spurts up, leaps, struggles, etc.

פוּז Action of *emitting sperm.*

פָּח PHEH. Everything which is drawn in, expanded, as *the breath;* all that which is unfolded in order to envelop and seize, as *a net;* thence,

פחה Every idea of *administration, administrator, state, government.*

The Arabic فِ constitutes an onomatopoetic and idiomatic root which describes every kind of hissing of the voice, snoring, strong respiration, rattling. When this root is strengthened in فخ, it signifies literally, *an ambush; a trap.*

פוח Action of *inhaling, expiring; respiring, blowing;* action of *inspiring, communicating* one's will, *governing.*

פחז (comp.) Every idea *of breath, of lightness, of unstable thing.*

פחת (comp.) *A yawn, an hiatus, a hole.*

פָט PHT. An opening, a pit; a dilation; a prorogation given to something.

The Arabic فت signifies literally, *to crumble;* ظ *to rise, leap.* From the latter word is formed فض which characterizes that which acts abruptly, with cruelty, etc.

פט Action of *opening* the mouth, *yawning;* figuratively, the action of *crying, chattering, ranting,* etc.

פִּי PHI. This root is the analogue of the two roots פא and פה; but its expression is more manifest.

פִּיה *A beak; the orifice* of anything; the prominent part, *an angle; a discourse,* and particularly, *a message.*

The Arabic فِي departs from the Hebraic root and instead of developing the primitive فِي *the mouth,* from the moral stand point; it develops it from the physical, characterizing that which is interior and opposed to the surface of things. The root فِي conceived abstractly, is represented by the adverbial relations, *in, into, within.* As noun, it designates the shadowy part of the body, *the umbra;* as verb, it signifies *to darken, to shade.*

פִּיד (comp.) *Ruin, disaster.*

פִּיח (comp.) *Soot.*

פַּךְ PHCH. Every distillation which comes from vapour suddenly condensed: *a drop of water;* metaphorically, *a lens.*

The Arabic فك signifies literally *to be dissolved.*

פַּל PHL. The emphatic sign, united by contraction to the root אל, symbol of every elevation, constitutes a root which develops all ideas of distinction, privilege, choice, election, setting aside: thence,

פַל Some thing *wonderful, precious,* which is considered *a mystery*: *a miracle*: *a distinguished, privileged* man whom one reveres; *a noble, a magistrate;* that which is set aside, hidden in all fruits, *the germ;* literally, *a bean.*

The Arabic فل has not preserved the moral ideas developed by the Hebrew. This root, inclining toward the physical sense, is limited to expressing that which is separated, extracted, drawn from another thing: that which is divided into distinct parts. In the modern idiom فل signifies literally *to drive away.*

RADICAL VOCABULARY 427

פלל (*intens.*) From the idea of noble and magistrate, springs that of *dominion, power*: thence, the action of *judging* others, *rendering justice, governing,* etc.

פם PHM. Root not used in Hebrew. The Chaldaic פום signifies *mouth;* the Arabic فم has exactly the same sense. As verb فوم, is *to bake bread, to cook;* in general, that which is related to food for the mouth.

פן PHN. The face of anything whatsoever, the front of a thing, that which is presented first to the view: that which strikes, astonishes, frightens: every idea of presence, conversion, consideration, observation, etc.

פן *The aspect* of a person, *his countenance, face, mien, air,* sad or serene, mild or irritated: action *of turning* the face, expressed by the relations *before, in the presence of, from before,* etc. Action *causing* the face *to turn,* expressed by *beware! no! lest! for fear of!* etc. That which imposes by its aspect: *a prince, a leader; a star, a ruby, a tower,* etc. That which is the cause of *disturbance,* of *hesitation.* See פון.

The Arabic فن has evidently the same primitive idea which has produced the Hebraic root; but although starting from the same principle, its developments have been different; they have inclined rather toward the physical than toward the moral, as can be remarked in general, of other roots. Thus, from the primitive idea deduced from the exterior face which things present, from their manner of being phenomenal, the Arabic idiom has drawn the secondary ideas of complication and of complicating; of mixture and of mixing; of variety and of varying; of specification and of specifying; of classification and of classifying; so that finally, considering as general, what had been particular, this same root فن is used to designate *an art,* or *a science* of some sort, because it is by means of arts and sciences that one can class all things and **examine** them under their aspects.

פס   PHS. That which comprises only a portion of the circumference or totality of a thing.

פס   *A part, a face, a phase.* Action of *diminishing,* of breaking into pieces.

The Arabic فص signifies literally to *examine minutely.*

פע   PHUH. Onomatopoetic root which depicts the cry of an animal with yawning jaws. Figuratively, a clamour; metaphorically, a diffusion.

The Arabic فغم characterizes the call of the shepherds.

פעל (*comp.*) Every kind of *act, work, action.* See על.

פעם (*comp.*) Every kind of *agitation, movement, impulse*: literally, *the feet.* See עם.

פען (*comp.*) Every kind of *augury, observation, phenomenon.* See פ.

פער (*comp.*) Every kind of *distention, relaxation;* action of *depriving, stripping, making naked,* etc. See ער.

פץ   PHTZ. Every idea of diffusion, loosening, setting forth, giving liberty. See פוץ.

The Arabic فص presents the same sense in general. In a restricted sense فص signifies to *examine minutely,* and فض to *break the seal.*

פק   PHCQ. That which opens and shuts; which is stirred by an alternating movement back and forth; that which is intermittent, inquisitive, exploratory, etc.

The Arabic فق has in general the same ideas as the Hebrew. As verb, this root expresses particularly the action of *releasing, opening, dilating,* etc.

RADICAL VOCABULARY

פק and פקק (*intens.*) Action of *passing* from one place to another, *being carried here and there, going and coming;* action of *obstructing, standing in the way,* etc. See פוק.

פר PHR. The emphatic sign replacing the sign of interior activity ב and united to that of movement proper ר, constitutes a root which develops all ideas of fructification, production, elementary generation.

פר Any *progeny,* any *produce* whatsoever; *the young* of any animal, particularly of the cow. That which is *fertile, fecund, productive.*

The Arabic ف, being applied principally to developing in the Hebraic פר the idea which had relation to the young of a weak timid animal, has characterized the action of fleeing; the flight, the fear which makes one give way; also the growth of teeth, dentition; the examination that is made of the teeth of an animal to discover its age, its strength, its weakness, etc.

פרה Action of *producing, bearing.*

פרח That which *vegetates, germinates, swarms*: a *seed, a flower.*

פרי *Fruit;* figuratively *an effect, a consequence.*

פרו or פרע Onomatopoetic root which describes the noise of a thing which cleaves the air, or strikes it with a violent movement.

פרך (*comp.*) Every abrupt movement which *breaks, bruises.*

פרם (*comp.*) *To rend* a garment.

פרס (*comp.*) That which *breaks;* that which *divides* in *breaking.*

פרץ (*comp.*) Action of *breaking* into many pieces; *reducing to powder.*

פרק (*comp.*) That which *tears,* draws forcibly from a place, *breaks* the bonds, *sets at liberty.*

פָּרַשׁ (comp.) Action of *dispersing, divulging, manifesting, specifying;* action of piercing: metaphorically, *a hunter, a horseman.*

פֵּשׁ PHSH. Every idea of pride, vanity, extravagance; of *inflation,* literally as well as figuratively. That which seeks *to extend, to put itself in evidence.* See פוּשׁ.

The Arabic نش is an onomatopoetic and idiomatic root which depicts the noise made by the air when escaping from the place where it has been confined, as when it comes from a bladder which has been pressed; thence, if one considers the bladder, the sense of *letting out the air;* if the air which escapes is considered, the same sense of doing a thing with vivacity, arrogance, passion, etc.

פַּת PHTH. Every idea of dilation, extending easily, allowing to be penetrated, opened; every divisibility, every opening; space, extent: thence,

פַּת *Space* in general, or *any space* in particular; that which is indifferent in itself, *impassive;* metaphorically, *a fop, a fool, a silly person, a simpleton*: action of *persuading, deceiving;* etc.

The Arabic ڧ preserves the radical sense of the Hebrew, without having the same developments. As verb, it is the action of *scattering, spreading here and there,* tearing into small pieces, etc.

צ TZ. This character as consonant, belongs to the hissing sound, and describes as onomatopœia, all objects which have relations with the air and wind. As symbolic image, it represents the refuge of man, and the end toward which he tends. It is the final and terminative sign, having reference to scission, limit, solution, end. Placed at the beginning of words it indicates the movement which carries toward the limit of which it is the sign; placed at the end, it marks the very limit where it has tended.

Its arithmetical number is 90.

צָא TZA. The final sign צ, as initial and united to that of power, characterizes in this root, that which leaves material limits, breaks the shackles of the body, matures, grows; is born exteriorly.

The Arabic صاما expresses with much energy the effort made by the young of animals to open their eyes.

צֹאן (comp.) *Flocks* and *herds;* in a broader sense, *a productive faculty.*

צוֹא Onomatopoetic root expressing a movement of disgust and repulsion at the sight of a filthy object.

צוֹא Every kind of *filth, obscenity, excrement.*

צָב TZB. Every idea of concourse, of crowd; that which rises, swells, stands in the way; that which serves as a dike; that which is conducted and unfolded according to fixed rules.

The Arabic صِبّ characterizes in general, that which flows after the manner of fluids; metaphorically, that which follows a determined inclination, which obeys an impulse. ضِبّ expresses every kind of emanation in general; that which belongs to, that which results from, another thing. In a very restricted sense ضِبّ signifies a species of lizard.

צָב *An army, a military ordnance; a general order* observed by a mass of individuals, *discipline*: thence, *honour, glory, renown.* Metaphorically *the host of stars, the harmony which regulates their movements.*

צָג TZG. Root not used in Hebrew. The Ethiopic ጸገግ (*tzagg*) signifies *to publish.* The Arabic جَصّ indicates the noise made by iron striking upon iron. ضَجّ signifies *a tumult; an uproar.*

צַד   TZD. That which is insidious, artful, double, sly, opposed, adverse, deceitful, seductive.

The Arabic صد presents in general, the same sense as the Hebrew; that is to say, every idea of opposition, defense. ضد expresses the state of quarreling, disputing.

צד   In a literal sense, very restricted, *the side;* in a broad and figurative sense, *a secret, dissimulating hindrance; an artifice, a snare.*

צוּד   Action of *setting snares; hunting, fishing, ensnaring* birds; *deceiving.*

צָהּ   TZEH. Root analogous to the root צָא and develops the same ideas.

The Arabic صه is an onomatopoetic root which characterizes the action of one who imposes silence; it is represented by the interjective relations, *hist! hush!* This root being reinforced at the end in صمع designates literally *silence.*

צהל   (comp.) *To neigh.*

צהר   (comp.) *Luminous ray; the splendour of midday.* See צר.

צוּ   TZOU. This very important root characterizes every kind of line drawn toward an end, of which the sign צ is symbol. It develops every idea of order, command, direction, impressed by the *primum mobile.*

The Arabic صو has departed much from the radical sense of the Hebrew, of which it has retained only certain physical developments. Thus صوا expresses a sort of natural humectation; and ضو, the impression which light causes upon the organ of sight. As onomatopoetic root ضوه denotes the sound of the voice.

צוה A *law, an ordinance; an order, a command;* that which leads to an end: *a precept, a statute, a maxim of conduct*: action of *ordering, directing, leading; impressing a movement.*

צוה (comp.) *To cry aloud.*

צול (comp.) *A thing which is propagated afar, as noise; depth,* literally and figuratively. See צל.

צום (comp.) *To fast.* See צם.

צוף (comp.) *To overflow.* See צף.

צוץ (comp.) *To blossom.* See צץ.

צוק (comp.) *That which presses; holds back forcibly.* See צק.

צור (comp.) *That which compresses, forms, conforms.* See צר.

צות (comp.) *To set on fire, to kindle.* See צת.

צץ TZZ. Root not used in Hebrew nor in Arabic.

As onomatopoetic root ضّ characterizes the inarticulate sounds emitted from closed jaws. Figuratively it is *to champ the bit.*

צח TZEH. *That which is dry, arid, exposed to the rays of the sun. That which is clear, serene, radiant.*

The Arabic ضح offers in general, the same sense as the Hebraic root and adds much to the developments of the moral side. In the Arabic idiom, it is the state of that which is sane, upright, pure, true, clean, rectified, etc. The verb ضح characterizes that which shines on account of its purity.

צחה *State of being exposed to the rays of the sun, being thirsty, dry, etc.*

צט TZT. Root not used in Hebrew. The Arabic ضلل designates *a strong man, a formidable adversary.*

צִי TZI. Root analogous to the root צָא and צָה, but develops the same idea with greater intensity.

صِا expresses a sort of lotion, libation, aqueous emanation. ضِي signifies literally *brightness*, every kind of luminous effusion.

צִיָה Every *place* exposed to the rays of the sun, and made *dry* and *glaring*.

צִיד (*comp.*) Every opposition which springs from artifice. See צָד.

צָךְ TZCH. Root not used in Hebrew. The Arabic صَكّ is an onomatopoetic root which depicts the noise made by two flat stones rubbed together to crush anything whatsoever.

צָל TZL. This root, composed of the final sign united to the directive sign, characterizes a thing whose effect is spread afar. This thing expresses, according to the genius of the Hebraic tongue, either noise, or shadow passing through air and void; or void itself, containing darkness: thence,

צָל Every *noise* that is striking, clear, piercing like that of brass; every *shadow* carried, projected a great distance into space; every obscure *depth*, whose bottom is unknown: metaphorically, *a screaming voice;* any kind of object extending overhead and making a shade as *a canopy, dais, covering, roof, veil;* every deep, obscure place, *a cavern*. See צוּל.

The Arabic صل has evidently the same radical sense as the Hebrew צָל, but this root, besides its primitive sense, having also an onomatopoetic sense, has received developments much more extended. According to the first sense, the verb صل characterizes the state of that which grows dark being corrupted, of that which imitates the darkness of shadow, which lengthens, gains, as a shadow, etc. According to the second sense, it is a prolonged sound, a cry which invokes succour, a prayer, etc. ضل expresses that which is prolonged indefinitely, wanders, disappears, etc.

צם TZM. That which is carried with avidity, with force, toward a thing; that which covets or seizes eagerly.

The Arabic صم has the same radical sense as the Hebrew. As verb, it is the action of obstructing, opposing forcibly the egress of anything whatsoever; state of being *deaf*, stupid, etc.

ضم expresses that which is strongly united; an aggregation, an agglomeration, *a mass*.

צם *Thirst.*
צמם *A knot, a braid, an indissoluble bond*: thence,
צום *Action of fasting.*

צן TZN. That which conserves, preserves, puts in safety.

צן *A dwelling* where one gathers for shelter; a *shield, an urn, a basket;* any sort of defensive *weapon*, etc.

The Arabic صن characterizes that which being shut up becomes warm and smells badly; figuratively, it is concentrated anger, *rancour.* ضن is the state of that which is sordid, tenacious, avaricious.

צס TZS. Root not used in Hebrew nor in Arabic.

צע TZUH. This root, analogous to the roots צא, צה, צי develops the same ideas of tendency toward a determined end; but adds to it the particular expression of the root עי, image of all material development: thence,

ץע   Every kind of *machine, automaton;* anything acting like clock work: that which is *wandering, irresolute, running to and fro,* etc.

The Arabic صم presents the same sense as the Hebrew and characterizes in particular, that which is supple, flabby, ungainly, slack, etc. As onomatopoetic root صم denotes silence, and the verb ضم, the action of bringing to uniformity that which tends to be dispersed.

ףצ   TZPH. Every idea of diffusion, profusion, overflowing; that which flows like water; which follows a steady incline.

The Arabic صف in departing from this last idea, develops the action of *putting in order,* arranging, co-ordinating, instructing, etc., and ضف, to put together, *to assemble.*

ףוצ   Action of *flowing, following the course of water, swimming, floating.*

ץצ   TZTZ. Root not used in Hebrew. The Arabic صص expresses the cry of small birds, by an imitative noise.

קצ   TZCQ. Every noise, every sudden clamour.

The Arabic صق expresses *clapping the hands.* In the modern idiom صق, indicates consent given by a hand clasp: *an engagement, a note.*

רצ   TZR. If this root is considered as composed of the final sign united by contraction to the elementary root רא, one perceives all universal ideas of form, formation, co-ordination, elementary configuration: but if it is considered as result of the union of the same final sign with that of movement proper, one perceives only the idea

RADICAL VOCABULARY 437

of a tight grasp, an oppression, an extreme compression. Thence,

צוּר   Every *formation* by the sole co-ordination of the elements, by their own aggregation, or by their artificial liaison and their limitation to a model; every *creation, fiction, picture, image, exemplar*: action of *forming, conforming, modeling, figuring, painting,* etc.

צוּר   Every *compression* by effect of an exterior movement which *pushes*, which *presses* the elementary parts upon each other toward a common point: that which *obliges, forces, oppresses, obsesses, besieges, presses upon, acts in a hostile manner; a violent adversary, enemy, competitor, rival*: that which causes *anguish, suffering*: *the point of a sword, the steepness of a rock,* etc.

The Arabic صر signifies literally, *to press, draw closer, link, knit, twist, pack,* etc., and ضر the action of injuring, wounding, offending, etc.

צוּאר   (*comp.*) That which holds to corporeal forms: in a restricted sense, *the neck*.

ציר   That which serves as bond: *the vertebræ;* the muscular and bony ligatures: *the hinges* of a door which fasten it to the wall: *the ambassadors* of a king; *a legation,* etc.

צש   TZSH. Root not used in Hebrew. The Ethiopic ፀዐሸ (*tzoush*) expresses that which is tortuous, bandy-legged, counterfeit.

צת   TZTH. Every impulse given toward the same end; every communicated movement; as is expressed by the Arabic صت.

צתה   A *conflagration;* the action of *setting fire*.

ק   KQ. This character as consonant, belongs to the
guttural sound. As symbolic image it represents a trenchant weapon, that which serves as instrument for man, to
defend, to make an effort for him. It has already been remarked, that nearly all the words which hold to this consonant in the greater part of the idioms, designate force
and constraint. It is, in the Hebraic tongue, the compressive and decisive sign; that of agglomerative or repressive force. It is the character כ entirely materialized;
the progression of the sign is as follows: ה, vocal principle,
sign of absolute life: ח, aspirate principle, sign of elementary existence: ג, guttural principle, organic sign: כ,
same principle strengthened, sign of assimilated existence
holding to forms alone: ק, same principle greatly
strengthened, sign of mechanical, material existence giving
the means of forms.

Its arithmetical number is 100.

קא   CA, KA or QUA. This is the analogous root of
קי which characterizes the expression of the sign. As onomatopoetic root it is a convulsive and violent effort;
to spue out, to vomit forth.

The Arabic ڡ which takes the place of the primitive root, reinforces all its acceptations. As onomatopoetic
root قاق depicts the croaking of a crow.

קוא   Action of vomiting.

קיא   Vomit.

קב   KB. The onomatopoetic root קא, united by
contraction to the sign of interior activity ב, expresses
all rejection, expurgation. Literally, it is *an excavation;*
figuratively, *an anathema, a malediction.*

But if one considers here the figure ק, as being contracted with the root אב, then the root קב characterizes
every object capable of and containing any kind of mea-

sure: literally, *genitalia muliebra;* figuratively, *a bad place.*

The Arabic ڧ is an onomatopoetic and idiomatic root expressing every effort that one makes to cut, carve, sharpen. It characterizes, in general, that which retrenches or is retrenched; thence, the idea of a prince, a magistrate; of any man or any thing which operates a line of demarcation. ڧ designates again, the principal sound of the musical system, *the keynote.* See כם.

קג KG. Root not used in Hebrew nor in Arabic.

קד KD. The vertical point, pole, summit, of anything whatsoever; the pivot, motive, point upon which all bears, turns.

The Arabic ڧ has evidently the primitive sense of the Hebraic root but develops, however, other acceptations. It is, in general, a line of demarcation, fissure, notch; in particular, it is *the figure* of anything whatsoever, the corporeal proportion, etc.

קוד In a restricted sense, action of *inclining the head.*

קה KEH. This root is the analogue of קו, to which one can refer for the real meaning of the sign. As onomatopoetic root it expresses the sudden cry which is given to frighten, to astound, put to flight. See קא.

The Arabic ڧ is an onomatopoetic root which depicts a sudden and immoderate burst of laughter.

קהה State of *being frightened,* by an unforeseen noise, *stunned, stupefied.*

קהל (*comp.*) A call *to gather* the cattle.

קו COU, KOU or QUOU. This root, as well as its analogues קא or קה, when they are not onomatopoetic, designate in general, that which is indefinite, vague, indeterminate, unformed: it is matter suitable to be put in action, the mechanical movement which acts upon it; the obtuse, vague, blind but irresistible force which leads it; *necessity*.

קִי   The mathematical *line* and that which represents it: *a level, a rule, a clew;* that which holds irresistibly to a point; metaphorically *desire, hope;* figuratively, *sound, echo.*

The Arabic ڧ is no longer used in its radical form, but one finds a great number of its derivatives, all of which hold more or less closely to the Hebraic root; such as قَاب *obedience*, and in general, every proper, analogous thing; قُوِي *force, valour, virtue;* قُوَه *faculty, power*, etc. This onomatopoetic root قَوَه, depicts as in Hebrew a resounding, prolonged sound, like that of the hunter's horn.

קָוֵה   Action of *stretching, being carried toward* an object, *desiring, becoming, mingling with, being formed* of it. That which is *obtuse;* that which *acts without intelligence;* that which, like an echo, *repeats the voice* or *sound*, without seizing or keeping it.

קִחָ   (*comp.*)   Action of *reaching out,* making effort to *seize* something. See קָה.

קִיט   (*comp.*)   Action of being *disgusted.* See קָט.

קוֹל   (*comp.*)   *Voice, sound.* See קָל.

קוּם   (*comp.*)   *Substance* in general. See קָם.

קִין   (*comp.*)   *Lamentation.* See קָן.

קוֹף   (*comp.*)   *An ape.* See קָף.

קִיץ   (*comp.*)   Action of *cutting, cutting off; pricking.* See קָץ.

קוּר   (*comp.*)   Action of *digging* a well, a snare; action of *surrounding, catching, destroying,* etc. See קָר.

קוֹשׁ   (*comp.*)   *A snare;* action of *entangling, setting a trap.* See קָשׁ.

קֶז KZ. Root not used in Hebrew. The Arabic قز indicates every kind of leap, assault; impetuous movement to overpower a thing. In the modern idiom, the verb قز signifies *to weave*.

קֶה KEH. The idea of an effort that is made toward a thing to seize it to comprehend it. See קוה.

The Arabic قه characterizes that which is pure, frank, sincere.

קֶט KT. This root develops the idea of resistance opposed to that of tension, of extension: thence in a very broad sense, the *Occident;* in a very restricted sense, *a stick*. See קוט

The Arabic قط is an onomatopoetic and idiomatic root which depicts every kind of cut made without effort, as with a knife, etc. This root employed as adverbial relation is represented by *only, only so much, so little*.

קִי KI or QUI. This root is the analogue of the roots קה and קו, whose power it manifests.

The Arabic قي signifies according to the radical sense, an arid, desert land; according to the onomatopoetic sense, *to vomit*.

קִין (comp.) *A lance*.
קִיר (comp.) *Wall of circumvallation, enclosure, fortified precinct*. See קר.

קֶךְ KCH. Root not used in Hebrew nor in Arabic.

קֶל KL. The root קו, image of that which is undefined, vague, unformed, united by contraction to the directive sign ל, produces a root which designates that which is deprived of consistency and form; sound, voice, wind: but, if this same root is conceived as formed by the union of the compressive sign ק , with the root אל image of all elevation and all superior force, it expresses then the action of roasting, parching, etc.

קל Every idea *of lightness, rapidity, velocity*: that which is *attenuated, slender, thin*: without consistency; of little value; *vile, cowardly, infamous*.

The Arabic قل presents the same radical sense as the Hebrew; but, as verb, it is in particular, that which becomes *less;* which is reduced, lightened; which loses ground; becomes rarefied, etc.

קול *Voice, sound.* The Arabic قال signifies literally, *to say, speak, state, express.*

קם KM. The root קו, being universalized by the addition of the collective sign ם , characterizes substance in general, undefined nature; a thing whose only properties are extent and necessity: thence,

קום Action of existing in substance, being *substantialized;* assuming stability; state of being *extended, established; constituted; strengthened;* qualified to assume all forms; action of being *spread out; rising* into space. Action of *existing, subsisting, consisting, persisting, resisting*: that which is *necessary, real; rigid, irresistible*: that which is *opposed,* is *raised* against another thing, shows itself *refractory, inflexible,* etc.

The Arabic قم has preserved none of the intellectual ideas developed by the Hebraic root. As verb, قم expresses the action of taking away the superficies of things, making them dry, clean, etc. In particular, it is the action of *sweeping.* The radical sense of the Hebrew is developed by the Arabic قام .

קים Every idea of *manifest opposition, insurrection*: that which is *adverse, rebellious;* matter in travail.

RADICAL VOCABULARY 443

קן KN. This root has two sources whose expressions are blended, as it were, in one. By the first, it is derived from the root קו, image of the blind force which moves matter, united to the augmentative sign ן ; by the second, it springs from the compressive sign ק, contracted with the root אן, symbol of all corporeal circumscription; thence,

קן That which *tends* with ardour toward a thing; that which is *envious, usurping, vehement, covetous* of gain and possession; thence,

קן That which is *centralized, concentrated* in itself.

From these two roots קין is formed, in which are assembled the opposed ideas of *appetent tension* and *compression, vehemence* and *closeness, power* and *density*. It contains *the central force, profound basis, rule* and *measure* of things; also *the faculty* which *seizes, usurps, agglomerates, appropriates* and *assimilates with itself*.

The Arabic قن although holding to the same root as the Hebrew קן, is however, far from preserving or developing so great a number of ideas. Nearly all of those which were intellectual have become lost. The verb قان, which partakes most of the radical sense, signifies literally *to forge* the iron, to strike it while it is hot; *to solder* metals, to unite them by means of the forge. قين is *a blacksmith*.

קן or קנן (*intens.*) In a literal and restricted sense *a nest, a centre; a cane, a measure, a reed; an abode, a possession, an acquisition, conquest; a possessor, envious person, rival; envy, hatred, jealousy; an affair, property, wealth*, etc.

קם KS. Every idea of hazard, fatality, chance, etc. The Arabic قس expresses the kind of jealousy that one feels when the thing that one desires is possessed by another.

קָע KH. Every idea of line strongly traced, of stigma; of violent disordered movement which wounds, displaces, deranges, etc.

The Arabic قع is an onomatopoetic root which depicts the sound of the voice made by one who drives away a troublesome animal. Figuratively, all that which repels; a strong *bitterness;* briny, brackish water.

קָף KPH. Every idea of condensation, concretion; that which is coagulated, congealed, thickened, etc.

The Arabic قف presents the same radical sense. It is literally, the image of a humid thing when *shrunken* by drought.

קָץ KTS. The compressive sign united to the final sign, constitutes a root whence develop naturally, all ideas of term, limit, extremity, goal, summit, finish, cessation.

קץ and קָצָץ. (*intens.*) That which *cuts, limits, terminates, finishes* a thing; that which is *extreme, final,* without anything beyond: action of *cutting, cutting off, amputating,* etc. See קוץ.

The Arabic قص signifies literally *to shear,* to cut with scissors; figuratively *to follow* the tracks of someone, *to continue* a movement; *to narrate* a thing, etc.

קָק KK. Root not used in Hebrew. It is, in the Chaldaic קוֹק, the name given to the pelican; in the Arabic قاق it is onomatopoetic and describes the clucking of chickens.

קָר KR. The compressive sign united to that of movement proper, constitutes a root which develops the idea of that which is incisive, penetrating, firm, straight;

RADICAL VOCABULARY 445

that which engraves or which serves to engrave; every kind of engraving, character, or sign fitting to preserve the memory of things.

The Arabic ذ presents the same radical sense as the Hebrew, but with a certain difference in its developments. As verb, ذ signifies *to fix* in some place, on some thing; to stop there, to remember it, to make an act of commemoration; *to designate, to avow.*

קר From the idea of *character* and *writing* contained in this root, has come that of *reading*, and from *reading*, that of every *oratorical discourse* spoken aloud; thence the divers expressions of *crying out, exclaiming, speaking, proclaiming, reading, naming, designating* a thing *by name*, by expedient *sign; to convoke, evoke*, etc.

In making abstraction of the sign or character, and seeing only the cause which marks it, or the effect which follows it, one finds the idea of *course, contingency, concatenation;* thence, that of the *course of events, fate of occurrence;* action of *happening, occurring, hastening, arriving*, etc.

קור, קור or קיר. The idea of *incision* has brought forth that of *cutting in;* thence, the idea of *well, fountain, ditch, trap, snare, abyss;* that which is incisive, penetrating, firm, causes a sensation which recalls that of *cold*: thence with the idea of *coldness*, that which can shield, as *a walled enclosure, grotto, tower;* by extension, *a city*.

קש KSH. Every idea of perplexity, confusion, difficulty; that which is mixed, hardened, tightened, compact inextricable.

קש and קשש. (*intens.*) State of being *perplexed, confused, heavy, hardened;* action of *clearing up, seeking to know, scrutinizing, exploring*, etc.

The Arabic قش offers in general, the same ideas; it is, in a restricted sense, *to clean, rub, sweep*, etc.

The word קש , *a bow,* is derived from the Arabic قاس which signifies a curvature; but the Arabic word itself is attached to the Hebraic root.

קת KTH. Root not used in Hebrew. The Arabic ث or ت develops in general, every idea of attraction, extraction, agglomeration.

ר R. This character as consonant, belongs to the lingual sound. As symbolic image, it represents the head of man, his determining movement, his progress. According to Boehme the letter R draws its origin from the igneous faculty of nature. It is the emblem of fire. This man, who, without any learning, has often written in a manner astonishing to the wisest, assures in his book of the *Triple Life of Man,* that each inflection, vocal or consonantal, is a particular form of central nature. "Although speech varies them by transposition, nevertheless each letter has an origin at the centre of nature. This origin is wonderful and the senses can grasp it only by the light of the intelligence."

As grammatical sign, the character ר is, in the Hebraic tongue, the sign of all movement proper, good or bad. It is an original and frequentative sign, image of the renewal of things, as to their movement.

Its arithmetical number is 200.

רא RA. The sign of movement proper united to that of power, forms a root characterized hieroglyphically by the geometric radius; that is to say, by that kind of straight line which departing from the centre converges at any point whatsoever of the circumference: it is, in a very restricted sense, *a streak,* in a broader sense, *a ray* and metaphorically, *the visual ray,* visibility.

The Arabic رٰ presents exactly the same radical sense as the Hebrew. The developments of this root, which are very numerous in the Arabic idiom, all have reference, in general, in راي, رٰي, روي etc., to the action of *seeing*, or to the state of being seen.

ראה   Action of *seeing, fixing* the eyes upon an object, *beholding, considering; sight, vision, aspect* of a thing.

ראי   *A mirror*: figuratively, *an observation, examination*.

ראת   (*comp.*)   *Prophetic vision; spectacle; admirable thing*.

ראש   (*comp.*)   *The head*. See רש.

רב   RB. The sign of movement proper, united to that of interior activity, or by contraction with the root אב, image of all fructification, constitutes a root whence are developed all ideas of multiplication, augmentation, growth, grandeur: it is a kind of movement toward propagation, physically as well as morally.

The Arabic رب does not differ from the Hebrew. It is, in general, that which dominates, augments, grows, usurps, possesses, gathers together, governs, etc.

רב and רבב.   (*intens.*)   That which is *large, broad, increased*, whether in number or in volume; *augmented, multiplied;* that which is expressed by the adverbial relations, *much, more, still more, many;* ideas of *multitude, number, quantity; strength* or *power* which is drawn from number, etc.

רוב   (*comp.*)   Action of being *carried in a mass,* of making an *uproar,* raising *a quarrel, a dispute*.

רג   RG. Every kind of movement in the organs: *?motion, commotion, disorganization.*

The Arabic رج offers the same sense as the Hebrew. It is the action of *agitating, stirring; talking with familiarity.*

רד RD. The sign of movement proper united to the sign of elementary abundance, or by contraction with the root אר, image of every emanation, produces a root whose object is to describe every kind of indefinite movement, as that of a wheel.

The Arabic رد holds to the Hebrew in its radical sense, although the accessory ideas which emanate differ somewhat. It is, in general, a repeated movement which turns to itself. In particular, it is the action of *returning, replying, restoring*, etc.

רד or רדד. (*intens.*) That which *spreads out, unfolds, occupies space, takes possession* of a thing, by effect of a movement which is propagated circularly: *a wheel, a sphere, a veil*.

רוד Action of moving with firmness, either for *ascending*, or *descending;* action of *persevering* in one's will: *the domination* which is the natural bent of steadfastness and strength of soul.

רה REH. Root analogous to the root רא whose effect it increases.

רהה Action of *dazzling, fascinating* the eyes; of *troubling*.

The Arabic ره departs from the radical sense of the Hebrew, and develops only the accessory idea of weakness which follows physical or moral dizziness.

רהב (*comp.*) Every idea of magnitude, grandeur, force. See רב.

רהט (*comp.*) *A course*. See רט.

רן ROU. Root analogous to the root רא, but which, taking a more material expression, instead of characterizing *a luminous ray*, characterizes often *a stream of water*, the channel of a river, a brook: thence,

רוה Action of *watering, drinking, drenching*, etc. See רי.

The Arabic رو characterizes literally the **action of** *considering* the consequences, *reflecting* before doing a thing. The compound روٴ expresses a long, mature deliberation.

רוֹב (*comp.*) *Tumult.* See רֹב.
רוֹד (*comp.*) *Strength of the soul.* See רֹד.
רוֹח (*comp.*) *Movement of the air, the breath.* See רֹח.
רוֹם (*comp.*) *Action of rising* in being dilated, of filling space. See רֹם.
רוֹע (*comp.*) *Material movement, evil* and *disordered.* See רֹע.
רוּף (*comp.*) *Action of being shaken by a sudden movement.* See רֹף.
רוּץ (*comp.*) *Action of moving* in skimming the ground, of *running.* See רֹץ.
רוּש (*comp.*) *Action of impoverishing, making poor,* being *needy,* of returning to the principle of nature. See רֹש.

רז RZ. Every idea of exhaustion, material annihilation, extreme thinness: that which becomes indiscernible.

ר In a figurative sense, *the secret* of the initiates.

The Arabic رز designates, in general, that which is secret, mysterious, concealed. It is an inner movement, a dull murmur.

רח RH. In the same manner as the roots רא and רה, considered as rays of the elementary circle, are related to light and fire; in the same manner, as the root רו is related to water, thus we see their analogue רח being related to air and depicting all its effects: we shall see further on רי and רע, related equally, the one to ether and the other to terrestrial matter.

The Arabic رخ holds to the same radical sense as the Hebrew, as can be seen in a great number of its derivatives: such as رابح , روح , which mean the same as the Hebraic analogues; but رح is still in the Arabic idiom, an onomatopoetic root which depicts the effort of wind upon a thing, and which characterizes, metaphorically, that which weakens, diminishes. رخ designates, *to flow in torrents, to fall in a mass,* in speaking of water.

רוח Every idea of expansion and ærial dilation: *wind, breath, soul, spirit*: that which *moves, stirs, animates, inspires, transports.*

ריח Every kind of *odour*. See רו.

רחב (*comp.*) Every kind of *distention, inflation*. See רב.

רחם (*comp.*) That which is *soft, faint, calm* as air; a long, drawn breath. Figuratively, *tenderness, compassion, mercy.*

רחף (*comp.*) That which is *moved, stirred* by an expansive, vital movement; to *brood over, to cherish.*

רחץ (*comp.*) Every kind of *ablution*.

רחק (*comp.*) That which *recedes, goes far away, vanishes* in air.

רחש (*comp.*) That which allows the air which it contains to escape by *boiling,* by *fermentation.*

רט RT. This root, in which the sign of movement proper is limited by that of resistance, characterizes a directed course; accompanied or turned by a dike, an embankment, etc. It is literally a *conduit, canal, promenade.*

The Arabic رط has not preserved the radical sense of the Hebrew; but in being attached to one of its developments, that of *a promenade,* this root has designated a confused crowd, a tumultuous movement. The Chaldaic

רטש has followed the same idea as the Arabic رط, and has rendered it even stronger in expressing a sort of shuddering, of terror.

רִי RI. Root analogous to the roots רו, רה, רא, רח; but more particularly applied to ethereal, fragrant radiations.

רִי Effluvium; a fluidic, ethereal, spirituous emanation; a fragrant exhalation. In a restricted sense, *a stream*.

The Arabic رى signifies literally *the lung*.

רִיב (comp.) A sympathetic, electrifying commotion given to a crowd: literally, *a tumult, an insurrection*.

רִיח (comp.) An aroma, a fragrant spirit, perfume: figuratively, *fame*.

רִיע (comp.) The sound of metals striking together.

רִיק (comp.) Ethereal space, *the void*. See רק.

רִיש (comp.) Original manifestation: in whatever manner conceived. In a mean and restricted sense, *poverty*.

רֹךְ RCH. Every idea of relaxation, indolence, dissolution, literally as well as figuratively.

רה That which is *thin, rare, soft, delicate, slender, frail, weak, infirm*.

The Arabic رك has in general, the same ideas as the Hebrew. By its analogue رق is understood *to make thin*.

רל RL. Root not used in Hebrew nor in Arabic.

רם RM. The sign of movement proper considered in its abstract mode, or in its different radical modifications, רי, רח, רו, רה, רא being here universalized by the collective sign ם, designates that sort of movement or action, by means of which any thing whatsoever, rising from the centre to one of the points of the circumference, traverses or fills an extent or place, which it has not occupied previously.

The Arabic رم has lost nearly all of the intellectual ideas developed by the Hebrew. This root reduced to the purely physical and material sense expresses in general, the action of *establishing, restoring, repairing,* etc.

רם or רמם (*intens.*) That which is *borne upward,* which *rises, dilates, mounts, projects, shoots up, increases rapidly,* follows a movement of *progression* and *ascension.*

רום Action of *rising* by expanding, of filling space; action of *being lifted up,* in speaking of anything whatever; state of *being in effervescence;* the superior part of a thing; *height, sublimity.*

רן RN. Every kind of noise, of sound which follows a commotion of the air. A chant, shout, clamour; the murmur of wind, water, fire; the clinking of metals, etc.

The Arabic رن has exactly the same sense. It is literally *to resound,* to make some sort of sound, *to groan,* etc.

רס RS. Every idea of break, fracture; reducing into *impalpable* parts, in drops, like *the dew;* that which is *submissive, reduced, subdued.*

This primitive root is recognized in the four Arabic roots, رس , رش , رص and رض where its divers acceptations are divided. By رس is understood in general, *to excavate the earth, to dig;* by رش, *to water, to sprinkle:* by رص *to stratify, to arrange in layers;* and by رض *to crack, to break.*

רע RH. We have seen the movement principle, acting from the centre to the circumference, modified in turn, by light, fire, water, air, ethereal fluid, according to the roots רי, רח, רו, רה, רא : now, here is this same movement departing from the root רו and degenerating more and more toward the material sense, to become in the root רע, the emblem of that which is terrestrial, obscure and evil. This is worthy of the closest attention.

רע and רעע (*intens.*) That which is *bent, bowed down;* that which is *brought together* to be *made compact;* that which becomes *fragile, brittle;* that which *breaks* and *is reduced* to *powder*: physical and moral *evil; misery, malignancy, misfortune, vice, perversity, disorder.*

The Arabic رع has preserved none of the intellectual ideas developed by the Hebrew. The only physical idea that this root appears to express in the Arabic idiom, is that of inertia. The derivative roots رعي , رعو , etc., have reference, as in Hebrew, to the care of flocks and pastures.

רוע State of being *perverted, evil, mischievous;* action of following a *material, false, disordered* movement.

רעה That which concerns *earthly cares; the pains, anxieties, sorrows* and *afflictions* which they involve: human society in general, and that of shepherds in particular: *a shepherd, a leader* of flocks; *a king.* The one who shares the same cares, *a neighbour, relative, comrade.*

רעו Every *disorder, rupture, infraction.*

רעי Pasture, property, possession: that which concerns the state of *shepherd, leader, king: pastoral.*

רעב (*comp.*) Hunger; state of *being famished.*

רעד (*comp.*) Fear; state of *being frightened.*

רעל (*comp.*) Horror, venom; state of *being filled with horror, infected with venom.*

רעם (*comp.*) A disordered, universalized movement: *thunder, lightning.*

רעץ Action of *breaking, smashing, acting with fury.*

רעש (*comp.*) Action of *shuddering, trembling, shivering.*

רף RPH. Every kind of mediation, reparation, recovery, redemption. It is the idea of a **regenerating movement.**

The Arabic رف holds to the same **radical sense, but** its developments are perceptibly altered. **As verb, it is the** action of *being refreshed,* of *eating abundantly.* رف **is** also an onomatopoetic root, which depicts the noise of a bird which beats its wings.

רף Medicine, remedy; health, the action of healing.

רוּף The sign of movement proper, united by contraction to the root עוּף, forms an onomatopœia which is applied to every rapid movement which *dislocates, disunites, relaxes beyond measure*: etc. See עף.

רץ RTZ. This root characterizes a sort of movement of vibration, recommencing and finishing; reptilian, which propagates in being divided: it is a dragging, painful movement.

רץ and רצץ (*intens.*) That which *is shaken into fragments,* that which *is broken, divided; a rupture, a piece.*

The Arabic رص signifies literally *to stratify,* to arrange in layers or in strata; by رض is understood *to crush, to break* in great pieces.

רוץ From the idea of a divided piece, springs that of *alliance,* of *friendship;* from that of intermittent movement, springs the idea of *concurrence*: thence the action of *being allied,* of *concurring.*

רק RK. Every idea of tenuity, rarity, expansion, giving way.

The Arabic رق has the same sense as the Hebrew.

רק That which *is attenuated, rarified;* which *gives way,* physically as well as morally: in a figurative sense, *time.* See ריק.

רר RR. Root not used in Hebrew nor in Arabic.

רש RSH. The sign of movement proper, united to that of relative movement, constitutes a root which is hieroglyphically symbolized by a point at the middle of a circle: it is the centre unfolding the circumference: the fundamental principle.

ראש *Every acting principle*, good or bad; *a venomous poison*, a very bitter, *gall;* that which is primary, initial; the origin, summit, top; *the culminating point* of all things; *the head* of man or of anything whatsoever; *the leader* of a people, *a captain, a prince, a king.* See רוש and ריש.

The Arabic رش holds evidently to the radical sense of the Hebrew רש, and the compound راس has the same acceptation as ראש. In the modern idiom, رش signifies *to sprinkle*.

רת RTH. Every movement arrested, chained, retained.

The Arabic رث, offers the same meaning. It is literally, the action of *retarding*.

רת That which *chains, coagulates, arrests;* that which *freezes* the blood: *a sudden terror, a dread*.

ש SH. This character as consonant belongs to the sibilant sound, and depicts in an onomatopoetic manner, light movements, sounds durable and soft. As symbolic image it represents the part of the bow from which the arrow is shot. In Hebrew, it is the sign of relative duration and of the movement attached thereunto. It is derived from the vocal sound ', become consonant by joining to its expression the respective significations of the consonants ז and ס. As prepositive relation, it constitutes a sort of pronominal article and is placed at the head of nouns and verbs, to communicate to them the double power that it possesses of movement and of conjunction.

Its arithmetical number is 300.

שׁא SHA. The sign of relative movement united to that of power, constitutes a root which is hieroglyphically characterized by the arc of the circle inscribed between two radii. The character ס is designated by the arc deprived of its radius or arrow, and closed by its cord. The character ז is designated by the radius or arrow indicating the circumference. The portion of the circle represented by the root שׁא, can be considered in movement or in repose; thence, the opposed ideas of tumult and of the calm which it develops.

The Arabic شا signifies literally *to desire*. As onomatopoetic root شا denotes the sound of calling the flocks to the watering place.

שׁאה *A whirlpool, a delirium;* action of making irruption, *tumult, fracas*: *profound tranquility;* state of being *empty, deserted, void; a gulf*, etc.

שׁוא That which is *vain, empty; ruined, devasted;* that which is *tumultuous, tempestuous, whirling; vanity, insolence*.

שׁאב (comp.) Action of *drawing water.* See אב.

שׁאל (comp.) Action of *interrogating, asking.* See של.

שׁאם (comp.) Action of *troubling, putting in disorder.*

שׁאן (comp.) State of *being calm.*

שׁאף (comp.) *To aspire*, figuratively as well as literally. See אף.

שׁאר (comp.) That which *tends* toward *consistency, solidity;* that which *remains; residue; remnant*: in a restricted sense, *the flesh.* See אר.

שׁב SHB. This root has two expressions according to its composition; if it is considered as composed of the sign of relative movement and of duration, joined to that of interior activity, it contains every idea of return toward a point of departure; if it is regarded as formed by the same sign united to that of the root אב, image of paternity, it designates the capture of a whole tribe, its captivity, its deportation outside its country: thence,

שב The idea of any kind of *reëstablishment*, of *return* to an original state, to a place from which one had set out; *a restitution, a reformation*: thence,

שב Every state of *captivity*, of *separation* from one's country: *a deportation; a capture.*

The Arabic ش characterizes in general, that which tends from the centre to the circumference, increases, grows, unfolds itself, returns to its original state after having been restrained; develops its strength, etc. The primitive sense of the Hebraic root is recognized in the Arabic root although its developments may not be the same.

שוב Action of *coming back*, of *returning* to its first state; of *remaking* what has been already made. Metaphorically, the action of growing old; that which is on the wane; *an old man.*

שג SHG. The sign of relative movement united to the organic sign, indicates a movement of the organ deprived of intelligence, a covetous movement; the same sign joined by contraction to the root אג, symbol of organic development, characterizes every kind of increase. Thence,

שג *Blind desire, thoughtless inclination;* figuratively, *error, degeneration;* action of growing, *augmenting* in number, volume, duration.

The Arabic شج preserves but little of the radical sense. It is, as onomatopoetic root the action of *splitting* a hard thing, of making upon it an incision, a scar; *scratching, furrowing,* etc.

שׁד SHD. This root, composed of the sign of relative movement united to that of divisional abundance or by contraction with the root אד, image of every emanation, characterizes productive nature in general, whose particular symbols are, a mammal and a field. Thence, the name of שׁדי, given to GOD, as principle of all good; *Providence*.

The Arabic شد characterizes that which acts with force, with energy, in good or in evil; that which overthrows the obstacles opposed to it; that which shows itself strong and powerful.

שׂד The effusion of the virtual faculties, *Nature*: the sign of abundance and fecundity; *a mammal, a field*. All physical property, *fortune, the genius* of the earth. *A song* of jubilee.

שׁדד (*intens.*) Action of returning to primal, brutish nature; that is to say, of *devastating, ravaging* the production of art, labour and industry.

שׁוד Every kind of *devastation*, or *profanation; pillaging* the fruits of nature.

שׁה SHEH. Root analogous to the root שׂא.

The Arabic شها characterizes every tendency, every persevering movement toward an object: action of *coveting, wishing, desiring.* etc.

שׁו SHOU. Root analogous to the root שׂא, but conceived principally under its relation of equilibrium, equality, parallel, similitude, fitness, proportion and measure of things.

The Ethiopic ሰው (*shony*) signifies literally *a man*. The Arabic شا characterizes the state of being struck with admiration.

שׁוה State of *being in equilibrium* in all parts, as every portion of the circle; state of being *equal, conformable, fitting, just, qualified* for something; etc.

שׂוה (comp.) That which is *inclined*, which *leans* toward any object.

שׂוט (comp.) Action of *following* something in its *contours*, of *bending*, of *doing the same*. See שׂט.

שׂוך (comp.) Action of *interring* completely, *covering* wholly, *burying*.

שׂום (comp.) Action of *placing*, of *arranging* one upon the other, in layers, as *an onion*.

שׂוע (comp.) *Clamour, outcry;* action of *calling aloud.* See שׂע.

שׂוף (comp.) Action of *pressing* hard, *suffocating*.

שׂוק (comp.) Every *amorous desire;* every *inclination*.

שׂור (comp.) Action of *being directed* according to fixed laws, *resting in equilibrium, in harmony; modulating* the voice, *singing*, etc. *Music*, in the very broad sense that the ancients gave to this word. See שׂר.

שׂיש (comp.) State of being in *good humour*, in *harmony* with one's self.

שׂות (comp.) Action of *placing* something. See שׂת.

שׁז SHZ. Root not used in Hebrew. The Arabic شز indicates a dry, arid place.

שׂח SHEH. Every kind of bodily effort to follow any direction; every effort of the mind to accomplish a duty, to acquire a virtue.

The Arabic شح holds evidently to the primitive sense of the Hebrew, but developing it from the purely material side; so that the effort indicated by the root שׂח, being turned toward egoism, characterizes only *tenacity, avarice;* desire to draw to one's self, monopolizing, etc. As onomatopoetic root شخ depicts the noise made by any kind of fluid falling down from above.

שׂחה Action of *being inclined, following an inclination, bending* to a law; in a restricted sense, the action of *swimming;* of following the course of the water. See שׂה

שִׂיח (comp.) *A conception, an impulse, a flight.*
שָׂהֵם (comp.) *Vegetation.*

שָׁט SHT. Every idea of inflection, inclination or similar movement. See שׂוּט.

The Arabic شط characterizes that which goes beyond, leaves the centre, is drawn away, is remote from its own place.

שִׁי SHI. Root analogous to the root שׂוּ whose power it manifests. In its literal sense, it is justice rendered, honour accorded for merit, etc.

The Arabic شي characterizes *any thing* in general, whatever it may be; a real and evident existence; that which is obvious to the senses.

שָׁךְ SHCH. The sign of relative movement, united to that of assimilated existence, or by contraction with the root אָךְ, image of every restriction, constitutes a root whence are developed all ideas of return to itself, of envelopment, exterior repose, consciousness.

The Arabic شك develops the idea of hesitation, of conscientious doubt. As onomatopoetic root شك signifies literally to *prick* with a goad.

שָׁךְ In a literal and restricted sense it is *an onion*: in a figurative sense it is *contemplation, profound meditation, speculation, physical sleep; shrouding*, literally, as well as figuratively. See שׁוּךְ.

שָׁל SHL. Hieroglyphically, it is a line traced from one object to another, the stroke which unites them; it is expressed by the prepositive relations *from, at.*

שָׁל That which follows its laws; that which remains in its straight line; that which is *tranquil, happy, in good order, in the way of salvation.*

The Arabic شل has not preserved the ideas of order developed by the Hebraic root except in the compound شله *moral force*, and in the analogue سالم, action of *saluting*, giving evidence of respect; but this root becomes confused with the following intensive.

שָׁלַל (*intens.*) That which goes out from its line *beyond* anything whatsoever; which falls into *error;* that which is *extravagant, fanatical, insensate;* that which ignores law and justice.

The Arabic شل or شلل has the same sense in general. It is, literally, the state of being crippled, crooked, maimed, impotent, etc.

שָׁם SHM. Hieroglyphically, it is the circumferential extent, the entire sphere of any being whatever, the total space that it occupies; it is expressed by the adverbial relations *there, in that very place, within, inside there.*

שָׁם *The name* of every being, *the sign* which renders it knowable; that which constitutes it *such: a place, a time, the universe, the heavens,* GOD Himself: *glory, eclat. splendour, fame, virtue;* that which *rises* and *shines* in space; which is *distinguished, sublime, remarkable.*

The Arabic شم has not preserved the same intellectual ideas developed by the Hebraic root, except in certain compounds and in the analogue سم. Its most common acceptations are confused with that of the following intensive root.

שָׁמַם (*intens.*) That which leaves its sphere, gives way to *pride;* enters into *madness. The inordinate idea* of making one's-self remarked, *ambition*: that which *troubles, upsets* the mind: *ravages, lays waste* the land.

The Arabic شم offers in general, the same sense as the Hebrew. In a very restricted sense, the verb شم signifies *to smell.*

שַׁן   SHN. All ideas of mutation, iteration, passing from one state to another; that which leads to diversity, variation, change.

The Arabic ﺷﻦ agrees with the Hebraic root only in certain compounds, and in the analogue ﻣﻦ. As verb, ﺷﻦ indicates the action of *triturating, crushing, making noise*.

שֵׁן   The number *two*. Literally, that which *cuts* and *divides* as the teeth; figuratively, *hatred*. That which *varies, changes;* that which *measures* and *divides* time; *a cyclic revolution, an ontological mutation;* in a very restricted sense, *a year*.

שׁוּע   SHUH. Every idea of conservation, restoration, cementation.

שׁע   In a literal sense, *lime, cement;* in a figurative sense, that which *consolidates, guarantees;* which serves as *safe-guard;* which *preserves*.

The Arabic ﺷﻊ has not preserved the radical sense except in certain compounds and in its analogue ﺳﻊ. By ﺷﻊ is understood *to radiate*, to spread here and there, *to disperse*. According to this acceptation, ﺷﻊ is attached to the following onomatopoetic root.

שׁע   Onomatopoetic root which depicts the cry of a person who calls loudly. See שׁוע.

שׁעט   (comp.)   An acclamation.
שׁעל   (comp.)   The closed hand.
שׁען   (comp.)   That which serves as *support;* action of *supporting, propping up*.
שׁעע   (intens.)   That which is *partial to, choses, conserves* carefully.
שׁער   (comp.)   A *shudder of horror;* or *an opening, a door*: according to the sense under which one considers the root שׁור.

שָׁף   SHPH. Every apparent, eminent, distinguished, prominent object: that which extends beyond, as *a hill;* appears on top, as *cream,* etc.

The Arabic شف designates in general that which becomes limpid, clear, transparent.

שַׁף   Onomatopoetic root, expressing the noise made in trampling with the feet. See שׁוּף.

שָׁץ   SHTZ. That which leads to a goal, to perfection, achievement, end.

The Arabic شص designates in general that which serves as means for catching fish, *a fish-hook, net,* etc.

שָׁק   SHCQ. All ideas of tendency, of sympathetic inclination to possess: that which seeks and joins; that which acts through sympathy, envelops, embraces, absorbs.

שׁק and שׁקק (*intens.*) That which *is united,* which *attracts* reciprocally: action of *soaking up, pumping water, sucking up.* See שׁוּק.

The Arabic شق has not preserved the radical sense of the Hebrew. It is an onomatopoetic root, which in the Arabic idiom signifies literally *to cleave, to split.*

שָׁר   SHR. This root admits of several significations, according to its composition. If it is the sign of relative movement which is united simply to that of movement proper, there results from this abstract mingling of the circular line with the straight line, an idea of solution, opening, liberation; as if a closed circle were opened; as if a chain were slackened: if one considers this same sign of relative movement, being united by contraction to the elementary root אר, then it partakes of the diverse expressions of this root and develops ideas of strength, vigour, domination, power, which result from the elementary principle; if finally, one sees in the root אר the root

שׂו, symbol of all harmonious proportion, joined to the sign of movement proper, one discovers here the expression of that which is directed according to just and upright laws; thence, according to the first signification:

שׂר That which *liberates, opens, brings out, emits, produces;* as *the navel, a field,* etc.; according to the second:

שׂרר (*intens.*) That which is *solid, firm, resisting,* as *a wall, breast-plate, chain;* that which is *strong, vigorous,* as *a bull;* that which is *dominating, powerful,* as *a king, a prince;* that which is *formidable,* as *a rival, an enemy,* etc.; according to the third:

שׂו, שׂרו or שׂיר That which is *measured, co-ordinate, just,* conformable with universal harmony, restricted to regulations, as *a musical song, a melody, a law, a poem, a system of government,* etc.

The Hebraic genius merging these three expressions in one, draws from it the most complicated and most abstract sense that any tongue can offer: that of a government, liberal, ready, indulgent, productive within; powerful, strong, redoubtable, dominating without, which extends its empire by directing it according to just, luminous laws modelled upon the immutable laws of order and universal harmony.

The Arabic شر does not agree with the Hebrew in the radical sense, except in certain of its compounds and in its analogues سر and سار. This root, in the Arabic idiom has become intensive, and has developed ideas wholly contrary, as has been seen often in the course of this vocabulary. Thus, instead of order and justice expressed by שׂו, the intensive verb שׂרר or شرر, characterizes the action of that which is inordinate, unjust, wicked, perfidious, contrary to harmony and public welfare.

שׁשׁ SHSH. All ideas of proportion, measure and harmony.

שׁשׁ The number *six*. That which is in harmonious relations, as the *colour white;* in consequence, *the albatross, the lily, linen, old age*: that which enjoys calm and happiness. See שׁישׁ.

The Arabic شش develops ideas entirely opposed to the Hebraic root, on account of the intensive form which herein dominates. The verb شوش designates in general, that which troubles, mixes, deranges, etc.

שׁת SHTH. This root, composed of the signs of relative and reciprocal movement, indicates the place toward which things irresistibly incline, and the things themselves which incline toward this place: thence,

שׁת *The depths, the foundations,* literally as well as figuratively; *the place* where the sea is gathered; *the sea* itself; every kind of *depth;* every kind of *beverage.*

The Arabic شت has retained only a portion of the radical sense, in that which concerns the movement of water, the separation of this fluid into drops, its distillation, dispersion. The other portion of the primitive sense is found in the analogue مث which designates in general, the bottom or the foundation of things, the seat and particularly *the buttocks.*

שׁות Action of putting *at the bottom, founding, seating, placing, disposing,* etc.

ת TH. This character as consonant, belongs to the sibilant sound. The ancient Egyptians in consecrating it to Thoth, whose name they gave it, regarded it as the symbol of the universal mind. As grammatical sign in the Hebraic tongue, it is that of sympathy and reciprocity; joining, to the abundance of the character ר, to the force of resistance and protection of the character ט, the idea of perfection and necessity of which it is the emblem. Although it does not hold a particular rank among the articles, it appears nevertheless too often at the head of words, for one not to suspect that it was used as such in one of the Egyptian dialects, where without doubt it represented the relation את ; in the same manner that the character פ represented the relation פא, פה or פי.

Its arithmetical number is 400.

תא   THA. Every idea of determination, designation, definition.

תאה   That which *limits, determines, defines, circumscribes.* It is, in a restricted sense, *the nuptial chamber.*

The Arabic ټ expresses a mutual desire.

תאב   (*comp.*) A mutual desire.

תאם   (*comp.*) To be double, twain.

תאן   (*comp.*) An occasion, occurrence; a reciprocal sorrow; a fig-tree. See אן.

תאר   (*comp.*) A description, an information, a plan.

תב   THB. Every kind of sympathetic union by affinity; a globe, a sphere; the vessel of the universe, the world, the earth; etc.

The Arabic ڗ is an onomatopoetic root which characterizes the movement of disgust with which one repels a thing: *for shame!* The verb ڗاب expresses the action of repenting for a sin.

תוב   Action of *turning, returning* upon one's step, following a circular movement.

The Arabic ڗاب signifies literally *to improve*, to return from wandering.

תג   THG. Root not used in Hebrew. The Arabic ج indicates a mutation, a fleeting action; *the course* of something. By ڗاج is understood, *a mitre, a tiara.*

RADICAL VOCABULARY

תד   THD. Root not used in Hebrew. The Chaldaic as well as the Syriac ܬܕܐ indicate equally *the breast*.

The Arabic تدا or تدى signifies *to moisten, to wet, to sprinkle*.

תה   THEH. Root analogus to the root תא; but whose expression, more moral, characterizes the influential and sympathetic reason of things.

The Arabic تها signifies literally *to be led astray*, lost in empty space. By the compound تهاية , *a vain thing;* by the verb تهة a thing which is liquified.

תהום (comp.) *The depths of universal existence.* See תו.

תו   THOU. Root analogous to the roots תא and תה, but of an effect more physical.

תו   Every idea of *sign, symbol,* hieroglyphic, emblematic *character: fable, recitation, description, book, monument,* etc.

The Arabic ت characterizes a simple thing, not compound, not complex, such as a blade of grass, a word of one single letter. It is also, in a restricted sense, *an hour,* an extent of time considered in a simple manner.

תוה Action of *designing, signifying, characterizing, describing,* etc.

תוך (comp.) *The middle, the between* of things, the point of contact. See תך.

תור (comp.) *A circular sympathetic movement; a row, order, turn.* See תר.

תז   THZ. Every general idea of vibration and reaction. In a restricted sense it is the action of cutting with the sword.

תה THEH. Root not used in Hebrew. The Arabic indicates an emotion which pertains to the weakness of the organs. In adding the guttural inflection, this root characterizes in تَهَ, the action of *slackening*.

תחת (comp.) That state of *submission* and of *dependence* expressed by the relations, *under, below, beneath*: that which is *inferior*. See תה.

תט THT. Root not used in Hebrew. The Arabic تَا expresses a state of infancy, weakness; imbecility.

תי THI. Root analogous to the root תה.
תים (comp.) *Mid-day.*
תיש (comp.) *A he-goat.* See תש.

תך THCH. This root characterizes the sympathetic point in which things are formed as to their parts, or united one to the other; the point of contact at which they touch; the central point toward which they gravitate. Thence,

תך or תכך (intens.) Every idea of *intermediary link, space between; the delicate point* of a thing, of a question; *the dexterity* with which it is seized; *the finesse* with which it is used: that which *tends* to the same point; that which *oppresses; a calamity;* etc. See תך.

The Arabic تَكَّ has preserved of the radical sense of the Hebrew, only the sole development which is connected with oppression, either physical or moral; as that of a man oppressed by drunkenness or by an attack of folly. The intensive verb تَكَّكَ or تَكْتَكَ signifies again to *trample under foot*, to cover with waves, *to overflow*.

תל THL. Every idea of piling, massing, accumulation; that which is heaped up; that which is placed one upon another.

The Arabic بَلَ holds to the radical sense of the Hebrew, in the greater part of its developments. In a restricted sense, the Arabic root signifies, nevertheless, *to raise;* by بَلَ is understood *to draw out* the earth in digging a well.

תל and תלל (*intens.*) *A heap, a mound;* a thing suspended, as a quiver, a trophy of arms, etc.

תם THM. This root, in which the sign of signs, symbol of all perfection, is found universalized by the collective sign ם, develops the idea of that which is universally true, universally approved; accomplished image of the universal mind: thence,

תם *Perfection, integrity,* either physically or morally: *truth, justice, sanctity,* all the *virtues.*

The Arabic تم partakes of nearly all the developments of the Hebraic root. In a restricted sense, it is, as verb, the action of *achieving, accomplishing, perfecting, finishing.* As adverbial relation, تمَّ is represented by *there, yonder.*

תמם (*intens.*) Every exaggerated, degenerated virtue become *an error, an imperfection, a ruin.*

תן THN. Every idea of substance added, of corporeity increasing more and more; an extension, an enlargement, a largess; in a restricted sense, *a gift.*

The Arabic تن signifies literally, *to put into two,* to carry number one to number two; *to compare together; to augment.* By تن, is understood dry grass, *hay.* As onomatopoetic root, تن depicts the noise of metals, the *tinkling* of sonorous chords.

תן Action of *giving;* an *offering,* a *present*: that which is *liberal, generous.*

תנן (*intens.*) Action of *growing, extending* beyond measure: *a monster, a dragon, a crocodile;* in general, the cetacean species.

תם THS. Root not used in Hebrew. The Chaldaic designates *a boiling, a fervour.* The Arabic نَسِ designates *race, lineage.*

תע THUH. That which is *false, illusory, vain;* that which has only appearance, semblance.

תעה State of being *abused, seduced, deceived* by specious exterior; *hypocrisy, fraud.*

The Arabic نَع holds to the Hebraic root only on the physical side, and indicates the state of that which is enervated, without vigour. As onomatopoetic root نَع depicts stammering, hesitation in speaking.

תוע Action of *mocking, laughing.*

תף THPH. Onomatopoetic root expressing the noise of a drum. Thence by analogy, the Arabic نَفَ *to spit;* metaphorically, every object which is disgusting and repulsive to the sight. In the Arabic idiom, دَنَ signifies *a tambourine.*

תוף The Chaldaic word signifies the action of *anathematizing, cursing.* The Arabic تَابَ indicates the state of being *culpable, disordered by crime, debased by vice.*

תק THCQ. Root not used in Hebrew. The Chaldaic expresses moral doubt, or physical effort. The Arabic نَق is an onomatopoetic root which is represented by *look out!* The verb تَاقَ signifies *to desire.*

RADICAL VOCABULARY 471

תר THR. Every idea of determination given to an element: in a very broad sense, *modality*.

תר In a restricted sense, every kind of *fusion, infusion, distillation*.

The Arabic ز or ذ holds to the Hebraic root only on the most restricted and most physical side. It is literally, that which has juice, that which gives liquid, that which distils.

תור Action of *modifying, changing; turning* from one manner to another; action of *converting, translating, distilling;* action of *surrounding, turning about in a circle;* etc. See תור.

תש THSH. Sympathetic ardour of nature, the generative fire.

תוש or תיש Symbol of animal fecundity, *a goat*.

The Arabic تش signifies literally *a wine-skin,* on account of the skin of the goat of which it is made; metaphorically, the air contained in the skin and which escapes by pressing. The compound word تشوش expresses a sort of transmutation, of passing from one state to another.

תת THTH. Root not used in Hebrew. The Arabic ث indicates a cleft, a furrow; a solution of continuity.

END OF PART FIRST.

www.ingramcontent.com/pod-product-compliance
Lightning Source LLC
Chambersburg PA
CBHW022055150426
43195CB00008B/147